MUSIC IN THE JEWISH COMMUNITY OF PALESTINE 1880–1948

Music in the Jewish Community of Palestine 1880–1948

A Social History

Jehoash Hirshberg

CLARENDON PRESS · OXFORD

Oxford University Press, Great Clarendon Street, Oxford OX2 6DP

Oxford New York
Athens Auckland Bangkok Bogota Bombay
Buenos Aires Calcutta Cape Town Dar es Salaam
Delhi Florence Hong Kong Istanbul Karachi
Kuala Lumpur Madras Madrid Melbourne
Mexico City Nairobi Paris Singapore
Taipei Tokyo Toronto
and associated companies in
Berlin Ibadan

Oxford is a trade mark of Oxford University Press

Published in the United States
by Oxford University Press Inc., New York

© Jehoash Hirshberg 1995
First published 1995
new as paperback edition 1996

British Library Cataloguing in Publication Data
Data available

Library of Congress Cataloging in Publication Data
Hirshberg, Jehoash.
Music in the Jewish community of Palestine 1880–1948 :
a social history / Jehoash Hirshberg.
Includes bibliographical references.
1. Jews—Palestine—Music—19th century—History and criticism.
2. Jews—Palestine—Music—20th century—History and criticism.
3. Music and society. I. Title.
ML345.P3H57   1994   780'.89'92405694—dc20   94-42448
ISBN 0 19 816651 6

1 3 5 7 9 10 8 6 4 2

Typeset by Best-set Typesetter Ltd., Hong Kong
Printed in Great Britain
on end-free paper by
Bookcraft Ltd
Midsomer Norton, Avon

Preface

'THE history of society is *history*, that is to say it has real chronological time as one of its dimensions . . . The history of society is, among other things, that of specific units of people living together and definable in sociological terms.' Those two premises have provided the point of departure for Eric J. Hobsbawm's discussion of the question 'how are we to write the history of society'.[1] The topic of the social history of music in the Jewish community in Palestine allowed me the rare luxury of being able to determine the precise point in time when it all started, 1880, the commencement of Jewish immigration to Palestine that was motivated by modern nationalism. Likewise, the unequivocal self-definition by the immigrants themselves spared me the difficulties social historians frequently face in defining the society studied.[2] Nor did I face a hard decision about closing the book with the momentous event of the declaration of the State of Israel in 1948.

Though under Ottoman and later under British rule, Jewish society in Palestine was near-autonomous in most respects, especially in the realms of culture and education. Having planted first seeds in a virgin land in 1880, by 1948 the people involved in music in Palestine had established a full hierarchy of an internationally recognized professional musical establishment, thus telescoping a complex social process against the backdrop of the stormy and crisis-ridden reality of two world wars, absorption of successive immigration waves, local skirmishes, and a full-scale national war.

The study required the application of diverse methodologies, further supporting Hobsbawm's claim that 'social history can never be another specialization . . . because its subject matter cannot be isolated.'[3] The complex array of methodologies inherent in the study of music in immigrant and refugee societies has been applied throughout the book.[4] Since the musical scene under discussion was created by a small professional élite, the methodology of collective biography (prosopography)

---

[1] 'From Social History to the History of Society', in F. Gilbert and S. R. Graubard (eds.), *Historical Studies Today* (New York, 1972), 10.
[2] Ibid. 11.   [3] Ibid. 5.
[4] See A. Reyes-Schramm, 'Music and the Refugee Experience', *World of Music*, 32 (1990), 3–21.

seemed appropriate.[5] When writing his essay Hobsbawm pointed out that compared with research of social classes, the study of 'more restricted social groups—profession, for instance—has been less significant'.[6] Since then Cyril Ehrlich's social history of the professional musicians in Britain established a new trend. He focused not on élite soloists but on the large group of rank-and-file musicians[7] and the present book follows in this direction. When I started my research in the mid-seventies, a significant number of the protagonists in the present book were still alive and active, allowing me to utilize ethnographic methods and supplement the study of the extensive archival material with numerous personal interviews.

The study of the music artefacts has been deliberately limited to semiotics of music as part of the comprehensive discussion of ideologies and policies. One of the goals of the present study is to dispel the myth of a homogeneous and unified 'Mediterranean' style. The highly pluralistic nature of the repertory of folk and art music produced in Palestine during that period calls for individual detailed monographs of composers and genres, of which only a few have been already published.[8] Any generalized discussion would lead to superficial generalizations.

The emergence of national schools of music in the nineteenth century has directed the interest of historians to the dialectics of local versus mainstream histories, in the cases of Czechoslovakia and Hungary. Though geographically removed from Europe, Palestine presented a direct continuation of the history of the European national schools with their inherent tension between the vision of individuality and the urge to preserve links with mainstream world music.

The book follows a diachronic progression, though synchronic divisions into separate chapters is used when discussing broad topics such as the history of the Palestine Orchestra, music in the kibbutz, or the folk composer. The first two chapters deal with music in Palestine under the Ottoman rule. Chapters 3–6 cover the 1920s. Chapters 7–10 discuss the momentous developments from 1931 to the end of World War II. The remaining chapters centre on the broad array of ideological and social polemics which dominated the musical scene for the entire period, with a special chapter dedicated to the kibbutz—the unique experiment of communal living.

---

[5] L. Stone, 'Prosopography', in Gilbert and Graubard (eds.), *Historical Studies Today*, 107–40.

[6] E. Hobsbawm, 'Social History', 16.

[7] *The Music Profession in Britain since the Eighteenth Century* (1985; Oxford, 1988).

[8] Such as A. Bahat, *Oedoen Partos, his Life and Works* (Tel Aviv, 1984); N. Shahar, 'The Eretz Israeli Song 1920–1950: Sociological and Musical Aspects', Ph.D. (Hebrew University, Jerusalem, 1989); J. Hirshberg, *Paul Ben-Haim, his Life and Works* (Jerusalem, 1990).

The style of contemporary verbal documents—including personal and business letters, reviews, commentaries, and ideological essays—ranges from flowery and excited rhetoric to cool, matter-of-fact statements. Whenever possible I have attempted to convey the original flavour of these documents through many quotations in fairly literal translations from the original Hebrew. The language of original documents is Hebrew unless marked otherwise in the footnotes.

Some of the concepts and terms used in the book have been heavily laden with changing connotations over the years. I have applied them as used in the period under discussion. The term 'Palestine' is strictly used in its territorial legal sense during the period of the British mandate, which comprises the bulk of the book. Capitalized 'East' refers both to the Near East as a geographical entity and to the visionary East contrasted to the West. I have limited the use of 'Orient' to the particular sense of romantic European Orientalism.

It has been the custom of Jewish immigrants, musicians included, to Hebraize their names at some stage after their immigration. When they made the change upon immigration, as in the case of Paul Frankenburger who Hebraized his name to Ben-Haim, I have used the Hebraized form throughout the book with initial reference to the original German name. When the immigrants Hebraized their names only upon the foundation of the State of Israel I have preserved the original name throughout the discussion. In the interim stage when the change was made within the period of the British mandate, I have marked the change at the appropriate chronological point in the book, as in the case of critic Menashe Rabinowitz who Hebraized his name to Ravina in 1938. I have limited the use of Hebrew terms in the text to the absolute minimum, placing them in footnotes whenever deemed advisable.

Acknowledgements

I AM most grateful to Professor Cyril Ehrlich who provided me through-out my work on this book with generous advice and constant encourage-ment. During the long period of research I have enjoyed the dedicated help of my research assistants Meira Liebersohn, Roni Granot, Hana Stern, Michal Ben-Zur, and Claudia Ott, graduate students at the Hebrew University, in the painstaking collection and sorting of large amounts of data. Maureen Tschaikov and Tamar Cohen, students at the Musicology Department, made important contributions through their penetrating archival research. The style editor, Dr Ora Segal, has been a constant source of help.

My colleagues Professors Amnon Shiloah, Moshe Sikron and Eliyahu Schleifer have kindly assisted me with information and valuable material. I am indebted to Professor Austin Clarkson for allowing me full use of the material and the facilities at the Stefan Wolpe Archive at York Univer-sity, Toronto, Canada. I would like to thank Bruce Phillips and David Blackwell for the interest they have shown in this book and their help in its preparation.

The research has been supported by a grant from the Basic Research Foundation of the Israel Academy of Sciences.

The book is dedicated to my wife, Israela, for her constant encourage-ment, love, and forbearance.

J.H.

Jerusalem, September 1993

I would like to thank Mr Michael Keinan for his kind help in proofread-ing the book for the paperback edition.

Jerusalem, May 1996   J.H.

Contents

List of Abbreviations

ACUM	Association of Composers and Authors in Palestine
AMLI	Americans for Music Libraries in Israel
CZA	Central Zionist Archive, Jerusalem
(H)	The reference is in Hebrew
IMI	Israeli Music Institute, Tel Aviv
IMP	Israeli Music Publications, Jerusalem
JNUL	Jewish National and University Library, Jerusalem
Memorial Volume	I. Adler, B. Bayer, and E. Schleifer (eds.), *The Abraham Zvi Idelsohn Memorial Volume* (Jerusalem, 1986) (Eng. and H; unless otherwise stated, refs. are to the English section)
MGG	Friedrich Blume (ed.), *Die Musik in Geschichte und Gegenwart* (Kassel, 1949–68)
New Grove	Stanley Sadie (ed.), *The New Grove Dictionary of Music and Musicians* (6th edn., London, 1980)
PBS	Palestine Broadcasting Service
WCJMP	World Centre for Jewish Music in Palestine

Notes

Monetary Units

The official coin in Palestine until 1926 was the Egyptian pound which had a value of 1.06 British pounds sterling. In 1927 the administration issued a Palestinian pound which equalled the British pound sterling. A Palestinian pound was divided into 1,000 mils.

Transliteration of Hebrew Words

I have used apostrophes in transliterations of Hebrew words to indicate the beginning of a new syllable, where this might not otherwise be clear. For instance, 'Do'ar' indicates that there are two syllables 'Do' and 'ar' rather than one, 'Doar'.

List of Music Examples

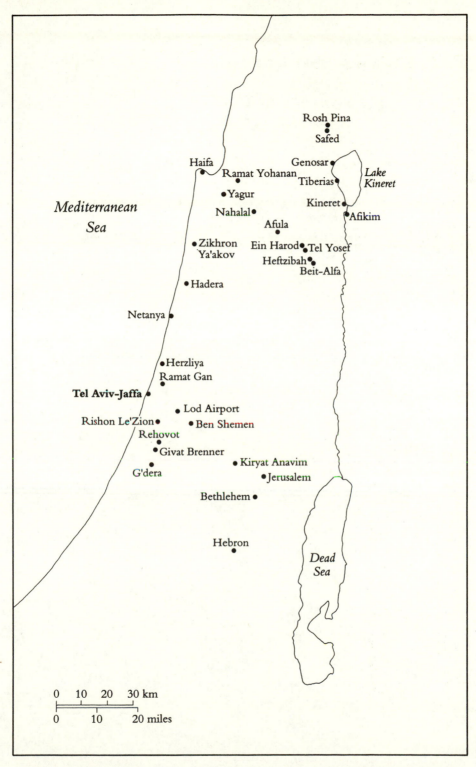

Rosh Pina

Safed

Haifa

Genosar

Lake
Kineret

Ramat Yohanan

Tiberias

Yagur

Kineret

Mediterranean
Sea

Nahalal

Afikim

Afula

Zikhron
Ya'akov

Ein Harod

Tel Yosef

Heftzibah

Beit–Alfa

Hadera

Netanya

Herzliya

Ramat Gan

Tel Aviv-Jaffa

Lod Airport

Rishon Le'Zion

Ben Shemen

Rehovot

Givat Brenner

Kiryat Anavim

G'dera

Jerusalem

Bethlehem

Hebron

Dead
Sea

| 0 | 10 | 20 | 30 km |
| 0 | 10 | | 20 miles |

A map of some of the towns and settlements in Central and Northern Palestine

1

Cultural and Ethnic Interaction in Ottoman Jerusalem

THE nineteenth century was a momentous period in the history of Palestine. Having suffered neglect for three centuries as an underpopulated remote province of the Ottoman Empire, the strategic location and economic potential of Palestine was revealed as a consequence of the Napoleonic and Egyptian invasions, although these occupations were brief.[1] The re-establishment of Ottoman rule was followed by major administrative reforms which effected a relative improvement of living conditions and encouraged immigration, pilgrimage, tourism, and interaction with European expertise and culture.

Palestine under Ottoman rule was a mosaic of religious and ethnic groups. While the Ottoman administration encouraged local participation in running the country, it 'did not remove the traditional barriers which had separated one ethnic group from another, and they continued to maintain their identities'.[2] The Jews took advantage of this policy and maintained a full autonomous educational system, which was to become a principal factor in the future development of Jewish culture in Palestine.

The reforms in Ottoman Palestine paralleled developments in the Jewish Diaspora which encouraged the renewal of a local Jewish community. In 1839 there were only 8,000 Jews in Palestine, most of them of the Sephardi community. By 1914 their numbers had swelled more than

---

[1] Napoleon's defeat in 1799 and the termination of Egyptian rule (1832–40) were largely effected by foreign pressures, esp. from Britain. See S. J. and E. K. Shaw, *History of the Ottoman Empire and Modern Turkey*, ii. *Reforms, Revolution and Republic—The Rise of Modern Turkey* (Cambridge, 1977), 56–8.

[2] D. Koshnir, 'The Last Generation of Ottoman Rule' in I. Kolat (ed.), *History of the Yishuv in the Land of Israel since 1882*, i. *The Ottoman Period* (Jerusalem, 1990), 74.

tenfold to 80,000, and the number of Ashkenazi Jews slightly exceeded that of the Sephardi.[3] The process involved two long-term stages.

At first a strict religious community, referred to as the 'Old Yishuv',[4] slowly emerged. The economy of the Old Yishuv was based on a well-organized network of distribution of charity collected in Jewish communities in the Diaspora, who considered it their sacred duty to support a dedicated Jewish community in the Holy Land.

The year 1882 marked the beginning of the second stage with the onset of a nationally motivated Jewish immigration to Palestine, which established the 'New Yishuv'. The national immigration, titled the 'First Aliya',[5] was initiated by diverse and often rival groups and organizations in Europe, including enlightened religious, secular socialists, political nationalists, idealistic dreamers, and refugees of persecutions and hardships.

At the turn of the century the Jewish community of Jerusalem underwent rapid socio-economic changes, which formed a favourable base for cultural institutions. A growing number of Jews abandoned the reliance on charity and started to work, mostly as shopkeepers and craftsmen. Some members of the younger generation of the Old Yishuv even became teachers at the new nationally oriented schools.[6] Nevertheless, the New Yishuv in Jerusalem was still a small minority compared with the Old Yishuv.[7]

The small potential audience for music was compensated for by the high proportion of the élite group of intellectuals among the immigrants, which included physicians, chemists, engineers, and teachers.[8] It was during the severe economic crisis which preceded World War I that the social balance in Jerusalem tilted in favour of the New Yishuv. The economic deterioration was especially hard on the Old Yishuv who had

---

[3] Yehoashua Ben-Arieh, 'The *Yishuv* in *Eretz Israel* on the Eve of Zionist Settlement', in Kolat (ed.), *Ottoman Period*, 75.

[4] 'Yishuv', lit. 'settlement', connotes the autonomous Jewish community in Palestine from 1840 to the establishment of the State of Israel in 1948. The term 'Old' referred to the traditional way of life rather than to the length of time of residence in Palestine.

[5] 'Aliya', lit. 'ascent', the term has invested the act of immigration with positive connotations. The Hebrew term for an immigrant to Palestine was 'Oleh', lit. 'the one who ascends'.

[6] M. Eliav, 'Notes on the Development of the "Old Yishuv" in the 19th Century', in Y. Ben Porat (ed.), *Chapters in the History of the Jewish Community in Palestine* (Jerusalem, 1973), 59. Jerusalem became a centre for a printing industry, which was closely connected to the development of local cultural activity. Y. Ben-Arieh, *Jerusalem in the 19th century* (New York, 1986), 396–8.

[7] Eliav, 'Notes on Development', 59.

[8] J. Eisenstadt-Barzilai, 'An Opinion about the State of the *Yishuv* in Palestine in 1894', *Ahiassaf Calender* (1894). This contemporary view has been supported by contemporary research, see Kolat, 'Introduction', in Kolat (ed.), *Ottoman Period*, 70.

been cut off from its traditional sources of charity, and many of its members left the country. By contrast, the nationally motivated intellectuals struggled to preserve the Jewish community, mostly through the modernization of education. The first Hebrew Teachers' Training College opened in 1904. The Bezalel school for arts and crafts was launched in 1906, followed by a school of commerce in 1907, by the Hebrew Gymnasium in 1909, and by a music school in 1911.[9] On the eve of World War I the total number of students in the Hebrew schools of Jerusalem reached 380, of whom about one hundred enrolled at the Teachers' Training College.[10]

Jerusalem, the largest town in Palestine, was a social microcosm of Palestine.[11] A run-down provincial town which numbered only 12,000 in 1840, it reached a population of 31,500 in 1880 and 70,000 in 1914. William Henry Bartlett, an English painter and traveller, wrote in 1855 that 'Jerusalem is rapidly springing up into new life'[12] and Lawrence Oliphant wrote in August 1885 that 'there is probably no city in the dominion of the sultan which has undergone more change during the last few years than Jerusalem'.[13] An important factor in the process was the quick growth of the Jewish community of Jerusalem. Bartlett wrote in 1855 that the 'Jews are . . . the most numerous body in Jerusalem'.[14] The population of the Jewish community more than trebled from 5,000 in 1840 to 17,000 in 1880, and had risen to 45,000 by 1914.[15]

European Enclaves in Jerusalem

Jerusalem, the administrative centre of Palestine, became the focus for the penetration of European culture. The most active catalysts of the process were the foreign consulates, which held extensive legal privileges over

---

[9] Ibid. 585. About the music school, see below.   [10] *Aherout* (26 Oct. 1914).

[11] The Christian community consisted of eight sects. See U. O. Schmelz, 'Population Characteristics of Jerusalem and Hebron Regions according to Ottoman Census of 1905', in Gad Gilbar (ed.), *Ottoman Palestine 1800–1914* (Leiden, 1990), 28.

[12] *Jerusalem Revisited* (1855; Jerusalem, 1976), 49.

[13] *Haifa or Life in Modern Palestine* (London, 1887), 309. Oliphant (1829–88) was a British author and journalist who encouraged Jewish immigration to Palestine.

[14] *Jerusalem Revisited*, 42.

[15] Ben-Arieh, *Jerusalem in the 19th Century*, 466. The role immigration played in the population growth was even greater due to the very high mortality rate among Jews in Jerusalem until the late 19th cent. See U. Schmelz, 'Some Demographic Peculiarities of the Jews of Jerusalem in the 19th Century', in M. Ma'oz (ed.), *Palestine in the Ottoman Period* (Jerusalem, 1975). On the difficulties of establishing reliable demographic data for the Ottoman period see Schmelz, 'Population Characteristics', 15–20.

their citizens permanently residing or temporarily staying in Palestine. Most of the Jewish immigrants chose to retain their foreign nationality, and consequently their European orientation.[16] Many of the consuls were appointed on the basis of their academic competence in oriental studies, archeology, and history. For example, George Rosen, the German Consul (1852–65) was an orientalist,[17] and Emil Botta, the French Consul (1848–55) was an historian and a surgeon. Their political power was so formidable that people used to say that the 'consul is second only to God'.[18] Mrs Finn, the British Consul's wife, noted the 'large number of intelligent Europeans'[19] residing in Jerusalem, which included Christian sects from the United States, Sweden, Germany, and Russia[20] who cultivated activities within their enclaves, as did the German Colony founded in 1872 by the Templars.[21] For example, there is a record of a Society for Music for Brass Instruments at the German Colony, which sponsored a concert by nine musicians at the lobby of Feil's Hotel.[22] A constant flow of diplomats, pilgrims, businessmen, professional advisers, and romantics attracted to the Orient further diversified the ethnically multifarious city. In 1842 Bartlett noted that Jerusalem was 'destitute of every European comfort and a very inferior Oriental city'. But 'the influx of so large a number of Europeans, . . . soon wrought great changes'.[23] The city sparked the imagination of European romantics who occasionally fashioned lofty enterprises which came to nothing. For example, at the turn of the century a German musician by the name of Alfred Lenz announced a plan for a *Festspielhaus* in Jerusalem, which would mount 'plays on ancient and biblical themes, mostly with music and songs. Lenz is an Ottoman citizen, so he hopes to encounter no difficulties in securing the necessary permit. Investors from Berlin would finance the enterprise.'[24]

[16] In 1905 14,000 Jews were Ottoman citizens, contrasted with 21,000 who were foreign nationals. Schmelz, 'Population Characteristics', 26.

[17] B. Neumann, *Die Heilige Stadt und deren Bewohner* (Hamburg, 1877), 231–3.

[18] Eliav, 'Notes on Development', 53. A. Blumberg, *Zion before Zionism* (Syracuse, 1985), 125, has noted that consular supremacy reached its zenith in the years 1853–66. England opened the first consulate in Jerusalem in 1838, followed by Prussia (1842), France and Sardinia (1843), the United States (1844), and Austria (1849). Other consulates opened later and were less influential.

[19] Bartlett, *Jerusalem Revisited*, 36. James Finn served as the British Consul 1846–62.

[20] Ben-Arieh, *Jerusalem in the 19th Century*, 276–367.

[21] A. Carmel, *German Settlement in Palestine at the End of the Ottoman Period* (Jerusalem, 1973). The German Colony of Jerusalem, though the smallest of the seven colonies of the Templars in Palestine, became an important enclave of European culture. Many of the original homes of the German Colony, which has retained its name to the present day, have been preserved by law.

[22] *Gazette de Jerusalem* (1882). The bandmaster was Christian Rohrer (1868–1934), who was a teacher in the Neu Lyzeum Tempelstift.

[23] *Jerusalem Revisited*, 39.   [24] *Hashkafa* (15 Mar. 1900).

The cultural changes in Jerusalem must have been confined to enclosed enclaves closed to outsiders. The traveller W. H. Dixon wrote in 1869 that 'there were no balls, no theatres, and no taverns. Gaieties of any kind are rare.'[25] F. H. Deverell reported as late as 1899 that 'as regards entertainment and amusement and what is generally understood as "life" there is no such thing'.[26] Yet, those travellers who were personally invited into European homes experienced an intense cultural activity by way of music soirées. The Europeans in Jerusalem were deeply infected with the 'piano mania' which had spread over Europe in the mid-nineteenth century,[27] and they must have clung to their cherished instruments as cultural and status symbols, as well as reminders of home. Mary Eliza Rogers, a highly perceptive young English woman who joined her brother for a prolonged visit in Palestine in 1855, observed that 'the centre table and its newspapers, the book-cases, the pictures, the pianos, and little works of art and nicknacks, proclaimed that Europeans had made homes there'.[28] It is of special significance that Miss Rogers mentioned 'pianos' in the plural,[29] since the transport of heavy objects to Jerusalem at that time was a major logistic undertaking. Regular steamboats from European ports to Jaffa began to operate only in the early 1850s.[30] Until the 1870s the only way to reach Jerusalem was on horseback for the rich, and by camels and donkeys for all others. The travel from Jaffa to Jerusalem took more than ten hours and required an overnight stay in Ramlah. Luggage was carried by camels, who were capable of carrying up to 300 kg.[31] The first pianos reached Jerusalem in this way, reminiscent of the 'journey endured by the instrument which Broadwood sent to Beethoven in 1818'.[32] Only Europeans on official missions, such as consuls or well-to-do businessmen, could afford the transport of costly instruments. In 1869 a dirt road was paved and two stage-coaches went daily between Jaffa and Jerusalem, still with an overnight stay.[33] It was only in 1892 that a French company started a train service from Jaffa to Jerusalem.[34] Thus, Palestine lagged behind Europe by more than fifty years in the development of the mode of transportation which had proved itself crucial to the dissemination of affordable pianos.[35]

[25] The Holy Land (London, 1869).   [26] My Tour in Palestine and Syria (London, 1899).

[27] Ehrlich, Music Profession in Britain, 71.

[28] Domestic Life in Palestine (1862; London, 1989), 35.

[29] M. Tschaikov, 'Musical Life in the Christian Communities of Jerusalem', MA Thesis (Hebrew University, Jerusalem, 1993).

[30] Consul Finn's family needed sixty-two days to go from London to Jerusalem. Ben-Arieh, Jerusalem in the 19th Century, 83.

[31] Ibid. 122.   [32] C. Ehrlich, The Piano (Oxford, 1990), 18.

[33] Yehoshua Ben-Arieh, 'Yishuv', 132.   [34] Ben-Arieh, Jerusalem in the 19th Century, 368.

[35] Ehrlich, Piano, 39.

On 11 November 1841 Michael Solomon Alexander was appointed the first Anglican bishop of Jerusalem. His wife brought along with her a harp and a piano and entertained her guests at receptions on Sunday nights. After the Bishop's sudden death the piano was sold to the Pasha, but there is no evidence that any member of his household ever used it.[36] It is likely that this was the same piano on which Colonel Hugh Rose, former British Consul in Beirut, played a recital at the Pasha's residence on 10 March 1851.[37] One of the celebrated travellers in Jerusalem was 'a nice old gentleman . . . Mr Broadwood'.[38] The German Consul George Rosen married Ignaz Moschelles's daughter, who frequently played the piano for her guests. Dr Titus Tobler reported that life in the Holy City was so boring that he used to visit Consul Emil Botta almost every evening to smoke hash and to play Beethoven's piano sonatas.[39] Thus Jerusalem acquired pianos when they were still rare in other parts of Palestine. Mary Eliza Rogers related an event which took place on 30 July 1856 in the tiny town of Haifa.

There were some additions to the European colony, and when Signor V., the Dutch Vice Consul called, he informed us that he had obtained a piano. It was the first which had ever been introduced into Haifa, and there was no one in town, excepting myself, who knew how to touch it. He invited all the Europeans to a soiree a few days after our arrival, that the new instrument might be inaugurated. . . . We found the Governor and about twenty Moslem gentlemen, in their richest embroidered costumes, assembled in the drawing room . . . The piano had been tried in turn by nearly all the guests, and they said: 'We cannot make it speak the same language which you cause it to speak, oh lady!' I handed to them some pieces of music, saying: 'Could you do so with the help of these?' It was very amusing to hear their exclamations and observe the surprise with which they watched my fingers. especially when they found that I looked all the while at the book before me. They are accustomed only to see small and portable musical instruments, and they wandered at my command over one so large, and said: 'The labourers at harvest time do no work so hard or move their hands so quickly.' They seemed to be more struck with the rapidity with which the keys were touched than with the sounds which were produced, until I played their national anthem, 'Abdul Medjid'. Then they all seemed roused, and a clear voiced singer . . . came forward immediately and sang, the rest of the company joined in chorus. One of the Becks seemed to appreciate music so much, that I told him if he would buy a piano for his wife I would teach her the use of it. He said: 'Oh, my sister, our women are not

---

[36] Tschaikov, 'Musical Life'.   [37] E. A. Finn, *Home in the Holy Land* (London, 1866).
[38] A. Blumberg (ed.), *A View from Jerusalem 1849–1858: The Consular Diary of James and Elizabeth Finn* (London, 1980). James Broadwood (1772–1851) was Johan Broadwood's eldest son.
[39] *Das Ausland*, 21 (1865). Dr Tobler (1806–77) was a Swiss physician and cartographer.

capable of learning—their heads are made of wood—it would be as easy to teach donkeys as to teach them.' By degree nearly everyone in the town became familiar with the sound of the piano, and it gave rise to many very pleasant soirees. This was the dawn of a new era in the history of the little European colony at Haifa, and music and singing were cultivated with energy.[40]

Occasionally music bridged the chasm between the Europeans and the Old Yishuv. In 1846 a young Jewish girl by the name of Rachel told Mrs Finn how much she enjoyed listening to the singing in church and to the missionary daughter's guitar. Rachel confessed that she had never heard the sound of a piano, and Mrs Finn introduced her to her friend, Mrs Wells, who not only played to her but treated her to free piano lessons as well. Indeed, Rachel proved to be 'a very apt pupil'.[41]

The responses of the Europeans to Arabic and Turkish music ranged from an outright rejection to a polite tolerance. Consul Finn entered in his diary on 26 December 1853 a reminder to make a request to the Turkish official 'not to allow the military music at the barracks during church time on Sunday'.[42] Mrs Finn complained that the brass band which played in the nearby barracks 'purposely make notes which are certainly discordant to our ears'.[43] Mary Eliza Rogers described a 'large party at the [French] Consulate. A number of English travellers came, and many of the European residents. In the course of the evening some Arab musicians were allowed to enter to play and sing for the especial entertainment the strangers present. Impromptu songs were sung in honour of the Imperial Prince.'[44] Although a fine musician herself, Miss Rogers made no further comment on the Arabic music. The missionary Josias Leslie Porter wrote a lukewarm report on Arabic music played in an open cafe: 'The notes are somewhat metallic, but not altogether unpleasant, and are generally accompanied by a slow nasal chant one might mistake for a funeral dirge. Yet, the natives of all classes enjoy it, and listen with rapt attention, as if it were the perfection of harmony and the masterpiece of a musical genius.'[45] The construction of the train station next to the German Colony in 1892 turned the peaceful enclave into a transportation centre which attracted Arabs to build a neighbouring Muslim section, and the Templars bitterly complained that 'the singing, or rather the screaming, of the *muezzin* is heard here day and night'.[46]

[40] *Domestic Life*, 351–2. Rogers, ibid. 85, estimated the entire population of Haifa at that time as numbering a little over 2,000, most of whom were Moslems, Greek Orthodox, and Greek Catholics.

[41] Finn, *Home in the Holy Land*, 290.

[42] Blumberg (ed.), *A View from Jerusalem 1849–1858*, 145.

[43] *Home in the Holy Land*, 158.   [44] *Domestic Life*, 292.

[45] *Jerusalem, Bethany, and Bethlehem* (London, 1887).   [46] *Die Warte* (11 Mar. 1897).

The American missionary William Thomson described what he heard in the open cafés in the 1860s as 'strange music from curious instruments, interspersed with wild bursts of song'.[47] Thomson also made drawings of the instruments, which turned out to be kanun, kamanjeh, oud, daff,[48] violin, and flutes.

High-quality charity concerts were occasionally held at churches in Jerusalem, such as the concert at the Erlösenkirche in 1904, in which two singers, two organists, a string quartet, and a chorus took part.[49] The consulates initiated musical charity events such as a concert sponsored by the wives of the Russian and of the British consuls in aid of the British Ophthalmic Hospital.[50] Such events were advertised in the Hebrew press. Still, they were infrequent and catered to a small segment of the Jewish population which could afford the donations expected at such events.

The European enclaves and the intellectuals of the New Yishuv shared a Eurocentric view. They were neither trained, nor motivated, to penetrate the walls of the compartmentalized Jewish and Muslim communities and to grasp the wealth of their musical traditions. Public musical life in the New Yishuv in Jerusalem during the Ottoman period was rudimentary.[51] Cultural evenings, which as a rule combined lectures, recitation of poems, music, and social games were sporadic and numbered no more than half a dozen per year. Young music-lovers among the immigrants who were unlikely to frequent the consuls' residences felt a void. In 1912 the poet Ya'akov Koplewitz wrote in his memoirs:

The one thing which I missed more than anything in Jerusalem was music. I was a music-lover since my youth. The Italian opera tunes which my old Polish friend Pan Kahl had played to me in my home town, and the pleasing Russian waltzes which the cavalry band used to play at dawn while riding for drills through the sleeping town, had awakened in me the desire for the art of music with its penetrating magic. I found nothing of all that in Jerusalem. Jerusalem revealed itself to me as perceived through vision and contemplation, but not through sound ... The Arabic ornamental singing which used to come out of old gramophones here and there in the Old City or at the Arab café near Jaffa Gate, and the eastern chanting of our brethren the Jews of Babylon and Syria,

---

[47] *The Land and the Book* (London, 1878), 683.

[48] The kanun is a large rectangular stringed instrument which is plucked by the fingers of both hands; the kamanjeh is a bowed instrument held on the knees; the oud is the progenitor of the European lute; and the daff is a large drum.

[49] *Hashkafa* (26 Nov. 1904) (notice printed in Hebrew and in German).

[50] *Hashkafa* (9 Feb. 1906) (notice printed in Hebrew and in English).

[51] See Ch. 2, below.

accompanied by their monotonous harp, did not sound to my ears as music at all, but as part of the exotic outlines of the environment. I could not hear them for more than a quarter of an hour without succumbing to oppressive feelings of alienation.[52]

Cultural Strife within the Jewish Community

The Old Yishuv led a strictly structured religious life. The quick growth of the Old Yishuv was accompanied by a process of fragmentation of the two large units of Sephardi and Ashkenazi into small communities, each practising its own musical heritage. Ashkenazi Jews were divided into Hasidic groups, each belonging to a specific Hasidic court in Europe, and Prushim.[53] From 1854 the Sephardis gradually split into Pure Sephardis, Yemenites, Mugrabi,[54] Georgians, Bukharans, Persians, Babylonians, Halebi, and several other small groups.[55]

Music was frequently practised among the Jewish communities of Jerusalem by regular bands of Klezmorim.[56] They performed on any festive occasion, especially at weddings, at times during the full seven days of festivities following the marriage ceremony. Ephraim Cohen-Reiss, who later became an innovative educator, reported that as a child he and his friends had attended every happy family celebration in town. 'But the central festivity used to be celebrated among both Sephardim and Ashkenazim on Saturday night. . . . We Ashkenazim, of course, preferred the music of Alter Fioler and Rabbi Haim Schernowitzer, but we also accustomed ourselves to listen to the Sephardi tunes with great Eastern pleasure.'[57]

The custom of instrumental music among the Ashkenazi Jews suffered a fatal setback shortly after Rabbi Meir Eurbach, a highly respected and wealthy religious leader, immigrated to Jerusalem in 1859.[58]

---

[52] Yeshurun Keshet, *Kedna Veyama* (*East and West*) (Tel Aviv, 1980), 34. Koplewitz (1892–1977, immigrated 1911) was a poet and a columnist who later used the Hebrew pen-name Yeshurun Keshet.

[53] A term signifying Jews opposed to the Hasidic movement in the 19th cent. (unrelated to the usage of the term in the period of the Second Temple). The same divisions have obtained to the present day.

[54] Lit. 'Western', referring to the Magreb countries (Tunisia, Morocco, Algiers).

[55] Y. Ben-Arieh, *A City Reflected in its Times, the Old City* (Jerusalem, 1977), 406. The fragmentation contrasted the official Ottoman policy which recognized the Chief Sephardi Rabbi as the sole representative of the Jews in Palestine.

[56] Lit. 'instruments of music', such bands, which frequently achieved a very high professional competence, existed in all Jewish communities in the Diaspora. Their instrumental combinations varied, but they usually included violin, clarinet, cello or double bass, and percussion.

[57] E. Cohen Reiss (1863–1933), *Memories of a Son of Jerusalem* (Jerusalem, 1967), 38.

[58] Ben-Arieh, *The Old City*, 416.

Rabbi Meir Eurbach and his court of law prohibited any instrumental music within the walls of Jerusalem which mourns the destruction of the Temple. Only drum beating was allowed. The Sephardim ignored the Ashkenazi Rabbi, but the Ashkenazim were forced to obey. . . . The weddings and the procession of the bride looked like funerals.[59]

The slow emergence of the New Yishuv represented an ominous threat to the small and frail Old Yishuv. Though frequently torn by internal strife and power struggles, the Old Yishuv was united in its antagonism to secular culture, to modernization, and especially to the revival of Hebrew as a modern literary and daily language,[60] all of which were the declared goals of the New Yishuv. The main target of the attacks of the Old Yishuv at the turn of the century was the amateur theatre which was considered by them as the most despicable, whether the Yiddish theatre which functioned as a nostalgic pastime, or the Hebrew theatre which served as a powerful educational and national tool. Yet, music was also frequently a source of conflict. A Jerusalem journalist witnessed a Hasidic Jew furiously tearing posters off the walls announcing a production of three short plays with music.[61] Yehiel M. Pinnes and Yoel Salomon, two moderate religious leaders who tried in vain to mediate between the opposing factions, were thus caught in a crossfire between the extreme forces of the Old Yishuv and Eliezer Ben-Yehudah,[62] the outspoken advocate of secular nationalism and of the modernization of Hebrew. Ben-Yehudah enlisted the support of the prestigious Sephardi educator Nissim Behar,[63] and thus mixed *Kulturkampf* with ethnic rivalry. Pinnes bitterly complained that 'Behar and Ben-Yehudah endeavour to constitute an "orchestra" in Jerusalem and the young Sephardi charlatans assist them and print "cards", attracting members to this honourable institute which they describe as "a source of pride to the Holy City" and they have already trapped a few Ashkenazis in their net.'[64]

[59] Cohen Reiss, *Memories*, 38. The powerful prohibition has been maintained to the present day in the ultra-orthodox circles in Jerusalem, though a single singer with percussion is tolerated. The ban has been occasionally circumvented by celebrating weddings outside Jerusalem. Y. Mazor and M. Taube, 'A Hassidic Ritual Dance: The *mitsve tants* in Jerusalemite Weddings', *Yuval*, 6 (1992), n. 4.

[60] Hebrew was considered in religious circles as a sacred language allowed for use only in services and learning. The Ashkenazi Old Yishuv used Yiddish as a daily language whereas the Sephardi communities used Judeo-Espagnol (Ladino) or Arabic dialects.

[61] *Ha'Zevi* (7 Feb. 1909).

[62] Eliezer Ben-Yehudah (1858–1922, immigrated 1881) founded and edited the Hebrew papers *HaZevi, Ha'Or, Hashkafa,* which acted as powerful political tools for his national ideology..

[63] Nissim Behar (1847–1931) was born in Jerusalem, where he founded and directed the schools of the Alliance israelite, in which he insisted on teaching in Hebrew. In 1897 he emigrated to the United States.

[64] A letter from Yehiel Mihal Pinnes (1843–1913) to Yoel Moshe Salomon (1838–1912), 1 Nov. 1896, quoted in A. R. Malachi, *Studies in the History of the Old Yishuv* (Tel Aviv, 1971), 313.

Idelsohn in Jerusalem

The potential of the Jewish communities of Jerusalem as an inviting treasure for ethnic studies led to a partial loosening of ethnic barriers and to the revelation of its wealth to outsiders. Thus, it was the imaginative and daring scholar, Abraham Zvi Idelsohn (1882–1938) who affected a major turning-point in the cultural life and status of Jerusalem.[65] Born in Latvia and trained as a cantor, Idelsohn also acquired extensive musical and general education in Berlin and in Leipzig. After a short period of work as cantor in South Africa, Idelsohn decided to devote his

strength to the research of the Jewish folk song. This idea ruled my life to such extent that I could find no rest. I therefore gave up my position and traveled to Jerusalem, without knowing what was in store for me. In Jerusalem, I found about 300 synagogues and some young men eager to study *Chazanuth* [cantorial singing and repertory]. . . . I started collecting their traditional songs. In the course of time the Phonogramm Archives of Vienna and of Berlin came to my help.[66]

Idelsohn came to Jerusalem early in January 1907. Eliezer Ben-Yehudah hailed the young musician's arrival and wished him success in his endeavour 'to revive the Jewish singing in the spirit of the ancient Hebrew song which flourished in the Land of Israel'.[67]

From the start Idelsohn worked simultaneously as a scholar,[68] a choral conductor, a composer and arranger,[69] author,[70] and a music teacher. He persisted despite the difficulties of research and of living conditions in

[65] For detailed analytical and critical studies of Idelsohn's life and work see *Memorial Volume*; I. Adler and J. Cohen, *A. Z. Idelsohn Archives at the Jewish National and University Library* (Jerusalem, 1976); E. Werner, 'Abraham Zvi Idelsohn: In Memoriam', *From Generation to Generation* (New York, 1969), 161–8; Amnon Shiloah, *Jewish Musical Traditions* (Detroit, 1992), 21–33.

[66] Idelsohn, 'My Life', *Jewish Music Journal* (1936), repr. in *Memorial Volume*, 18–23, with an introd. by Eliyahu Schleifer.

[67] *Hashkafa* (15 Jan. 1907). Earlier dates which have been presented elsewhere, as in I. Cohon, 'Idelsohn: The Founder and Builder of the Science of Jewish Music—the Cantor of Jewish Song', in *Memorial Volume*, 40, have ignored the precise press documentation of Idelsohn's arrival.

[68] On Idelsohn as a scholar see E. Gerson-Kiwi, 'A. Z. Idelsohn: A Pioneer in Jewish Ethnomusicology', *Memorial Volume*, 46–52, and R. Katz, 'Exemplification and the Limits of "Correctness"' *Memorial Volume*, 365–72. The Edison phonograph used by Idelsohn is on display at the National Sound Archives, Hebrew University, Jerusalem.

[69] S. Hoffman, 'A. Z. Idelsohn's Music: A Bibliography', *Memorial Volume*, Hebrew sections 31–50. J. Cohen, 'The Opera "Jiphtah" by A. Z. Idelsohn', *Tatzlil*, 15 (1975), 127–31.

[70] Idelsohn published a serialized novel and started another one, and completed a play, *Elijah*, (Idelsohn Archive, JNUL, Mus. 7 (656)). See E. Schleifer, 'Idelsohn: An Annotated Bibliography', *Memorial Volume*, p. 96, item 6, and p. 100, item 13. In 1921 he sent MSS of *Jephtah* and of *Elijah* to his close friend, the venerable poet Bialik, who criticized their scanty contents (Idelsohn Archive, JNUL, Mus. 7 (81)).

Palestine at the time.[71] His early publications soon reached Jewish scholars in Europe who asked him for material and advice.[72] His fieldwork was so intensive that after two years he presented a full manuscript of his work to respected professors in Germany, whose warm recommendations to publish the young scholar's work reflected the novelty of his in-context field work. Dr A. Berliner made a special note to the effect that Idelsohn had studied not only the 'accessible Polish-German or Sephardi-Italian traditions, but also the liturgies of the Yemenite, Moroccan, Persian, and other oriental Jews with special interest', and Prof. William Wolf pointed out that Idelsohn had worked with his informants not only in private but also recorded them during synagogue service.[73] While Idelsohn pursued his ethnomusicological work 'entirely by himself',[74] he enlisted the inter-disciplinary co-operation of members of the small scholarly community then residing in Jerusalem.[75]

Idelsohn earned his living in Palestine as a music teacher employed by the Hilfsverein der Deutsche Juden. The principal of the Hilfsverein schools was Ephraim Cohen-Reiss, whose special support of music education might have been a result of his childhood reaction to Rabbi Eurbach's prohibition of music in Jerusalem. Founded in 1901 in Germany, the Hilfsverein established a network of schools in Palestine, most of them in Jerusalem, with kindergartens, an elementary school, and a prestigious teachers' training college.[76] The very heavy curriculum combined the current German programme of humanities and sciences which was taught either in German or in Hebrew with Judaic studies taught exclusively in Hebrew. Music was a compulsory subject. The school maintained a religious orientation, and Idelsohn served as the cantor at the school's impressive synagogue. The Society paid adequate salaries according to the German rate, so that 'a position of a teacher at

[71] Irma Cohon, one of Idelsohn's close friends, reported that he suffered from severe health problems during his long stay in Jerusalem: 'Idelsohn', 40.

[72] A letter from David Magid, St Petersburg, 27 June 1913 (Idelsohn Archive, JNUL, Mus. 7 (398)).

[73] Letters from Dr P. Kahle, University of Halle, 30 Apr. 1911; Dr A. Berliner, Berlin, 5 May 1911; and Professor William Wolf, Berlin-Grünewald, Apr. 1911 (Idelsohn Archive, JNUL, Mus. 7 (326, 78, 641)).

[74] B. Bayer, 'The Announcement of the "Institute of Jewish Music" in Jerusalem', *Memorial Volume*, 25.

[75] Most importantly with linguist Dr Herz Torczyner (Naftali H. Tur-Sinai). See Schleifer, 'Annotated Bibliography', p. 107, item 24, and p. 148, item 77.

[76] The Hilfsverein competed with the Alliance israelite universelle and combined support of Judaic studies and Hebrew with the wish to disseminate the German language and culture. M. Rinot, 'Education in Eretz Israel', in Kolat (ed.), *Ottoman Period*, 652–64. Ben-Arieh, *Jerusalem in the 19th Century*, 427.

Ex 1.1. Idelsohn's right-to-left notation

the College in Jerusalem was prestigious on all accounts'.[77] Consequently Idelsohn's teaching position contributed to the immediate affirmation of his status in the local community and also acquainted him with the Jewish intellectual and political leadership. Idelsohn was also a music teacher at the School for the Blind and at the Bezalel school for arts and crafts.[78]

In his teaching Idelsohn emphasized the importance of music theory and of singing. In 1910 he founded a chorus which consisted of fifty girls and twenty boys from the Jerusalem schools and from the teachers' college.[79] The near-absence of any adequate Hebrew songs inspired him to publish a *Liederbuch* in Hebrew, in which he included his own original tunes as well as arrangements of Hasidic melodies and of two songs by Schumann and by Mendelssohn.[80] The collection was warmly received when it reached the Jerusalem bookstores as 'the book for which we have yearned for the past generation since the initiation of our national revival'.[81] Idelsohn had the music printed from right to left, in an attempt to overcome the difficulty of text underlay in Hebrew (see Ex. 1.1).[82]

---

[77] Rinot, 'Education', 656. Nevertheless, Irma Cohon has reported that Idelsohn paid his informants, and apparently had to cover some of the expenses of his publications, which accounted for his tight living conditions in Jerusalem. 'Idelsohn', 40.

[78] *Ha'Or* (5 Apr. 1910).   [79] *Ha'Or* (9 Apr. 1910).

[80] S. Hoffman, 'Idelsohn's Music', *Memorial Volume*. Hebrew section, 39. The Hilfsverein published the first volume in 1912, and apologized for the long delay (a letter of 31 May 1912 (Idelsohn Archive, JNUL, Mus. 7 (327)), so it appears that Idelsohn had completed the volume much earlier and gave it top priority. In 1912 Idelsohn published a methodological article on teaching music in Palestine (see Schleifer, 'Annotated Bibliography', p. 99, item 12).

[81] *Ha'Or* (21 June and 16 July 1912).

[82] Hebrew is a Semitic language written from right to left, and consequently music requires a cumbersome text underlay of syllable by syllable. Idelsohn's solution, which had been previously used only in old illustrations of masoretic accents, was not adopted by local musicians, with the exception of a few of his ardent admirers, and was completely abandoned after 1930.

Soon after his arrival Idelsohn became a regular contributor to Eliezer Ben-Yehudah's Hebrew newspapers. Idelsohn expressed his deep respect for Ben-Yehudah's dedication to the Hebrew language by the use of the Hebrew pen-name 'Ben-Yehudah' in most of his local publications.

The first stage of Idelsohn's research involved an extensive anthropological study of the principal communities of Eastern Jews in Jerusalem. Edith Gerson-Kiwi has pointed out that 'today it is difficult to realize that, at one time, Ashkenazi Judaism was the exclusive subject of historical, theological, and sociological study'.[83] Idelsohn's newspaper essays were permeated by a moralizing and occasionally even a sardonic rhetoric. It was soon after his arrival that he launched his first attack on the

prejudices held by Ashkenazi Jews towards their Sephardi brethren. . . . our enlightened brothers in Europe forget that they have family kins in Asia, and they ignore them. Really, what would an educated Jew have in common with people such as Yemenites, Sephardi, Persians, etc.? All European Jews are in agreement that whoever is not dressed in a tail and does not chatter in French is not a part of civilization. . . . Even I once held the false belief that the Sephardi Jews were musically incompetent, until I realized that the Sephardis were highly disposed to singing.[84]

Idelsohn's first study[85] which was completed within a few months of his arrival, was dedicated to the Yemenite community of Jerusalem, the uniqueness of which had been favourably underlined soon after their immigration began in 1882.[86] Idelsohn went beyond a mere ethnographic diary in his expression of compassion for the poverty-stricken community and his rebuke to the Ashkenazi Jews for their exploitation of the Yemenites as a cheap labour force. He emphasized the fact that despite their dismal conditions, the Yemenites remained proud of their ancient history and preserved their rich spiritual heritage, which included a mastery of Hebrew and a magnificent musical tradition. His pioneering study endowed the Yemenites with a special romanticized status both in Palestine and in the West for years to come. The philological and musicological section of his article instigated immediate responses among leading scholars in Europe. Prof. Wilhelm Bacher[87] questioned Idelsohn's

[83] 'A. Z. Idelsohn: A Pioneer in Jewish Ethnomusicology', *Memorial Volume*, 50.

[84] *Hashkafa* (19 May 1908). Idelsohn's target was the Jewish leadership in Europe rather than the local Jerusalem community, where the well-established Sephardi Jewish community had long constituted the French-speaking nobility.

[85] *Gazette de Jerusalem*, 14 (1908), 101–54; later fully replicated in the 1st vol. of the Thesaurus. A detailed summary in Schleifer, 'Annotated Bibliography', p. 93, item 2.

[86] Oliphant, *Haifa*, 311.

[87] Wilhelm Bacher (1850–1913) was a great scholar of Judaic studies and Semitic languages. His studies of the Hebrew and Arabic poetry of Yemenite Jews were the first in that field.

rubrics which accompanied the transcriptions. Protecting his methods, Idelsohn emphasized the significant difference between the Yemenites and all other Jews from Arab countries. The Jewish poets in Syria, for example, fit popular Arabic tunes to their sacred poems, 'and the tunes make the Jews like the Hebrew lyrics'.[88] Not so the Yemenites, whose 'Rabbis strictly prohibited them from singing Arab songs, and even more so from imposing an Arab tune on a sacred poem. . . . As a result each *Meshorer*[89] must invent his own tunes, . . . and the Yemenite tunes are in no way related to the Arab tunes.'

Idelsohn's initial encounter with Jerusalem gave rise to a multilayered personal transformation, the extent of which was revealed in his *Two Musicians*, a semi-documentary vignette which strongly betrays the style of Schumann's critical essays and of E. T. A. Hoffmann's Kapellmeister Kreisler tales. Idelsohn begins with a description of a piano recital held in a magnificent hall and attended by the high society of Jerusalem. A grotesque depiction of the women with their heavy make-up, with 'towers of straw, feathers, and flowers on their heads' leads to a Hoffmanesque poetic interpretation of the performance by an unnamed, long-haired, and demonic pianist.

I watch the audience for the effect of the Faustian playing on them. The men are glancing at their women and at their exposed necks, and the women are looking at each other: 'whose dress is prettier?'. I leave the hall engulfed in thoughts: 'Here is an audience, allegedly educated, "European", listening to European playing of the great masterpieces, and these people understand nothing . . .'. All of a sudden I hear the sound of playing echoing in the silence of the night. And in front of the gate, in a miserable shack, there sit Arabic farmers on low benches, smoking *nargilas* and drinking coffee from tiny cups, and in their midst there sits a musician absorbed in his song. . . . And the voice of the Arab musician swells. He tells about his beloved, her dark flashing eyes and her painted fingers, her straight figure and her pomegranate breasts. . . . His voice is full of yearning and outpouring, sadness and hidden pain, it touches the heart, and the Arabs answer with deep sighs 'Ah', 'Allah'. . . . the moon shines in the deep skies, all is peaceful and quiet. . . . And then I feel myself merged with the spirit of ancient times.[90]

Romantic orientalism, revolt against *petit bourgeois* values, and rejection of the social establishment and customs of European Jewry all combined to form the young musician's predisposition to undertake his monumental scholarly and educational programme.

[88] *Ha'Or* (30 Oct. 1910).
[89] The term *Meshorer* implies the Yemenite singer who both invents and performs the song.
[90] *HaZevi* (17 June 1909).

Idelsohn's comprehensive field work with the Yemenite community could not be replicated with all other Jewish communities in Jerusalem. He preferred to invite the informants to his study

which was at the far end of our house, and was most of the time full of guests. . . . Father stood at his high desk and made a quick transcription while they were singing. Frequently guests arrived during lunch and screamed various tunes. Father was engrossed in the music and did not touch his food.[91]

On 12 April 1910 Idelsohn published an excited appeal to all Jewish musicians in Jerusalem to gather for an as yet unspecified joint action.[92] A few days later Idelsohn and his assistant, Cantor Shlomo Zalman Rivlin (1884–1962), incorporated the text of the appeal into a longer and more specific *Announcement of the Institute of Jewish Music* in Jerusalem.[93] A few weeks later they asked the editor of *Aherout* to publish the detailed work plan of the Institute, which substituted a down-to-earth systematic description of the project for the 'high-flown, indeed bombastic, yet frequently awkward'[94] style of the initial announcement.

A. To collect all folksongs and tunes which have been practised in all ethnic groups of Israel, . . . and to gather all the singers and cantors of those groups who are now active in Jerusalem . . . The singers of each ethnic group will constitute a separate choir which will perform its own songs only. . . . In this way we will collect all songs and singers into one centre, and the specific spirit of each ethnic group will become known. This should enable us to compare them and to determine to what extent they stem from a common source. . . . In that way we would reach our second and cardinal goal:
B. To turn the singing of Israel into the stage of a living tradition. If the Jewish singers persist in living together and in singing in one centre, the various groups would inevitably influence one another . . . and the people of Israel would have a common song, a new–old song, and there will be no more Ashkenazi, Yemenite, Sephardi, Halebi song, but the song of Israel emanating from Jerusalem. . . . This is the scholarly part of the Institute. . . . But there is also a practical goal, which is the training of singers and musicians entitled to be called 'Hebrew' . . . The Institute will present plays with music based on the history of the people of Israel.[95]

---

[91] Memoirs of Idelsohn's daughter, Susanna, typescript, (Idelsohn Archive 1976 (no siglum), JNUL).

[92] *Ha'Or* (12 Apr. 1910).

[93] Hebrew original of the official announcement and an English trans. with an introd. by Bathja Bayer in *Memorial Volume*, 24–35. The article in *Ha'Or* comprises sections 1–8 of the *Announcement*, and it appears that the earlier publication was intended to raise expectations for the public presentation of the entire ambitious project.

[94] Ibid. 26.   [95] *Aherout* (25 May 1910).

Idelsohn and Rivlin added that they had by then taken the initial step, having established an Ashkenazi choir numbering forty members under Cantor Rivlin, a Yemenite choir consisting of twenty members under Levi Hamadi, and a Halebi[96] choir of fifteen members directed by Itzhac Adam. *Aherout* devoted an entire front page to the event. Using highly flowery rhetoric, the author linked the spirit of Israel with the 'song of Israel, that gentle voice of Israel, which is one of its most precious qualities, the pearl in its treasure'.[97]

Four months later the Institute made its first public presentation at a *Musaf* prayer, and Itamar Ben-Avi[98] wrote that

the experiment, as attested to by all experts present there, went very well. Three classes of singers, the Ashkenazis, the Yemenites, and the Halebis, sang together or in alternation, each group in its own style, and it all combined into a pleasant harmony. All those singers, seventy in number, were until a few months ago far from any scholarly conceived singing and far from one another, as are the disparate parts of the nation of Israel. . . . And this first attempt is of great importance to us, since it proves that Mr Abraham is right in his idea and in the prospects of carrying it out.[99]

Ben-Avi concluded his enthusiastic review with a warning that the promising project badly needed—and deserved—adequate financial support and a proper house. Yet, the Committee for Support of Jewish Farmers and Craftsmen in Syria and Palestine promptly cooled down the excitement when it turned down Idelsohn's application for lack of adequate funds which were needed 'for even more urgent purposes'.[100] Idelsohn soon encountered even worse obstacles on the social front. The ultra orthodox circles of Jerusalem, whom Idelsohn described as 'fanatics'[101] shunned any sort of co-operation with a member of the New Yishuv and blocked the charity funds of those Yeshiva[102] students who

[96] Haleb, Syria, had an ancient Jewish community which had its own distinct musical tradition.

[97] A. Levin, 'An Institute of the Song of Israel in Eretz Israel', *Aherout* (20 May 1910).

[98] Itamar Ben-Avi (1882–1943) was Eliezer Ben-Yehudah's son. He followed his father in his unceasing struggle for the cause of the Hebrew language and for national revival. He was a journalist and editor, whose writing was dominated by flowery rhetorics.

[99] *Ha'Or* (23 Aug. 1910).

[100] Letter from Menachem Ussishkin, 10 Nov. 1910 (Idelssohn Archive, JNUL, Mus. 7 (132)).

[101] Idelsohn, 'My Life', *Memorial Volume*, Hebrew section, 18.

[102] 'Yeshiva' (or 'Yeshivah') is a general term for any institute of high learning of Jewish theology. In the Orthodox Jewish communities the curriculum of the Yeshiva centres on an intensive reading and study of the Talmud as the font of Judaism. Learning at the Yeshiva is regarded as the highest fulfilment of the way of life of an observant Jew, and the Yeshivas are considered sacred.

were ready to cooperate with him. The Ashkenazi choir alone endured, whereas the Sephardi choirs led a merely sporadic existence.[103]

In 1913 the staff and students of the Hilfsverein schools became involved in a heated controversy concerning the use of German in the curriculum, which the advocates of exclusive Hebrew education opposed. The ideological conflict between the Hilfsverein and the Hebraists erupted in 1913 into a full-scale *Kulturkampf*. The supporters of Hebrew resigned and opened new Hebrew schools, attracting many of the pupils. Idelsohn joined them, although the principal of the Hilfsverein offered to double his salary.[104]

Despite his dedication to the local community, research and European contacts were at the top of Idelsohn's priorities. Soon after his arrival in Jerusalem he applied for an Egyptian passport which was issued 10 May 1907 and permitted him to depart from Port Sa'id to Europe,[105] although he first returned to Europe only seven years later. Upon the completion of the bulk of his fieldwork he became increasingly anxious to return to the mainstream of the musicological community. He sent the first collection of his annotated transcriptions to the venerable Prof. Oskar Fleischer who returned a warm letter in which he emphasized his personal interest in Idelsohn's hypothesis, which Fleischer himself had endorsed in his own research of ancient Greek and Christian traditions. Fleischer recommended that Idelsohn's work be soon published.[106] Erich von Hornbostel sent him a very detailed letter instructing him in the new methods of recording and transcription.[107] In December 1913 Idelsohn traveled to Austria where he presented the results of his studies to the Imperial Academy of Sciences in Vienna.[108] The Jerusalem press proudly reported that 'this has been the first time that an official Academy— indeed, one of the foremost in Europe—recognized the existence of

[103] Shlomo Z. Rivlin directed the Ashkenazi choir for many years after Idelsohn's departure, as told by Prof. Eliyahu Schleifer who has participated as a boy (personal communication, Feb. 1992).

[104] Idelsohn, 'My Life', *Memorial Volume*, 22. Idelsohn's decision might explain Ephraim Cohen Reiss's relatively cool attitude to Idelsohn's contribution in his autobiography *Memories of a Son of Jerusalem*.

[105] Idelsohn Archive, JNUL, Mus. 7 (677).

[106] Letter of 28 Apr. 1911 (Idelsohn Archive, 1976, JNUL, (yet uncatalogued)). Fleischer (1856– 1933) had published most of his studies of Greek and early Christian chant by 1904. W. Vetter, 'Fleischer, Oskar', *MGG* iv. 290.

[107] Letter of 2 Feb. 1913, (Idelsohn Archive, JNUL, Mus. 7 (279)). The letter followed Hornbostel and Otto Abraham, 'Über die Bedeutung des Phonographen für die vergleichende Musikwissenschaft', *Zeitschrift für Ethnologie*, 36 (1904), 222–33. See also B. Nettl, *The Study of Ethnomusicology* (Urbana, Ill., 1983), 359.

[108] The proceedings were published in 1917. For full details see Schleifer, 'Annotated Bibliography', p. 107, item 24.

Hebrew music. This is a victory to Hebrew culture.' The lecture attracted a large crowd, and its members were especially impressed 'by the musical examples he played on his phonogram recordings. We express our satisfaction with the great reputation which one of the dearest sons of Zion has achieved in the scientific community.'[109] On 27 June 1914 that venerable institution approved a grant of 500 kronen for the publication of the first volume,[110] which appeared in print in the same year.[111] The success in Germany, contrasted with the hardships and opposition he had met at home, led Idelsohn to a decision to stay in Germany, as alluded to in a letter of recommendation which Dr James Simon, representative of the Hilfsverein, wrote on his behalf. Having highly praised Idelsohn's accomplishments, Simon concluded that 'Mr Idelsohn intends to move to Germany in order to complete a series of musicological essays. We deplore his departure from our institutions and wish him all the best.'[112] Idelsohn extended his stay in Vienna for several months after the presentation of his paper at the Academy. In March 1914 the Jewish community of Posen invited him to serve as cantor and choir director at the Passover services.[113] It thus appears that his return to Palestine was affected by the outbreak of the war, which prevented him from pursuing his plans in Germany. Upon his return he resumed his work with the school choruses, with whom he performed pieces by Lewandowky and Haydn at a public concert on 4 December 1915.[114] He also participated in outdoor spectacles in solidarity with the Ottoman war effort.[115] Still, the war soon disrupted his work. As an Ottoman citizen he was drafted to the Turkish army, 'first as a clerk in a military hospital, then as a band-master'.[116] Indeed, during the war years he published only three studies, contrasted with twenty-one scholarly items and scores of newspaper articles which he had published during his first five years in Palestine.[117] His main occupation during the war years was the composition of his opera *Jephtah* and of the play *Elijah*. Although *Jephtah* was Idelsohn's most ambitious composition,[118] it was nevertheless an extension of his scholarly work.

---

[109] *Aherout* (9 Dec. 1913).   [110] Idelsohn archive, JNUL, Mus. 7 (328).

[111] *Gesänge der jemenischen Juden* (Leipzig, 1914). See Schleifer, 'Annotated Bibliography', p. 63, item 1, for full bibliographical data.

[112] Letter of 22 Jan. 1914 (Idelsohn Archive, JNUL, Mus. 7 (564)).

[113] Letter of 18 Mar. 1914 (Idelsohn Archive, JNUL, Mus. 7 (506)).

[114] Posters Archive (1961/1), JNUL.   [115] See Ch. 3, below.

[116] Cohon, 'Idelsohn', 41.

[117] Schleifer, 'Annotated Bibliography', p. 106, item 22; p. 107, item 23; p. 109, item 25. Item 24 of 1917 was a late publication of his 1913 presentation in Vienna.

[118] Hoffman, 'Idelsohn's Music', 43. An undated typescript in German of a play or an opera titled *Orientalische Liebe* is found in the Idelsohn Archive 1976, JNUL (no siglum).

Ex 1.2. Idelsohn, *Jephtah* (Yemenite melody)

(Praise ye Ba'al, God of the harvest)

Most of the opera music was based on the ethnic songs he had collected and on the Ashkenazi masoretic accents,[119] resulting in an 'eclectic mix' with 'naïve harmonization' for piano.[120]

Word about Idelsohn's grand project had spread as far as the United States, where it elicited the interest of the American music journalist Harry C. Plummer, who asked Idelsohn for information about 'the Hebrew system of musical notation' as well as about the use of 'ancient' instruments.[121]

Soon after the termination of the war in Palestine Idelsohn renewed his communal activities. He established the amateur Choir of the Hebrew Stage which was regularly invited to participate in various official and social functions.[122] Upon his birthday in 1918 the forty-eight members of the choir signed an ornate birthday card. The list features some of the prominent intellectuals of the New Yishuv, among them respected leaders of the Sephardi community.[123] Yet Idelsohn was no longer content with daily communal work and with teaching young children. He found himself increasingly hard-pressed to raise funds to continue his research and to advance the case of his opera and play. Löwit Verlag in Vienna was willing to publish the second volume of the Thesaurus, but due to the economic hardships of the post-war era in Austria, requested Idelsohn to

---

[119] Also called *te'amim*, the masoretic accents (from the Hebrew word *masoret* (tradition), are the traditional grammatical and melodic formulae used in the readings from the Bible at the synagogue service. They are marked by conventional symbols in the printed Bible. Whereas their grammatical functions are fixed, they have different significations among the numerous Jewish ethnic communities.

[120] J. Cohen, 'Jiphtah', 127–31.

[121] A letter of 2 Aug. 1915 (Idelsohn Archive, JNUL, Mus. 7 (497)). There is no record in the archive of any further communications with Plummer.

[122] Official letters of invitations, all of 1918 (Idelsohn Archive, JNUL, Mus. 7 (547, 659–61)).

[123] Idelsohn Archive, JNUL, Mus. 7 (131). Most prominent was Joseph Meyuhas (1868–1942).

find a financial source which would underwrite the printing costs.[124] Idelsohn applied in vain to his benefactor, the Imperial Academy in Vienna, for a grant of 4,000 kronen in order to renew his work on the phonogram collection.[125] He made impassioned appeals to institutes, Jewish organizations, funds, and sponsors in Vienna, Paris, London, and the United States, but to no avail.[126] His play *Elijah* did not fare any better. The Zionist leader Israel Zangwill, to whom Idelsohn had sent the manuscript, wrote from London: 'the subject of "Elijah" would not appeal to the ordinary proprietors of theatres in Christian countries. . . . Your play seems, however, just the thing we shall need in the National Theatre, Jerusalem, but it has not yet been founded.'[127] Attempts to promote a performance of *Jephtah* in Paris were likewise unsuccessful.[128] The only encouraging response was a stipend of £15 a month for one year which he received from the Zionist Federation on condition that he reduce his teaching load by the same amount. As a result Idelsohn's financial situation improved and he could devote more time to his research.[129] He then collaborated with the violinist Anton Tschaikov and the pianist Sidney Seal, who had arrived in Palestine with the British army. Jointly they opened the Jerusalem School of Music, which held its first public concert on 17 March 1919. Idelsohn taught voice and music theory, yet his failure to make any progress in his scholarly publications made him increasingly restive. In the autumn of 1921 he left Palestine for England on an impulse, allegedly in order to raise funds for the school of music, and in fact in order to find a venue to publish the next volume of the Thesaurus.[130] His unexpected absence created severe difficulties and aroused bad feelings among the staff members who had relied on his prestige and personality.[131] When urgent letters which were addressed to

[124] Idelsohn Archive, JNUL, Mus. 7 (392).

[125] Draft of a letter of 29 Aug. 1917 (Idelsohn Archive, JNUL, Mus. 7 (284)).

[126] Letters of 11 Aug. 1918 and 5 Sept. 1920, 14 Jan. 1921 (Idelsohn Archive, JNUL, Mus. 7 (388, 494, 545)).

[127] A letter of 4 Feb. 1918 (Idelsohn Archive, JNUL, Mus. 7 (656)).

[128] Hemda Ben-Yehudah tried to interest the Paris opera but was refused, allegedly because the work was 'too oriental' but more likely because of its inferior operatic qualities (Idelsohn Archive, JNUL, Mus. 7 (67–9)). J. Cohen, 'Jiphtah', 128. Idelsohn had the vocal score published at his own expense in 1922, allegedly in Jerusalem although he was no longer there.

[129] A letter from the Committee of Executives, 22 May 1918. Memoirs of Idelsohn's daughter (Idelsohn Archive, 1976, JNUL (unnumbered)).

[130] Letters from Sir Alfred Mond's secretary, 29 Sept. and from Maurice Myers, 26 Oct. 1921 (Idelsohn Archive, JNUL, Mus. 7 (438, 461)).

[131] Letters of 23 Nov. 1921, 20 Jan. 1922, and 19 Feb. 1922 (Idelsohn Archive, JNUL, Mus. 7 (377, 611, 612)). See also Ch. 2, below. Just before his departure Idelsohn became also entangled in a petty argument with the Federation of Teachers, which left him deeply insulted (Idelsohn Archive, JNUL, Mus. 7 (594)).

him remained unanswered, the school sent an angry cable to Jewish officials in London, warning them that 'Idelsohn remained abroad after beginning school year without permission, thus no longer our teacher',[132] and he consequently was not allowed to raise funds for the school. Even his close associate Cantor Rivlin expressed his sense of injury, having been left alone for many years to run the Institute with no communication from his adored colleague and mentor.[133] Idelsohn resumed limited contacts with a few colleagues in Palestine only after the publication of the second volume of the Thesaurus,[134] and upon his final acceptance of his new position at the Hebrew Union College. The chasm separating an exalted vision from a bitter reality was a dark omen of things to come.

[132] Idelsohn Archive, JNUL, Mus. 7 (529).
[133] Letter of 8 Nov. 1931 (Idelsohn Archive, JNUL, Mus. 7 (527)).
[134] *Gesänge der babylonischen Juden* (Jerusalem, 1922). See Schleifer, 'Annotated Bibliography', p. 70, item 1.

2

The Musical Scene in the Ottoman Period Initiatives and Rivalries

AT the turn of the century the New *Yishuv* was boosted by an immigration wave, known as the Second Aliya (1904–13). Pushed by the pogroms against Jews in Russia which broke out in Kishinev in 1903, most immigrants were young socialists motivated to reform the traditional Jewish way of life through the creation of a new, just society, with hard physical labour and collective effort elevated to the level of religious adoration. They numbered 35,000–40,000 persons[1] and their influence was especially prevalent in the political élite of the Yishuv for years to come.[2]

The gateway to Palestine was the small and primitive harbour of Jaffa. Having arrived there, the Jewish immigrants were faced with three options for resettlement. Some were attracted by the historical ambience and the intellectual vitality of Jerusalem. Others preferred to stay in the fast-changing Mediterranean port of Jaffa. The remaining immigrants strove to revolutionize their way of life and turned to new agricultural settlements, which by 1900 accounted for 10 per cent of the Jewish population in Palestine.[3]

The contrasting economic bases of the settlements deeply influenced their social and cultural nature. One group of settlements included those financially supported by Baron de Rothschild.[4] The Baron insisted on

---

[1] D. Gurevich and A. Gertz (eds.), *Statistical Handbook of Jewish Palestine 1947* (Jerusalem, 1947), 90.

[2] M. Lissak, *The Elites of the Jewish Community in Palestine* (Tel Aviv, 1981), 48.

[3] Altogether about fifty settlements were founded from 1870 to 1914, but some failed and many others remained very small, with no more than twenty families in each. D. Giladi, 'The Settlements outside the Baron's Sponsorship', in Kolat (ed.), *Ottoman Period*, 537.

[4] Baron Edmond de Rothschild (1845–1934) was a French–Jewish banker and philanthropist, who committed himself to pioneer Jewish settlement in Palestine.

Ex 2.1. 'Yah chai li li ha amali'

installing his own representatives as agricultural instructors and adminis-
trators, whose patronizing and at times even rude attitude frequently
triggered off resentment on the part of the settlers. The second group
consisted of settlements which were loosely sponsored by Jewish organizations in Europe, and as a result were economically less stable, yet socially
more homogeneous and independent.

   Documentation of the period of the Second Aliya manifests the extensive practice of group-singing which supported the ideology of collective
effort in all contexts of daily life:

Whenever several of them walked to work holding their spades, they would
unite in the song 'Ya chai li li ha amali' [Wake up, brethren, do not slumber, get
up to work; see Ex. 2.1].[5]

And when the bell tolled to stop . . . we would march in files to the settlement
singing songs to the public bath near the well.[6]

Night after night the workers would gather at our place, sit together in the
darkness, and sing.[7] 'El yivneh hagalil, 'el yivneh hagalil', thus the horra went on
and on in the small dining-hall of the small collective settlement in the Jordan
Valley.[8]

   Song, frequently coupled with dance, was regarded as a purifying
agent:

One of the tables started the song. The mood was that of a dance evening.
And then the 'last dance' arrived. It was the horra. They danced with excitement, with fervor, with fire, inspired by sublime spirit. It was as if the dance
liberated them from all suffering, from all troubles, dancing with one's hand on
the other's shoulder brings hearts together and purifies the soul. One frees
oneself from everything around oneself and concentrates on one's elevated
dream. This was the way they used to sing in Hadera.[9]

   [5] B. Habas (ed.), *The Book of the Second Aliya* (Tel Aviv, 1947), 368.
   [6] Ibid. 240.   [7] Ibid. 167.
   [8] 'The Lord shall build the Galilee'. The Galilee is the northern region of Palestine, then
considered the pioneer virgin land. Ibid. 451.
   [9] Ibid. 273. Hadera, about 50 km. north of Tel Aviv, was one of the earliest pioneer settlements,
founded in 1891. See Shahar, 'Eretz Israeli Song 1920–1950', 258, for a compilation of similar
quotes from Habas's book.

The Community Orchestra and the Music Society

In 1895 a group of farmers from the settlement of Rishon Le'Zion[10] initiated the first community orchestra in Palestine. It was a wind band which numbered 25 to 30 musicians, with the occasional participation of two or three violinists. Most of its members had turned to agriculture after their immigration, as one of them proudly declared at the first anniversary of Rishon Le'Zion Orchestra: 'We are all well dressed and we touch the harp, the drum, and the fiddle, as if our fingers were not bruised by daily toil.'[11] The instruments were purchased by a joint contribution of the farmers, which was matched by Baron de Rothschild. The orchestra took part in all the social functions of the village, especially those held on the Jewish holidays, when it mixed holiday songs in its programmes of light classics; a typical example was the orchestra's two Chanukah concerts in 1889.[12] The long programme opened with the Turkish anthem, followed by orchestral and solo arrangement of excerpts from *Carmen*, *Faust*, *La Juive*, *I puritani*, *Norma*, and *Il trovatore*, the traditional Chanukah song 'Maoz Zur', an aria from *Samson et Dalila*, and a pot-pourri of Serbian folksongs. The concert culminated with a locally written national skit 'Of the Life of Jewish Farmers in Palestine'.

Rishon Le'Zion Orchestra acted as a representative ensemble on special occasions, such as the memorable reception for Dr Herzl, upon his first (and only) visit to Palestine.[13] Herzl's refined musical taste coupled with his fierce opposition to Baron de Rothschild's tyrannical manners and his horror of the dismal condition of the settlers, most of whom had fallen victim to malaria,[14] blinded him to the social value of the orchestra. Indeed, his comments reflected the chasm between the dedicated excitement of the insiders and the observation of a detached outsider:

[10] Founded in 1882, 8 km. south of Jaffa, the settlement name (lit. 'The First to Zion') was derived from the biblical verse 'The first shall say to Zion, behold, behold them' (Isaiah 41: 27). The entire first street of the settlement, now a large boisterous city, has been preserved.

[11] D. Yodelevitch, *The Book of Rishon Le'Zion* (Rishon Le'Zion, 1941), 314. Yodelevitch (1863–1943) immigrated to Palestine in 1882. In 1887 he settled as a teacher in Rishon Le'Zion.

[12] Rishon Le'Zion Municipal Museum, 8/2, 27 and 29 Nov. 1889. The Feast of Chanukah, traditionally marking the victory of the Maccabeans over the Greeks as a religious miracle, was transformed by the national Jewish movement into a symbolic celebration of a heroic victory of a few freedom fighters over a mighty oppressor.

[13] Dr Benjamin Ze'ev (Theodore) Herzl (1860–1904) was the founder of political Zionism and of the Zionist Federation. His dedication to the vision of a Jewish state as the sole political solution to the Jewish problem earned the young and charismatic leader the admiration of the Jewish community in Palestine. Herzl arrived in Rishon Le'Zion on 27 Oct. 1898.

[14] Malaria was endemic in Palestine until the 1930s.

Meanwhile, news of our arrival had spread through the village. A deputation
came to invite me to the *Beth Ha'am* [Community Hall]. We were welcomed
by music which, unfortunately, was only well-intended. . . . Someone made a
speech in which he tried to harmonize their obligation toward the Baron
and their love for me, a harmony just as impossible as the one the conductor
tried to achieve between the violin and the flute. The big drum covered up
everything.[15]

Refined criticism notwithstanding, the orchestra was energetic and
dedicated, and was soon invited to perform in other settlements. In
September 1904 an honourable delegation of Zionist leaders from Europe
held a national conference at the village of Zikhron Ya'akov.[16] On the day
following the deliberations all the guests were invited to a picnic, 'and
they happily sang Hebrew songs'. The conference culminated in a
torch parade and 'Rishon Le'Zion orchestra played well after midnight'.[17]

The increasing activity of the orchestra angered the distinguished
leader, Moshe L. Lilienblum, who rebuked the settlers of Rishon
Le'Zion for 'often gathering at the Music House to listen to sounds of
singing and playing rather than to learn the history of their people or to
expand their knowledge in agronomy and economy which would be of
[more] help to them.'[18] Lilienblum's scathing attack fomented an angry
backlash. David Yodelevitch, one of the founders of the village, responded
in a long article overflowing with sarcasm.

I am not writing in order to argue now with uncle Lilienblum's notion that a
Jew has no need of 'flowers, toys, love songs and beautiful paintings' because 'the
Jew is not a Greek'. Certainly, dear uncle has searched and has investigated and
has discovered, that the five senses of the Jew are structured differently from
those of the Greek. . . . But what is my argument about? . . . I was seized with
a burning fever when I heard that Lilienblum, whom I have always admired as
the pillar of the fire of enlightenment in our time, . . . has been slandering the
broad-minded community of Rishon Le'Zion.

Yodelevitch then turns to arguments in support of the orchestra. He
begins by sketching a profile of the intense intellectual activities of the
small group of sixty regular members of the village.[19] In addition to

---

[15] *The Complete Diaries of Theodore Herzl*, ed. Rafael Patai, trans. Harry Zohn (New York, 1960),
740.

[16] *Zichron Ya'akov* (lit. 'In Memory of Jacob') which was founded in 1882 by immigrants from
Romania was sponsored by Baron de Rothschild who named it after his father.

[17] *Hashkafa* (4 Sept. 1904).

[18] Moshe Leib Lilienblum, *Ahiassaf Calender* (1901). A prolific author and columnist, Lilienblum
(1843–1910) was Secretary General of Hovevei Zion (Friends of Zion) Odessa organization, which
was the most active sponsor of Jewish immigration to Palestine at that time.

[19] i.e. sixty heads of families whose membership had been approved by the general assembly.

enjoying their orchestra, they subscribe to no less than sixty different newspapers and journals in German, Russian, French, Hebrew, and Yiddish, which reach them from Jaffa once a week. They meet every night in small groups for joint studies of various topics. They keep a large variety of books in their homes, as well as in the local public library. Every Saturday night they gather for lectures on a variety of topics from Jewish history, politics, science and education, to agriculture. Yodelevitch then bursts out again:

There are 168 hours per week, of which we waste—that is, a few of us, who have the talent—*six hours* in refreshing our souls with the sweetness of the great spirits, of the giant spirits: Halevy, Meyerbeer, Mendelssohn, Beethoven, Mozart, Wagner, and so on. . . . Only because I am a farmer, a vine-grower, a village settler, a poor worker in the Land of Israel, a certain philosopher allows himself to be cruel to me in the name of his ideals, as if my soul were no longer human like his![20]

Yodelevitch's blast against one of the most venerable national leaders signified the settlers' deeply ingrained need to complement their newly established class identity of pioneer farmers with the preservation of their intellectual pursuits in which the emancipated Jews of the Enlightenment traditionally excelled.[21]

Misgivings concerning involvement in music were also occasionally raised within the community. At the turn of the century the ageing Baron de Rothschild gradually transferred the financial responsibility for the Jewish settlements in Palestine to the Zionist organization JCA.[22] The prolonged process aroused apprehension in the settlements. Rishon Le'Zion Orchestra organized a concert with the intention

of somewhat alleviating the despair and the anxiety which have recently spread among our farmers and vine growers because of the changes in the economy of the settlements . . . the Orchestra Society, with the approval of the general assembly of the village, presented a concert on the holiday of Chanukah. The evening was sold out. . . . A few [members] have objected to the concert, arguing: 'Is this the right time, when our heart is full of worry about our future

---

[20] *Hashkafa*, 2 (1901), 16, 18.

[21] On the theoretical aspects of ethnic and personal identity see G. Devereux, 'Ethnic Identity, its Logical Foundations and its Dysfunctions'. in G. De Vos (ed.), *Ethnic Identity* (Chicago, 1975), 42–70, and G. De Vos, 'Ethnic Pluralism: Conflict and Accommodation', in *Ethnic Identify*, 1–41.

[22] JCA (Jewish Colonization Society) was founded in 1891 by Baron Maurice de Hirsch (1831–96), who planned to dispel the destitution of Russian Jews through their organized emigration to Argentina. In 1896 JCA changed its orientation and diverted funds also to Palestine. I. Margalit and J. Goldstein, 'Baron Edmond de Rothschild's Project 1882–1899', in Kolat (ed.), *Ottoman Period*, 496.

life and toil, to indulge in concerts? What will the people around us
say?' . . . But those in support of the concert have responded: 'On the contrary,
this is the proper time, especially on the holiday of Chanukah, when we should
be celebrating our magnificent past and infusing our people with hopes for a
better future.'[23]

Conflicts of opinion also touched on the owning and the use of
pianos. The inauguration charter of the village explicitly prohibited
jewellery, fine clothes, 'and all luxuries which deplete the resources of
our people',[24] and pianos were implicitly included. Nevertheless, several
families in Rishon Le'Zion did buy pianos from the German colony in
Jaffa or imported them from Europe. Around the turn of the century
there were two sisters who gave piano lessons in Rishon Le'Zion.
Nehama Belkind, one of the first locally born children,[25] reported that
as a young girl she had been in the habit of concealing the music
while walking to her piano lesson for fear of being ridiculed by her
schoolteachers.

The success of Rishon Le'Zion Orchestra inspired other settlements to
launch similar ventures. Zikhron Ya'akov purchased thirty instruments in
Europe and established a community orchestra of its own, the local
cantor serving as a conductor.[26] A year later the settlers of Petah Tikvah
followed suit, and even enlisted the help of one of the members of
Rishon Le'Zion Orchestra to coach the new ensemble.[27]

Rishon Le'Zion Orchestra suspended its activity in 1905 when its
conductor left the village. In 1912 a group of 'music-lovers' presented a
letter to the village committee in which they pleaded for the revival of
the orchestra, and forty of them promised to support the ensemble for
three years.[28] This time the orchestra was reinstated as a well-organized
society which collected dues and employed a salaried conductor. The
revived orchestra numbered about twenty members playing clarinets,
cornets, trumpets, one trombone, and a few violins. The orchestra assumed responsibility for instrumental instruction and became popular
among the young people of the village, who had to pass auditions if they
wished to participate.[29] It held four concerts per season which covered all
its expenses.[30]

---

[23] *Hashkafa* (3 Dec. 1903).   [24] M. Eliav (ed.), *The First Aliyah* (Jerusalem, 1981), ii. 37.
[25] Interviews with Nehama Belkind (b. 1900) and with Shmuel Ben-Ze'ev Abramowitch
(b. 1900), 1 Mar 1983.
[26] *HaZevi* (9 Oct. 1896).
[27] *HaZevi* (20 Mar. 1897). Petah Tikvah was founded in 1879, abandoned shortly after, and
resettled in 1892.
[28] *Rishon Le'Zion* Municipal Museum, 8/5, 26 Feb. 1912.
[29] *Rishon Le'Zion* Municipal Museum, 8/6, 21 Apr. 1912.   [30] *Aherout* (21 July 1914).

The Inception of a New Urban Centre

During the nineteenth century the port of Jaffa underwent a major transformation from a medieval walled fortress into a vibrant commercial harbour. New Muslim, Christian, and Jewish quarters were erected outside the walls.[31] Unlike Jerusalem, Jaffa had no Jewish community at all until the early twentieth century, when it numbered 8,500 Jews among its 50,000 inhabitants. The German-Jewish lawyer Arthur Ruppin has written that 'Jaffa differs from, let us say, Jerusalem, in not being under the pressure of an ancient and unproductive settlement, hostile to all innovation; [Jaffa] has therefore become the centre of modern Jewish life in Palestine'.[32] In 1910 a group of entrepreneurs founded the garden suburb of Tel Aviv north of Jaffa.[33] Although the founders of Tel Aviv numbered only sixty families, the event itself had far-reaching repercussions since it was the first Jewish urban quarter built in accordance with a comprehensive master plan. Characterized by broad streets and cosy residential homes, the new quarter soon became very attractive, and within four years the combined Jewish population of Jaffa and Tel Aviv had swelled from 10,000 to 15,000. It was an all-migrant society, which originated from an internal migration of Jews who rejected the enclosed religious life of the Old Yishuv.[34] This was the backdrop for an event spurred on by an ideological dispute which turned Jaffa almost overnight into the major cultural and educational centre of the Yishuv.

The settlements which came under the patronage of Baron Rothschild identified themselves with French language and culture,[35] but the intellectuals within them, especially the teachers, initiated a campaign for the implementation of modern Hebrew in all walks of life. Such a conflict was the harbinger of fierce ideological confrontations. At the end of 1905 a controversy broke out in the educational circles of Rishon Le'Zion between Francophiles and Hebraists over the curriculum of the first high school which was about to open in the settlement. The Francophiles

---

[31] The first new section was Neve Tzedek, founded in 1897. R. Kark, *Jaffa—A City in Evolution 1799–1917* (Jerusalem, 1984), 86 ff.

[32] 'The Picture in 1907' (an address delivered in Vienna in 1908), *Three Decades of Palestine* (Jerusalem, 1936), 5. Ruppin (1876–1943) was born in Germany. He was an economist and a lawyer who specialized in real estate. In 1908 he founded the Palestine branch of the Zionist Federation which was in charge of land purchase for Jewish immigrants.

[33] The suburb's original name was Ahuzat Bait, but it was changed to Tel Aviv within a few months. G. Bigger, 'The Development of the Urban Area of Tel Aviv 1909–1934', in M. Naor (ed.), *The Beginnings of Tel Aviv, 1909–1934* (Tel Aviv, 1973), 52.

[34] In 1905 only 12 per cent of the Jews aged 20–40 and 6.6 per cent of those above the age of 40 were born in Jaffa. Kark, *Jaffa*, 131, 163.

[35] Margalit and Goldstein, 'Baron Edmond de Rothschild's Enterprise', 481.

prevailed and the advocates of Hebrew angrily moved to Jaffa. There they founded a high quality Hebrew high school, which followed the model of the German gymnasium. The school was soon named Herzlia Gymnasium, after Dr Theodore Herzl. In 1910 the school reached full bloom when it moved to its permanent home, which was the first public building erected in Tel Aviv. The castle-like edifice dominated the skyline of the small town for many years and functioned as a multi-purpose social and communal centre.[36] The prestigious school soon acquired a reputation abroad and stimulated the immigration of pupils whose families wished them to receive a solid Jewish education away from the troubled conditions in Europe. Most of the school teachers were also active in the politics of the Yishuv, a fact which endowed the school with an image and a status of a national centre. Music was included in the curriculum as a compulsory subject, mostly on account of its unifying social properties. The school maintained a mixed choir, an all-boy wind band, and an all-girl ensemble of plucked instruments.[37]

It was the German colony in Jaffa and the European enclaves of Jerusalem which spurred the Jewish community to step up public musical activity. A joint concert of the Jaffa and the Jerusalem community orchestras provoked the columnist of *Hashkafa* to gloomy thoughts about the cultural state of the local Jewish community:

The sitting-room was packed with men and women, among them Germans, many Russians and Christian Arabs, and a few Jews, who came to listen to Wagner, Schubert, and Beethoven. The music was very beautiful, the organization was excellent, and the audience applauded after each piece. A young and lovely young German woman played very well with the orchestra. . . . At eleven the concert was over and all returned by carriages to their homes, which were far from the German colony. At that point, under the bright moon which could proudly compete with the electrical lights of the Parisian theatre, one observed a group of happy people, free of sadness and anxiety, and so rare in our neighbourhoods. We should be ashamed that we, the Jews, who outnumber the Germans, were not able to organize regular concerts, which could be of great help to our brethren here, who are detached from the sound of music and are constantly concerned with worries and hardships. . . . So that they may be distracted . . . and pass for a few moments to a more lofty world, the world of song and music.[38]

The realization of the elevating power of music set the stage for the inception of the Violin of Zion Society in Jaffa in June 1904. In 1908

---

[36] In the mid-1950s the school moved to a large new structure and the old historical building fell victim to a greedy development plan.

[37] B. Ben Yehudah, *The Story of the Herzlia Gymnasium* (Tel Aviv, 1960).

[38] *Hashkafa* (19 May 1902).

three instrumental teachers founded a branch of the Society in Jerusalem with a broad-ranging pragmatic platform:

The purposes of the Society are to disseminate the art of music in general and that of Jewish music in particular among the Jews, to organize concerts in Jerusalem as well as in other towns and settlements, to encourage music-making everywhere, to organize evening courses and to support those endowed with instrumental talent; to work toward the inauguration of a music school in Palestine, to attract musicians of international reputation from abroad, and to form liaisons with societies there.[39]

The ideological leadership of the New Yishuv, however, had much more elevated goals in mind. Hemdah Ben-Yehuda[40] spoke at a special event to which the Society invited the entire intellectual élite. She combined Neoplatonic views of the educational and the purifying powers of music with paraphrases of E. T. A. Hoffmann's poetic images expressing the superiority of music over language, an idea which she finally linked with that of national revival: 'Our violin, the Violin of Zion, broken and shattered, was cast away, on the rivers of Babylon . . . Let us have a new Violin of Zion! Indeed, the Violin is being built just now. It is a big violin, its base is in Judaea and its head is in the Galilee.'[41] On the following day the Society illustrated its interest in music education when it held a concert performed and attended by schoolchildren.[42] The Society also launched a fifteen-member community orchestra in Jerusalem.[43]

For about three years the Society sponsored most public concerts in Palestine. Straight recitals were rare. More typical was a mixed bag of music, literature, and scholarly lectures. It was stated in the advertisement for one of the earliest concerts that 'the English and the Germans organized many concerts in Jerusalem, but this concert would be purely Jewish and the proceeds would serve to help poor Jews'.[44] Hemdah Ben-Yehudah provided a detailed description of the event: 'The auditorium was decorated with green branches and well lit. Excellent organization. Men and women enter well dressed and are politely shown to their seats. . . . the curtain rises and reveals a beautifully set stage, lit with numerous candles placed in heavy silver chandeliers.'[45]

The concert was performed by four violinists and three pianists who alternated in music for piano solo, *quatre mains*, violin and piano, and

---

[39] *Hashkafa* (1908). The society offered violin, mandoline, and guitar lessons.

[40] Hemdah Ben-Yehudah was Eliezer Ben-Yehudah's second wife. She joined him in Jerusalem in 1892 and became one of the most dedicated promoters of his national-secular ideology, in which music held a prominent role.

[41] *Hashkafa* (22 May 1908).   [42] Ibid.   [43] *HaZevi* (7 and 23 Nov. 1909).

[44] *Hashkafa* (21 Dec. 1906).   [45] *Hashkafa* (26 Dec. 1906).

violin ensembles, including Chopin's Étude Op. 25 No. 11 and *Marche Funèbre*, an unnamed piece by Beethoven, a piano piece by Glinka, and Bruch's *Kol Nidrei*[46] which was soon to become a favourite in recitals. The performers were all 'new to the audience' and they were warmly applauded. The event also included readings from German and Hebrew literature. A special attraction was a virtuoso performance by four students of Bezalel art school who competed in drawing and painting to the rhythm of rapid piano-playing. The audience enjoyed a rich buffet in the interval, and was treated to a champagne reception at the end.

The concerts of the Society played a central role in the initial promotion of new immigrant musicians. In the small and enclosed community special talents were very likely to stand out, as was the case in a recital in which a recent arrival, the pianist Miriam Levit, made her Jerusalem début alongside the founders of the Society who played the harp and the violin. The press attracted the audience with an enthusiastic preview[47] without even bothering to provide any detailed biographical information. The next day the correspondent confirmed the fulfilment of all expectations, and the Society reaped its own benefits:

The connoisseurs felt as if they were in a large European city, at a major auditorium—faced with one of the greatest and most renowned musicians. The uninitiated listened to a real, rich and varied playing for the first time in their life. . . . These were divine moments . . . She played three pieces, and the listeners felt as if immersed in waves of poetry and dignity. They were obsessed by a single thought: more, more, more! But it was late. . . . The public slowly dispersed. Many surrounded Miss Levit, trying to catch a glimpse of the heroine of the day. This time the Violin of Zion Society won a full victory.[48]

Levit's accomplishment indirectly precipitated the process of professional stratification which differentiated between the good and the outstanding among local musicians. Levit's success was soon replicated in Jaffa, when she acquiesced in the wishes of the excited local audience and moved there, joining the faculty of the new music school. The event was considered of such import that it was reported in the Jerusalem press.[49] Author and poet Jacob Koplewitz described her playing as the best

---

[46] *Ha'Or* (20 Mar. 1912). Kol Nidrei is an introductory prayer to the sacred service of Yom Kippur (The solemn Day of Atonement). It was its position at the opening of the service and its sublime traditional melody which earned it special status which far surpasses its limited and even controversial religious significance. See I. Elbogen, *Der jüdische Gottesdienst in seiner geschichtlichen Entwicklung* (Leipzig, 1913), Hebrew trans. by J. Amir (Tel Aviv, 1972), 116.

[47] *HaZevi* (5 Aug. 1908).

[48] *HaZevi* (7 Aug. 1911). No details of the programme were listed in the review.

[49] *HaZevi* (11 Oct. 1909).

example of the tradition of the Moscow Conservatory, depicting her as a 'serious young woman, somewhat cumbersome in her movements, but graceful and warm in her peaceful smile. She was aristocratic and reticent. . . . One evening, when she played at home for three guests, myself included, I told her that there was something of Turgenev in her playing. She liked this characterization'.[50]

It was only on very rare occasions that visiting musicians from Europe were induced to undertake the arduous concert tour in the remote community. The first Jewish visiting artist was David Schor[51] whose trip came in the wake of a long spiritual process which he recorded in his diary:

Although I was no Zionist, I was among the first Moscovites who visited Palestine. An analysis of the musical composition in which I was occupied revealed to me the emotional and spiritual sublimity of the composers. It became clear to me that a great composer is also a great man. This is especially true of Beethoven. I felt an urge to go to Bonn, Beethoven's birthplace. In 1906, a year before my trip to Palestine, I went to Bonn. In front of me there is a letter sent from there on 27 August 1906: 'Here I am in Bonn! In the place I have dreamt of, the way a devout Moslem dreams about Mecca, or an orthodox Jew about holy Jerusalem. . . . I mention this inspiring trip because in a way it prepared me for my visit in Palestine. Bonn, Eisenach, Leipzig, and Berlin did not alleviate my musical doubts, and the national folk feeling which rose in me requested unceasingly: to the Land of Israel! . . . And when doubts assailed me: will the people succeed? will it overcome? will it understand the greatness of its task? I always discovered: yes, it will make it, it will overcome. I understood that the fertile land of national vision will also give birth to a comprehensive human vision. I believed that the excited and exciting workers would strive to achieve the acme of culture: to disseminate among all people spiritual and material treasures by way of uprooting all distinctions of class, nationality, and religion.[52]

Schor stayed in Palestine for five weeks and performed in Jaffa and in Jerusalem. His Jerusalem recital attracted 'almost all music-lovers in our town, Jews and Gentiles, locals and Europeans, men and women who themselves play instruments and understand music' to a programme of Bach, Beethoven, Chopin, and Mendelssohn. Schor was attentive to the sentiments of the small Jewish community. He invited the fine young violinist Rivka Zakoshinsky to collaborate in his recital, and the concert

[50] Y. Keshet (Koplewitz), *Kedma and Yama*, 68.

[51] Schor (1867–1942, also spelled Schorr) was a professor of piano at the Moscow conservatory, and a member of a piano trio with Krein and Ehrlich which was founded in 1892. His recital in Jerusalem took place on 10 May 1907. He settled permanently in Palestine in 1925 (see Ch. 5, below).

[52] *Davar* (5 Dec. 1933).

was warmly applauded.[53] Pianist Arie Niswitzky, who was among the founders of the Society for Jewish Folk Music in St Petersburg in 1908, made a concert tour of Palestine, during which he also took the opportunity 'to collect and notate folksongs which were popular in the Land of Israel'.[54] In 1912 *Ha'Or* published a sensational preview for the Jewish pianist, singer, and composer Florence Menkmeier who was introduced as a 'former student of Liszt and Anton Rubinstein'. The enthusiastic preview paid special attention to the programme which would include 'two vocal excerpts by Wagner. Since we are still far from having a great opera-house for the presentation of Wagner's sublime dramas, it will be an exceptional opportunity for us to listen to these songs.'[55] The programme included piano arrangements from *Lohengrin*, as well as short piano works by Chopin, Anton Rubinstein, and Menkmeier herself. The recital was so successful that she repeated it twice to accommodate the excited audience.[56]

Opportunities for socializing on such occasions were frequently utilized for fund-raising for schools, libraries, welfare groups, and hospitals. Such evenings served as entertainment and pastime. They presented mixed programmes of light classics played by the community orchestras and by recitalists, alternating with poetry-reading, skits, and social games. Some events had a more serious orientation and included lectures, such as an evening at the prestigious Lemel school, in which 'the audience was of the "élite". All enjoyed Mr Yellin's lecture on the Samaritans' which was followed by works for piano and for violin.[57] Such events were closely scrutinized in the Hebrew press. Even the venerable poet Bialik was severely rebuked when he disappointed a full house by choosing to read an old poem depicting rural life in Russia instead of a soaring new national poem which the audience had expected. The pianist who opened Bialik's performance, however, was warmly applauded.[58]

Such events, albeit popular and well-received, continued to be infrequent, as stated in the very detailed review of a 'great concert' in 1908.

The Violin of Zion Society announced a joint concert in Jaffa with members of the branches in Jerusalem, Petah Tikvah and Rishon Le'Zion. The word soon

---

[53] *Hashkafa* (14 May 1907).

[54] *Aherout* (18 June 1909). Niswiztky (1885–1984) settled in Palestine in 1921, where he Hebraized his last name to Abilea (see Ch. 4, below).

[55] *Ha'Or* (19 Apr. 1912).   [56] *Ha'Or* (24 Apr. 1912).

[57] *Aherout* (13 Dec. 1909). David Yellin (1864–1941) was an orientalist and a teacher, who founded and directed the Teachers' Training College in Jerusalem.

[58] *Aherout* (4 June 1909).

spread in town and elicited much interest among members of all nationalities, because the audience in Jaffa craved spiritual food, having missed entertainment for a long time. The members of the society gathered at 2 p.m. for a rehearsal, each group on its own: the violins, the pianists, and the orchestra. . . . At 8 p.m. the audience began to gather. . . . The curtain rose and a marvellous sight was revealed. Five members held their violins ready . . . the march started and the audiences applauded. . . . After the march the members of the orchestra took their seats. . . . The conductor, Kowalsky, stood in front of them and after the call one–two–three the orchestra played. Everyone wondered how Mr Kowalsky could organize such a large orchestra with so little money and with so much modesty. . . . After the concert the audience applauded once more and slowly dispersed. Several groups stayed behind and discussed the event. The players and the singers were surrounded on all sides by unrelenting enthusiasts.[59]

The typical programme included instrumental arrangements of operatic excerpts by Bellini and Meyerbeer, Mendelsohn's Violin Concerto (apparently only one movement), a few operatic arias, a 'Gypsy Song' for piano, and a 'piece for violins' by Stradella.

Some of the concerts occasioned bold social observations, such as a concert in which two women played the violin and the piano alongside two male violinists: 'According to my opinion women are more sublime than our brothers, the men, in the field of arts. Possibly it is embedded in their gentler nature. . . . Women are a "rarity" in sciences, but they have the capability to charm us in literature, singing, and playing.'[60]

One of the most important aspects of the musical activity in Palestine was the quick realization of its potential for national unification above and beyond local boundaries. At the turn of the century the old Sephardi Jewish community of Beirut, Lebanon, attracted young Jewish migrants from Russia, who maintained contacts with their comrades in Palestine. A large delegation from Jerusalem and Jaffa went to Beirut and organized a well-attended Purrim ball. The programme consisted of Hebrew choral songs, readings of Bialik's national poems, and music for violin and piano.[61]

Despite the general enthusiasm for cultural events, the initiators soon encountered the unavoidable difficulty of converting passive support into action. 'The expectations were very high but help was wanting.'[62] Personal conflicts further aggravated the situation, and the Society enlisted only thirty five members who paid dues. The worst stumbling-

[59] *Hashkafa* (9 Nov. 1908).   [60] Ben-Abraham, *Aherout* (5 Jan. 1910).
[61] Hashkafa (13 Mar. 1907). The holiday of Purrim as reported in the Scroll of Esther marks the miraculous deliverance of the Jews in Persia from Haman's extermination plans. It has traditionally been the happiest Jewish festivity of the yearly cycle.
[62] *HaZevi* (15 Nov. 1909).

block was the absence of adequate auditoriums. The Society held its concerts at schools, hotels, and at private homes. 'At times they relied on favours, at times they paid for the auditorium more than they collected at the door. Whoever was acquainted with the daily business of the Society knew how much agony, emotions, and incredibly hard work were needed to secure an auditorium for each performance.'[63] During the years 1908–10 the Society managed to hold a total of only twelve adults' and three children's concerts in both Jaffa and Jerusalem. The circle of active recitalists in Palestine consisted of about a dozen pianists and violinists, who gallantly avoided competition and shared the few opportunities to perform.

The musical activity, however infrequent, encouraged music education to such an extent that in 1907 Haim Mühlmann, music teacher at the Hebrew Gymnasium in Jaffa, announced the opening of a music store which promised to procure instruments and sheet music from Europe and to respond to mail orders.[64]

The fierce political rivalries within the New Yishuv did not spare the frail musical scene. The Zionist Jewish circles considered the implementation of modernized Hebrew a necessary condition for national revival. Consequently they were adamantly opposed to the continued use of Yiddish by Jews in Palestine. Yiddish was pejoratively labelled 'jargon', and the amateur theatre productions in Yiddish, popular with the older generation, were denigrated in the daily press and frequently even obstructed. The Violin of Zion Society sent a letter to the editor bitterly complaining that it had been unjustly censured for its participation in a Yiddish theatre production designed to raise funds for the Society, 'while there is not a single organization in Jaffa which has not used our services to raise money for its own purposes'.[65]

The use of European languages in vocal concerts was equally censured. A scandal erupted at a ball in Jerusalem: 'Mrs Stavinowsky's voice was ugly and screeching, and to make matters worse, she sang in Russian, at which the audience protested and she was forced to stop and leave the stage.'[66] A violent exchange took place at a concert in Jerusalem when a singer performed a song in French:

The audience protested and disrupted the performance. [The violinist] Mr Kowalsky approached one of the protestors, the teacher Mr Burla, and rudely pushed him back to his seat, with the intent of calming down the audience.

[63] Ha'Or (5 Apr. 1910).   [64] Hashkafa (8 Mar. 1907).
[65] HaZevi (14 Dec. 1908).   [66] Aherout (5 Sept. 1910).

Does Mr Kowalsky really think that if the audiences refuse to eat straw, they should be forced to do so?[67]

Still, a combination of a fine performance and a tactful attitude could bring about a certain tolerance. Pianist Miriam Levit charmed the Tel Aviv audience with her performance of Chopin, Brahms, and Tchaikovsky: 'It felt as if we were transported to another world, away from material worries, a wholly fantastical world.' The pianist then introduced a new immigrant, formerly an opera singer at St Petersburg, who presented a programme of songs in Hebrew. When the audience requested an encore, the singer apologized that she had exhausted her Hebrew repertory and could sing only in Italian. The entire audience consented to 'allow her to continue her performance, although the songs were not in Hebrew'.[68]

A careful planning could prove the power of music of temporarily bringing together rival factions. The correspondent of *Aherout* reported a concert in honour of the founder of the Violin of Zion Society which was held at an auditorium previously used by the French consulate. 'The organizers were right in holding the ball in a neutral place . . . Had it been held in Lemel school, the opponents of the Hilfsverein would have abstained, and had the Alliance auditorium been selected, the Vereiners and other anti-Alliance people would not have attended', whereas the Christian auditorium, 'for which 60 francs were paid only for rental' attracted 'the entire élite of Jerusalem, both Jewish and Christian'.[69] Yet, at times, internal strife prevailed over the unifying power of music. At the height of the fierce war of languages between the Hilfsverein and the Hebraists,[70] a concert sponsored by the music school in Jerusalem turned into a rampage. The audience noticed among the chorus members a young student, who 'had abandoned his friends and had stayed at the Verein. The appearance of this traitor on the stage roused fierce anger in the audience, and all the youngsters started to boo and whistle and disrupted the music' until the concert was called off.[71]

The Beginning of Professional Stratification

The dedicated work of the Violin of Zion Society and of the instrumental teachers paved the way for the inception of the first professional con-

---

[67] *Aherout* (24 Feb. 1913).   [68] *Aherout* (1 July 1914).   [69] *Aherout* (4 May 1910).
[70] See Ch. 1, above.   [71] *Aherout* (2 Feb. 1914).

servatory in Jaffa. The founder Shulamit (Selma) Ruppin was born in 1873 in Bromberg, Germany, to an educated Jewish family. She studied voice in Berlin and her goal was performing in the opera. However, her parents dissuaded her from such a career and she became, instead, a voice-teacher in Berlin. 'Thanks to a tremendous perseverance and a talent for music, she had succeeded in establishing herself by taking a job which, together with the income from private singing lessons, left her financially independent.'[72] In 1908 she married her cousin Dr Arthur Ruppin, and joined him in Palestine in 1910 after recovering from a difficult delivery of her first child in Berlin. The young artist found herself cast out of metropolitan Berlin into the small Mediterranean port of Jaffa. Yet, the first step she took upon her return to Palestine was to establish a school of music. 'A patron appeared . . . and supported the school financially.'[73] The internationally renowned Professor Henri Marteau of Geneva recommended his pupil Moshe Hopenko whom she invited and appointed director of the school and violin-teacher. Another member of the faculty also included the piano-teacher Gutta Weizmann and the highly popular Miriam Levit. Marcel Hammerschlag taught piano, theory, composition, and directed the choir. Hopenko was also listed as teacher for cello, double bass, flute, and oboe, but there was no enrolment to study those instruments.[74]

The painter-author Nahum Gutmann depicted violinist Moshe Hopenko's arrival as a poetic surrealistic dream:

The Arabic sailor placed his two arms, one under the passenger's knees, another behind his hips, and picked him up. The passenger who held a violin case in his right hand opened bewildered eyes. . . . Suddenly the sailor sent the passenger flying to the hand of a second sailor who was standing below in the boat. . . . The passenger and his violin sank into the boat together with parcels and luggage. . . . Having reached the shore, he walked erect . . . He walked as if he were sent to this place and had no time to spare . . . The chemist was sitting on the porch of the pharmacy. The violinist asked:

'do you know of any vacancy here?'

'Is there a violin in this case?', the chemist asked.

The violinist replied with a smile: 'The sailors thought it was a hand gun. And when I heard the donkey, I thought it was a broken gramophone. I feel as if a whale has cast me upon this shore.' . . .

The shutters in the chemist's home were wide open. Through the lighted window one could see the violinist, his chin attached to the violin and his right hand gently touching with the bow, like the breeze over the sands. . . . The

[72] A. Ruppin, *Memoirs, Diaries, Letters*, ed. Alex Bein (London, 1971), 142.
[73] Ibid. 144.   [74] First brochure, 1911 (CZA 785).

residents of the quarter took their seats on the fences around . . . The remote
houses were dark, and from the nearby homes people took out chairs. People lay
down on the sand all around. The miracle box—the chemist's house—opened
up. . . . This is what I said: 'Do we know how music can affect us? I feel as if a
big whale has cast this violinist on to our shore.'[75]

The first school year opened on 1 November 1910. Seventy-five pupils
enrolled, of whom thirty had been sent by their families from Europe
(mostly from Russia). Thus the Music School, like the Herzlia Gymnasium, acted as an immigration catalyst. The high professional level of
the small faculty also attracted the finest piano students from Rishon
Le'Zion, thus establishing Jaffa as the centre of music training. Nearly all
learned either violin or piano.[76] A relatively high proportion of twenty-
two left during the first year. The high prestige of the Music School
stemmed from the admiration for Shulamit Ruppin's daring initiative,
and from the intensive communal activity of the school.

Shulamit Ruppin's step was her own personal response to the trauma
of her immigration. Having lost her professional environment, she re-
claimed it through transplanting the model of the central European
conservatory. The opening of the school coincided with the inauguration
of the garden suburb of Tel Aviv, yet it appears that the two events were
unrelated. The socialist-oriented weekly Hapo'el Ha'tza'ir[77] published a
lengthy and sincere study of the role of Tel Aviv in the social life of the
Jewish community of Jaffa. The author, who used the pen-name Citizen,
reprimanded Tel Aviv for being a centre of self-centred intellectual
haughtiness, contributing nothing to its surrounding neighbourhoods.

The entire intelligentsia—teachers, authors, civil servants, political activists,
professionals—those who have served the community all their life—all settled in
Tel Aviv. . . . Yet, this Tel Aviv created nothing new. . . . The School of Music
and the School of Arts were formed by two energetic women unrelated to Tel
Aviv.[78]

Music education was considered a feminine field. Fifty-two of the
seventy-three pupils who enrolled in the first year of the school in Jaffa
were girls. When the school was threatened by the economic crisis of
World War I, Hopenko felt obliged to justify his application for financial
support with the comment that

our school trains its pupils to master a craft which provides a living, and in this
respect it is no different from any other vocational school. Many musically

---

[75] N. Gutman, Ir Ktanah Ve'Anashim bah Me'at (Tel Aviv, 1959), 39–41.
[76] There was one cello-pupil and one voice-pupil. Data from the detailed school bulletin, 1911.
[77] Lit. 'The Young Worker'.   [78] Hapo'el Hatza'ir (6 Aug. 1912), 18.

talented pupils from poor families receive in our institution a fully adequate preparation to make any honourable living. Experience has proved that poor pupils who were forced to leave school before earning their diploma now make a living as players and provide for their parents and kin.[79]

The need for a music school was frequently expressed in the small circle of music-teachers in Jerusalem, but it was Shulamit Ruppin who, encouraged by her initial success, realized their wish when she founded a Jerusalem branch of her school in November 1911.[80] The New Yishuv in Jerusalem welcomed her initiative

which would fill in a severe lacuna in our town, for it would provide the women of Jerusalem with the opportunity to develop their hidden talents and would in general direct the young generation of girls to aspire to new horizons and to a new life. Many of our lovely girls, who have so far passed their time in boredom, would now find the right challenge.[81]

In the predominantly conservative society of Jerusalem in which education of girls was viewed with suspicion, the intellectual circles of the New Yishuv realized the potential of the music school to raise women's social status and self-image.

Shulamit Ruppin directed the school in Jaffa for only two years. She died on 15 October 1912 of a blood infection following a stillbirth. The imprint of her personality during the mere two years of her activity in Jaffa was such that the memorial service 'was attended by a very large crowd, showing great respect for the departed'.[82] Moreover, the powerful personality of the independent and determined young woman affected a dramatic shift in social outlook, as reflected in an obituary written by a member of the Sephardi Jewish community:

Until recent times we, Eastern Jews, used to look down on our brothers from the West. We treated them the way the learned would treat the simple. Now, . . . they sometimes surprise us when they reveal to us their great spiritual richness. . . . and we are stunned. How is it that those people, who had been so far from us in their education, customs, and opinions, still preserve the holy fire of Jewishness, which bursts out and lights the way for us, the Jews of the East? . . . For a short while a Hebraic woman from the West, one may say the most Western of the Westerners, the late Shulamit Ruppin, lived among us. She had received a modern European education and mastered music well . . . How could she find anything in common with the land of Israel? . . . Yet, the incredible did happen. Since her arrival . . . she did everything to become one of

[79] Letter of 12 June 1916 (CZA 785).   [80] *Aherout* (20 Nov. 1911).
[81] *Ha'Or* (17 Nov. 1911).   [82] *Hapo'el Hatza'ir* (6 Oct. 1912).

us, to be a sister to her brothers and to distribute among them the spiritual possessions she had brought along with her from the West. But above and beyond all Shulamit displayed all the virtues of a Jewish woman. She deeply loved her husband and treated him as the head of the family. She, the teacher, always behaved as if her foremost duty was to gratify her husband, and she was likewise dedicated to her little girl. Whatever you say, modern innovators, women-liberators, and free-love advocates—I do consider the dedication of a woman to her husband and to her children to be an ideal far higher than the fake ideal of freedom.[83]

Sofer's writing was exceptionally candid and sincere for an obituary. The Sephardi Jews of Palestine prided themselves on their long lineage in the holy land. The Ottoman regime recognized the Sephardi *Hakham*[84] as the sole official representative of all local Jewish communities. The Sephardi Jews were deeply conservative, patriarchal, and the social fabric of their communities was based on the expanded family as the core unit. The growing immigration wave of Jews from Europe and the ideological pressures to place national unity above ethnic identity threatened the cherished Sephardi customs and traditions.[85] As such Shulamit Ruppin's contribution was remarkable, especially in view of the brevity of her activity in Jaffa. After Shulamit Ruppin's death the two branches of the school were named after her.[86]

The school in Jaffa was soon facing a challenge to transform the cultural scene in Palestine. A fine violin and piano recital triggered the request to increase the number of concerts and to lower ticket prices 'so that they could complement the education of the young generation and provide the youth with the warmth and sensitivity which they miss now'.[87] The school responded to the appeal and organized fortnightly faculty and student recitals. Each school year ended with public examinations which attracted a large audience.[88] The faculty recitals substituted the model of pure musical programmes for the earlier model of mixed musical and literary social events. For example, one of the first faculty recitals included a Beethoven violin sonata, Schumann's *Faschingsschwank aus Wien*, Chopin's *Fantasie Impromptu*, the first movement of a concerto by Viotti, and a violin concerto by Bruch (both accompanied by piano). Some concerts were devoted to a particular theme, such as a concert

---

[83] A. Sofer, *Hapo'el Hatza'ir*, 5–6 (1 Nov. 1912).

[84] Lit. 'the sage', who was the religious leader of the Sephardi community.

[85] In 1905 55 per cent of the Jews in Jaffa were of European (Ashkenazi) descent. Kark, *Jaffa*, 164.

[86] *Ha'Or* (23 Oct. 1912). Moshe Hopenko became the director in Jaffa and the Jerusalem branch became independent under pianist Marie Itzhaki. Dr Ruppin maintained his support to the two schools.

[87] *Ha'Or* (19 Mar. 1912).   [88] *Ha'Or* (16 Oct. 1912).

commemorating the fiftieth anniversary of Meyerbeer's death,[89] in which the school choir and the orchestra participated. The conductor Moshe Schalit who joined the school faculty in 1912 initiated concerts of 'Hebrew folk music', which included his own arrangements of diaspora Jewish folk songs, compositions by members of the Society for Jewish Folk Music in St Petersburg, and music by non-Jews using Jewish themes, most notably Bruch's *Kol-Nidrei*.[90] Some of the school events were honoured by the presence of Ottoman officials and enhanced the prestige of the small *Yishuv*.[91] The increasing regularity of the concerts also modified the promotion system in Jerusalem. 'Tickets will no longer be distributed as before, when honourable ladies laboured to bring them to each home, but will be sold in the two stores mentioned in the ad on first-come-first-served basis.'[92] On the eve of World War I the Violin of Zion Society in Jaffa operated in full co-operation with Shulamit School, and had seventy-one members who paid their dues.[93]

Dissonant chords of personal friction soon disrupted the harmony in the pioneer Shulamit school. The popular pianist Miriam Levit brought her grievances to public attention in a long letter to the editor of *Aherout*.[94] Writing in perfect Hebrew and beautiful calligraphy, the young pianist charged that Hopenko's attitude to his teachers was dictatorial and insulting, and that, although the number of violin pupils had reached fifty, Hopenko refused to hire additional violin-teachers with the result that lessons became short and superficial, with tuition of beginners mostly entrusted to the more advanced children who were ill trained to teach. She also objected to the allegedly exaggerated emphasis placed on the orchestra which allowed little time for developing individual talents. Miriam Levit concluded with an intention to resign. The public committee which ran the school angrily chided the dissident teacher for defamation of the school and fired her on the spot.[95] Miriam Levit responded by starting a small music school of her own, which in 1915–16 attracted thirty-nine piano pupils.[96]

---

[89] On 13 May 1914 (Posters Archive, JNUL, V 1961/1).

[90] 16 Mar. 1911 (Ravina Archive (R1/2/1), AMLI Tel Aviv). The programme also included works by Schalit, Engel, Levov, Schklar, Zeitlin, and Kopit.

[91] *Ha'Or* (13 Mar. 1912).   [92] *Ha'Or* (12 Mar. 1912).

[93] CZA S2 785. The Society used Shulamit School's letterhead.

[94] A letter of 16 June 1914 (Yariv Ezrahi Archive, Tel Aviv University).

[95] A letter from Dr Arthur Ruppin, Meir Dizengoff, and Sarah Tahon, 24 June 1914 (Yariv Ezrahi Archive, Tel Aviv University).

[96] A document of 1924 (no precise date) (House of Levites Archive, CZA M2/3). See Ch. 3, below.

The school in Jerusalem encountered severe difficulties from the start. The correspondent of *Aherout* bitterly reprimanded the Jerusalem public for its low attendance at a very fine teachers' recital, and bemoaned the very disappointing initial enrolment of only five pupils.[97] On the eve of World War I the number did not exceed thirty-seven.[98] The national circles in Jerusalem discovered to their dismay that the Sephardi well-to-do intellectuals preferred to enrol their daughters at the French monastery school of St Joseph's and at the schools run by the Italian nuns, where about one hundred young Jewish girls took piano lessons. 'It has been said that the Sephardi girls are attracted by the studies of French and handcrafts there, but the girls who would study at our own music schools would easily be able to learn French at the Alliance school.'[99] It appears that the Sephardim of the Old Yishuv felt that their daughters would be spiritually safer at the conservative Church schools in Jerusalem than if exposed to the enlightened spirit of the modern education of the New Yishuv. The Hebrew Gymnasium in Jerusalem attracted an equal number of girls and boys, but whereas the boys were almost evenly divided into Ashkenazi and Sephardi, only 18.5 per cent of the girls were Sephardi.[100]

The shaky school benefited from the moral and the material support of its friends in Russia. Upon his return to Moscow David Schor formed a committee which raised small funds for the music schools until the outbreak of the war.[101] Schor also maintained a lively correspondence with his new friends on matters of ideology and methodology. He wrote to Marie Itzhaki, director of the Jerusalem school, that 'the school should serve the Christian and Moslem communities. It must be a unifying agent for all religions.'[102] He also warned Mrs Itzhaki to 'avoid the current mistake. . . . Do not commence musical education with an instrument but only with singing. This is the only way to train a good and musical ear. For this purpose violin is preferable to piano. . . . A compilation of Jewish and of other folksongs will be best for that. . . . It will also be easier for the school to hold group lessons.'[103] Schor also tried to recruit new teachers for the Jerusalem school, but he encountered severe difficulties in convincing people to go, especially since he has

---

[97] *Aherout* (18 Mar. 1912).

[98] CZA J43/7, 9. Parents paid by the month, and a different number of pupils was reported in the financial records each month, reflecting the shaky economy of the school.

[99] *Ha'Or* (16 Nov. 1912).

[100] M. Rinot, 'The Education in Eretz Israel', in Kolat (ed.), *Ottoman Period*, 677.

[101] *Davar* (5 Dec. 1933).   [102] CZA J/43.   [103] 20 Sept. 1911 (CZA J/43).

failed to raise adequate funds to support the emigration of fine
musicians.[104]

The proximity of Idelsohn's work directly influenced the scholarly
orientation of some of the school teachers. Sachnowsky, principal of the
music school, presented a public lecture on ancient Hebrew music, in
which he used Idelsohn's research as evidence for the preservation of the
most ancient Hebrew cantillation in Yemenite music, as distinct from that
of the Sephardi.[105]

The stance of the music schools in the New Yishuv may be roughly
assessed by the proportion of their students within the total school
population. In the school year 1913–14 the number of children at the
elementary school system of the New Yishuv was 535.[106] Total enrolment
at the Shulamit schools in Jaffa and Jerusalem and at Levit's new studio
together reached about two hundred, amounting to 37 per cent of the
total school population.[107] Such astounding figures reflected a blend of
miscellaneous factors, such as the 'small village' conviction that enrolling
the child in the music school was considered the right thing to
do, the inner need to support any Jewish institutional initiative, the
scarcity of other outlets for youngsters, as well as a genuine devotion to
music.

The two schools were subjected to an assessment by the Jewish
composer Michael Gnessin who visited Palestine in 1914 for one month
as an official envoy of the Odessa Committee.[108] Upon his return to St
Petersburg Gnessin presented a well-attended public lecture, which was
published in the Russian weekly *Novi Waschod*. The editor of *Aherout*,
who printed a full Hebrew translation of the report, pointed out that
'Gnessin who was not a committed Zionist has discussed the topic with
no bias or prejudice, so that even the anti-Zionist *Novi Waschod* approves
of his report.'[109]

Gnessin judged the state of music in Palestine from three viewpoints:

---

[104] Letters from Schor to Itzhaki, Mar. 1913, 14 June 1913 (CZA J/43).

[105] *Aherout* (3 Mar. 1914).

[106] D. Gurevich, *Statistical Abstract of Palestine 1929* (Jerusalem, 1930), 240. The figures do not
include the orthodox system of Jerusalem, which did not take part in any secular activity.

[107] The number was even a little higher, since pupils who took private lessons, such as with the
piano teachers in *Rishon Le'Zion* were not included.

[108] M. Gnessin, 'An Autobiography', 1st pub. in R. Glazer, *M. P. Gnessin* (Moscow, 1961)
(Russ.), trans in *Tatzlil* 2 (1961), 120–1. The so-called Odessa Committee was a nickname for the
Society for Support of Jewish Farmers and Artisans in Syria and Palestine which was founded in
Feb. 1890 following a favourable change in the policy of the Russian government towards Jewish
organizations. Gnessin (1883–1957) was a member of the Society for Jewish Folk Music which Joel
Engel had founded in St Petersburg in 1908. See Ch. 5, below.

[109] *Aherout* (21 July 1914), which is the source of the following quotes.

a. From the viewpoint of a performer who investigates to what extent music has been grounded as art in Palestine, and whether it deserves support.
b. From the national viewpoint which requires a clarification of the extent of the contribution of musical performance in Palestine to national art.
c. From the viewpoint of folk music, which is distorted not only in Russia but in other European cities. The capitals, the centres, and large towns enjoy a profusion of music, whereas the deprived village dwellers subsist on mere leftovers from urban performance.

Gnessin pointed out that Shulamit School in Tel Aviv which then numbered 150 pupils,

caters to the well-to-do community of Tel Aviv and is economically safe and sound. The school relies on tuition alone, so its chances to expand and increase its enrolment are limited. . . . The school has no funds for scholarships; it cannot open departments for double bass, bassoon, and [other] wind instruments . . . and consequently cannot develop a full orchestra. The absence of scholarships leads to deplorable situations. In one case a boy who had no instrument has worked hard and built a violin for himself . . . and still could not be admitted since he could not afford the tuition.

Gnessin was much more pessimistic about the school in Jerusalem, since 'the poverty-stricken community in Jerusalem does not pay for education. Only two or three cantorial students come from the orthodox circles.' Broad-minded and sensitive, Gnessin took special notice of the importance of a constant liaison between the Jewish community and the neighbouring Arabs and Turks.

One should keep in mind the cultural role which musical life in the Land of Israel may play *vis-à-vis* the neighbours. Despite the existence of rich and superb folk music among the Arabs, and despite the attachment of Arabs and Turks to music, they have no public musical life, neither in Palestine, nor in Syria and Egypt. The Arabs frequently wish to enrol in the music schools in Palestine but the managements must turn them down because they cannot afford tuition.

A more favourable liaison was established with the Ottoman administration, which asked the music school in Jaffa for advice in coaching the military bands. The Ottoman Pasha commissioned the music school to organize a special reception for the respected aviator Nuri Bay on the occasion of his brief visit.

After an opening speech by the president of Tel Aviv committee, Mr M. Dizengoff, the orchestra played the overture to the *Marriage of Figaro* and the *Rondo alla Turca* by Mozart and a Mendelssohn [violin] concerto. All present, among them the Arab and Turkish dignitaries and all important consuls expressed their pleasure and asked to be regularly invited to the school concerts.

Gnessin was favourably impressed by the community orchestras of the settlements, especially with the Rishon Le'Zion revived ensemble. He pointed out that 'musical life in the settlements develops at its own pace, with no outside artificial encouragement. The school in Jaffa maintains a symphony orchestra which is frequently invited for concerts at the settlements.'

The intensification of musical activity which followed the formation of music schools was reflected in the growing market for second hand pianos which were advertised in the local press. Soon an agent by the name of Philip Kiefendorf exploited the market in Palestine and in Syria by importing Hoffmann pianos. Kiefendorf even used a jingle, *Das Lied vom Hoffmann Piano*, which opens with the following verses: 'In every town and country one hears music. But often it insults the ear, sounding bad and shrill. The player need not be an artist, if the instrument is good.'[110] The agent invited the smart customer to buy the waltz music for the Lied. Those who could not afford to buy pianos were invited to rent them at a Jerusalem store, which also sold violins, recorders, and mandolines.[111] Still, public organizations could not afford even commercial rentals. On one occasion a concert scheduled for the first night of Passover had to be postponed for a week because of a 'piano which a certain matron was reluctant to loan'.[112]

The general public endorsement of musical activity was explicitly justified as part of the forward-looking encouragement of national revival. Yet, it appears that it was equally motivated by the migrant state of mind, dominated by a sense of alienation and a nostalgic yearning for European culture, which occasionally burst out, as in the review of Miriam Levit's Jerusalem debut quoted above. A notice of a new community choir being formed in Jerusalem spurred a full enrolment, since 'one cannot exaggerate the need for it in view of the boring life in Jerusalem, where some spiritual preoccupation is required in order to refresh the souls weary of the difficult life and the struggle for survival.'[113] The Herzlia Gymnasium in Tel Aviv used to celebrate the end of each school year with a public ball which emulated the classical spirit in mixed programmes of music and of gymnastics. The ball in July 1914 was of special importance, first, since it hosted two large delegations of Hebrew teachers from Russia and from the Ukraine, and second, since the proceeds were earmarked for the

---

[110] 'In jeder Stadt in jedem Land | hort jetzt Musik man schon. Doch oft beleidigt sie das Ohr, klingt schlecht und schrill der Ton. | Der spieler braucht kein Kunstler sein, wenn gut das Instrument.' *Aherout* (14 Nov. 1913).

[111] *Aherout* (28 Oct. 1913).   [112] *Aherout* (21 Apr. 1914).

[113] *Ha'Or* (6 and 13 Mar. 1912).

exceptional purpose of purchasing the first aeroplane for the Jewish autonomous administration. The columnist wrote that

we, local residents, have grown accustomed to our balls with their recurring contents and structure and we are not especially impressed. But our guests are deeply affected. We miss the elaborate European stage, the great artistic talents of the world stage; but they crave the Hebrew stage, whatever it is.[114]

The author Asher Barash described a lecture by a visiting German professor on Eichendorff's Lieder, which was held in 1914 at the German Colony in Jaffa. Most Jews attended, since 'there was hardly a Jew who did not understand German' and they 'all felt the need for some cultural breath of air, to feel the breeze of the West'.[115] The lecture was illustrated by a young amateur singer from the German Colony. Barash's poetic description of gloomy Tel Aviv betrays his nostalgic image of a distant European city: 'It was midwinter and the sky was overcast with heavy rain clouds The *lux* shone in the mist. Piano-playing, mostly scale passages, was heard from some of the houses.'[116]

Music thus satisfied both the inner needs of the individual migrant clinging to his home culture and the collective urge for national revival. The nascent institutionalization and the gradually increasing frequency and standards of concerts by the year 1914 held a promising potential, which was shattered all of a sudden by the outbreak of World War I.

---

[114] *Aherout* (13 July 1914).

[115] A. Barasch, *Ke'Ir Netzurah* (Tel Aviv, 1945), 42. Asher Barasch (1889–1952, immigrated 1914), was a teacher, an editor, and a prolific author.

[116] Ibid. 43. The *lux* was a powerful kerosene lamp, which was the main device for external illumination at that time.

3

From Abyss to Recovery

THE four years of World War I left Palestine in a shambles. The Jewish community shrank from 85,000 in 1914 to 56,000 in 1918, and those who stayed suffered hunger, epidemics, and deprivation.

The leaders of the Yishuv were hard-pressed at the first stages of the war to dispel the image of a disloyal minority, the result of the large number of Jews who had maintained their foreign citizenships.[1] The routine, albeit modest, musical activity which had gradually established itself in Jerusalem before the war, was replaced by patriotic spectacles such as a fund-raising ball for the Red Crescent[2] which turned out to be an impressive rally of the Yishuv's solidarity with the Ottoman war effort. The entire Turkish administration as well as friendly consuls were present at the event, which attracted an estimated crowd of 1,500 people. The patriotic function occasioned a strange hotchpotch programme. Idelsohn conducted the combined choruses of the Hebrew schools who sang a Hebrew prayer for the Sultan, whereas the Arabic school chorus performed a Turkish national song. Then two pupils of the music school performed a Mozart violin and piano sonata, 'which roused the interest even of the plain audience bereft of sensitivity to European music, and they responded with thunderous applause'.[3] Idelsohn followed by conducting the Arabic chorus in the Turkish march song 'The Revenge', after which a young Jewish soldier performed a violin piece by Wieniawski. A young soldier sang a 'beautiful Arabic tune which charmed everybody',

[1] N. Efrati, 'The Jewish Community in Eretz Israel during World War I', PhD thesis (Hebrew University, Jerusalem, 1985), 67.

[2] The branch of the International Red Cross active in Arabic countries.

[3] *Aherout* (15 Sept. 1915). A more modest event was held in the summer. *Aherout* (1 July 1915).

followed by a violin and piano piece by Anton Rubinstein, the evening proceeding in this manner.

The war played havoc with the three music schools which had barely established themselves. The shaky school in Jerusalem was shut down in October 1914, and a piano which the school bought for 524 francs in 1914 was sold for only 447 francs a year later.[4] Miriam Levit's new studio closed down for three years in 1916. Shulamit School, however, was sturdier. Immediately upon the outbreak of hostilities Dr Arthur Ruppin dispatched an urgent letter to the German Consul, complaining that 'it appears that the Turkish government has started to detain all pupils who hold citizenships of hostile powers'.[5] The small Yishuv found itself disjoined from the Turkish viewpoint. The German citizens, like Ruppin, were on the allegedly right side of the Triple Alliance of Turkey, Germany, and Austria, whereas the Jews who retained Russian citizenship were suspected as loyal to the Entente powers which included Britain, France, Belgium, Russia, and Serbia. Consequently, the number of pupils in Shulamit School dropped from 120 to 40, and even those who stayed paid tuition with worthless Turkish banknotes. The war stopped the lines of support from Europe, and the school could not pay its rent.[6] The situation deteriorated even further when the British army invaded Palestine from the south. In March 1917 the Turkish government expelled nearly the entire Jewish population of Jaffa and Tel Aviv to the Turkish ruled zone in the north. Shulamit School maintained a minimal activity in the settlement of Petah-Tikvah. The British invasion of Jaffa in November 1917 enabled the Jews to return to their abandoned homes in Tel Aviv. This return coincided with the momentous event of Lord Balfour's declaration in favour of a national home for the Jews in Palestine.[7] Violinist Moshe Hopenko was the first to receive the happy news. The author and painter Nahum Gutman depicted the event in his poetic style:

The three windows of the house were open to the green street. It was no miracle that when Mr Hopenko returned home, he noisily opened the shutters to allow light into the house which had been sealed for many months. . . . It was no miracle that the violinist opened the black case and took out his good friend, the violin. For many months the case has been wrapped in rags for fear of arousing the curiosity of the Turkish soldiers. The violinist tuned the strings and drew the bow. It was no miracle that he felt happy and liberated. No miracle.

[4] *Aherout* (26 Oct. 1914) (CZA 43/9).   [5] Letter to Dr Brode, 29 Nov. 1914 (CZA 14).
[6] A letter from Hopenko to Dizengoff, chair of the Tel Aviv Committee, 12 Sept. 1915 (CZA S2 785).
[7] Lord Arthur J. Balfour, British foreign minister 1916–19, issued his declaration on 2 Nov. 1917.

His wife sat at the piano, wiped the dust off the keys, and the hitherto dormant sounds emerged.

No miracle? Yes, there was a miracle!

Since the music poured through the windows on to the green road and filled the air. It endowed everything with a certain festive light, which is seen but not grasped.

It was good fortune which brought along an Australian officer to the green pavement. Suddenly he stopped to the sound of the tune. He approached the window and listened to it until it was over.

With a shy smile the officer came to the door and enquired whether he could enter and thank the musician. For a long time he had not listened to good music. He was for many months on the road and in the desert, and always among soldiers. . . .

In that way the people of the neighbourhood were informed—on the very first day of their return—by the Australian officer about Balfour's declaration. . . . Mr Hopenko went out to the street very excited. He must share his feelings with other people. . . . He stopped the first people he saw, raised his gentle hands, and said: 'It is true.' When he saw that people were still doubtful, he added: 'Don't you believe? People who like music cannot lie.'[8]

The end of the war and the implementation of an internationally recognized British mandate aroused high hopes in the Yishuv. The British government entrusted the Jews in Palestine with an almost complete autonomy over their internal affairs, which were administered by an elected institutional hierarchy. Most influential was the National Committee[9] of twenty to forty members, who appointed an Executive Board which ran the daily life of the Yishuv. The autonomy was especially important in culture and education, allowing the dissemination of the unifying use of Hebrew and of national education. The need for ruling institutions gave rise to an experienced political, economic, and cultural élite.[10] The depressing depletion of the Jewish population during World War I was sharply reversed with the arrival of two successive waves of European Jewish immigrants. The first, known as the Third Aliya (1919–23), originated mostly in Russia (13,363) and Poland (9,158) and there was only a trickle of 469 from Germany and 497 from Austria.[11] About

---

[8] *Shvil Klipot Ha'tapuzim*, 78.

[9] Va'ad Le'ummi. The National Committee functioned from 10 Oct. 1920 until the establishment of the Provisional Government in May 1948.

[10] The British administration retained command over foreign policy, the judicial system, postal service, ports, and security. Lissak, *Elites of the Jewish Community*, 16.

[11] Gurevich, *Statistical Abstract of Palestine*, 46. Figures were provided by the Zionist Leadership in Palestine. The British administration provided slightly different figures for part of the period, but the proportions are virtually the same.

49 per cent of the Third Aliya immigrants were young and unmarried.[12] The Yishuv had such high demands from the immigrant artists that an immediate disappointment was unavoidable. The poet and columnist Yehudah Karni portrayed them as being

of two kinds: those salvaged from the fire who came here to make a living, and those who came to this country, explicitly to this country, to collaborate in the erection of a temple for the Hebraic art. The former disembark the boat and step instantly on the stage, attract audiences and entertain them. The latter go through agony and struggle, build and demolish and rebuild, and in the meantime they starve. We are not sorry for the former. If they do earn their daily bread, they will also enjoy their homeland. If they do not, let them go away. We are sorry for the latter. Not because they are hungry. They are hungry but happy, because they have something in them which makes them forget their hunger. But both groups have something in common: they do not create anything of lasting value for the art of the future. The former group has no interest. The latter one lacks focus.[13]

In the year 1924–6 the composition and size of the Jewish immigration changed to such an extent that the immigrants were treated as a new wave, later referred to as the Fourth Aliya. This was the first instance of a mass immigration into Palestine. About 50,500 Jews joined the Yishuv, most of them in 1925. About 40 per cent of this new wave of immigration, which originated in Poland, were granted entry certificates to Palestine under the category of 'capitalists', meaning applicants capable of settling by their own means with no public help, and therefore automatically eligible for entry. The label was distorted, since most of the immigrants were small shopkeepers and craftsmen who were hard hit by the economic policy of the new Polish government and had barely recovered their money from its crumbling economy.[14] The Fourth Aliya gave the demography of Palestine a strong urban orientation. One-third of this migration wave settled in Tel Aviv which had made an astounding population increase of 30 per cent. in 1924 and of 58 per cent. in 1925,[15] consequently turning from a green suburb into a vibrant commercial

[12] D. Gurevich, A. Gertz, and R. Bachi, *The Jewish Population of Palestine* (Jerusalem, 1944), table 4. B. Amikam, 'The Third Aliya', in B. Eliav (ed.), *The Jewish National Home* (Jerusalem, 1976), 289.

[13] *Hedim*, 1 (1922), 36. *Hedim* was the literary organ of the young poets and authors. It was published irregularly until 1928. Z. Shavit, *The Literary Life in Iretz Israel 1910–1933* (Tel Aviv. 1982), 74–6.

[14] D. Giladi, 'The Yishuv during the Fourth Aliya', Ph.D. thesis (Hebrew University, Jerusalem, 1968), 30; id., 'Tel Aviv during the Fourth *Aliya*', in M. Naor (ed.), *The Beginnings of Tel Aviv 1909–1934* (Jerusalem, 1984), 78.

[15] *Statistical Abstract*, 37.

urban centre. Although adjacent to Jaffa, the British administration encouraged the administrative separation of Tel Aviv from Jaffa.[16] This legal
step received an additional impetus from the unexpected bloody events of
1 May 1921 when Jews were attacked in Jaffa by an Arab mob. The
shocked Jews reacted by developing an independent economic infrastructure in Tel Aviv,[17] which further loosened their links with Jaffa. Tel Aviv
then acquired the status and the nickname of the First Hebrew City; thus
its unique character which contrasted with the unbeatable historical
prestige and cosmopolitan character of Jerusalem was established. In 1922
the Jewish population of Jerusalem numbered 34,000, (54 per cent of
the city population), whereas the Jewish population of Tel Aviv and Jaffa
put together reached only 20,200.[18] Yet there was a marked difference
between the Jewish community of Jerusalem, with its high proportion of
compartmentalized orthodox subcommunities which kept out of any
secular activity, and the mainly secular and nationally oriented community of Tel Aviv. Moreover, Tel Aviv took the lion's share of the new
immigration during the 1920s, with about 40 per cent settling there
compared with about 12 per cent who turned to Jerusalem.[19]

Between Vision and Illusion

The music schools signalled the recovery of musical activity after the war.
The faculty and the students of Shulamit Music School in Jaffa initiated
the resumption of concert activity after the war with a festive concert
at the newly founded Eden cinema.[20] In 1922 the number of pupils
reached 102, and by 1925 the comeback was complete with 125 registered pupils.

An analysis of the school's documents reveals a chasm between vision
and illusion, which touched on all aspects of the musical scene in the
1920s. On the surface, the economic recovery of the school after the war
was remarkable, as shown by comparing the financial records of the
school with the official statistical data for the year 1926. The average

---

[16] Effected on 11 May 1921.

[17] Bigger, 'Development of the Urban Area of Tel Aviv', 54–5.

[18] Gurevich, *Statistical Abstract*, 35, 37. Gurevich *et al.*, *Jewish Population of Palestine*, 82–4. In 1922
Tel Aviv, which originated as a green suburb of Jaffa, incorporated the older small Jewish sections
adjacent to Jaffa, thereby quadrupling its population. The Jews who still lived in Jaffa constituted
only 15.6 per cent of the population of the Arab town, but to all intents and purposes they were
culturally linked to Tel Aviv.

[19] Central Bureau of Statistics, *Census* (Jerusalem, 1948).

[20] 10 Feb. 1919. Founded in 1913. Eden was the first cinema in Tel Aviv.

monthly expenditure by a family of four was at the time £10.10 per month. Nearly 40 per cent of the salaried workers and civil servants earned £6–£10, 20 per cent reached £11–£15, 9 per cent made £16–£25, and only less than 2 per cent earned £26–£40.[21] Moshe Hopenko, the director who salvaged the school from the crisis, commanded a monthly salary of £35, and together with his wife, the piano-teacher Lena, the family earned an enviable monthly sum of £50. The rest of the faculty numbered seven teachers,[22] whose salaries ranged from £10 to £20, a salary for which they had to give a dozen pupils an hourly lesson per week, receiving a small bonus for each additional pupil.[23] Yet the attractive conditions remained a dead letter. After the war the Education Board of the Zionist Organization 'took the school under its protection and allowed it a monthly subsidy of £30, which was reduced owing to lack of funds to £25, and further to £10. During the last year the payment of even the latter amount was stopped altogether.'[24] Most pupils were expected to pay high tuition fees of £12–£15 a year, which ran up to 8–10 per cent of the parents' salary. Such high fees, particularly when requested of immigrants still involved in initial resettlement, called for trouble, and 'they were indeed collected with difficulties'.[25] As a result the school provided almost 30 per cent of the pupils with a discount of 50 per cent, and an additional 20 per cent were exempt from tuition. By the end of 1926 the debt to the faculty, excluding Hopenko and his wife, the piano-teacher Lena, reached the alarming sum of £463, amounting to 27.24 per cent of the salary, and consequently the teachers received only partial salaries. Hopenko and his wife suffered most, having contracted a debt of more than £1,000, which represented almost a two-year salary. The school received a small yearly grant of £19 from the Tel Aviv Council and earned £75 from rentals of its auditorium, but the small additional income was eaten up by the rental of the school building. The attempts to raise a contribution to purchase a house were brought to naught. The frustration of the teachers who never received their theoretically fine salaries resulted in a frequent turnover. The only ray of light was the appointment of two of Hopenko's own graduates, Atara Glückson and Yariv Krishevsky (Ezrahi), as his assistants, a fact which proved that the school had the potential of raising a locally trained professional

---

[21] Gurevich, *Statistical Abstract*, 172, 179.

[22] There were four piano- and two violin-teachers, one teacher for cello and one for theory.

[23] A contract with violinist Margery Bentwich, 26 Aug. 1921 (CZA S2 151).

[24] A letter from the school to Israel Cohen (in English) of 10 June 1924. The same information appears in a letter (in Hebrew) from J. Luria to the music school, 20 Sept. 1922 (CZA).

[25] Ibid.

corps.[26] By 1926 nearly all members of the small faculty of 1922 had changed. Hopenko flooded the Education Board in Jerusalem with pleading and threatening letters and personal calls. He emphasized the involvement of the school in the musical life of the community and drew attention to the free concerts it provided for workers, proving thereby that the school was 'not a luxury'.[27] It appears that the actual salary the teacher received hardly reached the estimated cost of living; as for Hopenko he earned his living from piano and music business as well as from concert management rather than from his teaching activity. Ironically, Hopenko himself sold a piano to his own school for £47, but could not recover the money.[28] The only support came from international soloists who donated fellowships for talented pupils. Pianist Benno Moiseiwitsch provided a yearly scholarship of £50,[29] and Jasha Heifetz contributed the proceeds of his sensational tour of 1925 to the cause of musical education in Palestine.

Hopenko's repeated references to difficult times in the country came in the midst of the euphoria over the mass immigration into Palestine, and made clear to what extent the image of a flow of 'capitalists' was a damaging illusion which misled initiators into taking unwarranted risks.

A different direction was taken in Jerusalem. Brigadier General Roland Storrs, Military Governor of Jerusalem, and the Jewish-British violinist Anton Tschaikov opened a new school of music with Marie Itzhaki, former director of Shulamit School, Idelsohn, and the young British pianist Sydney Seal. Seal (1898–1959) who had arrived in Palestine as a British officer, became devoted to the cause of the Jewish people. He married a Jewish woman, settled permanently in Palestine, and took Hebrew lessons 'in order to teach in Hebrew'.[30] Storrs was deeply involved with all aspects of the administration, including the purchase of furniture.[31] The directors secured an initial fund of £2,000 and instruction started in April 1919. One of their first actions was to ask the Education Board for exemption from the compulsory agricultural work for piano pupils.[32]

The school ran immediately into a crisis. Idelsohn's messy departure generated much anger and ill feelings,[33] and Anton Tschaikov took over

---

[26] The appointment took place in 1924. Document of 10 June 1924 (CZA). Yariv Krishewsky, son of one of the first Hebrew teachers at the Hebrew Gymnasium, soon Hebraized his name to Ezrahi. He married Hopenko's daughter, the pianist Lena.

[27] Letter of 4 Dec. 1921 (CZA S2 151).   [28] Document of 22 Jan. 1922 (CZA).

[29] Letter to Norman Bentwich, 20 May 1924.   [30] Ha'Olam (11 June 1920).

[31] A note to Marie Itzhaki, 14 Mar. 1919 (CZA J43/6).

[32] Minutes of a meeting on 12 May 1919. No record of the response has been found.

[33] See Ch. 1, above.

as director. By then the initial fund was used up, and the Education Board of the Zionist Federation decided to effect a major organizational change:

Since the proportion of Jewish students in the school far exceeds that of students of other denominations, the school, which so far has been an international institution, would now become part of the Board of the Zionist Administration in Palestine as part of its educational undertaking. Hebrew would be adopted as the language of instruction.[34]

The number of students at that time was fifty-nine, of whom thirteen were Christians.[35] The new management declared that enrolment would be open to all regardless of religion or nationality, but that the school 'would be closed on Jewish holidays'. The development was so quick that just a month later Tschaikov reported that the number of pupils had increased to seventy-four: fifty-three in the piano class, fifteen in the violin class, and only two in the vocal class.[36] Despite the frequent administrative changes, the school seems to have taken advantage of its location in the vicinity of the British Mandate administration, and Herbert Samuel, the first High Commissioner of Palestine (1920–25), accepted the honorary position of its patron.[37]

The Education Board had meant well, but it, too, ran into financial difficulties. Anton Tschaikov bitterly complained that the Board was constantly behind in meeting its financial obligations, that many of the parents did not pay their tuition on time, and that as a consequence the teachers could not receive their full salaries. After a few months Tschaikov gave up hope and returned to England, plunging the school again into a deep crisis. However, the pianist Sydney Seal valiantly stepped in. In a sincere letter which he wrote to the Education Board he applied for the position of director, on the basis of his professional qualifications, including a diploma of the prized Manchester College of Music and an Artist Diploma. In his letter Seal emphasized that

first of all I will see it as my obligation to shape the school as a totally Hebrew institution. I will do everything in my power to make sure our school will be as Hebrew as any other Hebrew institution. I, like all other progressive English people, acknowledge the revival of the Jewish people and therefore I recognize the revival of the Hebrew language, and I well understand that the duty of a

---

[34] CZA S2/142ii. Report also in *Ha'Olam* (11 June 1920).

[35] Letter from Anton Tschaikov to the Education Board, 9 Nov. 1920.

[36] CZA S2 597. The numbers add up to only 70, so there must have been an error, which cannot now be clarified.

[37] Letter from Anton Tschaikov to the Education Board, 12 Dec. 1920 (CZA S2 597).

director of a Hebrew music school in Jerusalem is to develop and revive Hebrew music.[38]

The Board agreed, and the school finally emerged out of its prolonged crisis. Yet the Board's share in its maintenance rapidly declined, and was finally eliminated altogether. By 1924 the teachers established a temporary committee to manage the school.

The school took a survey of the occupations of the pupils' parents and it turned out that of the thirty-three who responded there were nine professional musicians, eight civil servants, six businessmen, four teachers, and only one manual worker. Four were defined as 'various jobs' possibly referring to manual labour, and one was an orphan.[39] With only half of the families participating, no far-reaching conclusions can be reached. The school charged a tuition fee of £16, which was similar to the fee charged by Shulamit School in Tel Aviv, and the high number of the children of professional musicians may be accounted for by the decision to exempt faculty children from tuition fees.[40]

Until then the Jerusalem school catered to the New Yishuv. An opportunity to retry a link with the enclosed Old Yishuv which had been hostile to Idelsohn some fifteen years earlier presented itself upon Salomon Rosowsky's immigration in April 1925, when he proposed to launch a cantorial department. Rosowsky (1878–1962), himself a cantor's son, was among the founders of the Society for Jewish Folk Music.[41] The School committee pointed out that 'the proposal would interest many of the Jews of Jerusalem and its opening would create a new outlet for the young talents among the orthodox Jews of Jerusalem'.[42]

Unlike the cities of Tel Aviv and Jerusalem with a Jewish majority, the port town of Haifa was still at the time predominantly Arabic. The number of Jews in Haifa doubled from about 3,000 in 1914 to 6,230 in 1922, but even then they accounted for no more than 25 per cent of the town's population, which included 9,377 Moslems and 8,863 Christians.[43] Nevertheless, the community reached a size which enabled it to initiate its own musical activity, and the distance of more than 100 km. from Tel Aviv was considerable enough to support the development of independent local musical life. Haifa joined Tel Aviv and Jerusalem when the

[38] A letter to Luria, 4 Dec. 1921 (CZA S2 597). The letter was written in Hebrew, but apparently dictated to and polished by the secretary, whose handwriting appears also on letters from Tschaikov and Idelsohn.

[39] Document of 25 July 1922 (CZA S2 627).

[40] Minutes of a meeting on 12 May 1919 (CZA S2 147).   [41] See Ch. 5, below.

[42] Letter from the School to the Education Board, 15 June 1925.

[43] Census of 23 Oct. 1922. A. Carmel, *The History of Haifa under Turkish Rule* (Jerusalem, 1977), 173.

Education Board inaugurated a music school on 1 November 1918 under the directorship of piano-teacher Dunya Weizmann. The faculty consisted of two piano-teachers and one violin-teacher, and was soon augmented by a vocal teacher and another pianist. The school brochure indicated the denomination or the foreign nationality of all pupils.[44] Eighty-five children enroled in the first year, seven of whom were Christians and one Moslem.[45] The well-wishing Education Board fared in Haifa no better than in Tel Aviv and in Jerusalem, and in 1924 the faculty of the school in Haifa decided to run the school on its own, each member pledging to contribute 20 per cent of the tuition to cover administration expenses.

Miriam Levit reopened her Tel Aviv-based piano studio in 1919 after it had been closed for three years. She immediately attracted forty-four pupils, and two years later opened classes for voice, violin, cello, and theory. She enlisted a strong faculty, including J. Pewsner, a former student of the great teacher Leopold Auer, as the violin-teacher, and by 1924 her school nearly matched Shulamit School with its 105 pupils.[46] Levit offered a relatively high salary of £20, but required a teaching load of twenty-four hours, twice as much as the one requested by Shulamit School.[47] However, the same dismal chain reaction of parents failing to pay their tuition fees as a result of which teachers were not paid their full salary obtained in her school as well. The destitute Education Board, already in debt to Shulamit School, turned down Levit's application for public support, arousing unavoidable envy and ill feeling.[48]

Though fraught with chronic financial crises, personal difficulties within the faculties, mistrust of the Education Board, and lack of adequate housing, the schools provided the most enduring institutional infrastructure for the musical scene in the 1920s. The music schools were the only venue for regular positions in music, and they were deeply involved in dissemination of music in the community, whether by means of professional concerts or by public student recitals. Their social stance may be evaluated by the proportionate number of music students in the total school population. In the school year 1923–4 the autonomous Jewish school system of Tel Aviv numbered 3,332,[49] about 600 of whom were still at nursery-school age. The number of music students in the two

[44] JNUL, 34V 3570.
[45] School Brochure, JNUL. Thirty-five of the pupils left within the first year.
[46] Document of 1924 (n.d.), House of Levites Archive, AMLI Tel Aviv, M 2/3.
[47] A contract with the piano teacher Rachel Krugliakov, House of Levites Archive, 142/3.
[48] Letter from Levit to the Education Board, 14 Oct. 1925.
[49] Gurevich, Statistical Abstract, 240.

schools of Tel Aviv in the same year was about 230, an impressive 9 per cent of the Tel Aviv school population.[50] While a steep fall from the high proportions of 1914,[51] it represented a more natural norm of an urban society, as distinct from the village mentality of the pre-war years.

Music in the Press

The resumption of musical activity was strongly promoted and influenced by the nascent daily press and by the Hebrew periodicals. Reviews and commentaries on music were at first written by well-educated columnists, poets, and authors, who viewed music as one of the components of the broader cultural context of the Jewish community in Palestine. At times, however, they provided poetic interpretations of musical works, for example, Koplewitz's review of a performance of Saint-Saëns's Violin Concerto.

In the first movement one hears the struggle of the soul which strives to reach upwards. . . . The second movement introduces the song of calmness, happy and serene peace, the song of a shepherd in the mountains—a pastorale—in which the flute responds to the cello with a leading motive. The leading motive appears and reappears as if on the waves of light. This is the aspect of satisfaction, but for the soul this is not enough, and it looks for more than that. In its endeavour it reaches the abstraction of the third movement.[52]

The heroic reading betrays the strong influence of contemporary German criticism, such as Paul Bekker's interpretation of the 'poetic idea' in Beethoven's music,[53] which was very popular among critics and music-lovers at that time.

In 1924–5 the editors of the three Hebrew daily newspapers appointed regular music critics. Two of them, David Rosolio for *Ha'Aretz* and Menashe Rabinowitz[54] for *Davar* were to maintain their posts for a whole generation. The composer and pianist Jacob Weinberg who wrote for *Do'ar Hayom* emigrated to the United States in 1927.[55]

David Rosolio (1898–1963) was a member of the tiny immigration from Germany. He was brought up in an atheist family committed to German national values, and excelled at a young age as a pianist. After

---

[50] The total number was even higher, as there were a few private instrumental teachers active in Tel Aviv at that time, for whom no statistics are available.

[51] See Ch. 2, above.   [52] *Ha'Aretz* (2 Nov. 1919).   [53] *Beethoven* (Berlin, 1911).

[54] Rabinowitz (1899–1975) later Hebraized his last name to Ravina.

[55] More on Weinberg in Chs. 5, 10, 13.

having been drafted to the German army, he was seriously wounded on the French front. During his long recovery he went through a soul-searching process, which led him to join the Blau-Weiss Zionist youth movement, and in 1919 he took leave of his family and emigrated to Palestine. He turned to agronomy as a profession,[56] but since music continued to constitute his main field of interest, he happily accepted the post of a music critic as a part-time job. He was self-taught in music history and theory, making use of his fine library of German and English music books, and his powerful self-discipline. He was in the habit of meticulously preparing for each concert and then working late into the night on his long reviews. He insisted that they be published within a day or two after the concert, thereby keeping concert life under strict scrutiny.[57]

Unlike Rosolio, the Russian born Menashe Rabinowitz (1899–1968) was a professional performing musician, well-trained as choral conductor and theorist, and deeply involved in all aspects of the nascent musical life in the country.[58]

The *Palestine Bulletin*, an English daily, was launched in 1926. Compared with the excited rhetoric of the Hebrew papers, it maintained a cool tone of understatement, taking the British press as its model. Most of its musical items were very detailed chronologies of concerts and of music institutions, and the infrequent reviews were published unsigned. The English daily, the *Palestine Post* which replaced the smaller *Palestine Bulletin* in 1933, refrained from hiring its own critic, and instead published English versions of Rosolio's reviews.

Despite the modest scope of the daily newspapers which rarely exceeded four pages, critics and columnists were allowed to write relatively long articles and very detailed reports which frequently covered up to 15 per cent of the newspaper space, attesting thereby to the high regard in which the editors held the musical scene. The weekend issues, published on Fridays, included four-page cultural supplements, which on special occasions were fully dedicated to music, as on the anniversary of Schubert's death, when the entire supplement of *Davar* consisted of a lengthy heart-breaking biographical essay by Rabinowitz.

The short-lived and irregular journal *Theatre and Art* that appeared for three years was also committed to musical topics and to a detailed chronology of musical events.

---

[56] Rosolio later had a brilliant career in the civil service as a public accountant, and after the establishment of the State of Israel as the Chief of the Civil Service.

[57] Interview with his son Shaul Rosolio, Aug. 1991.   [58] See Ch. 5, below.

Rank-and-File Musicians Enter the Scene

The massive immigration wave of the early 1920s brought along young professional instrumentalists who considered performance rather than instrumental teaching as their main vocation. With no regular orchestra available to absorb them, the only immediate venues capable of providing them with a semblance of a regular income were the silent movie houses, the few Hebrew theatres, and the cafes, which acquired much popularity in the Mediterranean climate and in the flourishing urban life.

The immigration wave of 1924–5 increased competition and opened the way for the exploitation of musicians. The musicians soon reacted and in 1924 they formed the Union of Workers in Art.[59] Membership in the years 1926–8 reached sixty-three players, including twelve (19 per cent) women. The same proportion obtained in the entire urban workforce at that time, of which 20.50 per cent were women.[60] With the exception of one cellist, all women were pianists.[61] Not unexpectedly, the small group of rank-and-file musicians roughly matched the male–female proportions of professionally employed musicians in Europe and in the United States at that time.[62]

The most respected venue for employment were the Hebrew theatre companies, who used to employ small orchestras at the pit for most of their productions. However, throughout the 1920s they were crisis-ridden and short-lived. The relatively stable Theatre of the Land of Israel (TEI) set the model when it opened by putting on the biblical spectacle *Belshazar* with an elaborate score by the renowned violinist and composer Joseph Achron.[63] The Union and the management reached an agreement according to which the Theatre of the Land of Israel would maintain a regular seven member orchestra. The socialist workers' theatre, Ohel, opened in 1925 as a project of the Federation of Hebrew Workers,[64]

---

[59] The trade unions were mostly connected to the central Histadrut, Federation of Hebrew Workers, which was formed in 1920 as a union of workers' parties and organizations which until then acted separately and competed with each other. As a well-organized and politically motivated federation of all workers' unions in the country, it exerted considerable power in labour relations within the Jewish community. In addition to protection of workers' rights, the Federation was very active in education and culture.

[60] Data for 1926, Gurevich, *Statistical Abstract*, 168.   [61] Lavon Institute, 3227 (250/IV).

[62] e.g. the Vienna Philharmonic has traditionally been an all-male orchestra. The number of women in leading American symphony orchestras during the 1930s and 1940s ranged from none in Boston and New York to five in Philadelphia and eight in San Francisco. J. Mueller, *The American Symphony Orchestra: A Social History of Musical Taste* (Bloomington, Ind., 1951), 309; R. R. Craven (ed.), *Symphony Orchestras of the World* (New York, 1987).

[63] Premièred on 3 Mar. 1925. For Achron see Ch. 5, below.

[64] Ohel, lit. 'the tent', implying the opposite of the luxurious European theatres.

whose actors worked during the daytime in manual jobs and contributed their evening hours to the theatre. The economic depression in 1927 'eliminated all the theatres we had, with the exception of the semi-amateur Ohel'.[65] In 1928 Ohel became fully professional, but its funds remained scarce. It was only when the prestigious Hebrew-speaking Jewish Habimah Theatre[66] immigrated *en bloc* to Palestine in 1931 that a regular theatre orchestra could be relied upon as a small job outlet.

Most players had to turn to the two other venues which also set the stage for frequent industrial actions. Cafe-owners were in the habit of hiring a pianist or a piano violin duo on short-term contracts. The musicians had to perform from 5.30 p.m. until midnight, with a dinner break of one hour. The scarcity of jobs and the difficult conditions of employment set the stage for the intervention of the Union. As was the case in England, no industrial action by players could yield any result without the support of more powerful sectors. However, while the Unions in England enlisted the support of some of the famous music hall and theatre stars,[67] the small union of immigrant musicians in Palestine had to rely on the solidarity of other unions, most effective of which was the Waiters' Union which could shut down any troublesome cafe.[68] The two unions signed a co-operation agreement.[69] On 6 March 1926 the union was informed that Bar Kokhba café had fired its regular pianist 'for no reason' and hired a non-union pianist, 'who gets two pounds less'. The Union took action 'to remove her'.[70] The Union bitterly complained that the Maccabi Sport Association invited the British Police Band to perform at several of its public events, thus depriving Union members of job opportunities. Maccabi's response was that 'as to the British, you should understand that we must be kind to them since they are those who play football with us every Saturday'.[71] It appears that no serious political issues were at stake. The Union opposed the band not because it was British but because of the scarcity of jobs, whereas the sports association was reluctant to sacrifice its friendly relations with the British for the sake of the union's interests.

The young violinist Shlomo Garter (1904–86) was elected immediately after his immigration in 1925 to the post of union president.[72] He

---

[65] *Do'ar Hayom* (18 Nov. 1927).

[66] Habimah (lit. 'the stage'), the first professional Hebrew theatre was founded in Russia in 1918.

[67] Ehrlich, *Music Profession in Britain*, 142–85.

[68] Document of 30 Jan. 1926 (Lavon Institute, 3227).

[69] Minutes of a meeting, 30 Jan. 1926 (Lavon Institute, 3227).

[70] (Lavon Institute, 3227).   [71] 4 June 1926 (Lavon Institute, 3227).

[72] Shlomo Garter became one of the founders of the Palestine Orchestra, where he was leader of the second-violin section until his retirement.

pressured the Eden film theatre to expand the orchestra from four to six
players. The terms of the contract of 13 February 1929 obligated the
orchestra to perform every weekday as well as during two shows on
Saturday night. The matinées were accompanied by piano only. Garter
acted as conductor and arranger. He watched each film before the
première and selected the proper excerpts.

The repertory included classical music, and in the case of comedies, also tunes
from operettas. We usually played only excerpts, because of the need for frequent
alteration of the music according to the plot . . . In dramatic films we played a
Beethoven adagio arranged for a small orchestra, or Tchaikovsky and Gounod
for landscape scenes. There was a Russian movie about the Volga, and then we
assembled a small choir and enlarged the orchestra.[73]

Any proper opportunity to expand the role of music was taken, such as
the screening of the film *La traviata* in which the opera choir joined the
orchestra.[74] The orchestra, and at times also the choir, also performed
before the movie and during intervals, and its participation was strongly
emphasized in the advertisements. It appears that the owner considered it
as a source of attraction in its own right, at a period when few other
opportunities to listen to good music presented themselves.[75] Other
movie houses hired similar orchestras. The World Fair Theatre maintained
a band of two violins, cello, and piano.[76] Similar orchestras accompanied
films also at Zion Cinema in Jerusalem and at the Eden in Haifa.

   The sudden immigration wave of 1925 threatened to flood the job
market. The Union called an emergency meeting and requested that the
Jaffa Workers' Council inform the Jewish immigration agencies in Poland
of the deterioration in employment conditions, thus deterring potential
immigrants from coming.[77] Such a recommendation contradicted the
Zionist ideology, and an anonymous respondent angrily scribbled on the
document with red ink 'impossible to accept and approve'. A week later
the Union reached a compromise, asking to 'limit the immigration of
new players as much as possible until the next winter'.[78] After one year
things improved a little. The Union reported 'that the situation in our
Union is better than in others, and unemployment is not so bad. We
more or less help the unemployed by initiating symphonic concerts,

---

   [73] Recorded interview, 1975 (National Sound Archives, JNUL).   [74] 27 July 1929.
   [75] A similar attitude to music at cinemas obtained in England at that time. Cf. Ehrlich, *Music
Profession in Britain*, 196–8.
   [76] Document of 9 July 1926 (Lavon Institute, 3227).
   [77] Minutes of a meeting, 24 July 1925 (Lavon Institute, 3227).
   [78] Minutes of a meeting, 31 July 1925 (Lavon Institute, 3227).

increased ensembles in the restaurants, dance halls, etc.'[79] The relief sharply contrasted the general trend in Palestine, where the prosperity of 1924 and the first half of 1925 gave way to an acute economic crisis and severe unemployment.[80] Two reasons may be offered for the conflicting trends. First, the Union's report should be read with caution, since in reality the musicians could expect no more than mere subsistence, with no regular income in sight. For example, when the chorus and orchestra of the crumbling Palestine Opera[81] were invited to play at a workers' ball, the organizers could afford to pay only the chorus members. Although an act of solidarity with the deprived players was expected, the chorus members painfully apologized in writing for taking the pay since 'for the past year we have not worked for a single day, and our comrades are virtually starving, so we took [the fee] without the orchestra'.[82] Secondly, the economic crises mostly hit the large sector of construction workers, whereas civil servants and craftsmen suffered less.[83]

The increase in the number of cinemas incited competition which was a blessing for the musicians. The Ofir and Eden cinemas in Tel Aviv advertised their 'large', 'enlarged', and 'selected' orchestras with up to a dozen musicians each, at times with the choir of the Palestine Opera. When the Ofir screened *Pagliacci*, a 'large' orchestra conducted by the violinist Shlomo Bor played the 'entire score' of the opera, with the opera-singers Giurini and Har-Melah singing selected arias. In the same week the Eden featured the opera choir and an 'enlarged' orchestra, introducing each evening show with Tchaikovsky's *Pique Dame* overture.[84] Thus the cinemas offered evenings of combined entertainment at cheap prices. It all came at a time when hardly any other steady jobs existed on the musical scene, so the cinemas were the only source of daily and steady income for players and choir singers. The cinemas supported nearly half of the sixty Union members in the country.

The film with sound threatened to ruin it all. In April 1930, only three years after the sensational première in New York, the three leading cinemas in Tel Aviv and Jerusalem proudly advertised the 'revolution in art and technology', which invaded the entertainment scene in the first week of May. Having anticipated the danger, the Union requested the Federation of Hebrew Workers to bar the introduction of sound films. As in England, where moral considerations were raised against the 'Atlantic

[79] Minutes of a meeting, 26 June 1926 (Lavon Institute, 3227).
[80] Giladi, 'Yishuv during the Fourth Aliya', 180 ff.   [81] See Ch. 4 below.
[82] Letter of 28 Mar. 1928 (Lavon Institute, 3227).
[83] Giladi, 'Yishuv during the Fourth Aliya', 187.
[84] *Ha'Aretz*. (28 Feb. 1930).

deluge',[85] the Union enlisted the support of the intellectual circles, who warned against the crippling effect of foreign sound films on the dissemination of the Hebrew language.[86] In addition to the threat to jobs which was common to all countries, there was the additional peril of the sound film blocking the development of concert life, since the first sound films were dominated by songs and music. Unlike London, there were no local music halls in Hebrew[87] to counterbalance the American hits. Most sound films were in English which most immigrants did not speak, so that they had to rely on the projection of badly synchronized manually operated reels of awkward handwritten translation on the side of the screen, thereby leading to indifference to fine details of the replicas, whereas the intellectual élite in the country expected the audience to follow each nuance on the stage of the embryonic Hebrew theatre in order to improve awareness of fine modern Hebrew. As in all other countries, the sound film won an easy victory. Yet, all was not lost, and after prolonged negotiations the Union reached an agreement with the two principal cinemas in Tel Aviv whose managements consented to maintain their orchestras for preludes and intervals until alternative sources of employment would be found. The sharp shift in economy and in the pattern of immigration which took place in 1931 shortened the period of transition and the musicians were soon absorbed in other jobs. In that way the small community of immigrant musicians in Palestine was spared the 'catastrophic'[88] effect of the arrival of sound films which hit musicians everywhere. None the less, the sound film continued to be treated with suspicion and even hostility.

Though feeble and unstable, the small community of musicians in Palestine triggered the process of professional stratification and provided the infrastructure, over which a massive musical scene was about to evolve in the next decade.

---

[85] Ehrlich, *Music Profession*, 213.

[86] M. Rabinowitz, 'The Tonefilm', *Davar* (16 May 1930), Y. Ben-Michael, 'Sound Movie in Eretz Israel', *Halel*, 2 (1930). *Halel* was a short-lived and irregular music journal, which advocated the views of the most extreme supporters of 'purely' national music and theatre in Palestine. See Ch. 12, below.

[87] Cf. Ehrlich, *Music Profession*, 155.   [88] Ibid. 210.

4

The Temple of the Arts
Dream and Nightmare

IT must have been the state of euphoria of the impoverished Yishuv at the end of World War I which stimulated the author Jacob Koplewitz to claim that 'there are enough musical forces [in the country] for a joint musical venture such as the beginnings of opera, or serious symphonic music . . . but we badly need additional talents. May all those who chance our shores stay here.'[1]

The programme for an opera in Palestine was delineated simultaneously in Russia and in Palestine. The originator of the idea was the conductor Mark Golinkin (1875–1963). The Russian-born Golinkin received his musical education in Warsaw, since there was no professional music school in his home town Odessa. In 1896 he returned to Russia, where traditional discrimination against Jews severely limited his progress. Unable to resist his passion for the stage, he kept travelling wherever some meagre income could be had as a prompter or as a chorus coach. Yet he had to maintain his home in Odessa, which was within the pale of settlement.[2] On his visits home to Odessa he used to conduct long discussions with the circle of his close Jewish friends and it was there that the vision of new life in Palestine gained momentum. In 1917 Golinkin articulated his scheme in *The Temple of the Arts*, a small pamphlet modelled upon Wagner's programme for the German theatre,[3] in which Golinkin outlined a grand plan for the 'total institute' for Palestine.

[1] *Ha'aretz* (1 Nov. 1919).

[2] M. Golinkin, *From the Temples of Japheth to the Tents of Shem* (Tel Aviv, 1957), 28 ff. An interview with Golinkin's daughter, Mrs Sarah Golinkin-Mindlin, Mar. 1992. The 'pale of settlement' were the zones in which Jews were allowed to live. In Russia under the tsars Jews could enter and work in other zones, especially in Moscow and St Petersburg, only by special permits.

[3] Wagner, *Entwurf zur Organisation eines deutschen Nationaltheaters für das Königreich Sachsen* (1848), *Gesammelte Schriften und Dichtungen* (Leipzig, 1871–80).

It would be the sacred duty of the Jewish intellectuals, who would be entrusted with the task of laying the foundations for new cultural life in the Land of Israel, to commence with the creation of the cultural-national centre which would nourish all nationally educated world Jewry. . . . The cultural revival of the Land of Israel would retain a place of honour for the Arts, and especially for the theatre, alongside learning and science. . . . Such a theatre would be a prototype for all other Jewish theatres in the country and in the Diaspora. It must be as valuable to us as the Wagnerian theatre in Bayreuth is to the Germans and La Scala in Milan to the Italians. This would be the kind of institution which Diaspora Jews could not create in their dismal conditions. . . . The theatre in the Land of Israel would be not only a national Hebrew institution but also a theatre of vital aspirations rather than of decay. . . . The theatre project in the Land of Israel would enjoy a fresh start, since the conventions of the European stage which might hinder our healthy aspirations have no roots there yet. The core of this large-scale artistic endeavour would be the Theatre Institute, which would encompass all kinds of schools for music, drama, and the fine arts. The Institute would admit children from eight to ten with no prerequisites. In the elementary classes they would all study according to a general curriculum of sciences and arts. Only at the advanced level of studies would each student select a field of specialization in accordance with his predilections. Most courses would emphasize practical training . . . The curriculum would span sixteen years.[4]

Golinkin proposed that a solid economic base for the proposed institute be formed through the formation of a co-operative artists' colony, in accordance with the existing kibbutz model in Palestine. Through mutual help and communal work they would free each other from daily chores and would devote all their time and energy to art.

The visionary institute would radiate its influence in five concentric circles:

1. As an integrated centre for the cultivation of national arts in the Yishuv. As a first stage the Institute Orchestra would present two free concerts every week in public parks in each of the three major cities of Palestine.[5]

2. As an artistic centre for talented young musicians from the Diaspora, who would be attracted to the fine teachers of the Institute, in the manner in which the young musicians from America used to travel to St Petersburg to study with Leopold Auer.[6]

3. As a research centre, which would send scholars all over the world to collect and compile the ancient remnants of Jewish music.

---

[4] Golinkin, *Heikhal Ha'Omanut* (*The Temple of the Arts*) (Tel Aviv, 1927).   [5] Ibid. 24.
[6] Ibid. 25. A highly admired virtuoso violinist, pedagogue, and conductor, Leopold Auer (1845–1930) was head of the violin department at St Petersburg's conservatory from 1868 to 1917.

4. As a world centre for reform and innovation in music education.
5. As a centre for resident composers who would find there the ideal milieu for the cultivation of a genuine Hebrew art.

The key word in Golinkin's text is 'new'. Nowhere in the document is the idea of a transplant of European models, such as opera, mentioned. It is only through Golinkin's references to Bayreuth and to Milan that the centrality of opera in his vision is revealed. Golinkin explained his marked preference for opera and orchestral music over the Hebrew spoken theatre as an economic necessity, since 'all local population would come to listen to the orchestra and to the chorus: Jews, Arabs, European residents, and the many tourists who come to the country',[7] and music would override language barriers. Even so, opera was destined to act as a means rather than as an end, such as a major tool 'in the dissemination of the Hebrew language among the people'.[8] Despite the occasional utopian rhetoric, Golinkin's programme reflected an awareness of social conditions in Palestine, which he had never visited prior to writing his document. On the one hand he recognized the size and the intellectual potential of the non-Jewish audience in Palestine for reinforcing the economic base of the project. On the other hand he sensed the importance of joining forces with the powerful movement for revival of the Hebrew language as a major unifying force in the Yishuv.

After the Bolshevik revolution anti-Semitism was officially banned in Russia, and Golinkin's professional prospects there immediately improved. He was appointed conductor of the Folk Opera in St Petersburg. There he cherished the dedicated friendship and the support of the legendary, albeit tyrannical, bass Feodor Chaliapin, who included Golinkin in the limited circle of conductors he was willing to work with. Nevertheless, Golinkin's involvement with his vision did not diminish in the least. In 1918 he enlisted the help of a Jewish quintet which toured the country with benefit concerts for his new project. His enthusiasm even captured Chaliapin, who volunteered a benefit concert in St Petersburg in which he sang Jewish folksongs in Yiddish.[9]

Golinkin's first practical step was the preparation of Hebrew translations of opera librettos. His knowledge of Hebrew was virtually nil, so he enlisted the help of the poet Yehuda Karni[10] and of the journalist and

---

[7] Ibid. 24.   [8] Ibid. 12.   [9] Id., *From the Temples of Japheth*, 161.
[10] Karni (1884–1949) was a columnist and a poet. Born in Russia, he migrated to Palestine in 1921. In 1923 he joined the editorial board of *Ha'Aretz* daily as his regular position for life.

folklorist Alter Druyanov,[11] who read their Hebrew translations aloud,
allowing Golinkin to judge their suitability to the music solely by their
sound.

At about the same time in Palestine, columnist Moshe Freidmann
formulated the rationale for an operatic venture in the Yishuv:

Now that we have begun to disseminate music in our country we must first be
concerned with our own national music. All we can say at this point is that we
have none. There is no single tune in the whole world of which one may say:
this is Hebraic music. . . . The only way to obtain homogeneous national music
would be through folk music, which would be well defined in its style and
language. . . . The state of music in this country is very grim. We still have no
musical environment. . . . Instrumental and vocal practice among the people
would gradually lead to the emergence of a Hebraic folk music of the Land of
Israel. . . . One may assume that opera would play a leading role in our national
music, since our history provides an abundance of material for this musical
genre.[12]

The concept of opera as source for future national folk music was
further fostered by the venerable poet Chaim Nachman Bialik[13] who
wrote:

The Zionist movement would not succeed without singing for us. A great
popular movement would flourish while singing and sing while flourishing. The
Hasidic movement has created five thousand nigunim and they still fill our
needs. We must continue to cultivate our Zionist nigun in the Land of Israel,
and its cornerstone would be the Opera.[14]

A nigun[15] is a textless melody of Hasidic patrimony which is the apex
of Hasidic emotionalism. Composed by the adored rabbis of the many
Hasidic communities, they were regarded as the sacred revelations of the
rabbi's soul. Most Hasidic courts opposed the Zionist movement, which

[11] Alter Druyanov (1870–1938) was an author and a Zionist executive, whose principal contribution was a collection of Jewish folklore. He settled in Tel Aviv in 1921, where he collaborated
with Bialik in his research work.

[12] Ha'Aretz (14 Sept. 1921).

[13] Bialik (1873–1934) settled in Palestine in 1924. He had by then acquired the respected status
of the greatest living Jewish poet. He was also a scholar, an editor, and an educator, who was deeply
involved with the cultural life of the Yishuv.

[14] Davar (16 Aug. 1927). The Hasidic movement originated among East European Jews in the
17th cent. It advocated a direct emotional expression of powerful religious feelings through song
and dance contrasted with the orthodox emphasis of strict learning of the traditional texts. The
Hasidic movement soon gained enormous popularity among European Jewry, and the respect of
many non-Hassidic and unobserving Jews. Y. Mazor and A. Hajdu, 'The Hasidic Dance Niggun',
Yuval, 3 (1974), 136.

[15] Lit. 'the act of singing or playing a musical composition'.

they considered heretical. Bialik, who had a thorough knowledge of and respect for Jewish tradition aspired to combine traditional Judaism with the revival of Jewish national self-definition, hence his synthetic term 'Zionist nigun' and his wish that the nigun form a link between traditional Orthodox Judaism and the secular Jewish national movement. Bialik conceptualized the opera project as an integral part of the realization of the national dream.

The anomaly of a massive migration as the initial step for national revival, found its expression in the reversal of the traditional task of a national opera. According to the ideology of the European national schools opera was expected to derive its inspiration and material from traditional folk culture and music. Conversely, the initiators of the Palestine Opera expected the national Hebrew opera to act as a catalyst for the creation of the still-non-existent genuine folk music in Palestine.

The first step toward the fulfilment of the dream was the founding of the Hebrew Musical Association in August 1921. The inauguration concert was performed by visiting singers Arieh Friedemann-Levov and Yehudah Har-Melah with the Shulamit School student orchestra. The press hailed the event with the happy news of Har-Melah's decision 'to settle in the country and devote all his time to the operatic training of local musicians'.[16] The two singers then took another step and mounted an evening of entire scenes from Anton Rubinstein's *The Demon* and Tchaikovsky's *Eugene Onegin* staged with settings and costumes, with other soloists, an amateur chorus, and piano accompaniment.[17]

Soon after that the pianist Arieh Nisvitzky Abilea settled in the country.[18] Energetic and resourceful, he joined his old comrade, Har-Melah, and in October 1922 the new association mounted a concert performance of Gounod's *Faust*, with piano accompaniment. The Hebrew Musical Association used the favourable response to pave the way for Golinkin's arrival in Palestine on 7 May 1923, promoted by the press as a national event. All dignitaries of the small Yishuv signed a congratulatory scroll which was handed to him upon his disembarkation at the primitive port of Jaffa. Yet with the dissipation of the initial euphoria, Golinkin soon discovered the chasm between his visionary Temple and the reality of life in the impoverished Yishuv, as he wrote four years later: 'In accordance with the local conditions I was forced to alter my original programme. Rather than commencing with each com-

---

[16] *Ha'Aretz* (30 Sept. 1921).
[17] Performances in Tel Aviv, 29 Dec. 1921, and in Jerusalem, 5 Jan. 1922.
[18] See Chs. 2, 3, above.

ponent of the Institute separately, I turned at once to a full production of operas.'[19]

Golinkin must have realized that any painstaking work on each separate component of his visionary Institute would be of no avail in the frail financial and social conditions of the Yishuv. He preferred to respond to the high expectations raised by his conspicuous arrival with an immediate *coup de théâtre*: 'I took advantage of the young singers who happened to come here for concerts . . . adding to them eight members of the amateur chorus *Kadima* and twelve pupils of the local conservatory Shulamit who constituted the orchestra.'[20]

The availability of experienced soprano, tenor, and baritone led Golinkin to select Verdi's *La traviata* for launching the new venture. The festive première of the Palestine Opera took place in Tel Aviv on 26 July 1923, less than three months after Golinkin's arrival, followed by performances in Jerusalem (31 July) and Haifa (2 August).

The Tel Aviv première was held at the Eden cinema.[21] The house was sold out and hundreds of disappointed enthusiasts, many of whom naïvely arrived by foot or by horse-drawn carriages from neighbouring agricultural settlements, were turned away. Reviews by leading columnists reflected the far-reaching social and political overtones of the event. Gershon Hanokh wrote in the socialist weekly *Hapo'el Hatza'ir*[22]

Verdi's light music was directed, so it seemed, by a master hand. Even the most unmusical ear could sense the full co-ordination (and co-ordination is something new in this country) between the orchestra in the pit and the singers on the stage, as well as with the attentive audience. All this was new, and there was a sense of a genuine cultural achievement which justified the prevailing festive sensation of all, from the Tel Aviv aristocracy seated in the front rows to our comrades in the back. . . . Well, the West may be decaying, but until it does, what charm and exaltation is kept for all of us in the concept-symbol 'Opera— Hebrew Opera.'[23]

Some eleven years later the opera celebrated its anniversary in a well-attended party, in which columnist Itamar Ben-Avi[24] summoned his flowery rhetoric for an emotional speech:

---

[19] 'Arba Shnot Avoda Operait Be'Eretz Yisrael' ('Four Years of Operatic Work in Palestine'), in *Temple of the Arts*.

[20] Ibid. 29. 'Kadima' means 'forward'.

[21] Eden (lit. 'Paradise') was the first cinema in the Yishuv, founded in 1913.

[22] Lit. 'the young worker', this weekly served as the organ of one of the two workers' parties in Palestine at that time.

[23] *Hapo'el Hatza'ir*, 15: 38 (1923).

[24] Itamar Ben-Avi (1882–1943), was the founder and the editor of the Jerusalem daily *Do'ar Hayom* (Daily Post). See Ch. 1, above.

Indeed we all recall, don't we, this glorious night, first in Tel Aviv, and thereafter on the mountains of Zion, when our glowing eyes witnessed a magic spectacle which surpassed all our dreams. *La traviata* by the Italian Yoseph[25] Verdi, presented to us on the stage in our sacred language. . . . For many moments, or possibly several hours, we could not absorb the magnificent reality, which flooded our yearning ears with biblical words, as created by our forefathers in days of yore.[26]

Hanokh's evocation of Spengler's recently published treatise,[27] though whimsical, ensued from his migrant experience. While Spengler contrasted the decaying West with the emerging German spirit, his concept was soon employed to signify the emergence of a new alternative culture in the East. The operatic experience must have rekindled Hanokh's nostalgic links to his European heritage. By contrast, Ben-Avi carried the implications of the performance all the way to his cherished dream of achieving a national Hebrew culture.

The special magic of the opera persisted well after the exhilaration of the première, as indicated by one of the columnists: 'Even concerts the musical value of which supersedes that of the opera hardly attract even a shade of the same admiration and excitement.'[28] Yet the opera did not fully prevail over the small but noisy intellectual circle which called for a full repudiation of western values. B. Felix curtly stated that

opera in itself is not interesting. The interest in *Traviata* and in *Rigoletto* has waned even in Europe. Even more so in this country. The whole business of opera is shaky. Nowadays there is no use for the centre but only to its right or to its left. In our case: to the symphony or to the operetta.[29]

The most salient feature of the Palestine Opera was the consistent use of Hebrew. Printed Hebrew librettos were cheaply sold at every performance and were treated as independent reading material even by people who did not attend the productions.[30] Productions of operas in translations were a common practice in Europe. For example, German opera-houses used as a rule German translations of Italian and French operas. Translations acquired added connotations with the rise of nationalism, as in the extreme case of Mahler's insistence on productions in Hungarian during his tenure as musical director in Budapest (1888–

---

[25] Ben-Avi deliberately used the Hebrew biblical spelling rather than the Italian Giuseppe.

[26] *The Booklet of the Palestine Opera* (Tel Aviv, 1935), 11.

[27] *Der Untergang des Abendlandes* (Decline of the West), i (1917), ii (1922). The trans. of the title follows H. Kohn, *The Mind of Germany* (New York, 1960), 330.

[28] S. Yehudai, *Ha'Aretz* (9 Sept. 1923).   [29] B. Felix, 'Golinkin', *Hedim*, 3 (1923), 95.

[30] An interview with historian Shulamit Laskov, Aug. 1991. The Dutch-born (1916) Mrs Laskov immigrated to Palestine with her parents in 1922.

91). His bold decision effected a 'spectacular increase of audiences in the Budapest Opera House', although 'he did not speak Hungarian and had to communicate with many of the artists through interpreters'.[31] The situation, however, was far more complex in the migrant society in Palestine. Throughout the 1920s Jewish migrants outnumbered Jews born in Palestine. Yet about half of the immigrants from Russia in the early 1920s had been Hebrew-speakers prior to immigration,[32] and collective pressures to use Hebrew in daily life bolstered the natural urge of any migrant to learn the official language of the receiving country.[33] According to the few reliable censuses taken in Palestine in the 1920s, nearly 78 per cent of the Jewish adults were able to speak Hebrew. Yet a distinction should be made between 'ability to speak' and 'actually speaking'. The sociologist Roberto Bachi has pointed out that 'the results of the official censuses of 1922 and 1931 cannot be utilized, as they seem to have been affected by large misstatements, due to political propaganda, conducted with the purpose that all Jews should reply "Hebrew" to the census question on language'.[34] Likewise, ability to use basic daily Hebrew by no means implied the ability to follow Hebrew as sung on the operatic stage. Like most of his singers Golinkin himself could not speak Hebrew at all. Moreover, the Hebrew translations, which did not emanate from a natural context of a live modern Hebrew usage, were fraught with archaisms and a twisted syntax. The critics, readily willing to overlook defects in staging and decor, were uncompromising on the matter of the Hebrew language: 'Was it in Hebrew? I doubt it. . . . In vain did the translator indicate on the title-page 'do not reproduce or use without permission from the author. In my view no use of the present translation should be allowed even with the permission of the translator.'[35] Golinkin's insistence on the use of Hebrew was both a liability and an asset. The productions in Hebrew complicated the rehearsals, since the experienced singers were required to relearn their parts in a language which they hardly spoke. Yet, by subscribing to the vogue for Hebrew in Palestine, Golinkin gained the staunch support of leading political and literary personalities precisely at the crucial period during which the centre of

---

[31] E. Krenek, *Gustav Mahler* (1941; New York, 1973), 183.

[32] R. Bachi, 'Demography', *Encyclopedia Hebraica*, 6 (1957), 675.

[33] Full knowledge of Hebrew was declared in 1930 as one of the prerequisites for acquiring voting rights for the representative institutions of the Yishuv. E. Rubinstein, 'From *Yishuv* to a State: Institutions and Parties', in B. Eliav (ed.), *The Jewish National Home* (Jerusalem, 1976), 176.

[34] 'A Statistical Analysis of the Revival of Hebrew in Israel', *Scripta Hierosolymitana* (Jerusalem, 1956), 188.

[35] Ben-Yishai, *Ha'Aretz* (11 Nov. 1923).

cultural activity in the Hebrew language shifted abruptly from Russia to Palestine.[36]

Golinkin's choice of repertory relied primarily on the availability of cast. Yet it also reflected his own personal taste and expertise. In four seasons the Palestine Opera produced seventeen operas:

First season: Verdi, *Rigoletto*; Leoncavallo, *Pagliacci*; Gounod, *Faust* and *Romeo et Juliette*; Halévy, *La Juive*.

Second season: Verdi, *Aida*, *Il trovatore*, *Otello*; Puccini, *Tosca*; Mascagni, *Cavaleria Rusticana*; and Saint-Saëns, *Samson et Dalila*.

Third season: Anton Rubinstein, *The Maccabeans*; Bizet, *Carmen*; Dargomizhsky, *Russalka*.

Fourth season: Meyerbeer, *Les Huguenots*; Rossini, *Il barbiere di Siviglia*.

The typical repertory of the Russian opera houses where Golinkin had been trained granted Meyerbeer and national Russian works an equal share with mainstream Italian opera. Golinkin had personally met Rimsky-Korsakov and Cui in St Petersburg, and the first operas he conducted there were *Les Huguenots* and *Russalka*. Yet in the new context of the Palestine Opera the choice of certain operas was loaded with Jewish connotations. For example, the Jerusalem daily *Do'ar Hayom* heralded the production of *La Juive* with a detailed five-instalment monograph about Halevy.[37]

A rather anecdotal incident in the first season revealed the significant yet precarious position of the Palestine Opera in the Yishuv. The première of *La Juive* (17 June 1924) was well received, and Golinkin was ready for the remaining scheduled productions, when the British Commissioner James Campbell shocked him by putting an unexpected ban on all future productions of this opera, since 'certain circles find it insulting'.[38] It was the Latin Patriarchy of Jerusalem which complained about Cardinal Bruno's portrayal in the opera as an evil character. Golinkin replied that *La Juive* had been produced for nearly one hundred years in Europe with no reservations, and that he would not allow any alteration in the libretto. Still, Golinkin realized that the ban would ruin the young Palestine Opera which had invested all its meager funds in the new production, and he finally accepted a compromise: the Cardinal would wear a black robe without a cross instead of the red robe with a cross which had infuriated the Patriarchy. Moreover, Golinkin even agreed to the ridicu-

---

[36] I. Even-Zohar, 'Processes of Contacts and Synthesis in the Formation of the Modern Hebrew Culture', *Perspectives on Culture and Sociey in Israel* (Tel Aviv, 1988), 133.
[37] *Do'ar Hayom* (June–July 1924).   [38] *Do'ar Hayom* (29 June 1924).

lous request of renaming the opera *Rachel* when produced in Jerusalem.[39]
The Commissioner promptly lifted the ban. Yet Golinkin did not foresee
that his seemingly small concession would lead up to an even more
ominous crisis. The prestigious columnist Yitzhac Lufbahn reprimanded
the Palestine Opera which

did not fight the attack of a Catholic Inquisition on our spiritual life . . . and
instead tried to save the few coins paid as rental fee for the music materials from
Paris. . . . The culture-oriented public in the country hailed the Palestine Opera
as an impressive launching of an important Hebrew creative activity. The audience applauded in the initial steps even what was ridiculous. But if the Opera
cannot protect its honour and has no respect for feelings of the public, we would
show no interest whatsoever in it and in its productions.[40]

Lufbahn's scathing censure incited a backlash of support for Golinkin's
pioneering achievements. As usual in such cases, the polemic soon ran its
course with no immediate damage. Yet the incident revealed not only the
intensity of national and religious tensions in the local society, but also
the frail artistic position of the young company, which enjoyed only a
brief period of grace before it would no longer be excused for faults in
its performance.

Ticket sales for the six productions of the first season[41] reached 40,000.
Assuming that the same listeners attended all six productions, Golinkin's
audience amounted to at least 6,600 individuals. At that time the Yishuv
numbered nearly 90,000 Jews, of whom 35,000 had arrived since 1919.[42]
The potential audience consisted of the combined Jewish population of
Jerusalem, Tel Aviv, and Haifa, as well as of the small adjacent agricultural
settlements which were within walking or horse-riding distance from the
major cities. Productions in Jerusalem also attracted British officials, well-
to-do Arab intellectuals, and other Europeans residing in Jerusalem,
whose conspicuous attendance of the productions was favourably pointed
out as evidence for the broad public support for the opera.[43] All the same,
the figures should also be adjusted downwards, since the ultra orthodox
Jewish community of Jerusalem[44] never took part in secular activities. The

[39] *Palestine Bulletin* (25 June 1925).

[40] Yitzhak Lufbahn (1880–1948), *Hapo'el Hatza'ir*, 17: 38.

[41] 'Four Years of Operatic Work in Palestine', 30.

[42] Gurevich *et al.*, *The Jewish Population of Palestine* (Jerusalem, 1944), 24, table 1. Gurevich points
out that there was a constant conflict between the higher figures presented by the Zionist
Federation and the lower numbers provided by the British administration, due to certain inaccur-
acies of registration and political manipulations of statistics. For the present purpose the differences
are of little significance.

[43] *Do'ar Hayom* (15 Jan. 1924). Also personal communication by Mrs Shulamit Laskov.

[44] Gurevich *et al.* (eds.), *Jewish Population*, 4. Ben-Arieh, *Jerusalem in the 19th Century*, 608.

potential audience in Jerusalem consisted mostly of recent arrivals to Jerusalem who numbered less than 6,000. Hence the potential opera audience may be estimated at no more than 60,000. It follows that the regular opera audience comprised more than 10 per cent of the Jewish population. The Palestine Opera was launched on the eve of the large immigration wave of the years 1924–6.[45] The sudden rise in Jewish population was soon reflected in an immediate 25 per cent increase in the Opera box-office proceeds, which sold 50,000 tickets in the second opera season. The proportionally high size of the opera audience may be partly explained by the age groups and marital status of the members of the Yishuv. In 1925 nearly 70 per cent of the Tel Aviv community was between the ages of 14 and 69. The percentage of people aged above 70 was a negligible 1 per cent. It was a young population, consisting of single women and men (18,600) who outnumbered married individuals (14,200). The mild Mediterranean climate, the short distances, and the absence of any home entertainment, further encouraged regular attendance of cultural events.[46]

The Palestine Opera's brochure reported that the first season left earnings of about £1,000, which were paid as fees to the conductor and to the five leading singers. Each received an average of £28 per month, a sum roughly identical to the monthly salary of a high school teacher in Palestine at that time.[47] They could afford such relatively generous terms only owing to the co-operation of a twenty-three-member unpaid pupils' orchestra. Sarah Golinkin regularly played the harp part on the piano.[48] During the second season the orchestra increased to forty players, most of whom were paid professionals. No capital was left for the six new productions planned for the second season. The Zionist Federation turned down Golinkin's application for a loan of £500. Yet, Lt.-Col. Frederic Herman Kisch,[49] who attempted to establish a broader financial base for the opera, collaborated with several respected members of the business and judicial community and registered the Palestine Opera Company on 10 September 1924 with a capital of £5,050. The public was invited to buy the opera stocks, but the drive was poorly organized

[45] See Ch. 2, above.

[46] Cf. Max Weber's observation about the combined climate–culture factor, *The Rational and Social Foundations of Music* (New York, 1958), 124, as quoted in Ehrlich, *Piano*, 12.

[47] 'Four Years of Operatic Work in Palestine', 44.

[48] Interview, Mar. 1991. Such economizing was not exceptional in the 1920s, cf. Ehrlich, *Music Profession in England*, 208.

[49] Frederic Hermann Kisch (1888–1943) was a British Jew, whose family had served in the British colonial administration. Haim Weizmann appointed him in 1922 to head the Zionist Federation in Jerusalem.

and brought to naught. Golinkin later rebuked Col. Kisch for losing interest too soon,[50] but it appears that even a better organization could not induce investments among the members of the local migrant society.[51] Most migrants were petty shopkeepers and craftsmen who could not be expected to invest their limited resources in an opera.

At the opening of the third season Golinkin convened a press conference in which he spoke about the abyss between vision and reality: 'Every opera performance is celebrated in town, . . . but the realization of the vision is threatened by working conditions: we work under such difficult conditions that at times I am overcome with despair.'[52] Golinkin was forced to rely on the rentals of the three available cinemas in Tel Aviv, Jerusalem, and Haifa. The largest auditorium was the 1,000-seat Zion Cinema in Jerusalem, whereas the Eden cinema in Tel Aviv could accommodate only 600 patrons, so that even the capacity houses which the Palestine Orchestra usually had, could support the company only if a heavy performance schedule had been maintained. Yet, the owners of the cinemas reserved the preferred days such as the weekends for the popular silent films and limited the opera productions to no more than five nights per month. Consequently, the members of the orchestra and the chorus were forced to make a living elsewhere, thus further complicating rehearsal and performance schedules.[53] By contrast, Golinkin could not support his family with his small income, nor could he find extra jobs given his age, his heavy workload, and his special expertise. Fatigue started to spread among the overworked staff: 'The initial magic was gone. . . . Routine replaced enthusiasm, . . . and led to impatience, jealousy, suspicion. People started to complain about exploitation and working conditions.'[54] The Union protested at the despicable terms of employment and demanded that Golinkin raise the salaries of the players and of the members of the chorus by 25 per cent, which he could ill afford.[55]

The third season coincided with the sudden onset of economic depression. Within a few months the wave of new arrivals has been eroded, and in 1927 emigration exceeded immigration. At the opening of the fourth season all remaining funds were spent on an ambitious production of *Les Huguenots*. Golinkin closed the season with a gloomy evening of

---

[50] *Memoires*, 167.   [51] See Ch. 3, above.   [52] *Ha'Aretz* (7 Nov. 1925).

[53] 'Four Years of Operatic Work', 38.

[54] M. Gross-Levin, 'Opera in Palestine', *Journal de jeunesse musicale d'Israël* (1958), 4–5. Miriam Gross-Levin, then a pupil at Shulamit Music School and later a music-educator, played violin at the opera. See also 'Four Years of Operatic Work', 43.

[55] Letter of 31 July 1925 (Lavon Institute, 3227).

excerpts from Wagner's operas accompanied by piano and harmonium. Embittered and broke, Golinkin halted all activities and went to the United States for a fund-raising campaign. The cool report in the *Palestine Bulletin* contained an ominous premonition: 'Mr M. Golinkin . . . is proceeding to America to raise funds . . . Most of the artists are also leaving Palestine, and so we shall have no opera performance at all during the coming season.'[56]

A formal report of the Registrar of Companies in Palestine acted as an epilogue. The balance on 31 July 1929 was the grotesque £7. The Registrar reported that 'meetings were never attended properly and reports to the Registrar of Companies were sent irregularly. The Company was struck off the Register on the 25 April 1934, for reasons of inactivity.'

Ironically, the direct victim of the collapse of the Palestine Opera was the first original Hebrew opera, which had been the *raison d'être* of the opera project. Jacob Weinberg who settled in Palestine soon after the opening of the Palestine Opera[57] completed within a few weeks both the libretto and the music of *The Pioneers*.[58] By then the Palestine Opera was in severe financial difficulties, and a production of a new opera has become a distant dream. All that Weinberg could accomplish was two concert performances of a few excerpts from the opera (April 1925, May 1927). *The Pioneers* was finally produced in New York in 1934.[59] A few excerpts were broadcast on the Palestine Broadcasting Service in July 1941 leaving little mark.[60] It would take another twenty years before the first original opera—Marc Lavri's *Dan the Guard*—would reach the local stage.

[56] (15 May 1927). [57] See Chs. 3, above, and 5, below.
[58] Weinberg wrote the libretto in Russian, and had it translated into Hebrew by Joseph Markovsky, a resident of Jerusalem. A vocal score with Hebrew transliteration and English translation was published in the United States.
[59] Excerpts from the New York performance have been preserved on large size 78 r.p.m. records (National Sound Archives, JNUL), but the quality of the performance, in as much as it can be judged from the old recording, was rather poor. No reviews of the performance could be found in the contemporary Jewish press in the United States, and it is not clear whether it was a fully stage production. For more about *The Pioneers* see Ch. 15, below.
[60] *Ha'Aretz* (13 July 1941).

5

Music of the People
Music for the People

THE inauguration of the Society for Jewish Folk Music in St Petersburg in 1908 marked a turning-point in the modern history of the music of the Jews.[1] From Russia its sphere of influence spread to central Europe. It then invaded Palestine, and its reverberations were felt in America as well. Twenty years later the composer and scholar Salomon Rosowsky[2] recollected how as a young student he, together with the Jewish pedagogue Joseph Tamars and the pianist Arieh Nisvitzky (Abilea), approached Drotchevsky, Commissioner of St Petersburg, and asked him to grant official recognition to an organization they wished to name the Hebrew Music Society. The Commissioner wondered whether there was such a thing as Jewish music, and the delegation responded by stating that Jewish music existed as a distinct entity, independent of usage by Jewish musicians, and that it was written

not only by Jews like Rubinstein, Halévy, Mendelssohn, Meyerbeer, and Goldmark, but also by non-Jews: Glinka, Balakirev, Rimsky-Korsakov, and Mussorgsky, and that on Mussorgsky's tombstone is engraved a Hebrew tune which the late composer has used in his wonderful cantata *Joshua*. Yes, replied Drotchevsky, I also recall a Jewish tune which I have heard at a Jewish wedding in Odessa, but this was a folk tune. I think you should name your project the Society for Jewish Folk Music.[3]

The Mighty Five provided the prototype for the Jewish Society, and Rosowsky commended them for their personal support of the Jewish project: 'I recall now the declaration made by our great mentor Rimsky

---

[1] Trans. of the Russian title as given in A. M. Rothmuller, *The Music of the Jews* (London, 1953), 140.

[2] Rosowsky (1878–1962) emigrated to the United States in 1946.

[3] Rosowksy, 'The Twentieth Anniversary, i', *Ketuvim*, 3 (20 Dec. 1928).

Korsakov (may it be a prophecy!). Charmed by the special beauty of one of our melodies, in which the soul of the wandering nation is expressed, he said: "Hebrew music is yearning for a Glinka of its own." [4]

The tendency of the founders to concentrate on research of Jewish folk song was established in 1894, when Joel Engel, still a student at the Moscow conservatory, initiated the project of collecting and arranging Jewish folk songs. Joel (Julius) Engel (1868–1927) studied law in Kiev and Charkov and later composition with Tanejev and Ipolitow-Ivanov. His initial interest in Jewish music was that of a scholar rather than of a Jew immersed in folk tradition. He himself confessed that 'It is not that I collected, arranged, and studied the tunes because I was a Jew, but on the contrary: the more I studied and loved them, the more Jewish I became.'[5] Indeed, it was only in the course of his collection of folksongs that he learned Yiddish.[6] The Russian composer and critic Leonid Sabaneev considered such a state of affairs necessary for the formation of a national school, since 'so long as a man is wholly immersed in the atmosphere of the folk-life he does not notice the style of his nationality... To become alive to it he must get away from that state of existence... only then he is capable of artistic transformation.'[7] From 1897 Engel was the music critic of *Ruskija Wjedemosti*, one of Russia's most respected journals. He also edited the Russian edition of Riemann's Lexicon, and published several opera guides.[8] In 1900 Engel and his colleague, the folklore scholar P. S. Marek, decided to organize a lecture-recital of Jewish folk songs. In order to circumvent the requirement of getting a permit from the anti-Semitic government bureaucracy, they secured the sponsorship of the Moscow Society for Natural Science and Anthropology.[9] The favourable reception stimulated the young Jewish musicians in St Petersburg to establish the Society for Jewish Folk Music. Following its official inauguration in St Petersburg in 1908, the Society opened branches in Moscow in 1913, and later also in Kiev and in Kharkow.[10] The recognition of Jewish music by the non-Jewish officials,

---

[4] Rosowsky, 'The Twentieth Anniversary, ii', *Ketuvim* 3 (27 Dec. 1928).

[5] Engel, 'The First Concert of Jewish Music, 1900', *Theatre and Art*, 6–7 (1926–7), 9.

[6] In a letter of 24 July 1924. Printed posthumously in *Theatre and Art*, 8 (1927), 4.

[7] 'The Jewish National School in Music' (1924), Engl. trans. by S. W. Pring, *Musical Quarterly*, 15 (1929), 452. Sabaneev (1881–1968) was a distinguished composer and critic. In 1926 he left Russia for western Europe and later emigrated to the United States.

[8] J. Engel, 'Curriculum vitae', *Theatre and Art*, 8 (1927), 3. E. Gerson-Kiwi, 'Engel, Joel', in *New Grove*, vi. 167.

[9] Engel, 'First Concert of Jewish Music, 1900', 9.

[10] Partial lists of the composers among the members see Sabaneev, 'Jewish National School in Music', 448–68, and Rothmuller, *Music of the Jews*, 140, 144. Rothmuller erroneously lists Leo Nesviszky and his Hebraized name Arie Abilea as two different persons.

composers, and scholars triggered the extensive activity of the Society.
Rosowsky warmly recollected the 'ray of light: the attitude of affection
toward our project on the part of our teachers—the late Rimsky
Korsakov and Liadov, and Glazunov who is happily among us'.[11] In
addition to professional composers and critics, the Society also included
many amateurs, among them engineers and lawyers, who ardently supported its activities.

From the outset the Society for Jewish Folk Music encountered extreme opposition on all fronts.[12] Assimilated Jews belittled the value of the
folk tunes which the Society published. Orthodox circles disapproved of
the harmonic arrangements of the sacred liturgical melodies. Jewish
intellectuals opposed the involvement of the Society in concerts and
demanded that it should concentrate on research and study. The audience
at large, however, was very responsive to the concerts of the Society,
which consisted of highly communicative melodious arrangements, as
well as of virtuoso paraphrases in the best late romantic encore tradition,
mostly those by the violin virtuoso Joseph Achron.[13] In 1914 the Society
launched a publishing-house, which issued about one thousand items in
the course of ten years.

The Jewish heritage which was the rationale and object of study for
the Society was rooted in the numerous Jewish communities of eastern
Europe. The interest in Palestine was not inherent in the initial pro-
gramme of the Society. Yet, three prominent members, David Schor,
Leo Nisvitzky, and Michael Gnessin, had established initial links with
Palestine during their concert tours and official visits there before the war
and the revolution, events which suspended all outside connections with
Russia for a long time.[14] Soon after the war the Russian focus of the
Society gradually changed as a result of the emigration of several of the
most industrious members of the Society. The first who left after the war
was Leo (Arie) Nisvitzky (Abilea) who gained a high reputation as pianist
and pedagogue in Switzerland. The revolution resulted in the closing
down of *Ruskija Wjedemosti* in 1917, and Engel who lost his prestigious
critic position moved in 1922 to Berlin. There his Juwal[15] publishing
house benefited from the co-operation of the Jewish publishers Jibneh,
Ever, and Judischer Verlag. A new and lasting connection was reached

---

[11] 'The Twentieth Anniversary, i'.   [12] Ibid.

[13] Joseph Achron (1886–1943) was one of Auer's best violin students. He studied composition
with Liadov. In 1925 he immigrated to the United States. See W. W. Austin, *Music in the 20th
Century* (New York, 1966), 485.

[14] See Ch. 2, above.

[15] The name Juwal, 'the father of all such as handle the harp and organ' (Genesis 5: 21) was
frequently used as a label in Jewish musical circles.

when Engel met the cellist Joachim Stutschewsky at a concert of Jewish music in Berlin.[16] The meeting made Stutschewsky a staunch supporter of Engel's project.

In 1921 Hopenko invited Leo Nisvitzky for a concert tour in Palestine, following which the pianist decided to settle there,[17] Hebraizing his name to Arie Abilea. Another member of the Society, the pianist and composer Jacob Weinberg[18] immigrated in 1923. In the same year Michael Gnessin secluded himself for a few months in the wild mountain scenery of Bab al Wad[19] where he completed the first act of a projected five-act biblical opera, *Abraham's Youth*, 'which evidently must stand as an attempt at the creation of "Jewish Grand Opera" somewhat in the style of oratorio'.[20] Gnessin considered immigration, but he was disenchanted and returned to Russia after a few months.[21]

Soon after his arrival, Abilea formed a committee dedicated to pave the way for Engel's immigration to Palestine, in the hope that the arrival of the venerable scholar and musician would gradually turn Palestine into the essential centre for the research and the publication of Jewish music. After certain negotiations Engel accepted Hopenko's offer of a position at Shulamit School. Engel immigrated in December 1924, and within a few months he completed the transfer and formal registration of Juwal publishing house in Palestine.[22] Engel's arrival was publicly announced as a major national and cultural event. The festive spirit of Engel's arrival was further enhanced by Salomon Rosowsky's immigration in April 1925 and by the astounding success of Joseph Achron's concert tour in May, when the brilliant violinist 'stirred our hearts with his works in the realm of

[16] The concert took place on 2 Jan. 1923. Born in Russia, Stutschewsky (1891–1981) went to Leipzig to study cello at a young age. In 1914 he settled in Zurich. Stutschewsky moved to Vienna in 1924 at the suggestion of the violinist Rudolf Kolisch, with whom he formed the Wiener Streich Quartett which pioneered works by Arnold Schoenberg and his school. The quartet excelled in a rigorous rehearsal discipline, which included playing all repertory by heart. In order to avoid personal tensions, Kolisch and Fritz Rotschild alternated the roles of the first violinist. Stutschewsky immigrated to Palestine in 1938. J. Stutschewsky, *Memoirs of a Jewish Musician* (Tel Aviv, 1977).

[17] See Chs. 2 and 4, above.

[18] Weinberg (1879–1958) was a composer, a critic, a piano-teacher, and a chamber pianist.

[19] Lit. 'gate to the fountain', but in Hebrew *Sha'ar ha'gai* ('gate to the valley'). Now on route 1 to Jerusalem, it is a scenic pass which marks the start of the ascent from the lowland to the mountains of Jerusalem.

[20] Sabaneev, 'Jewish National School in Music', 465. The score, long believed lost, has been discovered in 1991 at the St Petersburg library by Rita Flomenboim, a doctoral student at the Musicology Department, Tel Aviv University.

[21] Rita Flomenboim could find no document explaining his reasons to leave Palestine. A paper read at the Annual Meeting of the Israeli Musicological Society, July 1993. Back in Russia, Gnessin soon became director of the Conservatory in Moscow. In 1929 he renewed the activity of the Society which was halted during the war and the revolution. *Ha'Aretz* (29 Jan. 1929).

[22] *Theatre and Art*, 2 (July 1925).

Ex 5.1. Achron, 'Hebrew Melody'

Hebrew folk music, in which he revealed himself as the saviour of a great genre of national art work'.[23] Achron's works, which combined the Jewish *melos* of eastern Europe with the Russian school of virtuoso violin-playing became extremely popular with most other great violinists of that time. Jasha Heifetz was especially fond of Achron's 'Hebrew Melody' (see Ex. 5.1) which he recorded on 78 r.p.m. records, and which also became popular with violin-teachers.

The massive presence of the Society members was overwhelming in the small musical community, and the concept of Jewish music soon became synonymous with theirs. In addition to entire concerts of their works it became a recurrent gesture to include a work by one of them in heterogeneous programmes, such as a recital by Judith and Verdinah Shlonsky[24] which included a song by Engel alongside works by Pergolesi, Rimsky-Korsakov, and Chopin.

In April 1925 Engel accepted the position of musical director of the newly founded Ohel theatre. The company started as a socialist-oriented workers' theatre, whose actors worked during the daytime and contributed their evening hours to the idealistic project. Engel joined them as a devoted volunteer.[25] Warm-hearted and sentimental, he became very friendly with the actors. Engel also published reviews and essays in the daily press and in the periodical *Theatre and Art*, for which the fees were minimal. Engel's close friends tried in vain to convince the Board of Education to appoint him as a superintendent of music education and pay him a teacher's salary of £20 a month. Engel's close friend M. Rosenstein later complained that the tight-fisted Board forced the venerable 56-year-old musician to overtax himself teaching young children.[26] Engel's frustration exploded when he wrote to his close friend, Professor David Schor, who was about to immigrate himself: 'Keep dreaming as long as you have not set your foot in the Holy Land. Here will come

---

[23] *Ha'Aretz* (27 Apr. 1924).

[24] On 10 Sept. 1925. Verdinah Shlonsky immigrated in 1931 and became a leading woman composer in the Yishuv. See Ch. 10, below.

[25] It was only after Engel's death that the theatre became fully professional, and even then it could afford to pay no more than a meagre salary.

[26] A lecture at the inauguration ceremony of the Nigun Hebrew Music Society, published in *Ha'Aretz* (19 July 1929).

the end to all dreams'.[27] Undoubtedly, Engel must have been deeply humiliated when a considerable part of his salary at Shulamit school was repeatedly left unpaid.[28] In vain did Hopenko try to secure funds to pay Engel's rent.[29] On 13 February 1927 Engel succumbed to the insupportable pressures, having worked in Palestine for barely two years.

Soon the Society's presence in Palestine suffered another loss. When the collapse of the Palestine Opera put an end to all hopes of production of *The Pioneers*, Jacob Weinberg endeavoured to organize an entire concert of his own compositions in April 1927, but he must have been disenchanted with the results, since four months later he left the country, allegedly 'to disseminate Hebrew music in America and in Europe'.[30] In reality, as he has confessed many years later, 'absolutely unable to have my works published in Palestine I was forced to go to America and to continue to work there'.[31]

The Vision of an International Centre for Jewish Music

Engel's project, however, was not lost. Immediately after Engel's death his Berlin representative M. Rosenstein hastened to Palestine to salvage *Juwal*. He found the books in total disarray and deeply in the red, and decided to stay and rehabilitate the publishing house.[32] A well-publicized Juwal Festive Concert marked the continuation of Engel's project. Works by Achron, Milner, Engel, Gnessin, Weinberg, Krein, and Rosowsky dominated the programme, alongside the increasing role of Ernst Bloch as the admired embodiment of modern Jewish music.[33] An exhibition of Juwal publications, which by then numbered two-hundred single items, followed.[34]

At the same time the venerable and energetic dreamer Professor David Schor took the lead. His immigration seventeen years after his first visit to Palestine[35] was the culmination of a prolonged emotional and ideologi-

---

[27] Quoted in D. Schor, 'Ein Harod', *Davar* (May 1941). Ein Harod was one of the first kibbutzim in Palestine. The article, written to mark the twentieth anniversary of the pioneer kibbutz, turned into the personal memoirs of the elderly musician.

[28] Shulamit Archive, CZA S2 151. See Ch. 3, above.

[29] Letter of 10 Nov. 1924 (CZA S2 150 II; draft in Yariv Ezrahi Archive, Tel Aviv University). There is no record of any reply.

[30] *Theatre and Art*, 9 (Sept. 1927).   [31] 'Autobiography', *Taztlil*, 4 (1966), 68.

[32] Letter to Stutschewsky, 2 May 1929.

[33] *Do'ar Hayom, Davar, Ha'Aretz* (17 and 19 May 1927).   [34] *Theatre and Art*, 8 (May 1927).

[35] See Ch. 2, above.

cal process which led him to a synthesis of socialist idealism, humanistic belief in the purifying powers of music, and a national vision. Schor was deeply impressed by the first stage of the Russian revolution, when

we learned to appreciate physical labour, and we discovered the great value of farming during the years of famine, when a sack of potatoes cost more than a costly piano. . . . We understood that there was no reason to prefer the so-called intellectual subjects over other crafts. We also understood that the farmer would easily survive without our help, whereas we would be lost without him.[36]

On his way to Palestine Schor stopped in Berlin, where 'as soon as I reached my modest hotel, my eyes caught a sign: "Entrance to Gentlemen Only". How much insult and humiliation to human honour were expressed in this announcement!'[37]

Schor's immigration was prompted by a grand vision:

I am going to Palestine with the object of establishing an academy of music which should be not only a school of music, but also a means of spreading the love of music among the people by means of lectures and popular concerts. In making Palestine the centre of Jewish work, we want to serve all the nationalities inhabiting Palestine, Syria, Arabia and even Egypt. We want to make it a centre of modern culture for the whole of the Middle East. Nothing can bring peoples together so much as art.[38]

Schor laboured simultaneously on two fronts. He collaborated with the few remaining members of Engel's group in perpetuating the projects of the Society for Jewish Folk Music. At the same time he began to implement his vision of the dissemination of great music among the people.

Encouraged by the intensification of activity in the realm of Jewish music in the principal European capitals, Schor and his colleagues founded Hanigun—Universal Society for the Promotion of Jewish Music[39] in the spring of 1929. The purposes of the new society as outlined in its brochure were

to form a lively link with those active in Hebrew music all over the world, to organize international conferences of our artists, to sponsor scholarly research of music of the East in general and of Hebrew music in particular, to found a periodical which would report on activity in that field, and finally, to find the ways and means to provide the composer of Hebrew music with proper con-

---

[36] Schor, 'Ein Harod'.   [37] Ibid.   [38] *Palestine Bulletin* (12 July 1925).
[39] 'Nigun' is a generic musical term, meaning a tune, the act of playing an instrument. It specifically implies a long and elaborate vocal Hasidic composition, usually invented by an admired rabbi of a Hasidic court. The nigun acquired a status of divine revelation.

ditions for his work, and to disseminate the works of Hebrew music in all Jewish homes.[40]

The inclusion of Hebrew music within the category of Eastern music marked the conceptual shift of the centre to Palestine, although for all practical purposes the repertory of the Russian group retained its prominent position in concerts and publications. The new society differed from the original Society for Jewish Folk Music and from Engel's Juwal not in substance but in its quest to turn Palestine into the centre of international activities in Jewish music. M. Rosenstein assumed responsibility for the publishing house, which operated in close co-operation with Universal Edition in Vienna. There were no adequate music printing facilities in Palestine and most work had to be done in Berlin and in Vienna. Despite frequent difficulties in international financial transactions, the publications yielded a small income, especially Achron's popular violin pieces.[41] Rosenstein gathered the 200 single items which Juwal had published under Engel into ten volumes according to categories, such as Yiddish songs, piano music, children's songs, etc., which he offered for a total of £10. He also contemplated the publication of a periodical. However, the momentum was lost again with the sudden outbreak of bloody attacks by Arab mobs on Jewish settlements all over the country in August 1929, 'which threw us off track. The events shook us not only morally but also financially.'[42] Still, four months later the Society renewed its work, and 'within two weeks fifty members joined, although there was a very depressing atmosphere'.[43] By the summer of 1930 membership had reached 300 and the Society started a season of five concerts of Jewish music. The yearly dues of £1 served as subscription fees for which a member could choose from the publications of the Society.[44] At first the new society dealt only with the old publications of the Russian compositions. In 1931 Hanigun reached a new stage with the proud first publication of a compilation composed and printed in Palestine which, in line with the pedagogical orientation of the Society was *10 Violin Studies—Variations on Hebrew Folk Tunes* by Gabriel Grad.[45]

---

[40] Stutschewsky Archive, AMLI Library, Tel Aviv.

[41] Letter from Rosenstein to Stutschewksy, 17 June 1929 (Stutschewsky Archive, AMLI Library, Tel Aviv).

[42] A letter from Rosenstein to Stutschewsky, 3 Oct 1929 (Stutschewsky Archive, AMLI Library, Tel Aviv).

[43] Letters from Rosenstein to Stutschewsky, 5 Dec 1929.   [44] Ibid.

[45] A letter from Rosenstein to Stutschewsky, 27 Nov. 1931. Grad (1890–1950) was a violinist and composer.

The activity of Hanigun whetted the interest of the Hebrew University. In 1929, four years after its inauguration, it emerged as a small German-oriented elite institution with eight professors, thirteen lecturers, and 187 regular students. The Faculty of Humanities consisted of the Institutes of Jewish Studies and of Oriental Studies, with additional courses in philosophy, history, and literature.[46] Schor proudly wrote that the 'Hebrew University has invited me 'to "run the music" in the country.' Schor's formal duties, which he shared with Rosowsky and Rabinowitz, included organizing lecture series all over Palestine, launching a music department at the National Library, collecting Jewish folk music, and directing the University chorus. Within three months Schor had given twenty lecture-recitals in towns and villages to capacity audiences, struggling with the Hebrew language which he had not yet mastered.[47] The Music Department of the National Library had 'developed with great strides' with the acquisition of a set of Eulenburg scores and of Bach–Busoni's edition, as well as an 'almost complete collection' of *Juwal*'s publications. The library was enriched by the activity of the Warsaw Committee of Friends, who sent donations of entire collections of modern French and German music, such as Debussy, Les Six, Mahler, Schoenberg, Hindemith, Bartok, and many others, as well as books on history and theory and some of the leading music periodicals from France and Germany, so that professional musicians could keep abreast with recent developments in Europe.[48]

The musical scene in Palestine in the 1920s was almost exclusively dominated by the members of the Society for Jewish Folk Music. Their contribution received a prestigious authorization with the publication of Leonid Sabaneev's extensive study,[49] which coincided with Engel's immigration. Critic Menashe Rabinowitz fully endorsed Sabaneev's methodology considering the creation of art music as the third and last stage in the evolutionary process of national music, following the initial stage of the recognition of folk music, and the second stage of its research and compilation.[50] In the particular case of the migrant members of the Society, an abnormal situation ensued, since they commenced their work in Palestine directly with the third stage, detached from the soil which gave rise to their work.

[46] Gurevich, *Statistical Abstract*, 244–5.   [47] A letter to Stutschewsky, 25 Feb. 1930.

[48] *Palestine Bulletin* (20 May 1930).

[49] Sabaneev, 'Jewish National School in Music', 448–68.

[50] M. Rabinowitz, 'The National Hebrew School in Music', *Davar* (21 July 1927). Rabinowitz read the newly published booklet while on a brief study leave in Germany.

The immigration of the musicians indirectly raised the question of the interpretation of Zionism. Engel wrote in one of his first letters to the committee which had initiated his immigration that 'I am no Zionist, but I regard the national element in general and in human creation in particular as of supreme importance, and this brings me closer to Zionism.'[51] David Schor urged Stutschewsky 'to convince Jewish artists to take an interest in Palestine. This is a land not only for Zionists, but for all Jews.'[52] The two comments indicated that Zionists were conceived at that time as a definite group of committed young pioneers, who immigrated to Palestine after a prolonged period of structured political and ideological indoctrination in Europe and were expected to turn to agricultural work. Such an image could deter the potential immigration of musicians, who were reluctant to give up their vocation. Indeed, all the professional immigrant musicians in the 1920s immigrated following privately reached decisions in which professional, humanistic, and ideological considerations interacted with and frequently conflicted with one another. Most of them were middle-aged experienced musicians, whose high prestige eased their initial resettlement, especially since their arrival has been publicly eulogized. Yet their hailed reception also led them to entertain high expectations which frequently resulted in agonized frustration, and, in some cases, angry emigration.

Music for the People and the Socialist Utopia

Upon David Schor's immigration Miriam Levit invited him to teach at her school, for which she adopted the flowery name 'House of Levites'. Idealistic, emotional, and unrelenting, Schor shifted the orientation of the school and in May 1927 started an extensive programme of adult courses.

On Passover I was in the North of Palestine, where for many years the people heard nothing other than the cries of the jackals and the mooing of the cows. A musical soirée (with a lousy upright piano) gathered hundreds of people from all over, who listened with moving attentiveness. . . . Lack of funds precludes me from doing much, and I intend to go to Europe in order to form an organization of Jewish artists, who would perform in Palestine at least annually. We are all ready for self-sacrifice here. Our pay is meagre. Our colleagues must understand that. None of us is allowed to consider oneself relieved of the duty to contribute to the national revival of the people, lest one would ignore one's Jewishness. Once it was a religion. Now it is a matter of national existence.[53]

---

[51] 24 July 1924. Printed posthumously in *Theatre and Art*, 8 (1927), 4.
[52] A letter of 26 June 1928.   [53] A letter to Stutschewsky, 8 Apr. 1928.

In view of his ambitious plans, Schor's sense of isolation increased his need to share his experience with his friends in Europe by means of a regular and lively correspondence, especially with Joachim Stutschewsky. The latter, who had by then reached the peak of his career with the Wiener Streich Quartett and with the pianist Friedrich Wührer, embarked on a series of concerts of Jewish music. He also wrote a regular column in the weekly *Die Stimme*, in which he reported on all facets of music in Palestine, so that his support of the project in Palestine was crucial.

Schor's excursions to the countryside led to the inauguration of the Institute for the Promotion of Music among the People, of which he wrote:

In nearly every settlement there are 'musicians', that is, people who play a certain instrument or coach choruses. There is a wind band in the Emek,[54] a mandoline orchestra in Herzelia,[55] and so on. The initiators are dedicated to their project and love their work, but they often lack the know-how and the experience. . . . We could not send our instructors to them, as they are too few in number. I therefore decided this year to gather all the settlers who have to do with music. The first attempt was a success. Eighteen people came to Tel Aviv and for a fortnight they studied eight hours a day. We also invited them to all lectures and concerts which were held during that time. On Saturday we convened four choruses (from Petach Tikvah, Rehovot, Nes Zionah and Tel Aviv).[56] Under Rabinowitz's directorship the choruses joined together in two Bach chorales and two Jewish folk songs.[57]

Schor's vision was nourished by innovative trends in musical education in Russia, where he had been among music educators who realized that the limited stage for international virtuosi had reached the point of satiety, and that an increasing number of eager and talented conservatory students faced bitter disappointment and unemployment upon graduation. The new trend strove to transform the conservatories into institutes for the training of fine and knowledgeable educators who would disseminate the love of music, with emphasis on folk music, in all social strata.[58] Schor realized that the scope of his vision would require a well coordinated team of music instructors spread all over the country. Together

[54] The Valley of Jezre'el, a fertile valley in the north of Palestine. Settled mostly during the 1920s, it was a source of pride of the Jewish agricultural settlement movement in the 1920s and the origin for heroic myths.

[55] A village founded in 1924, 8 km. north of Tel Aviv.

[56] The three villages were in the perimeter of Tel Aviv, the furthest being Rehovot, 20 km. to the south.

[57] Letter to Stutschewsky, 25 Feb. 1930.

[58] M. Rabinowitz, 'Musical Life in the Country', *Davar* (11 May 1929).

with Rabinowitz and Rosowsky he established regular courses for the training of instructors, who were periodically brought to Tel Aviv to take part in intensive courses in methodology, choral conducting, and general musical education. The Institute for the Promotion of Music among the People stressed active involvement in music, and Menashe Rabinowitz warned against exaggerated euphoria in view of the

numerous concerts, the full houses at the opera, the new compositions, the increasing number of students in the music schools. All those are not indicators of the musicianship of the people. . . . On the contrary—music is in danger, because the fountain which has fertilized the creators of music is being dried up, and the common people who placed words into the mouths of their poets are mute.[59]

The prototype for Rabinowitz's work with the network of choruses which the Institute organized was Professor Fritz Jöde's project, which Rabinowitz personally witnessed during his study leave in Germany in 1927, when

2,000 people learned five folksongs. Had we attained this stage, had we been able to teach the immigrants from Europe Yemenite and Arabic songs for several evenings, it would have been a step toward the fulfilment of our wish to create the Hebrew music, in which such songs would have undoubtedly constituted an important and significant element.[60]

In order to overcome the difficulties in the instruction of music notation, Rabinowitz recommended the adoption of the British tonic system which would facilitate music education.

The combination of socialist ideas, national aspirations, and advanced educational methods was complemented by the inevitable recourse to the ancient Greeks by way of Wagnerian thought. Rabinowitz devoted the leading article in the first brochure of the Institute for the Promotion of Music among the People to a detailed discussion of ancient Greek music, focusing on the point that 'the singing had been directed to the people. All citizens had to participate and to be educated through it. The concepts of music and of the people were interrelated.'[61] The brochure published reports from local representatives of about a dozen active choruses, mostly in small and isolated settlements, each having its own

[59] 'Music of the People', *Davar* (20 Dec. 1927).

[60] Ibid. Fritz Jöde (1887–1970) was appointed in 1923 as professor for school and church music at the Imperial Academy in Berlin. In 1926 he started the project of 'public community singing' with the intention of renewing the folk song tradition. Rabinowitz attended one of the earliest sessions of the project.

[61] 'The Chorus in Greece', *Music for the People* (Mar. 1931), 10.

character and difficulties. Not unexpectedly, the long tradition of musical
activity in Rishon Le'Zion was reflected in the respected position of the
choir which numbered fifty members 'from all walks of life' and participated in all festive events of the settlement. A militant report arrived from
a socialist kibbutz near Hadera:

The Institute sent us plenty of material, but it is irrelevant to us. We want
workers' songs, songs which would fit our life and wishes. The chorus is no
longer satisfied with Mendelssohn and with religious songs. A workers' chorus
is not allowed to develop a random art which is detached from the daily life of
the worker and from its struggle for a new culture. . . . It is not enough to cause
pleasure to the audience. The chorus must also enrich the spiritual life of the
worker.[62]

By 1930 the number of active choruses had increased to twenty.[63] The
ideology of music for the people received additional support with the
gradual renewal of some of the community's orchestras which had halted
their work during the war. Rishon Le'Zion, the proud initiator of
community orchestras in Palestine, maintained its dynamism, having
swelled to 2,143 inhabitants by 1927. The settlement revived its orchestra
for the third time in 1924, again with a hired professional conductor.[64] A
community string orchestra was formed in Haifa.[65] The Violin of Zion
orchestra in Petah Tikvah regrouped as a forty-member wind band.[66] The
pioneer kibbutz Tel-Yosef[67] launched a wind band 'which excites the
members to dance, plays the anthem on the right occasions, and even
dares to play fantasias, operatic overtures, etc. There are many who
strongly criticize the band and they are right, but the power of the
orchestra (which mostly plays forte) mutes the criticism.'[68]

David Schor was hard-pressed to maintain active lines of communi-
cation with Europe and especially with Berlin. He convinced the Jewish
Professor Adolf Weissmann, prestigious critic of *Berliner Zeitung am
Mittag*, to become president of the Institute. Aloof and reticent,
Weissmann was 'far from Zionism and was not interested in Hebrew
national music'.[69] Still, Schor's fervour was catching, and Weissmann

---

[62] Ibid. 13. The name of the kibbutz was not mentioned but it most likely was Gan Shmuel,
founded in 1913.

[63] *Hazman* (4 Mar. 1930).

[64] *Ha'Aretz* (10 July 1924). Gurevich and Gertz (eds.), *Statistical Handbook*, 56. See Ch. 2, above.

[65] *Iton Hatzafon* (Bulletin of the North) (20 Mar. 1927).

[66] *Do'ar Hayom* (15 Nov. 1927).

[67] Founded in 1921 in the Emek, the Valley of Jezreel, a fertile valley in the central-northern
region of Palestine.

[68] Rabinowitz, 'Musical Life in the Country', *Davar* (29 Apr. 1928).

[69] Id. 'Professor Adolf Weissmann', *Davar* (2 May 1929).

became increasingly interested in the Institute, and on 19 April 1929 he arrived in Palestine. His inspiring lecture at the Hebrew University was dedicated to Arnold Schoenberg, whom he considered the greatest living composer. Yet all hopes for future co-operation were shattered when Adolf Weissmann suddenly died on 24 April, barely a week after his arrival.

Salomon Rosowsky then turned to the prosperous Jewish community of New York for support. Soon enormous posters in the daily press announced the inauguration of the Palestine Institute of Musical Sciences.[70] Designed to combine research and teaching, it was established by the New York-based Society for the Advancement of Music in Palestine who appointed Rosowsky, Golinkin, Schor, and Harlamov as the staff of the new Palestine Institute. The curriculum was distorted from the start, since Harlamov was expected to teach all wind instruments and no piano or string classes were announced. Menashe Rabinowitz, who was left out, angrily terminated co-operation with his older colleagues. Not hiding his deep personal hurt, Rabinowitz also chided the entire project for what he considered to be an old-fashioned urban conservatory directed by Americans, which he contrasted with the innovative Institute for the Promotion of Music among the People with its net spread all over the country.[71] The new project never got off the ground and its place was soon taken up by the Palestine Conservatoire.[72]

The idealistic euphoria which accompanied the first steps of the Institute for the Promotion of Music also gave way to disenchantment and to loss of communication between organizers and students.

Excitement subsided after a short while. Many of the participants quit the courses and relations became strained. The high motivation to learn piano raised doubts among the organizers about the real aim of the students. It turned out that most of them never intended to instruct the people, but rather hoped to make personal progress. Some wished to learn the piano, others were interested in harmony and composition. Their intentions were good. . . . Yet, it was the duty of the Board of Education and of the Teachers' Federation to train them. . . . The Institute could not answer their needs. Its purpose was narrower and well defined: to train instructors for the disseminating of music among the people.[73]

The chorus directors repeatedly faced a conflict between the aspiration of its choruses to perform in concert situations and the educational goal of active popular participation. On one occasion the Institute embarked

<hr />

[70] *Palestine Bulletin* (27 Nov. 1930).   [71] *Davar*, (8 Dec. 1930).   [72] See Ch. 10, below.
[73] Rabinowitz, 'Musical Life in the Country', *Davar* (11 May 1929).

upon a reformed Passover workers' Seder[74] with the participation of one of its choruses. Yet the audience did not respond to the invitation to join the singing. 'What was the reason? It was the stage. . . . The chorus of the Institute for the Promotion of Music should not sing from a high stage. They should mix with the audience.'[75] The same difficulty appeared when the great poet Bialik initiated public gatherings on the Sabbath, which included lectures and discussions on religious and literary Jewish topics. Bialik asked Rabinowitz to organize a small choir as a catalyst for group singing, but to their chagrin the audience did not join but rather 'listened and applauded'.[76] Menashe Rabinowitz got to the crux of the matter:

It is nice to stroll with a large group in the moonlight from the beach . . . and to sing aloud, together . . . What to sing? Will a Russian peasant ask his friend what to sing? . . . Will a German woman wait to be asked, and will her friend refrain from accompanying her in fifths and thirds? And what about us? Often I happened to join a group of people who wished to sing, and after a long search gave up. One would start a Hasidic Nigun or a folksong, but with no response from his friends he would stop. All of a sudden they would all start a powerful, expressive Russian song. But the sounds would suffocate among the flat-roof houses, and with no echo would return tasteless and colourless to the singers and shut them up. It is nice to stroll with a large group in the moonlight. But something is missing. No singing. No sounds.[77]

[74] The Seder is a religious function held on Passover's eve, which consists of a joint reading of the sacred texts of the Haggadah and a festive dinner. Traditionally a family event, the pioneers attempted to convert the Seder into a large-scale celebration with additional texts and music. See Ch. 12, below.

[75] Letter to the editor, *Davar* (8 May 1929).   [76] *Ha'Aretz* (10 Dec. 1929).

[77] 'Musical Life in the Country', *Davar* (4 Apr. 1928).

6

Music in the Land of the Bible, Pure Music, and Good Manners

THE genre of the biblical oratorio maintained a special position in the heated ideological climate of the Yishuv. The solemn moralistic and educational stance of the oratorio since the times of Handel and Haydn had been enhanced by the opportunity to enact the biblical heroic stories *in loco*. The participation of large amateur choruses which have won the support of the music educators was an added benefit. Moreover, productions of oratorio concerts were financially much less demanding than the costly opera. One of the earliest oratorio concerts in Palestine featured excerpts from Saint-Saëns's *The Deluge*; Haydn's *The Creation*; Mendelssohn's *Elijah*; and Handel's *Samson, Judas Maccabeus*, and the 'Hallelujah' chorus from *The Messiah*. Hanina Karchewsky, the first music teacher at the Herzlia Gymnasium in Tel Aviv, conducted a combined chorus of 'more than two hundred performers'.[1] Such initiatives, however, remained sporadic and amateurish.

Menashe Rabinowitz has drawn an analogy between the events in England which led Handel from opera to oratorio and the decline of the Palestine Opera which cleared the way for the oratorio.[2] The first serious enterprise in the realm of oratorio came with the immigration of Fordhaus Ben-Tzisi,[3] who differed from the other immigrant musicians in his total identification with his deeply religious Hasidic family background. His ageing father had left his family in Russia and settled among the cabbalists in Safed[4] where he died far from his family. Fordhaus had

[1] *Ha'Aretz* (12 Apr. 1925).
[2] 'Musical Life in the Country, i', *Davar* (27 Mar. 1928). See Ch. 4, above.
[3] An interview with Fordhaus (1898–1981), 1976. Fordhaus was his original last name. After the death of his adored mother, Tzisi, he named himself *Ben*-Tzisi (Tzisi's son).
[4] The cabbala is a medieval system of Jewish mysticism, whose upholders used secret ciphers to interpret the Scripture and thereby predict the end of days. The traditional centre of cabbala was the isolated holy town of Safed in the northern mountains of Palestine.

immigrated in 1924 with his mother, who died three weeks later. According to Jewish customs, he refrained from musical activity during the year of mourning and devoted himself to religious studies at a Yeshiva in Jerusalem. In 1926 Golinkin employed him as coach and choral director of the crumbling opera, but Fordhaus was emotionally remote from the operatic stage which he treated merely as a necessary job. His spiritual world was a combination of Jewish religious fervour and romantic belief in the moral power of great music, headed by Mozart, Beethoven, and the great masterpieces in the genre of the biblical oratorio. He founded the Bible Chorus for the purpose of 'planting biblical music amongst us, making it an integral part of holiday celebrations, and bringing it into all the homes of the people of Israel'.[5] Fordhaus, like Golinkin and Rabinowitz, stated that 'we still do not have the genuine song which would be a direct expression of our roots in the country, with our past and future' and that a tradition of folk song should be deliberately fostered. Yet, he differed from Golinkin in considering the biblical oratorio rather than the national opera as the channel designed to 'purify the Yishuv from alien borrowed tunes, some of which were unpleasantly jarring due to the vulgarity brought over here from all corners of the world with the waves of immigration'.[6] Fordhaus wished the *Bible Chorus* to follow the Jewish yearly cycle[7] with appropriate oratorios, such as Haydn's the *Creation* which would be performed on the week in which the portion from Genesis is read. Though he was not explicit about it, his model must have been Bach's cycle of church cantatas. Fordhaus's sincere and naive excitement won the hearts and the utmost dedication of his chorus members.

The great oratorios, though composed mostly by non-Jewish composers, enjoyed the superior status of 'Jewish music' in the broadest sense of the word. Fordhaus treated the Hebrew translation and the interpretation as a sacred undertaking which called for occasional revisions and *contrafacta*, as in the case of certain sections of Lidley's Enlightenment libretto for Haydn's the *Creation*. Fordhaus and his translator, the poet Aharon Ashmann, substituted Psalm 92, 'A Song for the Sabbath Day', for the operatic love duet of Adam and Eve in part III which they renounced as sacrilegious. Haydn took his affect for the chorus which concludes the *Creation* (no. 26) from the opening sentence 'in joy we come with one

---

[5] *Ha'Aretz* (31 Mar. 1927), *Davar* (1 Apr. 1927).   [6] *Ha'Aretz* (7 Apr. 1927).

[7] Portions (*Parashat hashavua*) from the Torah (the Pentateuch) are regularly read in the synagogue according to a fixed weekly cycle as part of the morning service on the Sabbath as well as on Mondays and Thursdays. Observing Jews use the title of each Portion as references to dates.

accord' which is set 'Vivace'. Fordhaus interpreted the great moment differently and performed the music in a solemn 'Grave'.[8]

The *Creation* was Fordhaus's first production of a complete oratorio, which coincided with the collapse of the Palestine Opera in July 1927. The opera soloists had dispersed and Fordhaus could recruit only three soloists, who were forced to cope with the five solo parts in the work.[9] Rabinowitz hailed the production, which 'affects the public more than the symphony. The oratorio suits our life here much more than the opera, and the biblical themes of most oratorios bring us closer to the Bible.'[10]

Fordhaus temporarily suspended his project when he joined the international tour of the Habimah theatre as conductor. He renewed his activity with a performance of Mendelssohn's *Elijah* in 1932. A modest activity in the realm of biblical oratorio continued to be an integral and respected part of the musical scene in the Yishuv.

The Education of an Audience

A listener who brought his barking dog along with him to a symphonic concert in Jerusalem sparked a scandal and exposed the chasm separating high attendance in concerts from civilized manners and a true understanding.[11] An anonymous critic ironically suggested that the organizers of concerts 'print in the programme very clearly "here one applauds", "here one sits quietly", as the rubrics in the women's *Mahazor* which indicate "here one cries".'[12] Attempts to improve the attitude and manners of certain segments of the audience were frequently impeded by inexperienced organizers and inappropriate auditoriums. Menashe Rabinowitz complained that the first recital of the excellent pianist Bruno Eisner was held in a freezing, noisy hall with terrible acoustics, and that ticket prices were too expensive for students.[13] Too much familiarity was also a liability at times. Violinist Samuel Dushkin played a series of folk song arrangements for violin and piano, and Rabinowitz chided the listeners who

---

[8] Interview with Fordhaus, 1976.

[9] The parts of Gabriel and of Eve are for soprano, and those of Rafael and Adam for bass.

[10] 'Musical Life in the Country', *Davar* (27 Mar. 1928).

[11] *Ha'Aretz*; a report (27 Dec. 1923); letter to the editor (30 Dec. 1923).

[12] *Ha'Aretz* (28 Dec. 1923). The *Mahazor* is the Jewish prayer-book for the High Holidays, where special rubrics were added for the sake of women who were traditionally barred from the extensive religious education of men.

[13] *Davar* (17 Apr. 1929).

'missed the opportunity to gain a better understanding of the function of harmony and elaboration in folk song, since they started to hum the well-known tunes during the playing.'[14] In that, Rabinowitz the critic inadvertently contradicted Rabinowitz the educator, who called for an active involvement of the listeners in music-making.[15] Mary Itzhaki, former director of the Jerusalem Music School, warned Professor Schor upon his immigration that 'our audience is far from understanding good music, whether Jewish or European. Mr Golinkin helped us a lot, and everywhere one hears tunes from *Carmen*.'[16] Yet, Golinkin himself despised the superficial popularity of operatic tunes, and ignored calls to encore the entr'acte to the last act of *Carmen*, since 'we all know that Mr Golinkin would not deviate from his rule never to repeat separate numbers which would detract from the dramatic continuity'.[17] The contrast between a small group of initiated connoisseurs and a large public eager for entertainment but musically inexperienced made the members of the professional élite feel that they must assume the heavy responsibility of educating a new audience in the heterogeneous immigrant society.

In Search of an Orchestra

The box-office success of the Palestine Opera aroused the pianist Arie Abilea to issue a warning against an unbalanced musical culture: 'The Palestine Opera would be able to do much in disseminating music among the people. But has the audience done enough to spread the influence of music in public life? I refer especially to pure music, that is, chamber and symphonic music.'[18] Thus the Romantic aesthetics of instrumental music were enlisted as a guideline for the emerging musical life in the country.

Golinkin conducted the first symphonic programme in Palestine in Tel Aviv on 25 December 1923 and in Jerusalem on the next day. All available musicians were assembled into an *ad hoc* orchestra of forty-five players. Still some parts could not be filled.[19] The all-Beethoven programme included the Symphony No. 5 and the Violin Concerto with the recent immigrant from England, Margery Bentwich. The fine violinist ignored this concert in her fascinating memoirs of her sister, the cellist Thelma Yellin, probably because it did not match her high artistic standards.[20] The excited press labelled the event as Golinkin's second project. Yet more

---

[14] *Davar* (12 Apr. 1927).   [15] See Ch. 5, above.
[16] A letter to Prof. Schor, 9 Dec. 1925 (CZA J/43).   [17] *Ha'Aretz* (16 Nov. 1925).
[18] *Ha'Aretz* (21 Oct. 1925).   [19] *Ha'Aretz* (25 and 26 Dec. 1923).
[20] M. Bentwich, *Thelma Yellin, Pioneer Musician* (Jerusalem, 1964), 12, 47. See more, below.

than a dozen years later the critic David Rosolio released the secret that Golinkin's concert was occasioned by unforeseen circumstances.[21] The orchestral material for the second production of the Palestine Opera did not arrive on time and Golinkin hastily substituted the symphonic programme with no intention of continuing to divide his attention between two insurmountable projects.

All subsequent efforts to organize a regular symphony orchestra were caught in a vicious cycle. The total number of Union members, including pianists, reached sixty-three in 1927,[22] too many to make a living from available jobs in cafés and cinemas, yet too few to form a professional symphony orchestra. The terms of their employment, according to which they had to play at the cafés and films every night, were an additional impediment. After much pressure the employers reluctantly released the musicians for one evening per week in which they could perform in concerts. Even so, their small number required a 'general recruitment' of musicians from Tel Aviv and Jerusalem for each symphonic concert.[23] Hopenko complained that 'various orchestras are scattered here and there, but each operates unaware of the others'. He called for a conference of all representatives of the orchestras in Palestine with the purpose of collecting data about musicians.[24] Yet he must have entertained a vain hope, since these were the members of the same small group of overworked and underpaid players who kept moving from one odd job to another. Personal and institutional ambitions further hindered some of the initiatives,[25] as when the Union of Workers in Art demanded administrative control of Golinkin's proposed orchestra.[26]

As in the case of the opera, decisive individual action was required in order to pave the way for the first serious symphony orchestra. Max Lampel, a conductor and organist launched one in May 1926.[27] Lampel (1900–85) was born in Vienna and studied at the Academy of Music there. He worked with Alexander von Zemlinsky in Prague as a conductor and a concert organist, and then returned to Vienna as orchestral and choral conductor. Lampel immigrated to Palestine in 1925 and by January 1927 he had organized and conducted eight symphony concerts. Since there was no adequate auditorium available in Tel Aviv, he used a wooden shell placed on a dune of soft sand overlooking the beach.[28] Large

[21] Rosolio, 'The Story of the Music in Palestine', Ha'Aretz (25 Dec. 1936).
[22] Z. Carmi, The Trade Union in Israel (Tel Aviv, 1959), 45.
[23] Garter, recorded interview, 1975. See Ch. 3, above.   [24] Ha'Aretz (24 Mar. 1925).
[25] Document of 6 Jan. 1926 (Lavon Institute 3227).
[26] Minutes of the meeting on 30 Jan. 1926.   [27] Ha'Aretz (4 June 1926).
[28] Last remnants of the magnificent dunes of the Palestine coastal strip may still be seen in the vicinity of Ashdod in the south and in Caesaria in the north.

audiences of about 3,000 people attended each concert. Enthusiastic publicists took it as an indication 'that there is a great need for such musical events'[29] though the high attendance must have also been the expression of the need for social entertainment in the young immigrant community. The educational aspect of the project was emphasized when Menashe Rabinowitz was invited to introduce the first programme with a brief lecture.[30] Lampel was more-or-less capable of performing mainstream classical programmes. When he tried to cope with Mendelssohn's 'Scottish' Symphony Rosolio remarked that 'this symphony which belongs to the standard repertory cannot yet be performed here in the polished way it deserves',[31] and a daring shot at a difficult Romantic programme which included Wagner's *Tannhäuser* Overture provoked the rebuke that 'there is a great difference between an occasional gathering of players and a unified musical ensemble'.[32] The concerts remained sporadic, dependent on weather conditions, and on the availability of musicians. The fragile project was soon shattered by external economic and political circumstances.

Crisis and Self-Appraisal

The economy of Palestine during the 1920s was one of fits and starts. The relative prosperity of the mid-twenties, nourished by the unprecedented growth of Jewish population, gave way to three years of a deep recession coupled with a sharp decline in immigration.[33] Disillusionment instigated a sober re-evaluation of prospects and goals. The Critic Menashe Rabinowitz took a hard-and-fast look at the grim reality of the local musical scene, allowing hitherto hidden reflections to surface: 'Once upon a time there was an opera in this country. All of a sudden it blossomed, flourished, withered and died. Even at its heyday occasional thoughts used to come to one's mind: have we indeed reached the stage which would allow us to maintain an opera in this country?'[34]

Rabinowitz also pointed out that 'the opera attracted many fine musicians who might have been a blessing to the country, . . . but with

[29] 'Symphony Concerts in Palestine', *Palestine Bulletin* (Jan. 1927).

[30] *Ha'Aretz* (4 June 1926). The orchestra consisted of 13 first and second violins, 3 violas, 5 cellos, 1 double bass, 2 flutes, 1 oboe, 2 clarinets, 1 bassoon, 1 trumpet, 3 horns, 2 trombones, 1 tuba, and 1 percussionist.

[31] *Ha'Aretz* (15 Nov. 1926).   [32] *Ha'Aretz* (24 May 1927).

[33] In 1925 immigration exceeded emigration by about 32,000, contrasted with 1927 when there were 5,000 emigrants and only 3,000 immigrants. Gurevich *et al.*, *Jewish Population of Palestine*, 24.

[34] 'Musical Life in the Country, i', *Davar* (27 Mar. 1928).

the shutdown of the opera they turned to Europe and left us'.[35] The outcome was disastrous for the symphony orchestra which, though less costly than the opera, 'leads a wretched life here,'[36] both because the emigration of musicians depleted the orchestral ranks, and because the potential audience for the symphony was far smaller than that for the opera. 'And another rival to the symphony has appeared, the jazz band. Although it interests only patrons of the ballroom, the symphony already feels the scarcity of musicians, many of whom have turned for reasons of "economic necessity" to the affluent jazz band.'[37] Rabinowitz concluded with a sincere self-appraisal:

While musical life has declined, criticism has flourished. . . . Constructive and productive musical criticism is rare. In most cases the criticism excelled only in its arrogant tones, in vulgar phraseology, and a self-confidence, which raises suspicion as to the critic's competence and objectivity. Here we need only explanatory and educational criticism, and must refrain from evaluation.[38]

Rabinowitz's objection went unheeded, and luckily so, since the continuous critical scrutiny was the only protection against the danger of a provincial morass.

Self-appraisal, however, brought about a new attitude which instigated the Concert Ensemble. The initiator, conductor Zevi Kompaneetz, was involved in the composition of Jewish music and in the revival of Hebrew in Russia, which he bolstered through an ambitious production there of Saint-Saëns's *Samson et Dalila* in Hebrew translation. An astute 47-year-old musician upon his immigration, he substituted a realistic evaluation of the local musical scene for Golinkin's and Schor's high-flown idealistic vision:

Let us realize the strange disproportion between drama and music in this country. By contrast to four theatre companies in Tel Aviv which employ scores of actors, there is only one double bass player and no bassoonist in this country. . . . It is still impossible to organize a symphony orchestra due to the absence of many important instruments, but it is necessary to organize at least a fifteen-member ensemble, which must perform regularly every week. Let each music-lover know that on a fixed night every week a concert will take place. I would call such an institution 'a folk music stage'.[39]

The Concert Ensemble was launched in the summer of 1928 with fifteen members.[40] Its programmes consisted mostly of high-quality light

---

[35] Ibid. [36] Ibid. [37] Ibid. On the jazz band see Ch. 9, below.
[38] 'Musical Life in the Country, ii', *Davar* (4 Apr. 1928). [39] *Ketuvim* (23 Aug. 1928).
[40] 4 violins, 2 cellos, 1 double bass, 1 flute, 1 clarinet, 1 trumpet, 1 trombone, 1 percussion-player, with a piano and a harmonium which filled in the missing parts.

classics, such as Mendelssohn's Hebrides Overture, Ponchielli's *Dance of the Hours*, Weber's *Freischütz* Overture, Tchaikovsky's *Italian Capriccio*, and Sibelius's *Finlandia*. Only rarely did the ensemble venture to play longer works, such as Beethoven's Symphony No. 1 and a Mozart violin concerto. Some of the programmes included works by Jewish composers, among them Engel, Krein, and Kompaneetz himself. Saint-Saëns's 'Danse Macabre' and 'Bacchanal' from *Samson et Dalila* became popular encores in all concerts of the Ensemble. Anticipating financial difficulties, Kompaneetz was smart enough to let the leery Union of Workers in Art organize the ensemble in accordance with its socialist ideology, namely as a co-operative in which the players were required to cover all the expenses.[41] The official charter of the Concert Ensemble stated that the artistic and educational goal of maintaining a regular and popular concert activity would lead to the 'improvement of the standard of living of the professional musician and contribute to his social security'. An important clause promised retirement benefits 'as long as the ensemble exists'. However, the ensemble did not last long enough to put this promise to test.

The Concert Ensemble started with much ado, performing daily at the summer Levant Fair in Tel Aviv where it also accompanied movies. It then embarked upon a regular season of weekly concerts at Beth Ha'am (Community House), a large outdoor cinema erected on the same dune where Lampel had started his orchestral venture two years earlier, and covered with a roof in early 1929. Loyal to his educational goal, Kompaneetz kept the ticket prices down,[42] and indeed at the first concerts the 1,200-seat auditorium was filled to capacity, and the ensemble repeated the programmes at the auditorium of Herzlia Gymnasium. But despite all the precautions taken, the young venture was soon assailed from unexpected directions. The new auditorium turned out to be no more than a flimsy shade which let in draughts and rain, and during the winter of 1929 attendance in concerts dropped sharply. At first the Association of the Friends of the Ensemble tried to raise money in order to pay the players a minimal fee of £4 a month, but even this paltry fund was soon exhausted. The players returned to their old café and movie jobs, where the owners 'refused to allow them one free night per week for fear of competition'.[43]

---

[41] Document of rules and regulations (Lavon Institute 3227).

[42] Tickets cost 25–50 Palestine mils, compared with 49–200 mils for a concert of the Institute for the Promotion of Music in Jerusalem, 15 Apr. 1930. Daily wages for skilled labour ranged from 200 to 600 mils. Government of Palestine, Department of Customs, Excise, and Trade, *Statistics of Imports, Exports, and Shipping, 1937* (Library of the Central Bureau of Statistics, Jerusalem).

[43] Programme of the fiftieth concert of the Concert Ensemble, 1932 (Lavon Institute).

The summer of 1929 was marked by a political deterioration which culminated at the end of August in a sudden outburst of attacks by Arab mobs on Jewish communities all over Palestine. The alarming number of civilian casualties left the Yishuv shocked and depressed. The British administration imposed a temporary state of martial law, and the ensuing night curfew curtailed public musical activity for nearly three months, especially in Jerusalem where the tension had mounted.

The Concert Ensemble renewed its work only in 1931. Rejuvenated with twenty-five members, it proudly presented its fiftieth concert. Yet the long crisis had taken its toll. Kompaneetz bitterly reported to the press that despite all his efforts to settle in Palestine, no institutional support was forthcoming; consequently he returned to Russia in June 1932 and the ensemble disbanded.[44] Obviously, conductors who had been accustomed to the European pattern of state-supported orchestras and operas found it difficult to adjust to the added burden of fund-raising in an unstable immigrant society.

Chamber Music and the Vogue of Societies

The platitude that music brings people together was well illustrated by the proliferation of music societies in Jerusalem and Tel Aviv. Some of them were ephemeral, a few serious and enduring, and all strongly imbued by local patriotism. Rosowsky observed that a delicate balance had formed between Tel Aviv and Jerusalem: 'Tel Aviv is the musical metropolitan of Palestine, but the best musicians reside in Jerusalem.'[45] This situation may explain the unremitting success of the Jerusalem Musical Society, founded in December 1921 at the bold initiative of the young cellist Thelma Yellin-Bentwich, and her sister, violinist Margery Bentwich.

Thelma Bentwich was born in 1895 as the ninth child of an aristocratic and highly educated British Jewish family, all the members of which received professional instrumental training.[46] A highly gifted cello student at the Royal College of Music in London, she was admitted by Pablo Casals, then already at the height of his career, as a private student and took lessons with him during his frequent visits to London. During World War I she studied with André Hekking in Paris. After returning to London in 1915, she embarked on a vigorous concert schedule, highlighted by her participation in an all-woman trio with Myra Hess

[44] *Ketuvim* (30 June 1932).   [45] A letter to Stutschewsky, 13 May 1928.
[46] Bentwich, *Thelma Yellin*, 9–14.

and Jelly d'Arranyi.[47] The pressure of concert life finally took its toll on the sensitive and emotional young woman. In October 1919 she suffered a nervous breakdown. She accepted the professional advice of radically changing her lifestyle and joined her brother and two sisters who had already settled in Jerusalem. A year later she married the engineer Eliezer Yellin. Her older sister, the violinist Margery Bentwich, came from England for the wedding and stayed in Jerusalem.[48] Thelma Yellin's initial resettlement was expedited by the cosmopolitan character of the German Colony, of which she wrote in her diary: 'The German Colony is just like a country village, the population equally divided between English and Arabs. Also some Indian soldiers. I am more at peace than I have ever been, I think. For the first time the sense of competition has left me, and I am content to be in the cycle of human life.'[49]

Like Shulamit Ruppin, this competent, strong-willed, and professionally independent young woman reacted to her immigration by transplanting the European model which best suited both her personal condition and her new surroundings. She substituted a chamber music society for the strenuous virtuoso career she had cast behind. From her memoirs one learns that the milieu of the Jerusalem Musical Society was dominated by the powerful presence of Europeans, by old European architecture, and by romantic orientalism:

The first concerts were in Mrs Gatling's house in a private flat. They were sponsored by Sir Ronald Storrs who was the first patron of music in Jerusalem. . . . Next door to Mrs Gatling's house was the International Cinema, afterwards called the Kleber Hall, which boasted a grand piano and had a sitting capacity of 300. The concert season was limited to the winter; and as the roads of Jerusalem were not asphalted and the hall not heated, the audience usually arrived mud-bespattered, and sat through the concert muffled in heavy wraps. Lighting was provided by a 'Lux' lamp which often drowned the playing. Hall after hall was tried, the most attractive and the best for sound being the 'Governorate' (Government offices) near the Damascus Gate. Vaulted ceilings and carved stone pillars lent charm to this hall and made it ideal acoustically. With no radio to blare music good or bad . . . one was thrown back on local resources and ready to pardon dilettantism. The Police Band boys, organized by

---

[47] The British pianist Dame Myra Hess (1890–1965) played her memorable début in 1907 under Sir Thomas Beecham. By 1915 she had established her reputation as one of the finest pianists in Europe. The Hungarian violinist Jelly d'Arranyi (1893–1966) had by then toured Europe and England. The two artists continued their joint performances for many years.

[48] Bentwich, *Thelma Yellin*, 45.

[49] An entry of May 1920, quoted in Bentwich, *Thelma Yellin*, 37, where fascinating additional quotes appear.

the late Captain Aubrey Silver were a never failing source of reinforcement. . . .
No one wanted a fee—it was done for the love of the thing.[50]

Thelma Yellin's unique position in the country was attested to when
M. Rosenstein apologized to Stutschewsky that a première of the latter's
piece had to be postponed since Thelma Yellin, 'the only good cellist in
the country, cannot perform now because of the delivery of her baby'.[51]

The backbone of the Society was the Jerusalem String Quartet, the
first professional chamber music ensemble founded in Palestine, which
persisted despite occasional personal changes in the second violin and
viola, and a piano trio, in which the finest pianists in Palestine alternated
with Margery Bentwich and Thelma Yellin.[52]

By the third season the Jerusalem Musical Society organized seven
concerts, and their number increased to nine in the next season. Sir
Ronald Storrs[53] was the president of the Society, and was succeeded by
the High Commissioners Lord Plummer and Sir John Chancellor. By the
1928/9 season the Society numbered 183 members, whose dues covered
the artists' honorarium, so that the ticket sales provided a surplus of about
£100, of which £80 was spent on the purchase of a piano and the rest
used to establish a scholarship at the Jerusalem School of Music 'in order
to assist some deserving child'.[54] The 1930/1 season turned international
with four concerts by guest artists, foremost of whom was the French
pianist Alfred Cortot, whose concert was 'the musical event of the
season'.[55] The following season featured the French pianist Lazare Levi,
who included his own sonatinas in his well-received recital.[56] The Society
sponsored a broad range of activities in addition to its regular subscription
concerts, such as lectures at private homes and gala concerts with international soloists, like the venerable pianist Emil von Sauer.[57] Mrs Landau,
one of the members, hosted a *Hausmusik* evening at her home, in which

---

[50] Thelma Yellin, 'Our First Concerts', *Palestine Post* (18 Jan. 1946). Quoted in Bentwich, *Thelma Yellin*, 48. Mrs Gatling was a wealthy Austrian woman.

[51] A letter of 12 Feb. 1930.

[52] The original members of the Jerusalem String Quartet were Margery Bentwich, Osnas, Bloch, and Thelma Bentwich/Yellin. The pianists were Sidney Seal, Arie Abilea, Traute Grünfeld, Judith Rosenthal, Lucille Bartzi (who was half-Arabic), and Nadia Etingon. Bentwich, *Thelma Yellin*, 47, 50.

[53] Storrs was the governor of Jerusalem.   [54] Menashe Ravina Collection.

[55] The other guests were the pianists Frans Goldenberg from Belgium and Irma Schoenberg from Romania (see Ch. 9, below), and the Krettly Quartet from Paris. The remaining two concerts featured the Jerusalem String Quartet and a cello and piano recital by Thelma Yellin and Sydney Seal. 'Jerusalem Musical Society', *Palestine Bulletin* (18 Oct. 1931).

[56] *Palestine Bulletin* (22 Dec. 1931).

[57] The Viennese pianist and composer Emil von Sauer (1862–1942) was Franz Liszt's student and a professor at the Music Academy. In 1917 he settled in Dresden.

wind-players of the Police Band joined the Jerusalem String Quartet and played Beethoven's Septet. The Jerusalem Musical Society persisted for fifteen years.

The regular attendance of British officials and notables in the concerts received special notice as a source of prestige. A review of a well-received recital by the opera-singer Vittorio Weinberg proudly reported the presence of the 'Officer Administering the Government' with Lady Davis, the Chief Justice, the Attorney General, and the Acting Chief-Secretary.[58]

Thelma Yellin soon realized the pitfall of limiting the Society to a social élite, and in 1930 she made a bold experiment with her sister

to hold weekly chamber-music concerts, the Saturday Evening 'Pops' in the Cardinal Ferrari Hall of the Terra Sancta College. We were warned by well wishers that not a soul would turn up to the concerts on Saturday nights, hitherto monopolized by cinemas; but the regularity of the concerts and the low price of the tickets confounded the pessimists, and the hall was always filled.[59]

The Saturday Evening Pops, modelled after the Sunday evening popu-lar concerts in the London South Place Institute, opened with a full cycle of Beethoven's quartets in chronological order, a remarkable accomplish-ment for a single ensemble. There was nothing popular about the pro-grammes themselves, but the style of the programme notes indicated that the target audience was different from the Jerusalem élite. To illustrate, there was the pathos-filled introduction to a Bach programme: 'Bach occupies in the musical world the same position as Moses in the religious. He established its *Torah* on which everything else was subsequently built.'[60] Tickets were sold for 49 mils and 100 mils, twice as much as the exceptionally low rates of the Concert Ensemble, but still much cheaper than the rates of 200–300 mils charged for regular concerts, such as Thelma Yellin's own recital in St John's Hotel in Jerusalem.[61] The strain of being 'organizers and business managers as well as musicians (we were ourselves the mainstay of the programme) was too great. After two seasons the "Pops" became defunct.'[62] An indirect indication of the local audience's taste was given when the two sisters based the programme of the last concert on popular vote, which selected Bach's two violin concertos, Brahms's E minor Cello Sonata, Beethoven's 'Appassionata' Sonata, and Cesar Franck's Piano Quintet.

By contrast, there was little cosmopolitan participation in the wild array of music societies, most of them ephemeral, which kept emerging

[58] *Palestine Bulletin* (27 July 1930).   [59] Bentwich, *Thelma Yellin*, 49–50.
[60] Concert at Terra Santa College, 28 Feb. 1927 (English text).   [61] 29 Dec. 1928.
[62] Bentwich, *Thelma Yellin*, 50.

in Tel Aviv. After a few abortive attempts, a more enduring Hebrew Music Society was formed in Tel Aviv in January 1925 by forty of the leading local musicians, among them Hopenko, Golinkin, Abilea, and Rosowsky. The Hebrew Music Society, which soon reached a membership of 150, preserved the pattern of programmes established by the Violin of Zion, in which a group of individual performers and different ensembles shared concerts such as a programme of a Beethoven early quartet, Arensky's Piano Trio, and Lieder by Brahms and Arensky, as well as the inevitable bow to Joel Engel. In his review David Rosolio defined the genre of chamber music as distinct from and superior to all other musical genres. While praising the size of the capacity audience, he rebuked it for its behaviour:

One should sympathize with the artists, who wish to generate a serious and concentrated mood, and instead must suffer constant disturbances, the banging of doors, chatter in the auditorium, long intervals between movements, and unbearable late comers. The education of an audience is something which has barely begun here.[63]

The small intellectual élite of Tel Aviv soon reacted and formed its own version of the Jerusalem Musical Society, whose monthly intimate chamber concerts addressed the most sophisticated group of immigrants from Europe, one of whom was quoted by Rosolio as saying: 'This is the first time since my immigration that I sense the typical mood which prevails at the European auditoriums.'[64] The German-educated Rosolio felt at home there and was uncompromising in his demands. He praised a programme of trios by Mozart, Beethoven, and Brahms which 'delineated historical development'. On the other hand, he objected to a diverse combination of Beethoven's Quartet Op. 74, unspecified works for two pianos by Debussy, and Dvorak's Trio, since

taking a bit of everything to cater to all tastes breaks the integrity of the programme. In my opinion one of the most important duties of the Society is to preserve an inner order and a logical line of development in our concert programmes, in accordance with the gradual development of the music. The Society should be concerned not only with momentary pleasure but with education as well.[65]

The organizers must have concurred with Rosolio, and indeed the sixth concert was an all-Brahms programme, with an introductory lecture by Menashe Rabinowitz. The prestigious position of the German-Austrian

[63] *Ha'Aretz* (9 Feb. 1926).
[64] D. Rosolio, 'The Music Society and its Activities', *Ha'Aretz* (4 Dec. 1927).
[65] *Ha'Aretz* (4 Dec. 1927).

repertory from Bach to Brahms was thus firmly established a long time before the influx of German immigrants in the next decade.

Here Comes the Star

The short-lived euphoria of the mid-twenties gave rise to a surge of internationally renowned visiting artists, most of whom were Jews. Not unexpectedly, their concerts followed the pattern of the late Romantic virtuoso recital, starting with one or two long sonatas and moving to a series of virtuoso show pieces. Yet whenever possible they made a deliberate effort to present a Jewish item. Since symphony orchestras were hard to recruit, violinists often played solo concertos with piano accompaniment. Such was Henri Marteau's recital, in which Bach's D minor Partita and Mendelssohn's Violin Concerto were followed by Saint-Saëns's Rondo Capriccioso, Paganini's Caprices, and four show-pieces by Marteau himself. Rosolio complained that such programmes placed the virtuoso rather than the music at the centre of the concert and that 'such respected guests . . . should consider their main duty to educate the audience to listen to the great masterpieces which are so rarely heard here.'[66] Menashe Rabinowitz started a review of violinist Samuel Dushkin's recital by expressing the wish that

our guests enrich us not only with fine and pleasant playing, but also with a programme which deserves to be listened to. It was hard to sit through an entire evening of light pieces, such as by Boccherini, Tartini, and Wieniawsky . . . the audience allowed the delectable sounds of the Italian and Polish music to affect its nerves, and was not interested in classical music.[67]

For the two leading music critics 'classical' was synonymous with 'German'. Needless to say, local reviews had little effect on the programmes. Heifetz's recital in Jerusalem on 14 April 1926 opened with a sonata by Grieg, followed by a succession of short virtuoso pieces and arrangements, among them Joseph Achron's Hebrew Melody, Bach's Air on a G String, Debussy's *La plus que lent*, and Paganini's Caprice No. 24.

The number of visiting virtuosos rose from six in 1926/7 to nine in 1928/9. It allowed the connoisseurs among the immigrants to overcome the feeling of having been uprooted from the musical centres of Europe, whereas the uninitiated were exposed to the supreme technical and artistic mastery. The prestige of some of the soloists and the artistic spell they cast brought about the best in audience attitude. Heifetz's recital

[66] *Ha'Aretz* (9 Mar. 1926).   [67] *Davar* (12 Apr. 1927).

attracted 'a crowded hall—packed literally almost to the roof—with a large number of people incredibly silent during the throbbing periods of the playing.'[68]

Some of the leading local musicians, however, warned that there were no roses without thorns. Jacob Weinberg noted that the concerts by visiting artists initiated a dangerous trend of social discrimination:

The great aesthetic enjoyment of the concerts by the great artists was unfortunately limited to the rich and well-to-do minority among us. . . . Most members of the audience have not even reached the stage of feeling the need to attend a concert by such a virtuoso. For example, one of the respectful Sephardim, when inquired whether he had attended Heifetz's concert, responded: 'Why should I pay 40 piasters for two hours of music, when I can buy a record and listen to Heifetz with my family as much as I like?[69]

David Rosolio cautioned that the level of satiety might have been reached: 'The large number, the rich contents, and the high level in most cases—all united to bake a European pie. . . . But all concerts address the same limited audience, so a certain fatigue has set in, and in the recent concerts of Gabrilowitz and Marteau the auditoriums were half empty.'[70] Professor David Schor pointed out the even more serious danger to the cultivation of local culture: 'As you see, Palestine has become a centre of attraction, whereas our intention is to make it a centrifugal force, that is to say, that Palestine will not expect artists from Europe, but rather send its own artists, especially musicians, to the world.'[71]

Most of the international virtuosos reacted with emotional excitement to their encounter with the vibrant immigrant community. Leopold Godowsky[72] who toured Palestine in December 1925 assumed the chair of the New York Committee for the establishment of a Jewish Conservatory in Jerusalem, which came to nothing. Violinist Jan Kubelik announced that 'in view of the great cultural work and the difficult living conditions here I will give a charity concert for the establishment of a symphony orchestra'.[73] Arthur Rubinstein[74] gave a fund-raising concert for the purchase of land in Palestine. The 25-year-old Jasha Heifetz

---

[68] *Palestine Bulletin* (15 Apr. 1926).   [69] *Ha'Aretz* (1 Oct. 1926).

[70] *Ha'Aretz* (5 July 1929).

[71] A letter to Stutschewsky, 13 Mar. 1929 (Stutschewsky Archive, AMLI Library, Tel Aviv).

[72] Leopold Godowsky (1870–1938) was one of the greatest piano virtuosos of the turn of the century, a pedagogue, and a prolific composer of piano music. He was born in Lithuania, where he started a brilliant career at a young age. He immigrated to the United States in 1914.

[73] *Do'ar Hayom* (17 Dec. 1926).

[74] Arthur Rubinstein's (1887–1982) first performances in Palestine in 1925 was the beginning of a lifelong dedication to and friendship with the Jewish community of Palestine and later of Israel.

endowed all the proceeds of his tour in 1926 to music schools in Palestine.

Music provided a compromise solution to the touchy issue of the attitude of Diaspora Jews to Zionism.[75] Since the establishment of the British mandate the Zionist movement had emerged as a significant political factor in the Jewish world, and leading Jews were faced with the emotionally difficult choice of defining themselves as either Zionists or anti-Zionists. The fertile cultural soil the artists discovered in Palestine gave rise to statements such as Heifetz's 'I was not and shall not be a Zionist in the political sense of the word, but I have always had an interest in Palestine, and when I heard of the love for art and music that exists here, I decided to help.'[76]

The End of a Decade

The first decade of British mandate was marked by constant wavering between grand visions and bitter reality. The general depression caused by the political deterioration and the economic crisis strongly affected the musical scene which experienced recurrent frustrations as a result of the collapse of the most promising institutions, the precarious existence of other ventures, the failure of still others to get off the ground, and the emigration of several fine but frustrated musicians. Nevertheless, two achievements of lasting importance were reached during this decade.

The first achievement was the formation of a professional élite. Those musicians who refused to give up their vision constituted an experienced corps which was to help absorb the sudden influx of the 1930s. A social analysis of the musician élite of the 1920s indicates the existence of two different groups, the first including the conductors and composers, and the second constituted by critics and performers. In his study of the social élites in the *Yishuv* during the period of the British Mandate Moshe Lissak has indicated that most members of the group of authors and artists among the cultural élite 'immigrated to the country before the age of 25 (37.5 per cent) and, moreover, about 61 per cent immigrated before the age of 35. One may safely assume that the artistic career of the members of this group started in most cases in Palestine.'[77] Lissak's sample of the cultural élite includes mostly authors and a few painters, but no musicians. The situation was more complex in the case of the musician

---

[75] See also Ch. 5, above.
[76] *Palestine Bulletin* (15 Apr. 1926) (two misprints tacitly amended).
[77] Lissak, *Elites of the Jewish Community in Palestine*, 94.

élite, which was divided into two groups. The larger group included composers, Jewish music scholars, and conductors, who were all born before 1890 and whose careers were well established before their immigration. Indeed, in the most salient cases, such as those of Golinkin, Engel, Schor, and Abilea, their careers induced their immigration rather than the other way round. This group was complemented by the small group of veteran musicians of the Ottoman period who stayed in Palestine, most notably Hopenko and Levit. The group of younger musicians who immigrated in their twenties was smaller, and it included only two conductors (Lampel and Fordhaus), a small group of fine instrumentalists (like Thelma Yellin, Margery Bentwich, and Shlomo Garter), as well as the two leading critics Rosolio and Rabinowitz. Most other players were hardly involved in chamber music and solo performances. The difference in age and experience between musicians on the one hand and authors and painters on the other, may be explained by the heavy institutional demands of the music profession in the context of the immigrant society. The élite musicians were involved in setting up elaborate hierarchical institutions, which required prestigious and experienced leaders, whereas the work of authors and painters was of a much more individual nature.

The second achievement during the 1920s was the formation of the institutional infrastructure of professional music education, music stores and libraries, and relentless music criticism. The musicians in Palestine took the lead in the controversial ideological and scholarly search for definition of Jewish music. The persistent musical activity expanded the musical audiences and gained international recognition of the Yishuv as a viable community of music consumers worthy of attention and support.

Economic and social recovery began in the year 1930, fueled by the renewal of immigration from Europe, which averaged 3,000 per year until 1932. From 1929 to 1932 Poland accounted for about two-thirds of the immigration and consequently the cultural upbringing of the audience remained virtually unchanged. Then a momentous upheaval took place in response to the Nazi rise to power. Only 150 immigrants came from Germany in 1932, whereas in 1933 their number leaped to 5,750. In a whimsical comment, Professor Schor predicted that a cultural shock was in the offing: 'only the Russian Jews have properly understood Palestine. With our American and German brothers everything is confined to intellect.'[78]

[78] Letter to Stutschewsky, 9 Mar. 1930.

7

A Scene Change
Enter the Germans

IN March 1933 the violinist Moshe Hopenko, director of the Shulamit Music School, wrote to Joseph Achron:

Boats are arriving carrying families from Germany whose children studied music with superb teachers there. They escaped persecutions in Germany, and they would like their children to resume their music lessons even before they complete their resettlement. They ask and even request that I allow the children to study, and they promise to pay as soon as everything calms down in Germany and they receive their property. Also, there are several excellent musicians who escaped from Germany and are looking for a place for peaceful life and work.[1]

The new immigration wave, named the Fifth Aliya, was the largest in the history of the Yishuv. The Jewish population of Palestine increased from 156,000 in 1928 to 445,000 on the eve of World War II.[2] Although Poland remained the main country of origin for Jewish immigration, the Fifth Aliya was nicknamed 'the German immigration' because of the distinctly individual character of the immigrants possessing a central European cultural orientation, whose share in the immigration wave was 82,000–90,000.[3] The German immigration instigated a mixed reaction in Palestine. On the one hand, it was the first immigration wave of a community threatened by violent persecutions and finally by annihil-

---

[1] A letter of 30 Mar. 1933 (Shulamit Archive, CZA M1/5/5).
[2] Gurevich and Gertz (eds.), *Statistical Handbook*, 45.
[3] Including Germany, Austria, Czechoslovakia, and in many respects also Hungary, where besides Bartók's and Kodály's endeavours in Hungarian music all music education was German. The different criteria which have been applied by the various agencies in estimating the total number of immigrants from central Europe in the years 1931–45 have led to significant discrepancies in estimating the total number of 'German' immigrants. Y. Gelber, *New Homeland* (Jerusalem, 1990), 64.

ation. On the other hand, the deterioration of the condition of the Jews in Germany until the outbreak of World War II was gradual. The bulk of the immigrants arrived after a period of deliberation and some made an exploratory visit as tourists. Moreover, during its first two years the Nazi régime encouraged the emigration of Jews, allowing them to take some of their money and possessions, so that they were regarded by the local residents of Palestine as well-to-do immigrants, even though in reality most of them had limited means.[4]

The Jewish immigrants from Germany entered a musical scene infused with the central European attitude to music. Most of the earlier immigrant musicians from Russia had absorbed a significant dose of German education and tradition, whether in their schooling in Russia or through advanced studies in Germany, and the brief flourishing of Jewish culture in Germany during the 1920s motivated the Russian-born musicians to turn to Germany as their anchor in Europe. To illustrate, Joel Engel found Berlin most congenial for his research work.[5] Menashe Rabinowitz took study leave in Germany in 1927, and David Schor's principal European connection was Joachim Stutschewsky who had become totally immersed in German culture by the time he settled in Vienna.[6] The German immigrants found Jerusalem and Haifa especially influenced by European spirit because of the massive presence of British military and administration. The Jerusalem concert of the Haifa-based Grand Band of the Second Battalion, Seaforth Highlander's Band and Pipers under Arthur Brundsen at the YMCA auditorium included band music, Highland dancing, cello-playing by Thelma Yellin, and finally 'reached its climax in Ekersburg's grand descriptive fantasia, *The Battle of Waterloo*.[7] Mrs Davis, a British music teacher, expanded her small music school in Jerusalem into the Philharmonic College of Music which established a 'Jerusalem branch of the British Music Makers' Guild'.[8] Thus conditions were ripe for the assertion and the preservation of the ethnic identity of the German immigrants, the most pervasive expression of which was European art music.[9] Yet the admiration for German culture conflicted with an anxiety concerning the danger of a wave of well-trained musicians who would flood the already-saturated job market. Thus, David Schor reported that 'musicians from Germany have been arriving . . . We

---

[4] Ibid. 222–3.   [5] See Ch. 5, above.

[6] Stutschewsky spoke no German at all when he first came to Leipzig in 1914 as a cello student. *Memoirs of a Jewish Musician*, 42.

[7] *Palestine Post* (7 June 1933).

[8] *Palestine Post* (4 Oct. 1933). The Guild was first established in England in 1924.

[9] P. V. Bohlman, *The Land where Two Streams Flow* (Urbana, Ill., 1989), 100.

warmly welcome them, but they deprive the local musicians of their daily bread.'[10]

The music societies reacted to the immigration as the most efficient shock absorber, especially the venerable Jerusalem Musical Society which offered the German immigrants a 'home away from home'. The report of the Society for the season 1932/3 mirrored the major change in the pattern of immigration. One of the first immigrants from central Europe was the first violinist of the Budapest Quartet, Emil Hauser[11] who was invited immediately upon his arrival to join the Jerusalem String Quartet as the first violinist.[12] The Society presented an ambitious season of ten concerts, the highlight of which was Alice Ehlers's harpsichord recital which introduced the instrument for the first time to Palestine.[13] The Jerusalem String Quartet was the backbone of the season, performing four of the concerts. Its programmes were dominated by Haydn, Beethoven, and Schubert, but the Quartet also hailed the immigration of the German-born composer Erich Walter Sternberg[14] by a performance of his difficult Quartet No. 2. The Jerusalem String Orchestra, an *ad hoc* ensemble, opened the season with a programme of Corelli, Vivaldi, Bach, and Mozart. Another German immigrant, the bass singer and composer Karl Salomon,[15] performed a recital just after his immigration. The rich season was complemented by a programme of folk arrangements by the French singer Madeleine Grey. The Jewish repertory of Hanigun group, however, received merely a token recognition, with a single folk arrangement by Engel. In 1932/3 the Society numbered 216 members, in most cases two or more members of the same family, representing all sectors of the Jerusalem élite, including the respected ancient Sephardi families of Kokia, Valero, and Hakhmi-Schwili; most of the small faculty of the Hebrew University, headed by Provost Magnes; and Zionist leaders, such as Menahem Ussishkin. A public accountancy firm donated its services

[10] A letter to Stutschewsky, 21 June 1933 (Stutschewsky Archive, AMLI Library, Tel Aviv).

[11] The original Budapest Quartet, founded in 1921, included Emil Hauser, Imre Poganyi, Istvan Ipolyi, and Hary Son. Both Hauser and Son immigrated to Palestine with the Fifth Aliya.

[12] Emil Hauser studied with Sevcik at the Academy of Music in Vienna. The other members were Shlomo Garter, Jeny Schmerzler, who immigrated from Berlin, and Thelma Yellin.

[13] The Viennese-born Alice Ehlers was Wanda Landowska's first prominent student. She toured Palestine immediately after quitting her position at the Berlin Hochschule. H. Schott, 'Ehlers, Alice', *New Grove* vi. 77.

[14] Sternberg (1891–1974) was trained in Berlin and was close to the avant-garde circles. His arrival in 1931 signalled the onset of the immigration of composers from central Europe. See Ch. 10, below.

[15] Salomon (1899–1974), who later Hebraized his last name to Shalmon, immigrated in 1933. See Ch. 10, below.

and issued a statement to the effect that the Society maintained a balanced budget.[16]

The Jerusalem Musical Society established a lasting social pattern bordering on a ritual, as described in Philip Bohlman's field work report of a concert held in the mid-1980s.[17]

The hospitable reception in Jerusalem encouraged new initiatives which diversified the concert repertory. The composer and bass singer Karl Salomon grouped a small choir which performed the school-opera *Der Jasager* by Kurt Weill and Bertold Brecht, barely three years after its Berlin première. Salomon extended the unconventional character of his concert to the other half of the programme, which included 'examples of choir training'. The anonymous critic concluded that 'Mr Salomon's decision to make Jerusalem his home augurs well for the future musical activities of the city.' Such initiatives, however, further fragmented the Jerusalem audience, since only 'a few enthusiasts . . . attended the excellent performance'.[18]

The Heyday of the Piano

A salient feature of the immigration from Germany was the surge in the local piano market. The piano agencies which had dominated the small local market in the 1920s could not afford to specialize, and combined the import of various musical instruments with trade in sheet music, even dealing with concert management. Kowalsky, a piano-tuner by profession, started a general music store in Tel Aviv in 1914, which developed into a chain of music stores in Tel Aviv, Jerusalem, and Haifa. The growing market created by the Fifth Aliya paved the way for S. Kleinmann who founded in 1933 the first agency which specialized in piano business.[19] The sharp curves in the pattern of immigration from central Europe in the 1930s resulted in an erratic piano market, as seen in Table 7.1.

The total figures of pianos imported represent the expected lag between the demand created by immigration and the reaction of the few piano agents who could not afford to keep any unsold stock. The table indicates that the renewed immigration correlated with the sharp rise of

---

[16] Jerusalem Musical Society, Report for Season 1932–1933. Ravina Collection.
[17] *Land where Two Streams Flow*, 1–2.   [18] *Palestine Post* (31 Oct. 1933).
[19] Interview with Professor Zacaria Kalai-Kleinmann, 3 May 1991.

TABLE 7.1 The Import of Pianos to Palestine

Country of origin	1928	1929	1931	1932	1933	1934	1935	1936	1937	1938	1939	1940	1941
UK	3	3	2	11	13	49	133	37	23	12		6	
Germany	69	74	41	43	95	106	89	32	94	33	49	61	21
Austria	13	21	12	21	67	69	49	13					
USA	2	1	4	5			33	37			1		
France	28	18											
Czech		3	2	3	15	30	38	9		8		3	
Other	4	9	6	5	26	23	30	9	31	5	4		
TOTAL	119	129	67	95	216	294	372	101	148	58	54	70	21

Total pianos imported 1928–41: 1,744

Notes: There are no records for 1930. The import of pianos stopped completely in 1942 and was renewed only after the war. The category of 'Other' is irregular in the statistical reports, and data about countries from which no more than two or three pianos originated were added to this category in the source. In the present table, countries from which less than five pianos arrived during the entire period were grouped under this category.

Sources: Government of Palestine, Department of Customs, Excise, and Trade, *Statistics of Imports, Exports, and Shipping 1928–1945* (Library of the Central Bureau of Statistics, Jerusalem).

import in 1933–5. The agents maintained commercial links only with England and Germany. The sharp decline in imports of German and Austrian pianos between 1934 and 1935–7 is in inverse proportion to the sudden rise in immigration from those countries, which reached about 7,700 in 1934, and more than 6,000 in both 1935 and 1936.[20] The reason was that commercial piano imports were taxed by the British customs and were entered into the financial records, whereas immigrants who shipped their pianos as part of their personal luggage were exempt from duty, so that not all imported pianos were included in the customs statistics.[21] The Nazi government imposed a limit on the flow of money from Germany, and the Jewish emigrants resorted to a complex system of bank transfer.[22] This involved a certain pecuniary loss in return for the permit to take certain house effects out of Germany, of which pianos represented the most solid investment. The immigrants who were in need of ready cash for resettlement and frequently short of space in their crammed temporary lodgings, flooded the market with used pianos, thereby pushing prices down. It is almost impossible to establish any statistics or any pattern of decisions in such unstable circumstances. Some of the middle-class families decided to leave their pianos in Germany since they anticipated a radical change in their living space, so there was no correlation between the economic condition of the immigrants and the rate of piano imports. To illustrate, Mr Adin Talbar (b. 1921 in Berlin) reported that his mother, who was a fine pianist, left her piano behind since the family substituted a small three-room apartment for a spacious seven-room flat in Berlin upon their immigration in 1935.[23] A random survey taken among twenty-eight members of the Jerusalem branch of the Organization of Immigrants from Central Europe[24] indicated that six of them brought their pianos to Palestine, of whom four sold them immediately for economic reasons and one donated the piano to a school. Two of those who did not import pianos rented instruments soon after their immigration. The result of the new situation was that most of Kleinmann's business during the 1930s involved the purchase of second-hand instruments which were then reconditioned, if necessary, and resold. Consequently there was no need to import new German and

---

[20] Gurevish and Gertz (eds.), *Statistical Handbook*, 104–5.

[21] Pianos imported separately were charged a flat rate of £10 for an upright and £20 for a grand, regardless of quality and value.

[22] The Hebrew term was *Ha'avara* (transfer) which was legally controlled by the Jewish agency.

[23] A telephone interview, June 1992.

[24] A telephone survey, 1992, according to the mailing list in *Kurzbiographien von Mitgliedern der Israelisch-Deutschen Gesellschaft Arbeitsgemeinschaft Jerusalem* (Jerusalem, 1991). The survey does not aspire to statistical validity.

Austrian pianos.[25] Kowalsky, who sold only new pianos, advertised the expensive labels of Steinway, Bechstein, and Grotrian-Steinweg, but most of his business involved English pianos by Brasted of which he imported up to fifty per year. Prices of used pianos went down from £40 to £20– £30. A new upright sold for £60 but the agencies requested only a third of the price in down payment and the rest in forty instalments, so clients could overcome the price difference if they wished to have a new instrument. An average monthly salary of a civil servant was £12, and that of a policeman about £6, so even used pianos were by no means cheap. Yet the pianist Arthur Zavadi, who was at that time an employee at Kowalsky's, reported that the demand for pianos during the 1930s was relatively high and matched the supply, so that prices remained stable. Most buyers were parents who bought instruments for their children.[26] The clientele included members of the Arab aristocracy as well as British military personnel who bought pianos for use in their many camps.[27] The best quality Blüthner or Bechstein grands with a price tag of £120 were beyond the reach of nearly all customers, whether private or institutions. The Palestine Conservatoire in Jerusalem[28] purchased only one Blüthner upright piano for £40. Four additional upright pianos were given on temporary loan by friends of the school. The Conservatoire rented grands for certain concerts at a high cost, which was relieved only when the Hebrew University allowed the use of its Steinway grand.[29] The other music schools owned only cheap used instruments, and even the prestigious Palestine Orchestra could not afford the purchase of a fine grand. Aware of the demand, Kleinmann imported in 1937 two Blüthner concert grands, placing one in Tel Aviv and the other in Jerusalem. They were regularly on loan to the Palestine Orchestra for £2 per concert, and were moved from time to time to other locations.[30] The owners of the piano stores provided tuning and repair services for a relatively high rate of about £1 for tuning, providing them with a regular income in an otherwise unstable market.

The outbreak of World War II halted imports completely, but the thousands of pianos which had reached Palestine within about ten years of the war kept the second-hand piano market alive.

[25] In 1935 Kleinmann also imported a few American pianos by Winter and Janssen. See Ehrlich, *Piano*, 219–20.

[26] An interview with Mr Arthur Zavadi (b. 1912, immigrated 1934), June 1992.

[27] The outbreak of the prolonged Arab revolt in Apr. 1936 caused a massive deployment of British troops.

[28] See Ch. 10, below.   [29] Annual Report, 1943 (Hauser Archive, JNUL).

[30] It was only after the foundation of the State of Israel that Max Targ donated a fine concert grand to the orchestra, then already the Israeli Philharmonic Orchestra.

The popularity of the piano as a musical instrument, a status symbol and a culture symbol reached its peak in Palestine during the 1930s, sharply contrasting its abrupt decline in the United States and in Europe at the same time. Cyril Ehrlich has suggested three reasons for the crippling of the piano industry: 'alternative sources of entertainment, erosion of the instrument's social status, and the crash and depression of the 1930s.'[31] It is noteworthy that none of those three reasons obtained in Palestine at that time. As to alternative home entertainment, local radio broadcast commenced only in 1936, and even then Hebrew programmes were limited to about four hours per day. The motor car, which had become 'the most formidable rival' of the piano[32] was a rare commodity in Palestine, where only 6,700 private cars were registered in 1939,[33] and no young couple could ever conceive of getting one as a wedding present. As to the economic situation, it was precisely the capital brought in by the German immigration which helped in overcoming the depression of the late 1920s. Moreover, since the market was dominated by personal imports of second-hand pianos, it was not influenced by the extreme drop in production of new pianos in Germany and in the United States at that time.

Opera—The Grounded Phoenix

Having returned empty-handed from the United States, Golinkin was so encouraged by the economic recovery in Palestine that he immediately attempted a revival of the Palestine Opera. Yet the grand vision of the *Temple of the Arts* was no longer evoked. From that time on, it was merely an uphill struggle for survival. Golinkin turned to the traditional warhorse, Johann Strauss's *Zigeunerbaron*,[34] followed two months later by a daring production of Anton Rubinstein's *The Demon*. The columnist Y. Roschuk hailed the production as 'an evidence that there is no obstacle a true artist will not overcome'.[35] Yet the Russian expressionism which dominated the production no longer appealed to the younger audience who regarded the production as 'ridiculous'.[36] After yet another long interval Golinkin marked the tenth anniversary of the Palestine Opera

---

[31] *Piano*, 184.   [32] Ibid. 185.

[33] The Jewish population then numbered 474,000, that is, there was at most one car per seventy-two persons, but the actual proportions were much lower, because the figures included many official vehicles which belonged to Arabs. See S. Ettingen, 'Transportation', in *Encyclopedia Hebraica* 6, 958.

[34] Premièred in Apr. 1932.   [35] Y. Roschuk, *Ha'Aretz* (6 June 1932).

[36] An interview with the historian Shulamit Laskov, Aug. 1991, then a promising violin student.

with a double-bill of Leoncavallo's *I pagliacci* and Mascagni's *Cavaleria rusticana*. By then Golinkin addressed the new critical audience of German immigrants which was unaware of his pioneering achievements. In the summer of 1933 the composer and conductor Paul Ben-Haim (Frankenburger) came to Palestine for an exploratory visit in preparation for his immigration soon after. On the basis of his rich experience as a well-received conductor at Munich and Augsburg opera houses, he reported to his sister: 'Last night I attended what passes for opera here. . . . Among the singers, at least those who were not beyond their prime, there were a few who had good voices. The chorus is good but uncultivated. The conductor is mediocre. . . . The orchestra—no comment. . . . The staging and the decor are impossible.'[37] Golinkin's production of *The Barber of Seville* during the worst days of the Arab revolt of 1936 was praised as 'further proof of the Jewish strong will',[38] so that admiration of the conductor's persistence replaced admiration of his musical personality. Confidence in the operatic establishment was dissipated to such an extent that a radio broadcast of *Carmen* was referred to in the review as a 'substitute until we have an opera here'.[39]

Golinkin's admirers brought out a modest compilation of brief essays to mark the tenth anniversary of the Palestine Opera.[40] Beyond the expected extolling rhetoric, the essays reflected the conflicting expectations from the visionary opera. The prestigious poet Saul Tschernichovsky[41] deplored the absence of musicality in the modern Hebrew poetry and the outlandish accent of even local youngsters. He complained that each theatre had a Hebrew accent of its own. The opera was his last hope 'because it is all music, all ears'.[42] Abraham Zamir considered arts and culture in Palestine as a means for the transition of 'our ancient–new homeland' from an Asian to a European disposition, thus contradicting the entire eastward ideology.[43] The poetess Elisheva revived the socialist issue and happily reported that the comments made at the back rows during the production of *Rigoletto* had all expressed 'deep and direct involvement in the unfolding of the drama'.[44]

The immigration from Central Europe soon paved the way for a diversification of the operatic realm. In May 1934 the stage director Beno

[37] Letter of 13 June 1933. See Hirshberg, *Paul Ben-Haim*, 107.

[38] Roschuk, *Ha'Aretz* (31 July 1936).   [39] Hermann Swet, *Ha'Aretz* (21 Mar. 1937).

[40] *Hoveret Ha'Opera Ha'Arzisre'elit* (Tel Aviv, 1935).

[41] Tschernichovsky (1875–1943) had known Golinkin in Odessa. He immigrated to Palestine in 1931 and was very involved in political and cultural issues.

[42] *Booklet of the Palestine Opera*, 9.   [43] Ibid. 29.

[44] Ibid. 25. Elisheva (Elisabetta Jirkova, 1880–1949) was a non-Jewish Russian poetess who turned to Hebrew and immigrated to Palestine in 1925.

Frankel and the conductors Hans (Hanan) Schlesinger and Karl Solomon launched a new venture of a chamber opera with a modest and well-received production of Pergolesi's *La serva padrona* followed a year later by Mozart's *The Abduction from the Seraglio*. The Chamber Opera followed Golinkin in its insistence on productions in Hebrew. Yet the German-speaking singers did not fare any better than their Russian predecessors: 'Nothing of that which was sung on stage could be understood because of the appalling accent.'[45] Hebrew remained a most touchy issue, reflecting the chasm between the dream of the tiny literary elite and the reality of a heterogeneous multilingual immigrant community.

The fascination with the operatic dream persisted against all odds. Another short-lived attempt was made just before the outbreak of World War II. The composer and opera conductor Alexander Boskovitch (1907–1964) immigrated in 1938 from Cluj, Transylvania, where he conducted the fine local opera.[46] Young and energetic, he gained the support of his closest friend, the brilliant stage director Y. Daniel, and they jointly launched a new venture in May 1939 with a production of Offenbach's *The Tales of Hoffmann*. Critic M. Rabinowitz wrote with a mixture of cynicism and careful optimism, that 'had the founders of the Hebrew opera known of the difficulties encountered by the Palestine Opera, . . . they would have given up'.[47] Offenbach's opera was repeated five times on the crammed stage of Ohel Shem auditorium in Tel Aviv, thus hampering all dramatic illusion despite the fine singers. The critics were tolerant and supportive. Yet, with the opening of the next season all that Rabinowitz could wryly report was that 'a Hebrew opera was born in 1939. It is no longer alive.'[48]

As if in a surrealistic dream, Golinkin persisted, reacting to the outbreak of war in 1940 with a well-timed revival of Halevy's *La Juive*, instigating the comment that 'the relevance of *La Juive* which depicts the suffering and the hardship of the Jews brings the production closer to the heart of the audience.'[49]

Against the backdrop of the gloomy news from Europe a group of opera singers launched the Palestine Folk Opera, which opened with Johann Strauss's *Die Fledermaus* in February 1941. Well aware of financial pitfalls, the members of the group organized as a co-operative of 115 singers, orchestral players, dancers, and technical staff. The title 'folk' represented the intent to relieve the new endeavour of a grand ideology and to stress its appeal to the public. Indeed, the repertory of the

[45] M. Rabinowitz, *Davar* (23 May 1935).   [46] See Ch. 10, below.
[47] *Davar* (5 May 1939).   [48] 'Music in 1939', *Davar* (13 Sept. 1939).
[49] M. Rabinowitz, *Davar* (18 June 1940).

Palestine Folk Opera until 1946, which included seventeen operas, was heavily inclined in the direction of popular operettas by Lehar, Offenbach, and Johann Strauss the younger. Four conductors participated, and the ageing Golinkin was acknowledged through his appointment as honourary conductor. Still, the new opera earned the credit of the first production of a locally composed Hebrew opera, Marc Lavri's *Dan the Guard*.[50]

The Symphony Orchestra—More of the Same

The revival of immigration and the improved economic and political conditions encouraged renewed efforts to establish a regular symphony orchestra. Yet, the pattern of *ad hoc* recruitments was at its worst when new immigrant conductors began competing with old-timers for sponsors, musicians, and audience. A columnist writing under the pseudonym Abu-Dan reacted with a scathing reprimand:

Dear Friend, Indeed, you are green in this country. Three months ago you read in the newspaper that a philharmonic society was founded in Tel Aviv and now you wish to inquire about the society's activities. Which society? Three months have elapsed and you still think we have only one philharmonic society? Well, you are not acquainted with our tempo. Within three months we have founded three philharmonic societies. Our main worry now is which society to subscribe to?[51]

On a more serious note, the conductor Wolfgang Friedlander bluntly stated that no symphony orchestra would ever materialize without musicians who 'would be available at all times'.[52] Professionalism finally won over vanity, and after long and exhausting negotiations an agreement was signed for the unification of the disparate societies into a regular orchestra, the Symphonic-Philharmonic Union which started a concert series in November 1934. Mainstream Classical and Romantic repertory prevailed, with occasional new music, such as a suite from the ballet *The Demon* by Paul Hindemith,[53] whose brave opposition to the Nazi regime had won him the admiration of the Yishuv.[54] Four local conductors alternated, foremost among them was Michael Taube, who had been a member of the Berlin State Opera since 1924.[55] Yet, after a few successful

[50] Lavri (1903–67) immigrated in 1935. The production took place in 1945. See Chs. 10, 15, below.

[51] *Davar* (5 Apr. 1934).   [52] *Ha'Aretz* (23 Jan. 1934).   [53] *Davar* (3 Jan. 1935).

[54] M. Rabinowitz, 'Towards Final Deterioration', *Davar* (15 Jan. 1935). Hindemith moved to Switzerland in 1938, and emigrated to the United States in 1940.

[55] E. Thalheimer, *Five Years of the Palestine Orchestra* (Tel Aviv, 1942), 10.

concerts the critic M. Ravina suddenly discovered that the ensemble was skating on thin ice:

Having dropped in by chance on one of the rehearsals I realized that in reality we have no symphony orchestra. The existence of the orchestra depends on many factors which have nothing to do with music. I have found out that a significant group of players has been recruited from amongst the British military stationed in Jerusalem. . . . Undoubtedly they are fine music-lovers who eagerly foster a musical project in this country. But could such dependence on them become a regular state of affairs? . . . The conductor is frequently forced to select the programme and to schedule the concerts not in accordance with his own plans and with our social life, but according to the timetable of the army stationed in Jerusalem.[56]

The main snag was the near-absence of competent wind-players and the uneven string quality, compounded by lack of discipline and irregular membership and attendance, to the extent that the conductors lost control and occasionally were heard screaming at the players during the performances.[57] The severe immigration quota hampered the chance of attracting fine players of instruments which the orchestra badly needed. The British administration classified each application according to four categories, and only applicants who had a capital of at least £1,000 or professionals backed by local employers were granted certificates without any difficulty. Some entered illegally and many were refused. No orchestra in the country held a formal status to officially qualify as an employer. The shaky orchestra outshone itself when it played under the great guest conductor Oscar Fried, but even he could not overcome occasional awkward wind sounds and bad orchestral balance.[58] It appeared that all local potential of organization, fund raising, and selection of musicians has been exhausted with disappointing results. A dramatic coup from the outside was needed in order to rescue the stranded boat and shoot upwards to the desired goal of a fully professional and representative orchestra. And the coup did occur.

[56] 'Do We have an Orchestra?', *Ha'Aretz* (6 Feb. 1935).   [57] *Davar* (2 Apr. 1935).
[58] *Davar* (2 Apr. 1935). Oskar Fried (1871–1941) had just moved from Germany to Tbilisi in protest over the rise of the Nazi regime. Heinz Becker, 'Fried, Oskar', *MGG* iv. 945.

8

From Pan-Europe to the Palestine Orchestra

THE creation of the Palestine Orchestra was a milestone in the history of music in Palestine which was effected with dramatic international reverberations. The new orchestra revolutionized the musical scene, provided the infrastructure for professional musical education and for local composition, and marked the culmination of the process of the professional stratification of music institutions in Palestine. It soon set a model of institutional tenacity and stability in troubled times.[1]

Unlike previous ventures which were instigated by local immigrant musicians, the creation of the Palestine Orchestra was a daring enterprise from the outside. Its initiator, the violinist Bronislaw Huberman,[2] inadvertently followed the pattern set by Golinkin and Schor in that his project was conceived as a means to achieve a grand visionary goal. Yet Huberman commanded a high international prestige and an access to financial resources which provided him with a much better starting-point.

Huberman was an ardent advocate of the pan-European movement[3] in which he accorded a central role to the Jews, since he was always of the

---

[1] The Palestine Orchestra, later the Israel Philharmonic Orchestra, is the only performing institution described in the present book which has persisted to the present day with no significant structural change. See U. Toeplitz, *The History of the Israel Philharmonic Orchestra Researched and Remembered* (Tel Aviv, 1992); J. Hirshberg, 'Israel Philharmonic Orchestra', in R. Craven (ed.), *Symphony Orchestras*, 202.

[2] Huberman (1882–1947) was born in Czestochowa, Poland. In 1892 Joseph Joachim accepted him as his pupil in Berlin. He started a brilliant career as a child, which included a sensational performance of Brahms's Violin Concerto in the presence of the composer.

[3] B. Huberman, 'Mein Weg zu Paneuropa', *Paneuropa*, 2 (1925); id., *Vaterland Europa* (Berlin, 1932). See P. E. Gradenwitz, 'Huberman, Bronislaw', *MGG* vi. 815.

opinion 'that there is nothing more European than the Jews'.[4] Huberman
went as far as to define himself as a European in his national affiliation.[5]
He did not consider himself a Zionist and was even concerned that
Zionism might hamper the fulfilment of the mission of the Jews in the
world.

Huberman's first encounter with the Yishuv was his concert tour in
March 1929. The local audience, though by then spoiled with international soloists, was overwhelmed by Huberman's strongly individual
interpretation of masterpieces such as Bach's Chaconne and Beethoven's
Sonata in A major ('Kreutzer' Sonata). David Rosolio noted that
Huberman's powerful influence stemmed exclusively from his artistic
performance, since he lacked personal charisma.[6] Huberman's second
visit two years later turned out to be a festive event and his concert in
Jerusalem was attended by the High Commissioner. Yet in an interview
for the *Neues Wiener Journal*, Huberman reiterated his belief in a European
orientation and commented that 'it would be a tragedy if the Jewish
people sever its links with Europe'.[7] In his third tour in January 1934
Huberman played twelve concerts in eighteen days for excited capacity
audiences and found himself surrounded by warm friends. The moving
experience 'provoked a fundamental change in my attitude and interest in
Palestine', he later wrote.[8] It followed his refusal to perform in Nazi
Germany, which was widely publicized in the European media and in an
open letter in the *New York Times*. The rise of Fascism in Europe dealt the
death blow to the pan-European movement and diverted Huberman's
interest towards Palestine, where he found himself deeply inspired by the
'atmosphere of mysticism'[9] which contrasted with his inherent European
rationalism. Yet his final decision to endorse the Jewish endeavour in
Palestine emanated from the social transformation of the transplanted
culture: 'I believe firmly that Palestine will in a short time be the first
country where the human humiliation of a culture limited only to one
class or section will disappear, the first country where we shall witness the
miracle of an entire community culture.'[10] Upon his return to England
Huberman wrote in the *Zionist Record* that 'there are individual idealists
everywhere. But mass idealism, collective idealism, as it exists in Palestine,

---

[4] Huberman, 'An Address at the Home of Gershon Agronsky', Jerusalem, 22 Jan. 1934 (1st. pub.
in *Hadassah News Letter* (Jan. 1935), in I. Ibbeken and T. Avni (eds.), *An Orchestra is Born* (Tel Aviv,
1969), 8. Ida Ibbeken was Huberman's loyal personal secretary, and the book contains all
Huberman's letters and documents pertaining to the founding of the Palestine Orchestra, as
preserved in the Huberman Archive, AMLI Library, Tel Aviv.

[5] Huberman, 'Address', 8.   [6] *Ha'Aretz* (20 Mar 1929).

[7] Haifa, 14 Jan. 1931. Ibbeken, and Avni (eds.), *Orchestra is Born*, 7.

[8] Ibid. 9.   [9] Ibid.   [10] Ibid. 11.

cannot be found in any other country in the world. That is one of the reasons why I no longer see any incompatibility between my Pan-Europeanism and Palestine.'[11]

From that point on Huberman became fully immersed in the implementation of his grand social and cultural vision, embodied in the project of a professional symphony orchestra. Embittered by the growing wave of anti-Semitism, Huberman expected the orchestra to function as a most potent response: 'Can you imagine a pro-Jewish and pro-Zionist propaganda more effective than a concert tour of the Palestine Orchestra, undertaken in a couple of years throughout the civilized world and acclaimed both by Jews and Gentiles as amongst the best in existence?'[12] Huberman envisioned a series of impressive international festivals in which masterpieces on biblical themes would be presented in their 'natural historical surroundings'. Such festivals would not only increase the prestige of the Jews all over the world but would also contribute to the economy of the country.[13] Huberman also suggested an exchange programme with the Cairo Opera, which would provide the orchestra with additional engagements and increase the co-operation with the neighbouring countries.[14]

Turning to the local audience, Huberman's excitement about the social milieu in the country made him insist that the projected orchestra commit itself to regular series of low-priced concerts for workers and students.

An important factor in the project was the cultivation of professional music education, which would begin with a high school of music from the age of 10 and continue to a music academy. The musicians of the proposed orchestra were expected to teach at the academy. In a discussion with the leading local performers he expressed his opposition to virtuosity and to the raising of child prodigies, and wished to effect a return to the model of Bach's period when each musician had mastered several instruments and the figured bass.[15]

The response of the rank-and-file musicians in the country was no different from that of their cohorts in England who were afraid that the best performers of Europe would take over their limited job opportunities.[16] Yet they differed from the British musicians in that their

[11] Ibid. 15.

[12] A letter to Mr Zieff, 30 Apr. 1934 (ibid. 17).

[13] A lecture to members of the Palestine press, Dec. 1935 (ibid. 22).

[14] A letter to Mayor of Tel Aviv, Meir Dizengoff, 27 Jan. 1934.

[15] A discussion with Emil Hauser, Thelma Yellin, and the violinist Wolfgang Schocken, recorded by Thelma Yellin (Ibbeken and Avni (eds.), Orchestra is Born, 13).

[16] Ehrlich, Music Profession in Britain, 221.

concern was purely economic, since they could not relate to Jewish refugees as 'foreigners' or as people endangering 'native musical art'.[17] Huberman quelled their fear, claiming that the proposed orchestra would recruit not only immigrants but also the best local musicians, who would then leave their jobs in cafés and cinemas and provide openings for other musicians. In this way the proposed orchestra would indeed expand rather than limit the job market.[18]

Huberman first tried to use the existing Symphonic-Philharmonic Union as a nucleus for his projected orchestra. While rehearsing Bach's and Beethoven's violin concertos with them he 'took the conductor's baton, multiplied the number of rehearsals, and trained the musicians of the orchestra with patience and pedantic attention.'[19] Yet he was soon disenchanted with the low professional level and furious with the inadequate management of the local orchestra. Consequently, his initially friendly attitude became authoritative: 'I had to impose my will on them ruthlessly when I finally succeeded in convening a meeting of a few interested people . . . There all my proposals were accepted with acclamation.'[20] From that point on Huberman displayed increasing impatience with any bureaucratic snag, such as when he threatened Meir Dizengoff, the Mayor of Tel Aviv, that he would withhold the money raised at a benefit concert unless the projected orchestra be exempt from city taxes.[21]

Huberman embarked upon an intensive fund-raising campaign, to which he added correspondence with any international conductor or soloist whom he considered sensitive to the cause of the Jewish people or to his humanist ideology.[22] His enthusiasm was catching, and the brilliant young conductor Issay Dobrowen organized a fund raising concert in San Francisco.[23] Huberman's dedication to his project made him increasingly fearful of any semblance of competition. He therefore reacted angrily to the news of the pending plans to start a radio service in Palestine 'which would crush musical life here as it has done elsewhere'.[24] Huberman was not alone at that time in regarding radio as competitor rather than an audience-builder. As a travelling virtuoso, he must have

---

[17] Ibid.

[18] An address to the press, Tel Aviv, Dec. 1935 (Ibbeken and Avni (eds.), *Orchestra is Born*, 22).

[19] Yariv Ezrahi, *Turim* (8 Feb. 1934).

[20] A letter to Mr Sieff, 30 Apr. 1934 (Ibbeken and Avni (eds.), *Orchestra is Born*, 17).

[21] A letter to the Mayor of 27 Jan. 1934, and to Shlomo Lewertoff, 1 July 1936. The request was finally granted and became a legal precedent until the present day.

[22] See letters to Pablo Casals, Issay Dobrowen, George Szell, and others in Ibbeken and Avni (eds.), *Orchestra is Born*.

[23] An interview with Dobrowen, *Ha'Aretz* (29 Jan. 1937).

[24] A letter to Emil Hauser, 30 Sept. 1935 (Ibbeken and Avni (eds.), *Orchestra is Born*, 18).

been aware of the stormy public controversy about the role of the BBC in British musical life which burst out in 1936.[25]

The alarming news of the mass sacking of leading Jewish musicians from German orchestras effected a major change in Huberman's plans which turned more and more into a rescue operation. Huberman was stunned by the refusal of the European democracies to admit the refugees, who could have enriched the culture of their countries in the same way that the Huguenot immigration had been a blessing to Prussia and England. Huberman wryly commented that from the local point of view the catastrophe in Germany created the best conditions for the founding of a fine orchestra.[26] The conductors Michael Taube, Hans Wilhelm Steinberg, and Issay Dobrowen undertook the delicate duty of holding preliminary auditions for the scores of sacked Jewish musicians from central Europe who presented their candidacy, following which Huberman himself conducted the final auditions in three European cities. Huberman reached far beyond a direct rescue operation in Germany and held auditions in other European cities and on a few occasions he took the initiative to recruit musicians who had not considered Palestine their destination. When an audition in Budapest was announced, the great violinist and pedagogue Jeno Hubay instructed his brilliant 18-year-old Jewish student Lorand Fenyves to play for Huberman. Fenyves had just made up his mind to leave Budapest in response to a violent anti-Semitic riot of Fascist students at the Academy of Music and he had promptly signed a contract as leader of the Göteborg Synfoniker, Sweden. He played to Huberman 'without being aware of the reason for the audition at all'.[27] After a few days Huberman sent him a cable instructing him to be ready to leave for Palestine within a week. Fenyves's parents insisted that he honour his contract with Göteborg. Unable to make up his mind, the young violinist consulted the conductor Felix Weingartner whom he highly admired. The response of the famous German conductor indicated that Huberman had succeeded in forging a most brilliant image for his future project, since Weingartner unequivocally encouraged his young student to prefer the opportunity of playing with the best Jewish instrumentalists from Europe gathered under Toscanini to an appointment at the well-established and flourishing Göteborg Synfoniker.[28]

---

[25] Ehrlich, *Music Profession in Britain*, 221–2.

[26] Huberman's lecture to the press corps in Tel Aviv, Dec. 1935 (Ibbeken and Avni (eds.), *Orchestra is Born*, 25).

[27] An interview with Fenyves, Apr. 1993, Toronto, Canada.

[28] R. Haglund, 'Göteborg Synfoniker', in Graven (ed.), *Symphony Orchestras*, 301–4.

Time was short and Fenyves, together with his sister, the violinist and violist Alice, landed in Tel Aviv on the eve of the first rehearsal with Toscanini.[29]

In just a few cases Huberman auditioned young musicians who had immigrated to Palestine before the initiation of his rescue operation. The pianist and composer Joseph Gruenthal (Tal) had immigrated in 1935.[30] He used his training as a harp-player, purchased a 'small Erard harp with a specially fine tone' from a family of German immigrants in Jerusalem, and auditioned for Huberman at King David Hotel in Jerusalem. He had 'no intention of making a career as a harp-player' but only wished to play part-time as a substitute for the regular harpist, the Hungarian Clara Szarvas.[31]

At the same time Huberman took charge of all local arrangements mostly by sending impatient orders by post. A major obstacle was the absence of any adequate auditorium. The emergency situation prevented any long-term planning of a new hall and Huberman consented to extensive renovations which combined two pavilions of the Levant Fair on the Tel Aviv beach into a huge structure capable of seating 2,500 listeners. Only a few rows were equipped with comfortable seats, and most listeners were content with folding garden chairs.[32] Huberman involved himself with all aspects of the building process, knowing well that any snag such as wrongly placed entrance doors may ruin a perform- ance. He even selected the proper music stands and requested that the income of the buffet be channelled into the orchestra budget. His main concern was the acoustic shell, and he consulted experts in Europe who provided him with the best plans, which indeed assured the fine acoustics in the otherwise makeshift auditorium. The flautist Uri Toeplitz has reported in his memoirs that Huberman had serious reservations about the appointment of a permanent conductor and instead he advocated a policy of inviting guest conductors of the first rank.[33] He then made his most dramatic move in convincing the legendary Arturo Toscanini to conduct the first concert series. Toscanini had just contemptuously re-

[29] Fenyves (b. 1918) was one of the rotating leaders of the Palestine Orchestra for more than fifteen years, as well as a prominent violin-teacher at the Academy of Music in Tel Aviv. In 1957 he was appointed leader of the Swiss-Romande orchestra in Switzerland and soon after he be- came a professor at the University of Toronto and an internationally acclaimed virtuoso and pedagogue.

[30] See Ch. 10, below.   [31] J. Tal (Gruenthal), *Der Sohn des Rabbiners* (Darmstadt, 1985), 185.

[32] Toeplitz, *History*, 28, 30.

[33] Ibid. 66. Huberman's policy has been maintained almost uninterrupted until Zubin Mehta's appointment as music director in 1977. See Hirshberg, 'Israel Philharmonic Orchestra', 205.

jected Hitler's invitation to conduct at the Bayreuth Festival and his consent to inaugurate the new refugee orchestra in Tel Aviv was interpreted in the *New York Times* as a 'duty to fight for [the] cause of artists persecuted by Nazis'.[34]

The entire project was suddenly threatened by a series of grave crises. The outbreak of the Arab revolt in April 1936 caused the British army to impose martial law, and concert activity was severely impeded for more than two months, especially in Jerusalem which was subjected to a night curfew. The musical circles of Jerusalem did not give up. They organized concerts at a private home by invitation only and secured 'walking permits' for the members of the audience.[35] In August Huberman wrote that 'the past two days have been a nightmare, since I was told that a complete ban of immigration to Palestine is imminent, so that our musicians must leave immediately'.[36] In his letter to Siegmund Warburg in London Huberman admitted that the tension had brought him to the verge of collapse, but that he had finally convinced the High Commissioner to grant entry visas to the musicians regardless of the forthcoming ban.[37] The unbearable tension was further intensified by a few haughty musicians who demanded higher salaries and solo performances, requests which Huberman dismissed outright.[38] Fearful of Toscanini's stormy temper and uncompromising standards, Huberman appointed his close friend, the Swiss conductor Hans Wilhelm (William) Steinberg, to drill the new orchestra through more than sixty rehearsals in less than two months. Then there arose the problem of hospitality for the great conductor. There was no proper hotel in Tel Aviv and Huberman demanded Colonel Kisch to 'induce some owner of a very quiet and most comfortable villa to put it entirely at the disposal of Maestro and Madame Toscanini',[39] by which he meant that the owners would have to move out of their home for the entire period of Toscanini's stay.

Toeplitz has pointed out that the postponement of the inaugural concert to December was indirectly beneficial for the first stage of resettlement of the immigrants from Europe who were surprised by the comfortable weather conditions, having expected an intense Asian heat. Yet the powerful December rains made a hammering noise on the light roof of the pavilion and drops of water occasionally leaked on the instruments.[40]

---

[34] (23 Feb. 1936).   [35] *Ha'Aretz* (17 July 1936). The concert was held in early July.

[36] A letter Mrs Nierop, Amsterdam, 30 Aug. 1936 (Ibbeken and Avni (eds.), *Orchestra is Born*, 38).

[37] Letter of 16 Sept. 1936 (ibid. 40).

[38] A letter (correspondent name omitted) of 14 Oct. 1936 (ibid. 39).

[39] Letter of 18 Nov. 1936 (ibid. 44).   [40] Toeplitz, *History*, 28.

The inaugural concert on 26 December 1936 turned into a national holiday. All tickets were sold out within a few hours and Toscanini consented to open the dress rehearsal to the public. The festive concert was followed by the first subscription series and within eight days 15,000 listeners attended concerts in Tel Aviv, Jerusalem, and Haifa, whereupon the orchestra immediately went on tour in Cairo and Alexandria. The conductors in the first subscription season were Hans Steinberg, Issay Dobrowen, Malcolm Sargent, and Michael Taube. Sensitive to the plight of the finest violinists who had lost their high status in leading European orchestras, Huberman had the leader chair alternate between four violinists of equal status. Huberman himself refused to perform as soloist in the first season since he wished to focus all the public's attention on the orchestra.

The orchestra maintained the festive aura throughout the entire first season, characterized by Rosolio as 'unprecedented', and continued with a series of weekly outdoor summer concerts. Subscription sales for the second season soared despite 'the gloomy economic conditions, which forces the common people to save every penny before spending it on luxuries. We may draw an important conclusion for our public life: artistic enjoyment here is not mere entertainment but a vital need.'[41]

The orchestra continued to benefit from the interest and dedication of first-rank international conductors so that there was no danger of any let-down after the first season. Of special significance was Toscanini's return in 1938 which was taken as a proof of the maestro's confidence in the potential of the young ensemble. The second visit once more marked Toscanini's uncompromising anti-Nazi protest, since it followed his refusal to conduct in Salzburg.

As in the case of Toscanini, Hermann Scherchen's visit not only gave both the orchestra and the audience a profound professional and spiritual experience but also acted as a powerful anti-Fascist statement. Deeply committed to the political left and to the cause of innovative trends in music, Scherchen had left Germany for the entire period of the Nazi regime. He arrived in Palestine in May 1939 and stayed for two months, conducting two full subscription series and a sequel of outdoor summer concerts.[42] A great pedagogue, Scherchen displayed special sensitivity to and understanding of the tense emotional state of the musicians, most of whom had been in Palestine for barely two years, and whose process of

---

[41] Rosolio, *Ha'Aretz* (25 June 1937).

[42] B. von der Lühe, 'Hermmann Scherchen in Palästina', in H. J. Pauli and D. Wunsche (eds.), *Hermann Scherchen, Musiker* (Berlin, 1986), 35–41.

assimilation was still incomplete.[43] He also pointed out the difficulty of producing good sound and concentrating in the 'scorching Hamsin wind . . . We are covered with sweat already before the beginning of the concerts.'[44] Writing to Kestenberg at the end of his stay he pointed out that 'this orchestra is problematic: as an ensemble, in its stationing in Tel Aviv, and in the diversity of the aspiration of its members, as well as in their attitude to the country'.[45] Scherchen's consideration for the exposed nerves of the musicians showed in his planning of his intensive rehearsals. He started every day with a two-hour rehearsal with the winds and percussion, followed by a two-hour rehearsal for the strings and harp, after which he held a full rehearsal for two hours, 'so that the entire orchestra was never busy for more than four hours every day,'[46] while he himself could train the orchestra for a full six hours daily, ignoring his own exertion. Scherchen became deeply involved in the local musical scene. He held intensive auditions for the members of the orchestra who wished to perform as soloists, spoke in four lengthy press conferences, and directed a two-month conducting course. After his return to Europe Scherchen enthusiastically wrote to Professor Leo Kestenberg, by then the new director of the orchestra, that the Palestine Orchestra was the greatest achievement of the best Jewish musicians from Europe and that it had the potential of becoming one of the best in the world.[47]

Such relationships as the Palestine Orchestra established with conductors such as Toscanini, Steinberg, Dobrowen, and Scherchen were markedly different from a system of guest conductors. Most of the conductors stayed for extended periods, donated their services gratis, and treated their engagement as an artistic and political commitment. They all wished to return on a regular basis and a small group of the greatest international conductors thus provided a preferred substitute for a musical director. The chances for such a development were annulled by the outbreak of the war.

Resettlement and Emigration

Seventy-three musicians started the Palestine Orchestra, fifty-three of whom arrived from Europe. Toeplitz considered the Polish group as the largest with nineteen members compared with sixteen from Germany

---

[43] H. Scherchen, 'Hubermans Schöpfung, das Palestine Orchester. Meinem Freunde Leo Kestenberg', 1939 (Huberman Archive, AMLI Library, Tel Aviv); quoted in von der Lühe, 'Hermann Scherchen', 37).

[44]. Ibid.   [45] Ibid.   [46] Ibid.   [47] Quoted, ibid. 40.

and ten from Austria, the rest coming from Hungary and Holland (four from each). The remaining musicians were selected from among the local musicians. The makeshift auditorium was located at the northern outskirts of Tel Aviv which was then a narrow strip of three streets, and most of the immigrant members rented apartments or rooms there. They all communicated in German among themselves and with their neighbours who treated them with the utmost respect. The management was aware of the danger that migrants were more prone to illness than local people, thereby risking cancellations of concerts. An arrangement had been reached with local physicians who were ready to provide professional help at short notice, frequently in return for concert tickets. Toeplitz has indicated that the conditions of such an enclave facilitated the immediate resettlement of the orchestra but in the long run isolated it from the cultural life of the country.[48]

Some of the immigrants must have treated Palestine as a temporary asylum in the first place and the conditions of a German-speaking enclave further enhanced such an attitude. Within the first three seasons, eighteen of the best players accepted positions in South and North America. Most left at the end of the 1937/8 season when the management relayed the disappointing news of financial difficulties and postponement of any plans for a salary increase.[49] Zionist activists in Palestine reprimanded Huberman for wasting precious certificates on 'birds of passage' without checking their Zionist commitments.[50] Yet Huberman left no gap unfilled and forty-five additional players soon arrived. Forty-four of the founders remained in the orchestra when it became the Israel Philharmonic in 1948. Excluding five players who died during this period, the turnover amounted to about one-fourth of the ensemble. Though damaging to the idealistic image the ensemble wished to foster, one should keep in mind the fact that Huberman saved also the lives of those who used Palestine as a mere outlet from the looming danger. By the outbreak of the war Huberman had rescued nearly one hundred musicians and their families from extermination.

Financing an Orchestra in Troubled Times

Huberman's persistent fund-raising provided the high initial investment which made possible the inauguration of the orchestra. The quick politi-

[48] Toeplitz, *History*, 28–9.   [49] Ibid. 69.
[50] B. von der Lühe, 'Von Orchester der Einwanderer zu einer nationalen Musikinstitution Israels', *Das Orchester* (1993).

cal deterioration limited any additional fund-raising,[51] so that the orchestra was forced to rely on the erratic box office. In the 1938/9 season 55 per cent of the budget came from subscriptions and 29 per cent from single tickets. The remainder came from the Orchestra Society. Whereas similar organizations in the United States and in Europe depended as a rule on affluent patrons, no such upper class existed in Palestine and the Society comprised about 2,500 dedicated subscribers who each donated £1–£5 annually, in return for which they had their names printed in a special brochure and were allowed precedence in seat selection. The musicians received monthly salaries which ranged from £12 for most members to £15 for section leaders, roughly equal to the salary of senior civil servants and high school teachers. In that way the Palestine Orchestra became the first performing institution in the country providing decent living conditions to a large group of musicians.

The outbreak of the war and the ensuing economic crisis in Palestine caused a sharp decline in sales of subscription tickets. In the third season the orchestra moved from the spacious pavilion to the small auditorium of Haohel theatre seating only 650 patrons. Toeplitz has deemed the move, allegedly taken for security reasons to a central venue, as a mistake, since the small and stuffy theatre with its bad acoustics could not cover the expenses even when sold out. The orchestra countered by an increase in the number of concerts to fourteen subscription series per season in the three cities, complemented by concerts in smaller settlements. The orchestra also continued its well-paid regular tours in Egypt, playing to a mostly European audience and a few Egyptian notables.[52] The British forces provided an important outlet for concerts, to the extent that fifty-four of the 225 concerts of the Palestine Orchestra during the 1940–2 seasons were given in military camps in Palestine and in Egypt. The Orchestra also sent chamber ensembles, nicknamed 'musical commandos', to perform in remote camps in Egypt.[53] During the summer the orchestra presented concerts of light classics both in the small auditorium of the Haohel theatre and at public parks. The intense heat and humidity of the summer seasons in Tel Aviv took their toll and several times exhausted musicians fainted on the stage.[54] The rising inflation forced the musicians to complement their salaries and some of them used to rush from the

---

[51] Difficulties were compounded when Huberman was seriously injured in an air crash in 1937, in which he fractured his ribs and both arms and hurt his lungs. It took more than a year before he overcame the trauma and returned to active performances; during this time, however, his contacts with the orchestra were extremely limited.

[52] An interview with Lorand Fenyves, 1993.

[53] Dr Peter E. Gradenwitz, *New York Times* (16 Aug. 1942).   [54] *Mishmar* (22 Aug. 1945).

morning rehearsals to play at cafés in the afternoon, and then dash to concerts. The musicians also used to purchase cheap products in Egypt and sell them in Palestine where prices were higher. Toeplitz has recalled that the overworked and financially pressed musicians became irritable and the discipline deteriorated.[55] Daily work was further hampered by the lack of a library which Huberman had considered an unjustified high expense. When the war severed contacts with libraries in Europe, the orchestra was frequently forced to have entire sets of parts copied by hand.[56]

One of the last musicians who immigrated from Nazi Germany before the war was the pianist and educator Leo Kestenberg[57] who was the most senior official in the German administration among the musician immigrants. Huberman, who could no longer supervise the orchestra, appointed him artistic director. Kestenberg's appointment coincided with the onset of deterioration of contacts with central Europe. Concerned about the professional standards of the Palestine Orchestra, Kestenberg turned to his former friend and colleagues who had immigrated to the United States. Writing to Alfred Einstein at his New York address, Kestenberg asked the great critic and musicologist to keep him informed of any orchestral scores by Jewish American composers worthy of performance by the Palestine Orchestra. He also asked for his opinion of the chances to engage any of the first-rank American conductors, such as Koussevitzky, Stokowsky, and Ormandy.[58] Kestenberg's desperate effort was in vain since the war spread and Palestine was cut off from Europe and America. Yet the small group of local conductors proved itself capable of taking over. The seasons 1939/40 and 1940/1 included one concert each in which the orchestra dispensed with conductors and 'conducted itself'.

Detached from Huberman's domineering personality, relations between the musicians and the management deteriorated. Playing more than two hundred concerts a year, with tiring journeys to Jerusalem, Haifa, Egypt, and other locations, the players were exhausted and overworked. While the ticket sales covered about two-thirds of the budget, the players' salaries were hardly adjusted to the soaring cost of living. The musicians protested against what they considered an inflated and costly

[55] *History*, 92–5.   [56] Ibid. 22.
[57] Kestenberg (1882–1962) was a socialist advocating the dissemination of music among the people. In 1918 he was appointed as artistic adviser and referent at the Prussian Ministry of Science, Culture, and Popular Education, which allowed him to bring about major reforms in musical education in Germany.
[58] A letter of 17 July 1939 (Ger.) (Kestenberg Archive, Tel Aviv University).

administrative staff. Kestenberg tried to quench the trouble, but all he could do was to send urgent appeals to Huberman, who was not in a position to intervene. Soon after the termination of the war, resentment turned into an open revolt. The players turned the festive one-thousandth concert with the Mayor as the guest of honour into a 'dinner-jacket strike', playing in casual dress. Totally disenchanted, Kestenberg sent a long letter to Huberman announcing his resignation:

The lack of conductors and soloists from abroad and the necessity to concentrate on box office appeal when drawing up the programmes have resulted in making the rehearsals very boring for the musicians. So you have a situation in which on the one hand there is an enormous amount of concert activity to bring in at least the 60 per cent of the budget which concert income must cover plus inadequate payment to the individual musicians . . . and on the other hand there is no artistic impetus or growth to offset the above draw-backs. Then one must remember that of the orchestra of about 68 musicians about 40 of them are soloists with their constant demands for solo appearances and their inevitable dislike of 'team' work. . . . Every day was a battle. I might mention here that for a long time I have been under doctor's treatment for high blood pressure and these constant clashes were affecting my health also.[59]

Soon after Kestenberg's resignation the musicians refused to renew their contracts and instead reorganized as a public company, which distributed an equal number of shares to the players and to representatives of the National Committee, the Jewish Agency, and the Federation of Jewish Workers. The players appealed to the associations of the Friends of the Palestine Orchestra to buy shares and continue to support the orchestra.[60] The organizational reform was in the long-run a stunning success which made the Palestine Orchestra the most stable and enduring performing ensemble in the country.

Repertory Quagmire

The young orchestra found itself facing a bewildering array of requests and expectations. First and foremost was the reliance on the audience which provided almost the entire economic backing. The orchestra addressed a heterogeneous public, ranging from those who had never heard a live performance of a professional symphony orchestra to the most sophisticated and demanding central European audience reinforced by the Fifth Aliya.

[59] Letter of 8 Mar. 1945 (Engl.) (Kestenberg Archive, Tel Aviv University).
[60] Mishmar (2 July 1946).

Critics and music educators expected the orchestra to provide the much-needed training of a serious musical audience. Indeed, it had taken the unrelenting Rosolio less than three months after the inaugural concert to reiterate his demand that the repertory be selected in a manner which would 'provide the audience not only with pleasure but also with educational values . . . whereas the programmes so far look like a random selection'.[61]

Next was the consideration of the need to select a repertory which would integrate the immigrant players into a unified ensemble under a system of guest conductors. Huberman expected the orchestra to master the mainstream repertory within a short time as the best means for its rigorous professional training.

The most touchy issue concerned the pressure from composers and critics to encourage Jewish music in general and local composition in particular. Salomon Rosowsky protested against the 'intention of the orchestra's directors to turn Palestine into the capital of German music. Despite the greatness of German music in the past, one should keep in mind that during the recent decades other nations have burst into world music and the audience in this country is interested in this development.' Rosowsky admitted the anomaly of having most Jewish composers living outside their national centre, but nonetheless requested that the orchestra 'dispatch a letter to all Jewish composers and encourage them to compose for the orchestra'.[62]

Less than six months after Toscanini's festive concert the young orchestra was subjected to a public discussion which simulated a court case. Held at the Ohel-Shem auditorium in Tel Aviv on 2 June 1937 with Judge Tzidkiyahu Harkavi presiding, critics and educators submitted their case for and against the orchestra. The prosecutor, D. Levin, raised the question of whether the Palestine Orchestra wished to 'be a refuge to any spirit except those of the Land of Israel'. The critic Menashe Ravina was called as a witness for the prosecution, blaming Toscanini for inaugurating the Palestine Orchestra with a work by Rossini rather than with a Jewish composition. The musicologist Dr. Hans (Hanan) Steinitz spoke as council for the defence. Questioning the availability of a high quality repertory of true Jewish music, Steinitz stated that the duty of the Palestine Orchestra was 'to create a general spiritual milieu'. Further, Steinitz made the daring statement that Beethoven's works were permeated with a Jewish spirit more than pieces by Jewish composers.[63] The jury refrained from any overt criticism of the Palestine Orchestra. Praising the project as

---

[61] *Ha'Aretz* (23 Mar. 1937). [62] *Ha'Aretz* (1 June 1937). [63] *Ha'Aretz* (4 June 1937).

a major contribution to the national endeavour, the jury commended the orchestra for performing works by the Jewish composers Weprik and Sternberg in its first season and expressed the hope that additional Jewish works would be gradually integrated into the programmes.

Huberman responded much later, claiming that

As the only orchestra in the country. . . this body was bound first to give its audience an idea of the foundation upon which modern music has been built. . . . Up to now the really great Jewish composers like Mendelssohn had written in the musical idiom of the country in which they lived, and it was in Palestine proper where a really inspired *Jewish* composer would be brought forth.[64]

Huberman's attitude angered the local composer community. The cellist and composer Joachim Stutschewsky sent a petition signed by thirteen composers to the violinist on the occasion of his visit in January 1940 (which turned out to be his last). Huberman passed on the matter to Professor Kestenberg who tried to evade the issue by blaming the troubled wartime for the neglect of local composition.[65] Kestenberg also referred to the performance of Sternberg's *The Story of Joseph* as proof that the orchestra was responsive to new Jewish works. The composers who expected a reply from Huberman himself were hurt, and the issue remained a source of tension between local composers and the orchestra for years to come.

The structure of the repertory of the Palestine Orchestra in four representative seasons is shown in Table 8.1.

The repertory undoubtedly depended on Huberman's preference for German-Austrian mainstream Classical and Romantic works. Toscanini's long inaugural programme included only one Italian piece, a Rossini overture, and was otherwise heavily German with Schubert's Symphony No. 8, Brahms's Symphony No. 2, Mendelssohn's Incidental Music to *A Midsummer Night's Dream* and Weber's *Oberon* Overture. Toscanini's next concert was an all-Beethoven programme. Yet the other prestigious visiting conductors brought about significant diversity. Issay Dobrowen explicitly stated that his criterion for shaping the third subscription concert of the first season was to counterbalance Toscanini's predominantly German programmes with works by Berlioz, Debussy, Liadov, and Tchaikovsky. Malcolm Sargent, who visited Palestine for three consecutive seasons, conducted works by Delius and Elgar in each of his concerts.

[64] An interview with Huberman, *Palestine Post* (16 Dec. 1938).
[65] Letter of 5 Mar. 1940 (CZA 6751).

TABLE 8.1 Repertory of the Palestine Orchestra

Category	1936/7	1939/40	1943/4	1945/6	Total 1936–47
Baroque	9 (7%)	20 (10%)	21 (9%)	25 (6%)	215 (7.6%)
Class.[a]	23 (18%)	27 (14%)	30 (13%)	33 (8%)	282 (10.0%)
Rom. G. A.[b]	57 (45%)	99 (51%)	105 (47%)	161 (39%)	1,150 (40.9%)
Rom. I. F. E.[c]	15 (12%)	14 (7%)	20 (9%)	81 (20%)	418 (14.9%)
Rom. Rus.[d]	14 (11%)	16 (8%)	1 (0.4%)	36 (9%)	275 (9.8%)
Jewish[e]	4 (3%)	0 (0%)	18 (8%)	26 (5%)	98 (3.5%)
Pal.[f]	3 (2%)	4 (2%)	13 (6%)	16 (4%)	116 (4.1%)
Contemp.[g]	3 (2%)	15 (8%)	17 (8%)	55 (13%)	260 (9.2%)
TOTAL	128	195	225	410	2,815

[a] Classical (Haydn to Beethoven).
[b] Romantic German, Austrian, including Mahler.
[c] Romantic French, Italian, English.
[d] Romantic, Russian, including the Mighty Five.
[e] music by Jews composed in Europe, mostly by Bloch and by members of Engel's group.
[f] new music composed in Palestine.
[g] early twentieth century, including Stravinsky and Bartók.

Beethoven's music, which had enjoyed a special ideological status since the beginnings of David Schor's educational endeavour, loomed very high in the repertory. Eight of Beethoven's symphonies were performed within the first two seasons. With the ensuing first performance of the Ninth under the conductor Eugen Szenkar the Palestine Orchestra reached a musical and human high point. Nine thousand listeners attended the four performances and 'heard the message "all mankind are brothers", felt its appropriateness in our days, accepted it as a solace and as an incentive for the future.'[66] Loyal to the old principles of the Palestine Opera and the Bible Chorus, Friedrich Schiller's ode was sung in the Hebrew translation of the poet Aharon Ashmann. David Rosolio, who had the highest praise for the soloists and for Fordhaus's Oratorio Choir, observed that the event also contributed to the absorption of the new immigrants:

Perhaps we may divide the music public of Palestine into its two chief components: those who have long been 'people of the country' and have seen the gradual raising of its standards on the one hand; and those who have come from abroad only recently, still preserving in their memory the best of musical tradition in the cities of Europe on the other... The former realized that a standard previously undreamed of has been achieved, while the latter noted with astonishment that Palestine is no longer a distant corner of the world.[67]

[66] Rosolio, 'Musical Coming of Age', *Palestine Post* (1 Feb. 1939).   [67] Ibid.

The orchestra was eager to face additional difficult challenges, such as a performance of Mahler's monumental Third Symphony.[68] The daring pioneer spirit compensated for the incomplete ensemble, since 'it was impossible to recruit eight horns, a second harp, and a children's choir which is very important in this work.'[69] Even more daring was Hermann Scherchen's performance of Arnold Schoenberg's complex *Pelleas and Melisande*, which was treated as a special event because of the obligation to great Jewish composers.[70] The oboe-player Heinz Berger indicated that the music sounded 'ultramodern for our public'.[71] One of the most dedicated promoters of new music, Scherchen followed the performance with a brief lecture and then performed the entire composition once more.

The proportion of contemporary music in the orchestra's repertory, while very low at first, gradually improved and reached 15 per cent in 1946/7.

The statistics indicate that the orchestra was not oblivious to the local composers. The proportion of local works was small judged by percentage points, as shown in Table 8.1, but the absolute number of 116 newly composed local works performed within eleven seasons was a respectable achievement for a young orchestra in an extremely troubled period. Indeed, nearly every significant orchestral composition written in Palestine was performed within no more than a year or two of its completion.

The direct link between the founding of the Palestine Orchestra and the rise of Nazism loaded the repertory policy of the orchestra and its founders with political connotations. Huberman rejected Dobrowen's proposal to include a composition by Richard Strauss on his programme since 'we cannot accommodate a person who has a Jewish daughter-in-law and a Jewish librettist on the one hand, and for material benefits has been the President of the Reichmusikkammer'.[72]

The orchestra scheduled a performance of Wagner's *Meistersinger* Overture for the end of November 1938. The outbreak of violence against Jews in Germany known as the Kristallnacht on 9 November 1938 instigated an appeal by a group of subscribers to cancel the performance as a symbolic protest against anti-Semitism and the orchestra complied. Uri Toeplitz has observed that the direct association with Nuremberg as the centre of activity of the Nazi regime acted against the particular performance more than a total rejection of Wagner, and that at about the

---

[68] Davar (15 Dec. 1938).   [69] Toeplitz, *History*, 75.
[70] Menashe Ravina, *Davar* (17 May and 2 June 1939).
[71] A telephone interview with Barbara von der Lühe, 'Hermmann Scherchen in Palastina', 38.
[72] A letter to Dobrowen, 27 Sept. 1936 (Ibbeken and Avni (eds.), *Orchestra is Born*, 42).

same time the Palestine Orchestra performed the Bachanalle from *Tannhäuser* in Egypt. Yet the cancellation inadvertently initiated a lasting boycott of public performances of Wagner's music. The decision resulted in mixed reactions. David Rosolio, while paying tribute to Wagner's greatness as a composer, justified the decision 'in consideration of the mood of the public'.[73] Menashe Ravina first expressed his hope that the decision applied to Wagner's music only, and not to German music in general. He then commented that

Wagner is one of the most salient examples of a contradiction between an artist and his work, and therefore one finds it difficult to agree to the revenge taken against the magnificent overture for a crime committed by its composer. We'd better not elaborate on the matter any further and avoid such incidents in the future.[74]

Upon the tenth anniversary of the Palestine Orchestra Rosolio noted that in his view the ensemble's most important achievement was its contribution to the musical consciousness of the local audience. While not ignoring the stormy applause and the capacity houses, Rosolio emphasized that in his opinion the major indicators of the orchestra's success had been that on a morning after an important concert he heard 'a passer-by whistling a theme from a Brahms symphony,' and that names of composers . . . became common knowledge'. Most importantly, Rosolio was happy with the many young people who crowded the standing spaces, thereby 'negating the claim that the immigrants were those who imported the interest in music . . . A musical standard has been reached, a predominating musical milieu which penetrates all walks of society, adults and youngsters, urban and rural people, even breaking the ethnic barriers.'[75]

The Triumph of Chamber Music

The concentration of seventy-odd experienced and regularly salaried instrumentalists had immediate reverberations in the realm of chamber music. The availability of musicians encouraged complex ventures, such as a performance of Beethoven's Septet and Schubert's Octet,[76] as well as

---

[73] *Palestine Post* (18 Nov. 1938); *Ha'Aretz* (17 Nov. 1938). The boycott has continued up to the present day on the public stage, although Wagner's music has been freely studied and discussed in academic institutions, sold in record stores, and in the 1990s also occasionally broadcast on the Israeli radio and screened in film versions.

[74] *Davar* (21 Nov. 1938).   [75] *Ha'Aretz* (31 Jan. 1947).

[76] On 8 May 1937. Rosolio, *Ha'Aretz* (19 May 1937).

first encounters with previously unavailable instruments, such as a virtuoso programme by the harp-player Clara Szarvas, an immigrant from
Hungary.[77]

An important step towards institutionalization of the chamber concerts
was taken when Meir Dizengoff, the first Mayor of Tel Aviv, bequeathed
his two-storey private home to the people of Tel Aviv who converted
it into a small art museum. The directors of the museum responded to
the inauguration of the Palestine Orchestra with a fortnightly series of
chamber music concerts in its central hall, which offered an intimate and
pleasant ambience for about two hundred music lovers, with heavy-
framed traditional European paintings hanging on the walls and the
musicians seated in the centre flanked on three sides by the audience. The
series was inaugurated with a programme of chamber music by members
of Bach's family, the harpsichord being played by Frank Pollack[78] as the
central attraction. The highly charismatic Pollack had purchased a
Neupert harpsichord in 1933 which he imported to Palestine upon his
immigration two years later.[79] This started Pollack's frequent harpsichord
recitals all over Palestine which were as a rule sold out. Performing
chamber works with members of the Palestine Orchestra, Pollack had
difficulties reaching a balance with the mellow strings 'which obviously
belonged to another period'.[80] An admirer of Wanda Landowska, Pollack
strove to make the harpsichord part and parcel of modern concert life,
stressing on the one hand its distinctness from the piano, and resisting on
the other hand any 'scholarly' image, so that he ardently supported the
modernization of the harpsichord as a means of increasing its sound.[81]

Soon after his immigration the young violinist Lorand Fenyves started
a piano trio with Ilona and Laszlo Vincze. Yet the crown of the chamber
programmes was the Viennese quartet repertory. Three new professional
string quartets joined Emil Hauser and his veteran Jerusalem Quartet.
Foremost among them were the 'Hungarians', the violinist Lorand
Fenyves and his sister Alice, the violist and composer Oedoen Partos,

[77] *Davar* (13 Nov. 1938).
[78] Pollack (1910–68) who later Hebraized his name to Pelleg, was both a harpsichordist and a
brilliant solo and chamber pianist who specialized in contemporary music, a conductor, and a
composer of incidental music. He also excelled as a radio commentator and lecturer.
[79] Data kindly provided by Mrs Pelleg and reported by the musician's daughter Mrs Daniela
Glass. An interview, Apr. 1993.
[80] Menashe Ravina, *Davar* (13 Nov. 1938).
[81] F. Peleg, 'The Harpsichord, Past and Present', *Tatzlil*, 9 (1969), 157–9. When his Neupert
disintegrated after about twenty years of concerts all over the country, Pollack ordered a modern
harpsichord from the British builder De Blaise whom he had known in the 1940s when De Blaise
was a flautist at the radio orchestra in Palestine.

and the cellist Laszlo Vincze. They were also dedicated to performing contemporary music.[82]

The museum series was complemented by so many other venues and organizations that Menashe Ravina complained that 'chamber music has spread beyond all proportions to other genres. Each large and small auditorium is ready to present intimate music to anyone who wishes to listen. The trouble is that there are not as many listeners to this special genre.'[83] Ravina counted no less than eight institutions which were involved in chamber music, each trying to distinguish itself from the others. For example, the Circle of Chamber Music in Tel Aviv presented chamber concerts dedicated to one composer each. The Circle also sponsored a series of lectures in preparation for the concerts of the Palestine Orchestra by the German immigrant Dr Hans Steinitz, a musicologist and a pianist who used to illustrate his talks by playing entire symphonies from memory. Thus, Tel Aviv soon matched Jerusalem in having a highly sophisticated chamber music audience in the central European tradition.

BBC and PBS

The inauguration of the Palestine Broadcasting Service in March 1936 was a major turning-point on the musical scene. Unlike other cultural projects in Palestine, the broadcasting service in Jerusalem was an initiative of the British Mandate administration, which took the BBC as its model. With a single channel directed to a diverse audience, the PBS was divided into English, Arabic, and Hebrew departments. While the news service was fully controlled by the Mandate authorities, the Hebrew department enjoyed full autonomy with respect to cultural, artistic, and educational programmes. Flight-Lieutenant Crawford McNaire, the British director of the PBS, was himself a gifted conductor, so that music played a central role in the broadcast schedule.[84]

Only a small portion of the music programmes were transmissions of records. Most of the music was broadcast live by the Studio Players. Versatility was a *sine qua non* for appointment to the small staff of the music department. Karl Salomon received the post of programme director since he had mastered German, English, and Hebrew, and as a

[82] See Ch. 10, below.   [83] *Davar* (25 Sept. 1938).
[84] When World War II broke out, McNaire joined his troops in Egypt, where he regularly conducted the Palestine Orchestra.

musician he was a composer, a dexterous arranger, a bass singer, and a conductor. Karl Salomon was also in charge of the music broadcast in the English department, occasionally triggering accusations of double loyalty.[85] The pianist Arieh (Erich) Sachs[86] was a skilled sight-reader capable of accompanying guest artists in various genres, including Lieder, cantorial repertory, folk songs, and jazz. He also played the harpsichord. The leader was the British Philip Sharp, and the flexible ensemble numbered seven musicians, who participated also in live broadcasts on the English programme. The meagre funds of the Hebrew programmes limited the invitation of guest artists save for occasional singers, and the Studio Players were forced to shoulder most of the workload, frequently resulting in 'poor and colourless programmes'.[87]

In its incipient stage the PBS broadcast time was limited to a total of five hours. For example, on 21 November 1937 the station got on the air at 5.30 p.m. and started with a children's programme in Hebrew. The Arabic programme ran from 6.10 to 7.15. The 'Hebrew Hour' then took over. The columnist Herman Swet's started with a commentary on current concerts followed at 7.35 with a thirty-minute live broadcast of the Studio Players featuring Jewish music. The Hebrew programme concluded with sports and the evening news. The English programme received the prime time from 8.30 to 10.35, one hour of which was a music broadcast. The Hebrew press provided no details of the Arabic programme but did so for the English which was accessible to most of the European immigrants. One might claim that music functioned as a convenient time-filler for a new and impoverished radio station. Yet music continued to play a major role on the radio also when broadcast time expanded to four hours of Hebrew programmes. For example, on 19 September 1938 seventy minutes were allotted to music programmes, accounting for 27 per cent of the Hebrew broadcast on that day. Together with the English broadcast the radio provided about two hours of diverse music broadcast daily, thereby effecting a major change in the availability of music. The launching of the Palestine Broadcasting Service brought about a dramatic increase in the number of radio sets in Palestine from 12,000 in 1935 to 21,000 a year later, to 49,000 in 1941, of which 36,000 were owned by Jews,[88] that is, roughly one radio set per three or four families. Radio-owners used to welcome relatives and friends who joined them to listen to the radio, especially since the tense political situation made people listen endlessly to the news service. Consequently, PBS

---

[85] Tal (Gruenthal), *Der Sohn des Rabbiners*, 189.
[86] See Bohlman, *Land where Two Streams Flow*, 173–5, for a detailed case study of Arieh Sachs.
[87] Hermann Swet, *Ha'Aretz* (4 Apr. 1937).   [88] *Ha'Aretz* (30 Mar. 1941).

resembled the BBC in being a powerful educational tool. Indeed, music critics and columnists subjected the music broadcasts to the most stringent scrutiny in long and detailed reviews.

The model of the BBC orchestra was followed when the Studio Players expanded into a forty-member radio orchestra at the end of 1938.[89] The musicians were civil servants who, though badly paid, at least did not have to rely on box-office proceeds. The radio orchestra held weekly public concerts at the YMCA auditorium which were broadcast alive, and also participated in short live broadcasts from the studio. Like European radio orchestras, it was officially committed from the outset to the dissemination of national music, whether composed in the Diaspora or by local composers. For example, in 1943/4 the radio orchestra performed twenty-eight German-Austrian Romantic compositions (19 per cent of the season repertory) compared to nineteen local works and ten works by Diaspora musicians (18 per cent), which strongly contrasted with the proportions in the repertory of the Palestine Orchestra as presented in Table 8.1. The PBS also established a chamber choir which numbered a dozen members. The PBS Orchestra could not afford the engagement of international stars, nor did it enjoy Huberman's prestige which attracted guests to donate their services. The impoverished radio ensemble employed a local resident conductor, Hans (Hanan) Schlesinger, who alternated with the programme director Karl Salomon. Joseph Gruenthal frequently performed piano concertos with the orchestra. During his first performance in Palestine of Brahms' First Piano Concerto Salomon failed to cue the clarinet-player who missed his solo over the piano accompaniment. Gruenthal reacted immediately and improvised his own melody and no one in the audience noticed the incident.[90]

Relations between the PBS and the Palestine Orchestra were uneasy, mostly because of Huberman's inherent hostility to the radio, which was translated into excessive financial demands for broadcast privileges. The press supported the public's rights to enjoy the Palestine Orchestra,[91] and the radio did broadcast Toscanini's concerts, with the result that 1,300 new subscribers paid the radio tax.[92] Relations improved after a few years and the number of live broadcast concerts increased.[93] Yet no regular

[89] The permanent BBC orchestra was formed in 1930. See Ehrlich, *Music Profession in Britain*, 215, and J. Hirshberg, 'Jerusalem Symphony Orchestra', in Craven (ed.), *Symphony Orchestras*, 200. Unlike the Israel Philharmonic Orchestra, the Jerusalem Symphony went through several radical personnel and organizational changes.

[90] Tal (Gruenthal), *Der Sohn des Rabbiners*, 208.   [91] Hermann Swet, 10 Jan. 1937.

[92] *Ha'Aretz* (31 Jan. 1937).   [93] Swet, *Ha'Aretz* (30 Mar. 1941).

policy was established and the broadcasts of the Palestine Orchestra remained erratic for many years.

Despite the different circumstances, a striking similarity may be discerned between England and Palestine in the 1930s. Sir Thomas Beecham in London and Bronisław Huberman in Palestine took bold personal initiatives in starting new orchestras which transformed orchestral life 'from fustian mediocrity to undoubted excellence'.[94] Likewise the public broadcast services in both countries established orchestras of their own. The BBC model was directly transplanted to Palestine. Huberman's model was German, but he benefited from the successful developments in Britain by gaining the support and confidence of the Mandate authorities.

The eastward ideology permeated the radio programmes, as signalled by the inauguration broadcast which included vocal compositions by Milhaud, Bloch, and Ben Haim alongside a performance of traditional Yemenite songs by the singer Bracha Zephira.[95] Arabic music, though easily accessible on the Arabic programmes of the PBS, was also regularly performed on the Hebrew programmes by two Jewish immigrants from Iraq, the oud-player Ezra Aharon and the violinist Rahamim Amar.

A by-product of the inauguration of radio broadcast was the public Gramophone Recording Concert which the firm of Schlesinger & Springer, German immigrants who founded a music store in Tel Aviv, started as a publicity ploy. The first concert, held on 26 October 1936, included works by Bach and Beethoven, and the legally minded entrepreneurs pedantically marked the recording labels on the programmes. Rosolio reported that the packed auditorium proved that 'music lovers no longer sneer at the gramophone . . . The record nowadays is one of the most important means of education for and dissemination of good music'. In his detailed review Rosolio also commented that HMV records sounded better than Columbia's, and commended the organizers for the low ticket prices of 36 mils.[96]

The season 1936/7 marked a major turning-point in the history of concert life in Palestine. Until then the total number of concerts held in the 1920s and early 1930s remained surprisingly stable despite the extreme social and economic changes.[97] There was a slight increase from

---

[94] Ehrlich, *Music Profession in Britain*, 215.   [95] See Ch. 9, below.

[96] About 3 pence. A daily paper cost 6 mils at that time. *Ha'Aretz* (3 Nov. 1936).

[97] Sources for the statistics were announcements, chronicles, and reviews of concerts in the daily press, Menashe Ravina's Archive, AMLI Library, Tel Aviv, and the Poster Archive, JNUL. Concerts in *kibbutzim* and little-advertised concerts in small settlements could not be included. Yet although the total number of concerts in the country was somewhat higher, the margin of error must have been similar for the entire period.

154 concerts in 1924 to 164 in 1925, after which the number stabilized until 1928. A drop to 131 in 1929 has been accounted for by the prolonged state of martial law from August which nearly halted concert life for more than three months. The stable total number, though, covered a constant shift in the distribution among genres. The year 1925 was the heyday of opera with fifty-seven performances compared to merely two orchestral concerts. The proportions were reversed in 1928 with only twelve opera productions but thirty-five orchestral concerts, indicating a stable balance of supply and demand. The full effect of the establishment of the Palestine Orchestra presented itself in 1938 with a sudden rise up to 447 concerts, including 110 orchestral and 197 chamber concerts, complemented by 325 live music broadcasts. The increase in quantity was enhanced by the finalization of the process of professional stratification which dominated the musical scene in Palestine for years to come.

9

Inventing a Tradition
of Folksongs

THE New Yishuv, a mostly secular and ethnically heterogeneous immigrant society, was in urgent need of a set of unifying cultural symbols, and the local composers were expected to form them. The vision of the return to and resettlement in the biblical Land of Israel required that they be oriented to the past, whereas the drive to build a new, better society called for future-oriented symbols. Consequently, both folk and art music were heavily loaded with ideological expectations. Folksongs and dances were designated to extol the spirit of the pioneer settlers, whether rural or urban; to depict the romanticized scenery of the land; to enhance the revival of Hebrew through settings of both biblical texts and modern lyrics; and to unify people through communal singing.[1] Art music was required to create a new system of communicative musical symbols connoting national ideology, to endow the cultural life of the Yishuv with international prestige, and to infuse the musical scene with a spirit of creativity.

Composition during the Ottoman period had been limited to a handful of musicians who were also committed to other musical endeavours, such as A. Z. Idelsohn, for whom composition was a secondary occupation.[2] A regular and continuous creative activity commenced in the 1920s in the realm of folk song and expanded to art music with the immigration from central Europe in the 1930s. There was a marked distinction between the groups of composers in the two realms in several respects:

1. Their pre-migration background and conditions.
2. The level and extent of their professional training as musicians.
3. Patterns of their resettlement in Palestine.

[1] See Ch. 2, above.   [2] Ch. 1, above.

With very few exceptions, the entire community of composers in Palestine consisted of immigrants from eastern and central Europe. The eastern European composers were apprenticed mostly in Germany and in France, whereas the Germans were raised on a solid German background.

The Core Group of Composers of Folk Music

The need for a unifying tradition of Hebrew folk songs stemmed simultaneously from the grass roots and from the leadership of the Yishuv. Consequently, the new folksong repertory was deliberately designed and expected to function as an 'invented tradition' as defined by Eric Hobsbawm who has observed that "traditions" which appear or claim to be old are often quite recent in origin and sometimes invented.'[3] Deliberately created by folk composers, systematically disseminated by the political and cultural leadership of the Yishuv, and in part received by the community, the new folksong tradition corresponds to Hobsbawm's definition according to which an invented tradition 'includes both "traditions" actually invented, constructed, and formally instituted and those emerging in a less easily traceable manner within a brief and datable period—a matter of a few years perhaps—and establishing themselves with great rapidity'.[4]

Folk music has been defined as 'inevitably a performed music', though there remain the questions of 'who performs? To whom are performances directed? Is folk music shared broadly throughout a community? Or is it maintained by a small group of specialists?'[5] The ideologists of the Yishuv never doubted that the new national folk song of Palestine would fulfil its goal only when actively sung by all strata of the heterogeneous society. Consequently, the scope of dissemination has been a basic determinant in distinguishing a 'folksong' from a printed setting merely conceived as a folk song which, however, remains on paper.

Composers of folk songs in Palestine ranged from prolific professional musicians who were fully dedicated to composition and dissemination of the new repertory to amateurs and school-teachers who occasionally composed a few tunes. An attempt at a definition of the repertory of folk songs and of the 'core group' of folksong composers has been based on

[3] 'Inventing Tradition', in id. and T. Rank (eds.), *The Invention of Tradition* (Cambridge, 1983), 1.

[4] Ibid.

[5] P. V. Bohlman, *The Study of Folk Music in the Modern World* (Bloomington, Ind., 1988), 53.

the quantifiable indicator of song prints.[6] By 1949 a total of 4,073 songs appeared in compilations of varying sizes, most of them anthologies of songs by different composers.[7] A statistical analysis of the entire collection has been based on the correlation of the number of reprints of each item and the nature of the publisher.[8] The analysis has suggested a division into three groups:

1. The 'repertory group' of songs which were frequently reprinted and distributed by official agents over ten years at least. This group consisted of nearly one thousand items which could properly qualify as folk songs.

2. The 'interim songs' which appeared in less than four reprints and were used within limited social groups for a short period of a few years.

3. The 'paper' songs which were printed only once and hardly reached beyond the immediate social group of the composer.

The entire output of more than 4,000 songs was the work of 189 composers whose names were mentioned in the publications. Yet most of them contributed less than three songs each, whereas three-quarters of the total were written by thirty-two composers, each of whom composed from twenty to a hundred songs each.[9] Moreover, those thirty-two composers created 85 per cent of the 'repertory group', so that there existed a high degree of correlation between high productivity and broad dissemination.

Nathan Shahar has attempted to classify the folk song composers according to their occupation, coming up with the results that ten to twelve of the thirty-two composers of the core group were employed as public school-teachers, seven were kibbutz members, and eleven worked as professional musicians.[10] Mordechai Ze'ira (1905–68) worked after his

---

[6] Shahar, 'Eretz Israeli Song', 126. Shahar's research has concentrated on printed sources. An ongoing research project directed by Jacob Mazor at the Jewish Music Research Centre, JNUL, has proved that there existed oral traditions of songs well known and practised over long periods of time in certain settlements. They were, however, of markedly local nature and their existence does not seem to detract from Shahar's criteria which gauge the national diffusion of the songs.

[7] The Hebrew term for such an anthology has been *shiron*, a newly invented declension of *shir*, namely 'song' (pl. *shironim*). A few of the anthologies were published in and geared to Diaspora communities.

[8] Shahar, 'Eretz Israeli Song', 21. Shahar has devised a set of sixteen parameters according to which he has quantified the 'weight' of each song as received by the society. The indicator of number of reprints as criterion for reception has been broadly used in studies of renaissance madrigals and of operatic arias.

[9] Ibid. 161–2. Many songs were designated as 'traditional' or 'folk' with no composers' names.

[10] Ibid. 167 and app. B. Kibbutz members used to shift fields according to the demand, but some of them also worked as music-teachers.

immigration in 1924 as construction worker and as fisherman, and from 1933 at the Electrical Company.[11] The occupational fields were by no means clear-cut in the unstable economy of the Yishuv which forced musicians to take part-time jobs in order to make ends meet. Whatever the occupational distribution, most of the folksong composers were placed in suitable positions, from which it was possible to disseminate the repertory in general and their own songs in particular.

Those folksong composers who acquired professional music degrees in Europe before their immigration differed in their personal background from that of the composers of art music. Such was Daniel Sambursky (1909–75). Though born in Königsberg in Eastern Prussia, his parents were Russian Jews who had immigrated to Germany in 1896,[12] and the eastern European melodies and the Yiddish and Hasidic songs dominated the development of his musical style. His father was a devoted Zionist and the spoken language at home was Hebrew. As a child Daniel Sambursky studied piano, cello, and theory at the Leipzig Conservatory, and then went to Berlin to study medicine and music. His professors were Curt Sachs, Ernst Hornbostel, and Friedrich Blume, and he considered the composers Hans Eisler and Kurt Weill as his 'spiritual teachers'.[13] Hans Eisler (1898–1962) rejected middle-class values and had just expressed his dedication to writing music for the proletarian revolution.[14] In this vein Sambursky wrote songs and choruses for an ideological play advocating immigration to Palestine which was produced several times in 1932/3.[15] Having produced the play in Switzerland, Sambursky decided against returning to Nazi Germany and in May 1933 he landed in Palestine, which he found amenable for his image of the folk composer. He worked as music instructor at teachers' training colleges and published seventy-five songs, thirty-four of which were classified by Nathan Shahar as belonging to the 'repertory group'.[16]

[11] M. Ze'ira, *111 Songs*, ed. S. Kaplan (Tel Aviv, 1960). His Russian name was Mitia Grebin. His friend, the poet Aharon Ashmann, whimsically nicknamed him Zeira (lit. *petit*) because of his small build and he then adopted it as his official Hebraized name. An interview with Mrs Zeira, the composer's widow, the Israeli Television, Apr. 1993.

[12] Referred to as *Ostjuden*, they were looked down on by the German Jews, and therefore tried hard to absorb both German culture and Zionist values. See the reference to their 'unesthetic exterior' in Ben-Haim's letter to his father of 23 May 1933, Hirshberg, *Paul Ben-Haim*, 104.

[13] D. Sambursky, 'Autobiography', *Tatzlil*, 9 (1969), 180.

[14] H. Eisler, 'Our Revolutionary Music' (1932), in M. Grabs (ed.), *Hans Eisler: A Rebel in Music* (New York, 1978), 59. In 1933 Eisler escaped to the United States. Austin, *Music in the 20th Century*, 499–500.

[15] Sambursky commented that paradoxically, the incipient Nazi regime ordered that productions of the play go on because it called for emigration of Jews from Germany.

[16] 'Eretz Israeli Song', app. A.

The initiation period of Yitzhac Edel (1896–1973) was, like Sambursky's, a fusion of cultural contrasts. Born in Warsaw to an orthodox Hasidic family, he started to play the violin by ear, emulating the *klezmers* he used to hear at weddings.[17] During his adolescence he rebelled against his orthodox education and went to Kiev in the Ukraine, where he pursued general subjects and music. In 1922 he returned to Poland and enrolled at the National High School for Music in Warsaw, then under Karol Szymanowsky as director. There he encouraged performances of music by Engel's group which he had discovered in Russia. He was deeply affected by his work with the legendary pedagogue Dr Janusz Korczak (1878/9–1942), 'who turned me into a teacher'. In 1929 he joined his parents who had voluntarily immigrated to Palestine. Edel worked throughout his life as a music teacher at Levinsky Teachers' Training College in Tel Aviv.[18]

The majority of the folk song composers, however, had no formal musical training and they turned to composition at an older age, as was the case of Ephraim Ben-Haim:

Born in 1895 in a small town in Ukraine, I received a religious education. As a child I was interested in music (there were several cantors in my family). For a short while I sang at the synagogue choir. As a boy I learned how to play the violin by ear, and also took a few violin lessons with the local *klezmer*. I used to improvise, but it was all forgotten when I left the small town and moved to Kiev and Odessa were I worked as a chemist. When the Russian revolution broke out . . . I joined a group of pioneers who worked on a farm, preparing to immigrate to Palestine. I used to walk from the farm 8 km. every Saturday to listen to the famous cantor Minkowsky with his choir and organ. I also went to the city opera. . . . I immigrated with the group in 1921 and settled with them at kibbuz Kiryat Anavim.[19] I took on myself many duties. . . . We were so involved with work that we could think of nothing else. In 1932 a young man with a violin visited us and rekindled my memories. I bought his violin for £1 and started to play again. I improvised but I did not know how to notate the music. The kibbutz granted me £2 for twenty music lessons in Jerusalem. I also took a few lessons on and off with [Paul] Ben-Haim and with [Alexander] Boskovitch. In 1933 I started to compose song tunes and dances. I soon met the PBS people, Karl Salomon and Efraim Goldstein, who broadcast

[17] The *klezmer* (lit. 'musical instrument') was the professional musician at the Jewish communities in the Diaspora, especially in eastern Europe. The *klezmers* provided instrumental music for communal and family occasions. Their popular instruments were violin, cello, clarinet, and percussion.

[18] Y. Edel, 'Autobiography', *Tatzlil*, 8 (1968), 57–62; M. Brod and Y. W. Cohen, *Die Music Israels* (a revd. edn. with a second section *Werden und Entwicklung der Music in Israel*) (Kassel, 1976), 55.

[19] About 15 km. west of Jerusalem, founded 1920.

my songs, some of which were printed in the anthology *Songs of Labour and of Homeland*.[20]

Matityahu Weiner (Shelem) was a shepherd in kibbutz Ramat Yohanan. His narration of his road to composition reads like an Arcadian pastoral:

The month of May came and the days of shearing arrived. Joseph and I were happy to undertake the task although we were not yet well trained. The shepherd from the neighbouring [Arab] village joined us as our instructor. . . . He hummed all the time. We responded. Nigunim, prayer chants, Ukrainian folk songs were all mixed together. . . . Joseph and I agreed that we should have had our own shearing songs, but there were none either in Hebrew or in Yiddish. . . . The shearing was nearly finished and we set a date for the Shearing Feast. . . . All day I was in an elevated mood and rhymes and tunes came to my mind. I deliberately kept away from people when going with my herd so as to be able to sing loudly to myself. This was my first shearing song. I decided to introduce it as a surprise at the party. I started with hesitation but I gradually gained confidence and finally all joined me.[21]

Distributing an Invented Tradition

The invention of a new tradition of local folksongs within a short period of time required a deliberate act of distribution. After the codification of the song in print it was as rule distributed in some or all of the following venues and methods:

1. Sales of cheap prints.
2. Teaching of new songs at the music periods in public schools.
3. Organized sessions of coached communal singing.
4. Performances of polyphonic arrangements of folk songs for amateur choruses or for semi-professional mixed vocal–instrumental ensembles.
5. Records.
6. Radio broadcasts.

The position of the public school music-teacher, though low in prestige and in pay, placed the composers in an influential position. The subject of music in the public school system of the Yishuv was designated 'singing lesson' and, indeed, the music teachers devoted most of the time

[20] E. Ben-Haim, 'Autobiography', *Tatzlil*, 5 (1965), 125–6. There were no family connections between Paul Ben-Haim (Frankenburger) and Ephraim Ben-Haim.

[21] M. Shelem, 'The First Shearing Songs', *Tatzlil*, 7 (1967), 180. Ramat Yohanan is a kibbutz a few kilometres east of Haifa, founded in 1932.

to class singing, which frequently included coaching the children in new Hebrew songs. Notation was little used and the songs were transmitted orally.

Many of the anthologies of folksongs were sponsored and their contents selected by officials in the cultural leadership of the Yishuv. Most active were the Cultural Centre (Merkaz Le'Tarbut) of the Federation of Hebrew Workers (Histadrut) and the Jewish National Fund (JNF).[22] Others were printed as private enterprises of composers and poets.

Many of the tunes of the Yishuv in the Ottoman period were brought over by the immigrants from eastern Europe, particularly Hasidic tunes and European popular and folk songs.[23] Yet, by the early 1920s the growing number of native children raised on Hebrew as their first language sparked opposition to the continual use of foreign tunes. Kindergarten teachers complained that 'there is too much Germanism in our kindergartens'[24] and that 'most tunes are beautiful and pleasant but they lack their essential component which is the Hebrew spirit. . . . Let a visitor determine our identity according to the singing in our kindergartens! We would be identified as anything except Hebrew.'[25] During the 1920s 'the dependence on imported songs disappeared'.[26] The process of modernization of the repertory may be illustrated through a comparison of the contents of three printings of the first commercially distributed song anthology, *Kinor Tzion*, which included thirty-one songs.[27] In the seventh printing of 1922 seventeen of the songs of the first printing were removed and forty-four locally composed new songs were added.[28]

During the years 1924–32 the repertory group numbered 200 songs, of which 118 were ascribed songs composed in the Yishuv and only seven songs were composed by identified composers abroad.[29] The proportions did not change during the 1932–41 period in which 207 of the 288

[22] The JNF (Keren Kayemet Leyisrael) was established by the Fifth Zionist Congress in Basel in 1901 for the purpose of raising funds to purchase land for the settlement of Jewish immigrants in Palestine. In 1922 the JNF established its headquarters in Jerusalem. Shahar, 'The Eretz Israel Song and the Jewish National Fund', *Studies in Contemporary Jewry*, 9 (1993).

[23] 'Eretz Israeli Song', 71.

[24] 'Minutes of the general assembly of the *Association of Kindergarten Teachers in Palestine*', *Ganenu*, 4–5 (1922), 173–9.

[25] T. Katinka-Gurevich, *Ganenu, a Journal of Children's Education at the Kindergarten and at Home*, 1 (1922), 100.

[26] Shahar, 'Eretz Israeli Song', 88.

[27] A. Moshe Lunz (ed.), *Kinur Zion* (Jerusalem, 1903). Only lyrics were printed since no facility for music setting was available in Palestine. The tunes, all well known, were referred to by their European titles.

[28] Shahar, 'Eretz Israeli Song', 89.

[29] Ibid. 99. The composers of seventy-five of the songs have not been identified in the prints.

repertory songs were composed by local composers as opposed to twenty-two which were composed abroad.[30] It followed that the bulk of the folksongs of the Yishuv was a newly composed local repertory.

The Jewish National Fund devised an ingenious tool for dissemination of songs through postcards, in which the lyrics and the music of the song substituted for the customary landscape photograph. The intensive correspondence between the immigrants and their families and friends abroad assured the dissemination of new songs in the Jewish Diaspora, whereas post inside the country was almost the sole method of communication in a period when the primitive telephone network was limited to official administration and major businesses.

The first series of a dozen postcards was announced on 28 March 1932. By the end of the year the entire printing of 4,690 sets was sold out, and the Jewish National Fund issued four additional sets by June 1933.[31]

The network of choirs[32] provided the professional musicians among the folksong composers both with jobs and with a venue for distribution of choral arrangements of the songs, which were regularly published by the Cultural Centre of the Federation of Hebrew Workers in the form of low-priced sheet music. In that way the Cultural Centre became the largest music publisher of sheet music in Palestine.

Evenings of Communal Singing—The New Venue

While spontaneous and natural in small homogeneous communities such as a kibbutz or a youth movement, group singing of folksongs required an initial stimulation in heterogeneous larger communities, especially in the fast-growing urban centres which resulted from the Fourth and Fifth Aliyas. The clear line of demarcation separating the institutionalized public concert from the in-context singing of folksongs[33] was blurred and a new venue of semi-formal 'public singing' was formed. Sponsored and initiated by central authorities such as the Cultural Centre or local councils, they resembled formal concerts in that they were held in auditoriums and directed by a 'communal singing coach', yet the entire audience actively participated in the singing. Most of the coaches were folksong composers themselves, who were thus placed in the ideal position to have their new compositions tested directly with the target audiences of folksongs. Singing and playing the piano or the accordion, the coaches used to divide the evenings between communal singing of

---

[30] Ibid. 111.   [31] Shahar, 'Jewish National Fund', 85–6.
[32] See Ch. 5, above.   [33] Ch. 2, above.

well-known folksongs and the joint learning of a few new songs, the lyrics of which were distributed on mimeographed sheets.

The new venue filled in an important vacuum in urban entertainment. Though largely secular, the Yishuv maintained a consensus enforced by municipal regulations by which public entertainments such as films, concerts, and theatres, shut down on the eve of the holy Sabbath. Public lectures and communal singing, however, were not considered as entertainment, so that they presented the sole opportunity for urban people to go out on Friday nights.

One of the first singing coaches was the composer Daniel Sambursky, who directed such events nearly every Friday at Brenner Hall, the cultural centre of the Federation of Workers' Unions in Tel Aviv from 1935 until 1950.

This was the only public event on Friday nights in Tel Aviv and the entire *intelligentsia*, including those of Northern Tel Aviv, used to attend. There they listened to interesting lectures and then sang with full devotion for more than an hour. Since the demand for tickets far exceeded available seats, each person had to stamp a membership card and was admitted only on alternate weeks.[34]

Sambursky's ironic comment about the Northerners stemmed from the social division of the small city. Tel Aviv developed northwards and the population of the more modern new sections was more affluent and hence considered among the socialist circles of the Federation of Hebrew Workers as haughty bourgeoisie alien to folk values. Their enthusiastic participation in the communal sessions reflected not only the wish of the secular people for social interaction on Friday nights but also their identification with the cause of the national folk songs. With little chance to absorb them by daily encounter at work, they turned to the new formal venue. Tickets for such evenings were sold for a token price of about 5 pence and the sponsoring agent paid the coach.

The singer and musicologist Moshe Bronzaft (Gorali) held more than a hundred such sessions in Jerusalem in which about 330 songs were sung.[35] The coaches also participated in the periodical conferences of kindergarten and public school-teachers who enhanced the quick dissemination of the new songs. The song anthologies of the late 1930s were explicitly directed for such occasions. Moshe Bronzaft wrote in the introduction to one of the most extensive anthologies: 'Public singing has

---

[34] Sambursky, 'Autobiography', 182.

[35] Shahar, 'Eretz Israeli Song', 105. After the establishment of the State Moshe Gorali founded the Haifa Music Museum and AMLI Library. He was the editor of the musicological yearbook *Tatzlil*.

Ex 9.1. Zeira, 'Ah, bne hagalil'

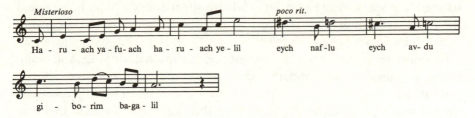

Ha - ru - ach ya-fu- ach ha - ru - ach ye - lil   eych naf -lu   eych av- du

gi - bo- rim ba-ga - lil

(The wind will blow, the wind will wail, how did the Galilee heroes fall, how were they lost?)

acquired an important position in our life. . . . The songs compiled here have become over the years the property of the people. Some are the most known and popular among the public, and others have been composed in the past few years and even just before publication.'[36]

Nathan Shahar has pointed out that the 'repertory group' acted in a circular way, both anticipating and affecting public taste.[37] The introduction to one of the anthologies placed communicability as the principal criterion in that 'simple and short songs were selected in order to enable the public-at-large to learn the song within a short time. Lyrical songs were not included because they suit individual singing or a limited group.'[38] Such an observation was well grounded in reality. In December 1938 the Jewish National Fund launched a fund-raising project for which Nathan Bistritzki, Director of the Youth Section, commissioned a song glorifying the Galilee. Nathan Shahar has observed that the song 'Ah, bneh hagalil' (Brother, build the Galilee) 'was doomed to failure from the outset' due to S. Shalom's high-flown poem and Mordechai Ze'ira's through-composed melody,[39] which is also filled with chromatic turns and spans a broad melodic range which ill-suited group singing (see Ex. 9.1).

The folksong composer B. Hatuli introduced his kibbutz holiday anthology with the statement that 'in selecting the material we were not attracted to the mere beautiful song. More than a few songs which could become popular with the audience were not included since they do not suit the function of basic material for the *Hebrew public* who wishes to revive its original culture.'[40] Still, the influence of the publishers was quite limited since the public was also exposed to the influence of the café

[36] *125 Songs for Public Singing and Choirs* (Jerusalem, 1940).
[37] 'Eretz Israeli Song', 108.   [38] Introd. to *Se'u Zimra* (Sing ye) (Tel Aviv, 1938).
[39] Shahar, 'Jewish National Fund'. Correspondence in CZA/KKL 91. Zeira, *111 Songs*, ed. S. Kaplan, 15.
[40] *Hag Umo'ed* (Holiday Celebration) (Hakibbutz Ha'artzi, 1940). Original italics.

music, the radio, records, and sound films. Indeed, Hatuli also reprimanded 'the spirit of the film hits and the street songs'[41] which pervaded the youth gatherings who rebelled against the 'national' taste propagated in the anthologies.

In contrast to the popular success of communal singing and song prints, attempts to disseminate songs by records did not get off the ground. In 1934 a small factory for manufacturing phonographs and records was established in Tel Aviv. The JNF expressed interest in using the new venue as a means for dissemination of folksongs as well as speeches of the leaders of the Yishuv.[42] Sample records were soon sent to JNF national offices in Europe with an attached brochure stating that 'every Jewish houshold that purchases an Eretz Israel phonograph disc brings into the home an important promotional tool for the Land of Israel'.[43] The factory took advantage of the Levant Fair of 1934 where the records were played to the large enthusiastic crowds. The excitement, however, was short-lived. The number of orders from abroad was disappointing, the quality of the records was poor, and the number of phonographs owned by people in the Yishuv was so negligible that commercial demand was virtually nil. The project was shelved for more than ten years. Fully commercial distribution of folksongs commenced only after the establishment of the State of Israel.

[41] Ibid.
[42] CZA 6203. Shahar, 'Jewish National Fund'.   [43] A letter of 20 July 1934 (CZA 6203).

10

The Immigrant Composers Transform the Musical Scene

THE already-limited compositional activity in the field of concert music during the 1920s nearly came to a halt with Joel Engel's death and Jacob Weinberg's emigration to the United States in 1927.[1] The renewed prospect of the arrival of first-rank Jewish composers was welcomed by the ideological circles in the Yishuv, as when rumours spread that Arnold Schoenberg, 'the founder of the modern school . . . who became famous all over the world, considers immigration to our country . . . Perhaps very soon out of Zion shall go forth music? . . . Let the lost sons return to their people'.[2] Ironically, Schoenberg's preference for the United States was more ideologically motivated than the choice of Palestine by other Jewish composers from Europe.[3] In contradistinction to the folksong group, almost none of the art music composers were declared Zionists prior to immigration. The entire group of immigrants were trained under renowned composition and performance teachers in Europe, providing them with the highest credentials. Unlike Engel's group which emulated the Russian Five as a national school, the new group of immigrant composers neither belonged to any single school nor formed one in Palestine. They had been trained in different musical environments, did not know each other before immigration, and none of them was able to exert authority over the others. Affected by powerful circumstances, they were a random gathering of strong-minded displaced individuals struggling to restate their professional and national identities, while caught in an ideological whirlpool which pushed them on to a rugged road leading to a vague, controversial, and undetermined goal.

[1] See Ch. 5, above.
[2] Y. Ezrahi, 'A Year of Music', *Turim* (20 Oct. 1933). The author paraphrases Isaiah 2: 3.
[3] A. Ringer, *Arnold Schoenberg: The Composer as a Jew* (Oxford, 1990), 116 ff.

Ex 10.1. Sternberg, 'At the Synagogue' from *Visions from the East*

Pre-Migration Conditions

Brief biographical outlines of the pre-migration circumstances of the most salient immigrant composers would contrast their extreme multifariousness with the absence of any predisposition to the immigration to Palestine which was common to all of them.

The oldest member of the German immigrants was Erich Walter Sternberg (1891–1974). Born and brought up in Berlin, he earned a law degree before pursuing composition studies under Hugo Leichtentritt.[4] Sternberg was deeply influenced by the innovative trends, especially by Hindemith and Schoenberg, and his compositions were well received in the avant-garde circles in Berlin.[5] His early works, ultra-chromatic and dominated by expressionistic melodic rhetoric, were rich in quotes of Jewish folksongs and cantillation patterns such as a Yiddish folksong and the *Shema Yisrael* formula in his First String Quartet (1924), and the 'At the Synagogue' movement in his piano cycle *Visions from the East* (see Ex. 10.1).

Paul Frankenburger (1897–1984) who Hebraized his name to Ben-Haim upon his immigration in 1933, received his professional training as pianist, conductor, and composer at the Munich Academy of Music. His composition teachers were Friedrich Klose (1862–1942) and Walter Courvoisier (1875–1931).[6] He was strongly influenced by the traditional spirit of the musical scene in Munich, dominated by Richard Strauss's

---

[4] Sternberg, 'Autobiography', 177. The term 'autobiography' is somewhat misleading. In this context it referred to a series of brief yet highly valuable autobiographical sketches and statements which the Hebrew musicological yearbook *Tatzlil*, edited by Moshe Gorali (Bronzaft) and published by the Haifa Music Museum and AMLI Library, solicited from composers in Israel. Hugo Leichtentritt (1874–1951) was a composer, a prolific musicologist, an influential music critic, and a teacher in Berlin. Being a Jew, he immigrated to the United States in 1933 where he was appointed professor at Harvard University. Nicholas Slonimsky, 'Leichtentritt, Hugo', *MGG* viii, 506.

[5] His second string quartet (1924) was performed by Amar Quartet in which Paul Hindemith played the viola.

[6] Hirshberg, *Paul Ben-Haim*.

powerful personality. After a short period of apprenticeship as coach and assistant to Bruno Walter in Munich, Frankenburger started in 1924 a successful career of Kapellmeister at Augsburg Opera. He also revealed himself as a prolific composer of about eighty Lieder, chamber, and orchestral works which were well received by the press and by the performers. In 1928–9 Frankenburger was encouraged by his friend, the committed Jewish composer Heinrich Schalit (1886–1976), to turn to the field of Jewish music, and indeed he composed several vocal works of Jewish character to biblical texts,[7] with his setting of Psalm 126 highly applauded at the Nürnberger Sängerwoche in July 1931. However, his involvement with Jewish subjects remained peripheral and constituted an expansion rather than a change in his style. In June 1931 the newly appointed opera manager, an advocate of the Nazi party, discontinued Ben-Haim's contract, allegedly for economic reasons. Left unemployed, Ben-Haim still viewed his situation as a temporary crisis. He kept looking for openings and in the mean time dedicated himself to composition, mostly of the large-scale oratorio *Joram*.[8]

In sharp contrast to Ben-Haim's ingrained order and self-discipline, Stefan Wolpe (1902–72) was a born rebel who never earned any formal diploma and instead led the bohemian life of a leftist avant-garde composer.[9] In addition to atonal music he also composed simple revolutionary songs for workers' theatres and arrangements of folk songs of Jews from eastern Europe.[10] With the Nazi rise to power, the storm troopers immediately turned to annihilate the communist groups and Wolpe's life was in imminent danger. Penniless and afraid of being recognized on the street, he managed a dramatic escape to Zurich via Czechoslovakia with the help of his friend and future wife, the Romanian pianist Irma Schoenberg, who also retrieved his manuscripts.[11] In May 1933 he went to Moscow to the International Workers' Theatre Olympiad and considered settling there, but 'some instinct prompted him to attend to the inner needs that he had so long neglected'.[12] From September to

---

[7] Ibid. 51 ff.; id., 'Heinrich Schalit and Paul Ben-Haim in Munich', *Yuval*, 4 (1982), 131–49.

[8] Based on Rudolf Borchardt's modern version of the Book of Job, the monumental oratorio was premièred only in 1979. Hirshberg, *Paul Ben-Haim*, 93.

[9] A. Clarkson, 'Stefan Wolpe's Berlin Years', in E. Strainchamps and M. Rika Maniates (eds.), *Music and Civilization: Essays in Honor of Paul Henry Lang* (New York, 1984), 371–93. A comprehensive study of Wolpe's unique personality will be Austin Clarkson's forthcoming *Stefan Wolpe, a Handbook*, which will also include an English edition of Wolpe's lectures and documents. The original scores and papers are in the collection of the Paul Sacher Foundation at Basel, Switzerland.

[10] *Ostjüdischer Volkslieder*, Op. 14, first performed in 1925. The *Ostjude* were Jews from Poland and Russia who immigrated to Germany. They never assimilated into the genuine German Jewry.

[11] Clarkson, 'Stefan Wolpe', 391. Irma Schoenberg was not related to Arnold Schoenberg.

[12] Ibid.

December 1933 he studied in Vienna with Anton Webern who taught him gratis. Despite the short duration of their encounter, there is ample evidence that Wolpe was deeply influenced by Webern's aesthetics and technique.[13] He then went with Irma Schoenberg to Romania, and five months later she convinced him that the only place to go was Palestine,[14] where her well-received recital as a guest of the Jerusalem Musical Society in 1931[15] had left her with favourable memories of the Yishuv.

Though born in Riga, Lithuania, Marc Lavri[16] (1903–67) received his entire musical training in Germany, where he studied composition at the Leipzig Conservatory under Paul Graener (1872–1944)[17] and conducting as Hermann Scherchen's private student. In 1926, after having been an opera conductor in Saar-Brücken for two years, Lavri settled in Berlin. He first worked as a musical director and conductor with Rudolf von Laban's dance theatre and composed music for Reinhardt's theatre productions and for films. In 1929 he became the conductor of the Berliner Sinfonie Orchester. The wheel then turned, and his concert in April 1932 was his last with the orchestra[18] which dispersed soon after. In April 1933, two months after the Nazi rise to power, Lavri returned to Riga, which was the target of a Fascist coup a year later, and he made up his mind to emigrate. Lavri was no Zionist and he hesitated between Palestine, Russia, and the United States. Like Ben-Haim two years earlier, Lavri secured a tourist visa and went to Palestine as his first station for preliminary exploration.[19]

The other composers from eastern Europe preferred Paris for their advanced studies. Alexander U. Boskovitch[20] (1907–64) was born in Cluj, Transylvania, to a deeply religious and highly respected family, whose ancestors were important Hasidic rabbis.[21] His general educational background was Hungarian, with strong influences of the ethnically hetero-

---

[13] M. Zenck, 'Das Revolutionäre Exilwerk des Komponisten Stefan Wolpe—mit kritischen Anmerkungen zur Musikgeschichtsschreibung der dreisziger und vierziger Jahre', *Exilforschung*, 10 (1992), 134–5.

[14] Austin Clarkson's interview with Irma Schoenberg-Wolpe, 4 Oct. 1976 (Stefan Wolpe Archive, Toronto).

[15] *Palestine Bulletin* (11 May 1931).

[16] He changed his original name, Lavritzki, while still in Europe.

[17] M. Lavri, 'Autobiography', *Tatzlil*, 8 (1968), 74–7. Graener was a prolific late Romantic composer, aesthetically close to Richard Strauss and Max Reger. L. K. Mayer, 'Graener. Paul, *MGG* v. 663.

[18] A typed comment by Lavri on the programme of the last concert (Lavri Archive (private)).

[19] An interview with Mrs Helena Lavri, the composer's widow, 9 Apr. 1986.

[20] The composer himself variously spelled his name Boskovics, Boskowitch, Boskovich.

[21] 'Boskovitch', *Encyclopedia Judaica*, iv. 1260. J. Hirshberg, 'Alexander U. Boskovitch and the Quest for an Israeli National Musical Style', *Studies in Contemporary Jewry*, 9 (1993).

geneous and multilingual region.[22] He took advanced piano lessons for a
short time in Vienna and then went to Paris, where he studied piano with
Lazare Levi and composition with Paul Dukas, who strongly influenced
his lifelong predilection for French music. Having returned to Cluj in
1930, he joined the local opera as a coach and later as a conductor. He
also founded a Jewish amateur orchestra named after the Jewish composer
Karl Goldmark (1830–1915). In 1936 Boskovitch joined a young group
of Jewish Zionist and communist intellectuals who strove to revive the
Jewish national identity in Transylvania. He undertook a fieldwork expe-
dition to remote Jewish villages in the Carpathian mountains which
inspired him to compose *Chansons populaires juives*, a suite of arrangements of Yiddish folksongs.[23] In 1937 he collaborated in a volume of
essays on Jewish topics, contributing his first study of Jewish music,[24]
which reflected the young composer's thorough knowledge of recent
achievements in Jewish music, such as Engel's group, and the music of
Ernst Bloch, as well as the proceedings of the Cairo Conference of
1932.[25] Boskovitch concluded with practical recommendations to develop
research, publication, instruction, and the dissemination of Jewish folksongs among the Jews of Transylvania, but made no reference whatsoever
to immigration to Palestine.

Oedoen Partos (1907–77) was born in Budapest. His grandfather was
a devout Jew but his parents were completely assimilated in the Gentile
society and as a young man he was indifferent to Jewish matters, whether
religious or national. He studied violin with Jeno Hubay and composition with Zoltan Kodaly at the Franz Liszt Academy during the
heyday of this venerable institution. A brilliant instrumentalist, he graduated at the young age of 17 and for the next two years was the leader of
the Lucerne Symphony. After an interim period in Budapest he settled in
Berlin in 1929 where he performed as a violinist with orchestras and

[22] Transylvania passed from Hungarian to Romanian rule after World War I. The region was
populated by Hungarians, Romanians, Germans, Gypsies, and Slavs. Most Jews spoke Hungarian,
and the extreme orthodox used Yiddish. Romanian was spoken by only about 5 per cent of the
Jews.

[23] Boskovitch used the transcription as presented in F. M. Kaufmann, *Die schönsten Lieder des
Ostjuden* (Berlin, 1920). The suite was later published under the title *The Golden Chain* by the Israeli
Music Institute.

[24] (Sandor) Boskovics, 'A Zsido zene problemas' (The Problems of Jewish Music), in *Kelet es
Nyugat Kozot* (Between East and West) (Cluj, 1937: a publication of the Jewish Students' Relief
Society), 31–7. The essay also included the music of Boskovitch's arrangement of the Jewish
folksong 'Yismach Moshe' (Moses will rejoice). Only two copies of the limited edition have been
located in Israel. A photocopy of Boskovitch's essay is kept at the Boskovitch Archive, JNUL.

[25] The Cairo Conference where Middle Eastern musicians and European scholars met for
discussions and recordings was a landmark in the history of ethnomusicology. See Ch. 11, below.

chamber ensembles. There he composed chamber works and also turned to composition for theatre, film, and cabaret which had reached its peak under the Weimar republic. Shortly after the Nazi rise to power he returned to Budapest. Huberman was interested in auditioning him but for unspecified reasons Partos suspended his reply and in 1936 he accepted an offer for a position in Baku, Azerbaijan, which appealed to his political tendencies as a youth and his interest in Asian music which had been aroused by his training under Kodaly. A brief close encounter with the Soviet system sufficed to change his mind, and when pressured to join the Communist party he resigned and returned to Budapest. He was about to sign a contract as leader and soloist in Lima, Peru, when Huberman invited him for an audition in Florence. The experience was so inspiring that he decided on the spot to accept the offer and in 1938 he settled in Palestine.[26]

Immigration and Resettlement Pangs

The only composer stemming from a committed Zionist family was Verdinah Shlonsky (1905–90) who differed from all other immigrant composers in the manner of her immigration and resettlement. She was born in Russia to a well-educated family imbued with Hasidic tradition and national commitment, signalled by her grandmother's immigration to Palestine during the Ottoman period. The entire family followed in 1921, leaving only Verdinah in Berlin where she studied piano at the Hochschule under Egon Petri and Arthur Schnabel. Verdinah's brother, Abraham Shlonsky (1900–73), excelled as an innovative Hebrew poet, editor, and critic, who dominated literary life in Palestine. The young pianist made a visit to her family in Tel Aviv in 1925, performed with her sister, the singer Judith Shlonsky,[27] and met Joel Engel who encouraged her to make her first folk song arrangement. From Berlin she went to study composition in Paris with Darius Milhaud. Her first composition, a Hebrew song cycle titled *Images palestiniennes*, was composed there and won the Nadia Boulanger Composition Prize.[28] Although she officially settled in Palestine in 1931, Verdinah Shlonsky returned to Paris a year later to continue her studies under Edgar Varese. In 1934 she returned to Palestine and became involved with composition of incidental music and songs for variety shows and also turned to symphonic music. Still, in 1937 she went again to Paris, most probably

[26] A. Bahat, *Oedoen Partos, his Life and Works* (Tel Aviv, 1984), 13–33.
[27] See Ch. 5, below.   [28] Paris, Édition Salabert.

feeling the need to 'recharge her spiritual and emotional batteries'.[29] Stranded in Europe, she escaped to London and returned to Palestine only in 1944.[30] Her international success as the sole woman composer active in Palestine attracted special attention.[31] She thus differed from the other immigrant composers for unlike them she had spent most of her formative years in Europe.

Egon Kunz has established the distinction between the anticipatory and the acute refugee. The former

leaves his home country before the deterioration of the military or political situation prevents his orderly departure. He arrives in the country of settlement prepared, he knows something of the language, usually has some finance and is informed about the ways in which he can re-enter his trade or profession,[32]

whereas the latter has little time to lose before facing imminent danger to his well-being and even to his life. The pre-migration conditions and the immigration experience of the immigrant composers ranged widely between the two. Unlike the performers whose admission to the Palestine Orchestra from 1936 until the outbreak of the war[33] secured them entry certificates, the composers had to find ways of bypassing the prohibitive-immigration Ordinance which classified applicants according to a set of categories. Only persons of independent means or assured income were not restricted. About one-half of the immigrants came under the Labour Schedule which required the Jewish Agency to 'submit to the Government once in six months an immigrant proposal indicating those economic branches in which the immigrants were expected to be absorbed.'[34] The list of required skills was frequently altered but 'musicians' never qualified, so that the immigrant composers used various ingenious schemes in order to enter Palestine. The only composer who entered as member of the Palestine Orchestra was the virtuoso violinist and violist Oedoen Partos (1907–77). The Polish violinist Joseph Kaminsky, one of the leaders of the Palestine Orchestra who held the post in rotation, turned to composition only in 1939 after his immigration.[35]

---

[29] Testimony by the pianist Yahli Wagman, the composer's nephew, 'Verdinah Shlonsky—In Memoriam', *IMI News* (Apr. 1990).

[30] A handwritten CV, kindly provided by the composer (Russ.).

[31] Moshe Gorali (Bronzaft), *Dvar Hashavua* (26 Feb. 1948).

[32] 'The Refugee in Flight: Kinetic Models and Forms of Displacement', *International Migration Review*, 7 (1973), 132.

[33] See Ch. 8, below.   [34] Gurevich and Gertz (eds.), *Statistical Handbook*, 94.

[35] Bahat, *Oedoen Partos*; J. Kaminsky, 'An Autobiography', *Tatzlil*, 12 (1972), 69–71; J. Stutschewsky, *Memoirs of a Jewish Musician* (Tel Aviv, 1977), 210.

The initial stage of entry by three of the immigrant composers was expedited by their previous reputation. Joachim Stutschewsky had been regularly corresponding with Professor David Schor, whom he had never met in person before his immigration, and with other members of Hanigun since 1929 and was well versed in the local musical and social scene.[36] Stutschewsky had a *Nansenpass* which meant that he had no protection of any government in case of emergency. Anticipating the impending difficulties, he hastened to leave Vienna in February 1938 for Zurich, his previous place of residence and work, where he received the news of the Anschluss. Although he was a dedicated Zionist, even he could not avoid an internal conflict:

Where should I turn, I, the wandering Jew? . . . America would probably provide me with economic security. I would find there work as a teacher. But the way of life there, the attitude ('time is money'), the completely different outlook of life . . . I decided against it. Russia? Once more I had many reservations. My father kept writing [from Russia], hoping for my return. But it was inconceivable that I, the pioneer of national Jewish music, the Zionist, would get an entry visa to Soviet Russia. I could not even reach any Soviet consulate. The road is blocked. Switzerland might be superb for me. They wanted me in Basel as teacher, chamber musician and soloist. I hesitated. I did not want to go on living and working in an atmosphere of hatred and contempt ('a tolerated foreigner') . . . Well then. The Land of Israel. Here I had to ignore objective circumstances. There was something else which called for Aliyah.[37]

Stutschewsky's poetic description of his internal conflict did not fully reflect the severity of his true condition. His *Nansenpass* was to expire in June 1938. After the Anschluss he could not renew the passport in Austria, nor could he extend his stay in Switzerland without a valid passport. Immigration to Palestine was his only outlet.[38] Yet he 'had no savings whatsoever' and could not make the security deposit required by the British consulate.[39] The columnist Hermann Swet tried to convince the PBS British director to form a special position of Director of Jewish music for Stutschewsky[40] and Dr Abraham Katzenelson, one of the prominent personalities in the National Committee, intervened on his behalf. The certificate then arrived within just a few weeks. In May 1938 Stutschewsky disembarked at Jaffa port where a delegation of colleagues waited to greet him and to offer him hospitality for the first few days.[41]

[36] Ch. 5.   [37] Stutschewsky, *Memoirs*, 193.
[38] Letters to Hermann Swet and Salli Levi, 8 and 12 Mar. 1938, WCJMP, quoted in Bohlman, *The World Centre for Jewish Music in Palestine 1936–1940* (Oxford, 1992), 107, 130.
[39] Ibid.
[40] Letter of 8 Mar. 1938. Archive of the WCJMP, JNUL. Stutschewsky, *Memoirs*, 193.
[41] Stutschewsky, *Memoirs*, 195.

Stutschewsky was primarily a performer, a collector of Jewish music, and a cello-teacher, in addition to which he invested much time and love in the organization of concerts of Jewish music, so that his work as a composer was relegated to a secondary place during the first period of his life in Palestine.

Sternberg had made himself known in Palestine through annual visits from 1925 onwards. His friends in the Yishuv welcomed his immigration in October 1931 with two concerts fully dedicated to his works. In a long preview David Rosolio introduced Sternberg to the public as an established composer of 'modern' music, 'which does not use the paved roads, as, for example, the classical or Romantic harmony... our world nowadays is not so harmonic that the artist who expresses his attitude to this world may do so with Mendelssohn's smooth and sweet sounds'.[42]

Boskovitch's immigration was likewise well prepared. Following the rise of Fascist government in Romania in 1938 he lost his position at the Cluj Opera and was unemployed. Desperately, he sent the orchestration of his *Chansons populaires juives* to the Jewish conductor Issay Dobrowen who accepted the work for performance in his forthcoming series with the Palestine Orchestra as the first première of a Jewish composition by the newly founded ensemble. The management invited Boskovitch to attend the event, and thus he earned the entry visa. He was met at the port of Haifa and was the guest of the orchestra for a few days.[43] Having no professional anchor in Cluj, he lingered in Palestine attempting to use the momentum of the performance to establish himself there. He had no difficulty in getting his new orchestral composition, *Four Impressions*, performed by the PBS orchestra.[44] Yet, they brought him little income, and he soon suffered the letdown of being unemployed in a new place at the grim initial period of World War II. For months he shared shabby rented rooms with friends, and at times was even forced to pass his nights sleeping on a bench in the public park.[45] His opera project ran aground after a few performances of Offenbach's *The Tales of Hoffmann*.[46] For a short while he worked as a music teacher at an elementary school and complemented his meager salary by private theory and composition lessons, gradually attracting young students who admired his charismatic

---

[42] *Ha'Aretz* (4 Oct. 1931). A chamber concert was held on 5 October, followed by a performance of Kompaneetz's *Concert Ensemble* two days later.

[43] Boskovitch later stated that the piece 'saved my life', in a paper at the Fourth Congress of the Institute for Liturgical Music, Jerusalem, 1964. A recording of the presentation is found at the National Sound Archive, JNUL.

[44] The première took place in Dec. 1938. The first movement was an orchestration of a short piano piece composed in Cluj.

[45] Communication by the composer's widow, the piano professor Miriam Boskovitch, May 1978.

[46] See Ch. 7, above.

personality. From 1944 the Habimah theatre commissioned him to write incidental music for which he received about £40 per score, a sum slightly surpassing an average monthly salary at the time.[47] Yet, the commissions were much too far apart, and Boskovitch maintained a bohemian way of life until 1946, when the new Academy of Music in Tel Aviv finally provided him with a small regular salary.

None of the other immigrant composers had even the limited benefit of previous notice of their arrival. Paul Frankenburger decided to emigrate soon after the Nazi rise to power, a year and a half after losing his position at the Augsburg Opera. In May 1933 he went to Palestine for a two-month exploratory tour, entering the country with a tourist certificate which did not allow him to make himself known through public performances. The adroit violinist and concert manager Moshe Hopenko convinced him to change his last name from Frankenburger to Ben-Haim in order to be inconspicuous.[48] He soon arrived at the bitter realization that 'despite my success and status in Germany, in this country I was in every respect an absolute nonentity, standing at the beginning of an unknown, mist-shrouded path (at the age of 35!)'.[49] During the next two months he proved himself to be a fine recital accompanist and was assured of a teaching position at Shulamit School. He felt encouraged when he realized that communicating in German with the local musicians presented no difficulty. He was utterly disenchanted with the low standard of the Palestine Opera,[50] by the absence of a professional symphony orchestra, and by the 'fierce competition' for piano pupils. Still, the situation in Germany tilted the balance in favour of immigration, although 'this would not be easy. Everyone has close links with the country in which he grew up'.[51] He tried to soften his trauma by making plans to use Palestine as an outpost for peaceful creative work, earning a modest living as an accompanist and theory teacher and looking forward to 'annual two-month visits to Europe (if I don't, living here will be unbearable) . . . Furthermore, my decision to transplant myself here does not commit me for the rest of my life!'[52] After a short return to Munich to settle his affairs Ben-Haim immigrated to Palestine in October 1933, securing a visa on the basis of his owning a capital of

---

[47] Boskovitch Archive, JNUL. Gurevich, *Statistical Abstract*, 141.

[48] Hirshberg, *Paul Ben-Haim*, 105. 'Ben-Haim' means 'Haim's son', which is the Hebraized form of Heinrich, Paul's father.

[49] 'My Immigration to the Land of Israel', *Tatzlil*, 11 (1971), 185.   [50] See Ch. 4, above.

[51] A letter to his father, 27 June 1966, Ben-Haim Archive, JNUL, quoted in Hirshberg, *Paul Ben-Haim*, 110.

[52] A letter to his father, 26 June 1933, ibid. See ibid. 97–148 for a detailed documentation of Ben-Haim's immigration and resettlement process.

£1,000 which represented all his savings from his work as opera conductor in Augsburg.

Equipped with a tourist visa only, Marc Lavri was more hard-pressed. Moshe Halevi, director of the Haohel theatre, wrote to Moshe Shertok, director of the Political Department of the Jewish Agency, that he was employing Lavri as a composer of incidental music and asked him to exert his influence and prevent the imminent deportation 'of such a talented and indispensable person'.[53]

Younger composers faced added hardships in their immigration process. Joseph Gruenthal (b. 1910)[54] had just graduated from the Staatlische Akademischen Hochschule in Berlin where he studied piano as well as composition under Paul Hindemith. Gruenthal stood no chance of securing a visa as a pianist. He found out that the British immigration authorities approved of his favourite hobby of photography as a skill and he hastened to enrol in a training course for a year and a half and in that way entered Palestine in 1934. He first worked at a photographer's shop in Haifa and later lived for over a year at the kibbutz Gesher.[55]

Born in Lithuania, Yehudah Bernstein (1911–89) studied piano with Alfred Cortot and composition with Nadia Boulanger in Paris. Unlike the other immigrant composers who were anticipatory refugees, Bernstein went through the trauma of a refugee in flight. He was an illegal immigrant, who started his arduous journey with the outbreak of the war in 1939. He made his way on foot with a few friends to the Black Sea, where he fell very sick with malaria. He then sailed for many weeks in a shabby Greek ship which ran out of food. Weak and undernourished, he nearly died on board. The British interned him at first in a refugee camp, following which he reached Tel Aviv ill and penniless. Ironically, the first person who came to his aid was the Lithuanian Consul who had known his father.[56]

Only a few composers immigrated with their families at a young age, establishing initial roots in Palestine prior to pursuing professional train-

[53] A letter from Moshe Halevi, 2 July 1936 (Lavri's Archive (private)). Moshe Shertok (Sharett, 1894–1965) later became minister of foreign affairs and second prime minister of the state of Israel.

[54] Gruenthal Hebraized his name to Tal after the foundation of the State of Israel. He has become the pioneer of the avant-garde in Israel, as the founder of the first studio for electronic music at the Hebrew University, where he was among the founders of the first department of musicology in the country (1965).

[55] A recorded interview with Prof. Joseph Tal (Gruenthal), 14 Feb. 1976. Tal, *Der Sohn des Rabbiners*, 139. Gesher is a kibbutz in the Jordan Valley, founded 1939 mostly by immigrants from Germany.

[56] An interview with Mrs Bernstein, 21 Apr. 1992. Bernstein immigrated to the United States in 1953 for personal reasons, adopting the name Julian Bern.

ing in Europe. The Polish Menahem Mahler-Kalkstein (Avidom, 1908–95) came in 1925, and a year later enrolled at the American University in Beirut. He then entered the French orbit studying composition in Paris for three years and returning to Palestine in 1931, on the eve of the mass immigration wave. The younger Mordechai Starominsky (Seter, 1916–94) immigrated from Russia with his family at the age of 10. In 1932 he went to Paris where he studied under Paul Dukas and Nadia Boulanger, and returned to Palestine in 1937. Despite their early immigration, both commenced their compositional activity together with the immigrants of the Fifth Aliya.

Earning Daily Bread

The forced migration interrupted the most crucial stage in the development and career of the immigrant composers. Most of them were in their thirties, on the verge of establishing themselves in regular teaching or performing positions, and the younger ones had to stop their academic studies. The sudden surge of nearly forty immigrants created fierce competition for the few available jobs, some of which were also open to performing musicians and to teachers.

Nearly all the immigrant composers settled in Jerusalem and Tel Aviv. Joseph Gruenthal (Tal) who joined the kibbutz Gesher soon encountered the difficulty of the young and struggling collective to recognize music as a required profession and returned to urban life. The contrast between Tel Aviv and Jerusalem deepened with the decision to anchor the Palestine Orchestra in Tel Aviv. Joachim Stutschewsky who first settled in Jerusalem wrote a moving profile of Tel Aviv upon his immigration in 1938, when he was still living in Jerusalem:

In the summer months I used to travel every week to Tel Aviv, the home of the homeless, of those deprived of their homeland. Whereas those left with no homeland who settled in villages and kibbutzim sent deep roots into the soil of the Land of Israel and were absorbed in their new home, the residents of Tel Aviv continued to lead the life of displaced persons. Tel Aviv is a magnet for new immigrants. They stick to Tel Aviv and are happy there. Tel Aviv at that period was not a garden town. There was little room there for peaceful meditation, for balanced thinking, for a purifying solitude. Still, there was something in the pace of life of this city. It stemmed not from its size but from its being an all-Jewish city.[57]

---

[57] *Memoirs*, 207. Stutschewsky refers to the original design of Tel Aviv as a garden suburb of Jaffa.

The Palestine Orchestra provided a secure income to the few of its members who became increasingly involved in composition,[58] and the newly founded music department of the PBS provided regular positions to just a few who could also conduct and make arrangements.[59] No other salary-paying institutions existed as yet, and the composers had to create the infrastructure for their own employment.

Occasionally, outside circumstances inadvertently created temporary job opportunities for adroit composers with a good training in improvisation and light music. Shortly after the outbreak of the war the hard-pressed British army converted Palestine with its supportive Yishuv into an enormous military base. The sudden presence of thousands of British, Australian, and Indian soldiers fuelled the crumbling economy and indirectly served as a blessing to some of the younger musicians who could barely make ends meet. Hotel bars and cafés employed musicians who played dance music. The pianist and composer Haim (Heinz) Alexander (b. 1915, immigrated 1935) played 'jazz', which implied music played exclusively for the dance floor, either by him alone, or with his friends, the composers Shabtai Petrushka and Herbert Brün who played the trumpet and percussion. Their repertory included popular American and English songs as well as Latin-American dances, such as rumba and *paso doble*. The only exception was the Hesse restaurant which was out of bounds for the rank-and-file. The more sophisticated officers who frequented the place expected Alexander to play Beethoven and Chopin.[60]

Private pupils could provide no more than pin money, and in the crisis-ridden economy of pre-war Palestine parents often could not afford to pay tuition for their children. Eager to communicate their expertise and knowledge, composers usually did not reject highly talented needy pupils, as was the case of Paul Ben-Haim who did not charge 12-year-old Moshe Lustig for his theory lessons.[61]

The immigrant composers hoped at first to be able to preserve a semblance of their European professional status, and at the same time be protected in their new land. In 1933 the young folk song composer Moshe Wilensky composed a successful hit for the review theatre

[58] Oedoen Partos, Joseph Kaminsky, and Heinrich (Hanoch) Jacobi. Joseph Gruenthal was a substitute harp-player.

[59] Karl Salomon, who was a conductor, arranger, and bass singer; and Hans (Hanan) Schlesinger who was a conductor and arranger.

[60] Interview with Professor Haim Alexander, Apr. 1992.

[61] P. Ben-Haim, 'Autobiography', *Tatzlil*, 13 (1973), 172. Moshe Lustig who died prematurely (1922–58) indeed excelled as a pianist and as composer.

Hamatate.[62] Wilensky seized an opportunity to issue a record of the song in London. Upon his return the theatre director claimed the rights to the song. Wilensky took him to court and the theatre lost the case. The affair caught the attention of an unemployed entrepreneur from Poland by the name of Markewitch who initiated the local version of the British Performing Right Society[63] and the Austrian Autoren, Komponisten und Musikverleger[64] which was named ACUM from its first informal action in 1934.[65] The official inauguration of the Society took place in 1936. For about two years Markewitch ran the endeavour from his rented room in Tel Aviv, pressuring the newly founded PBS to pay royalties for the limited broadcast on the Hebrew Hour. Markewitch was known for not keeping books, and whenever a composer or a poet met him on the street he used to pay him in cash on the spot. The improvised manner of payment angered the experienced composers, and the fiery Stutschewsky angrily took an action leading to the election of a new board, which included the composers Yedidiah Gorochov (Admon), Paul Ben-Haim, Menahem Mahler-Kalkstein, Joachim Stutschewsky, and Nissan Cohen-Melamed. In 1940 the Society was officially registered with the Mandate administration.[66] The board set rules and rates and negotiated agreements with the PBS and the Palestine Orchestra.[67]

Proliferation of Music Criticism

Encouraged by the growing number of new daily papers and periodicals, the field of musical criticism opened up to include new critics, whose official number soon reached sixteen.[68] The professional separation between composers and critics was, however, maintained and all critics came from the domain of musicology, performance, and education.[69] Born in Russia and trained as a pianist in Vienna, Olya Silbermann first collaborated with Rosolio in *Ha'Aretz* and later became a regular music critic for the socialist daily *Mishmar*. The locally born violinist Yariv Ezrahi first wrote in the literary periodicals *Ketuvim* and *Turim* and later

---

[62] Lit. 'The Broomstick', this popular theatre mounted review shows which consisted of political and social satire.

[63] C. Ehrlich, *Harmonious Alliance* (Oxford, 1989).   [64] Stutschewsky, *Memoirs*, 212.

[65] ACUM stands for Agudat Compositorim Umehabrim (Society of Composers and Authors). P. Yorman, *The ACUM Story* (Tel Aviv, 1977), 9.

[66] Ibid. 16.

[67] Stutschewsky, *Memoirs*, 212–13, Yorman, *ACUM*, 12. Menahem Avidom was elected president of ACUM in 1955 and held the position until his retirement.

[68] *Guide to Music in the Land of Israel* (Tel Aviv, 1942).

[69] The first professional composer who became critic was Alexander U. Boskovitch in 1956.

became the music critic of the conservative daily *Haboker*.[70] The field of music criticism was further bolstered with the immigration of Max Brod (1884–1968) in 1939. Born in Prague, Brod became in 1924 the theatre and music critic of the *Prager Tagblatt*. In 1930 he arranged for the publication of Franz Kafka's works. A versatile scholar, critic, and author,[71] Brod brought along the best tradition of a *Hausmusik* pianist. Having been appointed to the post of artistic advisor to the Habimah theatre, Brod turned to practical composition, taking lessons with the composers Ben-Haim and Boskovitch, who became his close friends and admirers. The musicologists Peter E. Gradenwitz and Paul Riesenfeld wrote reviews and critical essays in the local German press and, as long as conditions allowed, were correspondents of music periodicals in Europe and in the United States.

A prominent outcome of the immigration was a rejection of grand visions resting on flimsy grounds which had dominated the music scene in the 1920s. Most of the immigrant musicians lacked sympathy for old crumbling projects and they received the support of members of the first generation of locally born musicians. Reviewing the musical scene of 1933, the young critic Yariv Ezrahi resorted to a sardonic tone when writing about the venerable David Schor:

Various organizations: a depressing situation. Year by year—new plans, and each institute lives for twelve months, sometimes even less, and dies with no obituary. Just like that. Across the fence, as if committing suicide.[72] Strangely enough: sometimes the dead is suddenly resurrected. Professor David Schor is especially good at that. So far he has been: (*a*) Director of a music school (occasionally alive), (*b*) The president of the Institute for the Promotion of Music among the People, (*c*) The president of a 'chamber music Society' (defunct), (*d*) The president of Hanigun (dead but not buried yet, may rise to life at the proper time, (*e*) One of the directors of the Institute of Musical Sciences (dead, but recently infused with a donation, capable of rising again), (*f*) A music lecturer of the University (the only activity and institution which still really exists).[73]

Stratification of Professional Training

The most important long-term contribution of the immigrant composers was the infusion of new life into the professional music education. While

---

[70] Lit. 'The Morning'.

[71] Brod published historical novels, children's books, and numerous essays on Judaism, theatre, and music.

[72] Ezrahi alludes to the Jewish tradition of burying those who killed themselves outside the cemetery perimeter, suicide being banned by the Jewish religion.

[73] 'A Year of Music', *Turim* (20 Oct. 1933).

most of the best instrumentalists settled in Tel Aviv, it was the more academic-oriented Jerusalem which provided the drive towards a final stratification of professional music education in Palestine. The Hebrew University opened an Extension Division of Music in the spring of 1933, and in October of the same year the violinist Emil Hauser founded the Palestine Conservatoire of Music and Dramatic Art. Eighty-five pupils enrolled when the school opened and their number had doubled by the end of the first year and trebled by 1935. Twenty were 'Christians and Arabs'.[74] The new Conservatoire differed from the earlier music schools in the diversity of its programme and in the size of its faculty, which started with twenty-three teachers and soon numbered thirty-three. The Annual Report explicitly stated that eleven were immigrants from Germany who brought along with them new fields of study such as eurhythmics,[75] recorder, and guitar. The core of the curriculum was the individual instrumental instruction, but advanced pupils were also required to participate in theory and ear-training courses, chamber music, and orchestra. The school also launched a music teachers' training department and offered occasional courses in dance and stage directing. An important step was taken when the Conservatoire announced the opening of an Academy division for its fifteen advanced students who aspired to a professional career. Despite its heavily central European orientation, the Conservatoire appointed Ezra Aharon, a great oud-player and composer to teach Arab music.[76] The Conservatoire also invited the music publisher Benno Balan from Berlin to establish a printing plant 'which brought a small profit'.[77]

The only field of study which met with reservations was a proposed cantorial department. Salomon Rosowsky started a cantorial school in 1928 with money raised in the United States, but was forced to close it a year later when the funds ran out. Emil Hauser revived the project in 1936 when the renowned cantor and opera singer Hermann Jadlovker indicated his will to immigrate. Hauser wrote to Bialik Institute in Jerusalem and asked for financial support, since Jadlovker requested a monthly salary of £25 at least, much above the meager £10 which the Conservatoire could afford.[78] Apparently no action was taken since Hauser renewed the application more than two years later in a letter to

---

[74] First Annual Report 1933/4 (CZA S7/160). The category of Christians referred to European citizens, since some of the Arab pupils were also Christians.
[75] Taught by Käthe Jacob, a graduate of Dalcroze Seminary in Berlin.
[76] See Ch. 11, below.
[77] A letter from Dr Helen Cagan to the Jewish Agency, 11 June 1936 (CZA S7/296).
[78] A letter of 23 Dec. 1936 (Hauser Archive, JNUL, Mus. 54).

the Zionist leader Itzhac Grinbaum, who pencilled his negative response on the letter.[79] None the less, Hauser did open the course, but halted it two years later because of high costs.[80] While it is true that funds were hard to come by at that time, it appears that the project fell between two stools. The orthodox establishment which might have been interested in training cantors was not ready to co-operate with the secular establishment to which the Conservatoire belonged, whereas the financially hard-pressed Zionist leadership had no interest in training cantors.

The High Commissioner Sir Arthur Wauchope consented to become Patron of the Conservatoire and to head its Association of Friends. None of the eighty-odd members was affluent since their annual contributions ranged from £1 to £5 each, totalling no more than 8 per cent of the budget. The violinist Bronislaw Huberman, who had by then become deeply involved in the local musical scene,[81] raised the impressive amount of £141 at a single benefit chamber concert with Emil Hauser, Wolfgang Schocken, and Thelma Yellin, thus covering nearly 10 per cent of the first-year budget. By 1936 the school absorbed seven additional immigrants from Germany, most notably Stefan Wolpe.

The immigration Ordinance category of 'students whose maintenance is assured' enabled educational institutions to become actively involved in securing entry certificates for young applicants whose studies in Germany had been disrupted by persecution. The Conservatoire obtained the permission to grant certificates[82] and within a few months the school arranged for the immigration of nineteen pupils from Germany and five from Poland. The conditions of rescue operation under which the process worked have been described by one of the German students, Herbert Brün. Born in 1918 in Berlin, he was banished from school soon after the Nazi rise to power and for three years he worked as an apprentice at the firm of Reicha & Vogel which produced stage effects for opera houses. Having noticed a small newspaper notice of scholarships for the Palestine Conservatoire he secretly went to the audition which was held at a private apartment. He was immediately notified that he had earned the scholarship and was instructed to inform his shocked parents that he must leave Germany within one week. In September 1936 he travelled to Palestine via Genova, together with a few other students, among them Heinz (Haim) Alexander and Hans Block. Brün's scholarship covered his piano lessons with Arieh Abilea but left him barely any funds for his daily needs. Three months after his immigration he started playing the piano at

[79] A letter of 7 Feb. 1939 (Hauser Archive, JNUL, Mus. 54).
[80] Report of 1941/2, typewritten (Hauser Archive, JNUL, Mus. 54).
[81] See Ch. 8, above.   [82] An undated document (apparently 1936) (CZA S7/160).

a café in Jerusalem with a jazz band which included two violins, a trumpet, a double bass, and percussion. Working on a six-month contract and moving from one café to another, he played daily from 5 p.m. till midnight, earning his daily bread and leaving him most of the day for his music studies.[83]

The British administration requested that the school guarantee the maintenance of each pupil for the first year by a high deposit of £63 which the pupil or his parents had to pay back after their immigration. The complex methods of money transfer from Germany caused long delays until reimbursement,[84] pushing the economic situation of the school to the verge of a 'catastrophe'.[85]

With the outbreak of the war some of the older students were drafted to the British army, and consequently the development of the Academy division was hampered and the number of advanced Jewish students remaining was only sixteen. Still, the reputation of the Conservatoire attracted advanced students from Egypt, Syria, and Turkey,[86] and in 1941/ 2 the number of pupils reached 376.[87] The concentration of thousands of soldiers of the allied forces in Palestine boosted the 'amateur' classes with soldiers, 'who are pressed for time and wish to begin lessons immediately. Some of the refugees from Egypt during the German occupation took lessons during their stay in the country.'[88] The outbreak of the war halted the wave of immigration, and the proportionate number of locally born Hebrew-speaking pupils increased. The Conservatoire co-operated with Beno Balan in sponsoring the publication of the first music theory manual in Hebrew by Joseph Gruenthal (Tal),[89] who reported that the isolation of the country from Europe

doubled our zeal to maintain our work. Teaching was hampered by lack of professional literature. Scores could not be imported. I had modern works which were available in no more than a single copy photographed page by page and projected on the wall. An English officer allowed me to use his small Kodak projector which I used in countless lectures.[90]

The final step for professional stratification was taken in October 1944 when the Conservatoire opened a branch in Tel Aviv. After some ad-

[83] Herbert Brün left Israel in 1955, and after two years in Paris he went to Munich where Fritz Kortner employed him as composer for the theatre. In 1963 he settled in the United States as professor of composition at the University of Illinois, Urbana, Ill. An interview with Professor Brün, Apr. 1993, Toronto, Canada.

[84] A letter from Emil Hauser to Dr Landauer, 4 Aug. 1936 (Hauser Archive, JNUL, Mus. 54).

[85] A letter from Dr Helen Cagan to the Jewish Agency, 11 June 1936 (CZA S7/296).

[86] Annual Report, typewritten, June 1943 (Hauser Archive, JNUL, Mus. 54).

[87] *Guide to Music in the Land of Israel.*   [88] Ibid.   [89] Ibid.

[90] *Der Sohn des Rabbiners,* 216.

ministrative squabbles the branch became an independent Academy, dominated by the group of immigrants from Hungary, all graduates of the renowned Franz Liszt Academy in Budapest. The founders were the violinists Alice and Lorand Fenyves, the violist and composer Oedoen Partos, the flautist Erich (Uri) Toeplitz, and the cellist Laszlo Vincze, who were joined by the great piano pedagogue Ilona Vincze-Krausz and the composer Alexander U. Boskovitch.

The proliferation of numerous small music schools which had begun with Miriam Levit's resignation from Shulamit School in 1912[91] was reversed as a result of the pressure for tighter and more powerful organizations. Professor Leo Kestenberg initiated the unification of four of the small music schools of Tel Aviv into the Hebrew Conservatory, which by 1941 numbered fifty teachers.[92] Using his diplomatic experience, Professor Kestenberg prevented any loss of status in that the four former principals retained the titles of co-directors. Kestenberg himself was content with the position of chairman of the Pedagogical Board.

The venerable older music schools in Palestine, however, maintained proud independence. The oldest of them, Shulamit, made sure to indicate its inauguration year 1910 on its logo. In 1945 the school celebrated its thirty-fifth anniversary. World War II had just ended and the school boasted of the international success of its best locally born pupils, such as the pianist Penina Salzmann, who had just returned from an eight-month-long concert tour in England and Australia,[93] and the violinist Yiphrah Ne'eman.[94] Likewise, Professor Schor in Tel Aviv and Sidney Seal in Jerusalem also refused to merge with any new school.

The need to protect the rights of instrumental teachers, who were until then organized in several loose local associations, intensified with the new immigration. In 1941 the separate associations formed the Federation of Associations of Artists and Music Teachers in the Land of Israel. The first directory of the Federation listed the membership in the three cities. Tel Aviv took the lead with fifty-two piano-teachers compared to thirty-eight in Jerusalem and twenty-four in Haifa. Jerusalem listed thirteen violin-teachers and Tel Aviv only eleven, but almost none of the members of the Palestine Orchestra felt the need to register with the Federation although most of them gave instrumental lessons at home. Likewise, three cello-teachers registered in Jerusalem and two in Haifa, but most members of the cello section of the Palestine Orchestra taught as well, so that Tel Aviv took the lead in instruction of piano and strings.

---

[91] See Ch. 2, above.   [92] *Guide to Music in the Land of Israel.*
[93] *Haboker* (9 Feb. 1945).   [94] *Haboker* (13 July 1945).

The directory contained no names of teachers of wind instruments which attracted a very limited interest at that time. There were nine voice-teachers listed both in Tel Aviv and Jerusalem, compared to three in Haifa.

The majority of the immigrant composers and musicologists register-ed under the category of 'composition, conducting, musicology, and theory'. Once more Tel Aviv took the lead with thirteen teachers, com-pared to nine in Jerusalem and three in Haifa. Thus the process of making Tel Aviv the centre of music performance in Palestine continued.

The Wolpe Case and the Bastion of the Avant-Garde

The local music scene first encountered the hard core of European avant-garde with the immigration of Stefan Wolpe. His brief period of activity in Palestine was unusually intense even for the boiling cauldron of the local music scene, and his hasty emigration to the United States in October 1938 deprived the local composer-community of a powerful and committed personality. Tracing the circumstances which caused the fail-ure of Wolpe's resettlement sheds light on some of the more hidden facets of a musician's life in Palestine at that time.

Unlike Ben-Haim who reacted to the Mediterranean sound and the sights of Jaffa with the fascinated curiosity of a German tourist faced with the Levant,[95] Wolpe experienced a severe emotional shock. Irma Schoenberg has disclosed that he reacted to the first sounds of Arabic which he heard in Jaffa with the excited exclamation 'this is my sound' and he loved 'not the Jewishness but the native atmosphere' of Palestine. On the other hand he was 'in such a state of anxiety that he could not cross a street. He was absolutely lost for a few months'[96] and needed professional help before he resumed composition in late 1934. In 1935 Wolpe went to Brussels to attend a course in orchestral conducting given by Hermann Scherchen.[97] Thus Wolpe's regular activity in Palestine must have begun no earlier than the autumn of 1935 and lasted barely three years.[98]

---

[95] Hirshberg, *Paul Ben-Haim*, 103.

[96] Irma Schoenberg-Wolpe, an interview with Austin Clarkson, 1976 (Stefan Wolpe Archive, Toronto).

[97] Martin Zenck, 'Das Revolutionäre Exilwerk des Komponisten Stefan Wolpe', 135.

[98] See ibid. 132–3 for a catalogue of Wolpe's works 1933–45, to which *Four Ballades for a Mixed Chorus*, poems by M. Lifschitz (Jerusalem, 1938) should be appended.

Wolpe made a conscious distinction between two channels of musical activity.[99] He felt most content in the instruction of folk composers and in the venue of the kibbutzim. The other, in which he felt as though he were banging his head against a brick wall, was his professional activity as composer and teacher in Jerusalem.

In his farewell letter to his colleagues[100] Wolpe described his travels with his harmonium strapped to his back in order to organize and conduct choruses in the kibbutzim Merhavia, Usha, and Kiryat Anavim as the happiest hours of his activity in Palestine.[101] In his last lecture, given at the World Centre, Wolpe pointed out that musical consumption in Palestine was 'quantitatively astonishing; and this is for the greatest part in the hands of obsessed amateurs who—the whole lot of them—under different social circumstances, would have become professionals'.[102] The severe security conditions in the country jeopardized his efforts to gather the kibbutz musicians for regular courses. He therefore adopted David Schor's decentralized method and stated that training instructors 'carrying out a kind of mobile schooling should be the top priority of the professional musicians in the country'.[103] Despite transportation difficulties and security hazards there was a group of kibbutz members, among them Efraim Ben-Haim, Shalom Postolsky, and Mordecai Zeira, who took private lessons with Wolpe. Having acquired the financial approval of his kibbutz, Kiryat Anavim, Efraim Ben-Haim went to study composition in Jerusalem where he met 'the famous Stefan Wolpe. I invited him to direct the kibbutz choir, and took a few harmony lessons from him on those occasions, until he emigrated.'[104] Wolpe soon earned the reputation of a folk composer, as may be indirectly deduced from a reaction to a local kibbutz concert published in an internal publication. There one of the members anonymously warned against the danger that the kibbutz collective ideology might lead to a rejection of European music: 'Do we really have to abandon European cultural values? The recent programme included Mozart alongside Engel and Wolpe. The European culture is not superfluous for us.'[105] Wolpe's socialist world-view was rewarded when he composed music for the Mayday celebration of the kibbutz movement in the Valley of Jezre'el (Emek). The serene

---

[99] A lecture to the World Centre for Jewish Music, Aug. 1938 (Stefan Wolpe Archive, Toronto).
[100] 12 Sept. 1938, typescript (Stefan Wolpe Archive, Toronto).
[101] Letter to Colleagues, Jerusalem, 12 Sept. 1938 (Stefan Wolpe Archive, Toronto).
[102] Sept. 1938 (Stefan Wolpe Archive, Toronto).
[103] Ibid. For Schor, see Ch. 5, above.   [104] 'Autobiography', 127.
[105] Quoted in *Davar* (9 Dec. 1938).

memories of his kibbutz experience persisted after his emigration, and he observed that 'in Palestine there exists a closer co-operation between the composer and the people, as a result of which the composer becomes the guide of the amateurs, gradually heightening the musical values and preventing the stagnation of musical folklore'.[106]

The main arena of Wolpe's work, however, was urban Jerusalem. In 1936 Wolpe was appointed to the Conservatoire in Jerusalem as the first and only composition teacher. The Conservatoire paid the teachers according to the number of students they taught, causing petty jealousy and competition among the teachers. Wolpe soon realized that the office seldom referred students to him. Heinz (Haim) Alexander, Herbert Brün, and the youngest of them, the 14-year-old Peter J. Korn, came to Wolpe as private students and paid him from their scanty scholarships and their irregular earnings as café musicians.[107] Most of them also took piano lessons with Irma Schoenberg whose method they deeply admired, or with her assistant and close friend Elie Friedmann, so that Wolpe's home soon turned into a musical enclave and an informal school detached from and increasingly hostile to the Conservatoire. Asked about musical life in Jerusalem at this time, Irma Schoenberg replied that 'we were the musical life . . . Jerusalem has a certain way of making people cluster around a central personality and out of touch with other groups.'[108] The entire group of composition and piano students met once a week at Wolpe's home and once a month held an open concert of new music, whether at home or in a rented auditorium.[109] The repertory of those semi-private concerts included works by Debussy, Alban Berg's Piano Sonata, Max Reger's *Variations on a Theme by Mozart*, and Bartók's piano music. The group also used to listen to Bruno Walter's recordings of Mahler's symphonies. Peter J. Korn noted that 'anybody who would enjoy a Bartók work or even Stravinsky was considered radical. We had little or no twelve-tone music at all, and of course no way of getting it'.[110]

On 29 December 1935 Wolpe's circle attempted to launch the Palestine branch of the International Society for Contemporary Music with a concert held at the Conservatoire. The entire programme which included

---

[106] Stefan Wolpe, an introductory speech to a concert of his works, given in the United States, 1941 (Stefan Wolpe Archive, Toronto).

[107] Interview with Professor Haim (Heinz) Alexander, Jerusalem, Dec. 1992, with Herbert Brün, Toronto, Apr. 1993. Austin Clarkson's interview with Peter. J. Korn, Munich, May 1985 (Stefan Wolpe Archive, Toronto).

[108] Austin Clarkson, an interview with Irma Schoenberg-Wolpe, Apr. 1976 (Stefan Wolpe Archive, Toronto).

[109] An interview with Herbert Brün, Toronto, Apr. 1993.

[110] Austin Clarkson, an interview with Peter. J. Korn (Stefan Wolpe Archive, Toronto).

Stravinsky's Capriccio for Piano (in the two-piano arrangement) and *Four Russian Peasant Songs* as well as Wolpe's *Hölderlin Lieder* (1924) was fully repeated after the interval.

With no financial means to run the Society, Wolpe and Irma Schoenberg organized their later concerts under other auspices such as that of the Friends of the Palestine Conservatoire and the Jerusalem Association of Musicians which were not favourable to the cause of avant-garde music so that the programmes balanced works by Wolpe, Heinrich (Hanoch) Jacoby, and Stravinsky through the inclusion of works by Purcell, Debussy, Brahms, and Reger.[111]

The creation of an enclosed enclave of avant-garde devotees and semi-private concerts was an emulation of contemporary European groups which might have persisted for an extended period of time. Yet a series of acute incidents sparked a crisis which led to Wolpe's decision to leave the country. Having escaped the violence of the SS troopers, Wolpe felt increasingly fearful of the Arab Revolt[112] and concerned about the impending war in Europe.[113] In late 1936 Wolpe went with friends in a car which was side-swiped by an Arab car and driven into a ditch, following which he was hospitalized for some time.[114] His composition student Zvi Kaplan has noted that Wolpe was in a permanent state of fear of a war[115] and the violent accident was traumatic especially since Wolpe was convinced the Arab driver had deliberately caused it.

Initial reactions to Wolpe's works deepened his feelings of alienation especially when they took the ideological route. An anonymous reviewer (signed T.) of a performance of Wolpe's Passacaglia[116] and *March with Variations* at the Conservatoire was mildly favourable to those specific pieces. Yet, erroneously regarding Wolpe as Arnold Schoenberg's student, he renounced the entire style and spiritual world which they represented:

this music is especially alien to our life here, in Palestine . . . Wolpe has written also a few Palestinian songs and he directs several workers' choruses. Let us hope that he will depart from the road traveled by Schoenberg, Webern, and their

[111] Concerts held on 28 Mar. and 1 May 1938.

[112] The Arab Revolt which broke out in Apr. 1936 was directed both against the Yishuv and against the British administration. The revolt which resulted in many civilian casualties all over the country was repressed by the deployment of large British forces in Sept. 1936.

[113] Austin Clarkson, an interview with Zvi Kaplan, Apr. 1985 (Stefan Wolpe Archive, Toronto). Also stated in a personal communication with Prof. Austin Clarkson, quoted in P.V. Bohlman, 'The Immigrant Composer in Palestine 1933–1948: Stranger in a Strange Land', *Asian Music*, 17 (1986), 164.

[114] Austin Clarkson, an interview with Peter J. Korn.

[115] Austin Clarkson, an interview with Zvi Kaplan. Apr. 1985 (Stefan Wolpe Archive, Toronto).

[116] The last movement of *Four Studies on Basic Rows* (1936, pub. by Merion Music Inc.).

followers, from music whose roots are in the post-war decadence in western Europe, and that he will then breath the air of revival which surrounds us here, with all its delight and agony.[117]

Such a review must have been deeply insulting for Wolpe since the anonymous author totally misconstrued Wolpe's spiritual world in which his socialist-oriented activity in folk songs and amateur choruses could not be separated from his dedication to the avant-garde, both being expressions of his revolutionary urge to participate in the creation of a new world.

Wolpe's high hopes sparked off by the inauguration of the Palestine Orchestra soon faded when the management failed to invite Irma Schoenberg as piano soloist and rejected Wolpe's proposal to perform the orchestral version of his *March with Variations*. Composed in Romania on the eve of his immigration, the new work was very close to his heart and he took the refusal very badly. Irma Schoenberg performed the piece with Joseph Gruenthal (Tal) in a two-piano public recital at the YMCA auditorium but this did not heal the wound.[118] A slow official recognition of his importance was nevertheless forthcoming when on 5 July 1938 the Hebrew Hour of the PBS devoted a full thirty-minute programme to a live broadcast of Wolpe's songs for biblical and modern Hebrew poems,[119] complemented by his March, Op. 10, played by Irma Schoenberg. Yet this was too little and too late. Wolpe felt both alienated from and superior to most of his colleagues among the composers and arrangers whom he depicted as 'small people unwilling to spend their energies. Their limited talent forces them to think in unlimited analogies of musical cliches'.[120]

The last straw was a showdown with the Conservatoire. In late 1938 Wolpe took Irma's advice to air his grievances in a personal meeting with the management, which soon deteriorated into a shouting match,[121] following which Emil Hauser sent the couple an angry reprimand. On 12 September 1938 Wolpe reacted to Hauser's letter in a long document addressed to his colleagues.[122] He opened by introducing himself as a

---

[117] *Ha'Aretz* (7 Aug. 1936).

[118] An interview with Herbert Brün. Held on 12 Feb. 1938, the recital also included Feruccio Busoni's *Duettino concertante* as well as works by Brahms, Mozart, and Chopin. The concert is described in Tal, *Der Sohn des Rabbiners*, 197. The two-piano version has been published by Peer Southern Concert Music, New York.

[119] Texts from *Song of Songs* and poems by Rachel and by Zrubavel Gilad.

[120] 'Notiz über die musikalishe Situation', typewritten document (Jerusalem, 1938) (Stefan Wolpe Archive, Toronto). No record of any distribution of the bitter document has been preserved.

[121] An interview with Herbert Brün.

[122] An incomplete six-page single-spaced typed copy at the Wolpe Archive. It is not clear who if any received a copy of the letter. Hauser's letter has not been found and its contents are known only through the reference in Wolpe's response.

representative of the German avant-garde and as a morally committed 'professional maximalist'. An expression of warm gratitude to his many friends in the kibbutz movement followed. The bulk of the document revealed that the crisis was sparked off not only by personal conflicts but mostly by a deep ideological chasm between him and his colleague at the Conservatoire. Wolpe regarded the composition teacher as fulfilling the role of the 'conscience' of the conservatory, required to maintain the absolute professional standards not effected by the administration and by personal politics. He then angrily quoted derogatory comments made by his principal colleagues who ridiculed atonal music in general and his own *Four Studies on Basic Rows* and *Song of Songs* in particular. Most painful for him had been Hauser's disclosure that he had appointed Stefan Wolpe and Irma Schoenberg against the advice of the entire faculty. Wolpe wondered whether appointments should be made according to faculty consensus or by judgement of professional expertise. He then stated that Hauser's demand for group co-operation should be limited to the economic running of the school, whereas each teacher should have the absolute rights for ideological independence.

Wolpe's loyal students organized a farewell concert of their works in October 1938, representing the fruits of less than two years of studies with their admired teacher. Wolpe introduced the evening with a moving speech in flowery German in which he expressed his sorrow that he would not be able to continue 'to lead their vigour any longer towards a new, bold disorder'.[123] The students prepared extended programme notes in which they pointed out the social isolation of the contemporary artist and praised Wolpe's attention to the individual personality of each of his students. With the exception of the 13-year-old Hemda Davis who was born in England, his other students consisted of a group of German immigrants of varying ages.[124] The excerpts from their student works reflect Wolpe's avant-garde predilections, as in Peter J. Korn's violin and cello Duo (see Ex. 10.2).

Wolpe's emigration deprived both the nascent avant-garde and the musical scene of the kibbutz movement of their most committed and qualified spokesman. His abrupt decision stemmed from three reasons: a deeply ingrained fear of war and violence, disappointment with the

---

[123] 'Dass ich ihre Kräfte nun nicht mehr in neue, kühnere Unordnung bringen darf...'. Mimeographed programme notes, kindly provided by Prof. Haim Alexander.

[124] Wolpe's students, as mentioned in the programme notes, were Hemda Davis (b. 1925); Heinz (Haim) Alexander (1915); Ernst Hirsch (b. 1918); Werner Sussmann (b. 1910); Peter Jona Korn (1922); Herbert (Zvi) Kaplan (b. 1916); Wolf Rosenberg (b. 1915); and Dr Salli Levi (1894–1951). The material has been kindly provided by Prof. Haim (Heinz) Alexander.

Ex 10.2. Korn, Duo

Palestine Orchestra, and his break with the Conservatoire. While the first reason was beyond anyone's control, it appears that his reaction to the two other factors was unfortunately too emotional and subjective. While the Conservatoire undoubtedly did not fit Wolpe's professional and moral principles, he and Irma nevertheless were surrounded by a loyal group of fine students unmatched by any other musicians in Palestine which could have served as the basis for a small school of their own. Moreover, while deeply sensitive to the difficulties of amateur musicians in the kibbutzim, Wolpe was oblivious to the precarious institutional and personal situation of the newly founded Palestine Orchestra, which the outsider Hermmann Scherchen noticed immediately on his arrival a year later.[125] Wolpe ignored the need to allow the heterogeneous and still transient new ensemble a little time to build its performance expertise playing the standard repertory and to stabilize its subscription audience. Moreover, though highly regarded within his own circle, the 34-year-old Wolpe had not yet established his reputation in Germany and should not have expected a traditional artist such as Huberman to accept his first proposal immediately.[126]

Thelma Yellin, Max Lampel, and Arie Abilea whom Wolpe quoted as ridiculing his avant-garde style were all of earlier immigration vintages. They had been raised on different traditions and must have felt threatened by the new wave of immigration. Yet their conservatism was not shared by the entire local community. Ironically, Wolpe's emigration precisely coincided with the bold initiative taken by Erich Walter Sternberg, Mahler-Kalkstein, Frank Pollack, and Joachim Stutschewsky,[127] who revived the Palestine branch of the International Society for Contemporary Music with a well-prepared concert dedicated to the memory of Maurice Ravel. The Society continued with a regular concert series which soon formed its own élite enclave, emulating similar circles in Berlin and

---

[125] See Ch. 8, above.

[126] A view shared by Prof. Lorand Fenyves, an interview, Apr. 1993, Toronto. See Chs. 8, above, and 13, below for a discussion of the repertory distribution of the Palestine Orchestra.

[127] *Palestine Post* (14 Oct. 1938).

Vienna. Most concerts took place at the private home of Dr Shalom Hildesheimer. Though an eager advocate of music for the masses, the critic Menashe Ravina (Rabinowitz) supported the new series because of its educational nature and went as far as insisting that the programmes 'should by no means cater to the taste of the broad public. It is undesirable to expand membership and for a while at least the concerts should be limited to a certain circle of listeners wishing to study and familiarize themselves with the new repertory.'[128] Ravina even questioned the inclusion of Debussy's *Danses sacres et profanes* in the series, because 'it may be played at any regular concert'.[129] The series, though financially limited to no more than a concert every two or three months, maintained a high artistic level. The performers used to repeat one of the pieces at the end of the programme in accordance with the audience's request, such as when Oedoen Partos repeated the Sonata for viola solo by Paul Hindemith.[130] The series became a venue for the innovative immigrant composers such as Sternberg whose piano work *Visions from the East* was performed in the third concert. The newly founded 'Hungarian' quartet[131] featured works by Kodály and Leo Weiner in the fifth concert. The two leading critics differed in their evaluation of audience attendance in the Society's concerts, possibly because of the frequent alternation between small public auditoriums and Hildesheimer's residence. David Rosolio stressed the 'large attendance' at the second concert[132] whereas Ravina complained that the number of listeners 'was even smaller than could be expected', and commended the participants, 'who not only addressed themselves to others but played for their own satisfaction'.[133] Rosolio must have been more realistic in his expectations, since contrary to his colleague, he observed an 'increase in the number of listeners to those concerts'.

With the notable exception of Stefan Wolpe, the immigrant composers overcame the trauma of resettlement. Some never completed the process of assimilation. Erich Walter Sternberg and Hans Schlesinger never overcame the difficulties of Hebrew and kept communicating only in German and English. Others had to reorder their priorities, as, for instance, when Boskovitch and Ben-Haim minimized their activity as conductors and concentrated on composition and teaching. Yet, against all odds they followed Ben-Haim's firm decision: 'Look ahead, not back.'[134]

[128] *Davar* (6 Jan. 1939).   [129] Ibid.   [130] *Davar* (28 Apr. 1939).
[131] Lorand and Alice Fenyves, Oedoen Partos, and Laszlo Vincze.
[132] *Ha'Aretz* (20 Jan. 1939).   [133] *Davar* (26 June 1939).
[134] A letter to his father, 27 June 1933. Hirshberg, *Paul Ben-Haim*, 110.

11

My Heart is in the East

RABBI Yehudah Halevi's verse 'My heart is in the East and I am at the edge of the West'[1] embodied the dream of the Diaspora Jews to return to their ancient homeland. The national revival has transformed the East from a dream into a reality, urging artists in all fields to abandon vague orientalism and face the properties of the real East.

Idelsohn's emigration to the United States in 1921[2] suddenly deprived the country of its only great music scholar. For the following dozen years the quest for the East was pursued by ideologists, practising musicians, and critics, who acted under extreme ideological pressures to present quick results. They were faced with the challenge of determining the properties of a still non-existent national style based on the barely mapped field of the music of the eastern communities which, unlike Idelsohn, they were untrained to study.[3] This unfavourable starting-point inevitably resulted in vagueness and in heated debates. To illustrate, Idelsohn's study endowed the Yemenites with a mythical aura. Yet, a deep chasm separated a scholarly study of Idelsohn's printed transcriptions from an immediate penetration of elements of live Yemenite music into concert life. The main difficulty was how to acquaint western-educated musicians and concert-goers with the genuine musical heritage of the eastern Jewish communities in general, and with the Yemenites, who were at the centre of attention, in particular. None of the immigrant composers and

---

[1] Yehudah Halevi (c.1075–1141) was one of the greatest Jewish poets and philosophers in Spain during the Moslem period. Trans. in T. Carmi (ed.), *The Penguin Book of Hebrew Verse* (Harmondsworth, 1981).

[2] See Ch. 1, above.

[3] See R. Katz, 'Exemplification and the Limits of "Correctness"', *Memorial Volume*, 367 for an analysis of Idelsohn's rigorous method.

performing musicians in the country had the basic training in anthropology and in fieldwork techniques required in order to enter the enclosed Yemenite communities and interact with their music in the proper context. The music of the eastern communities was bound to the life-cycle and the yearly cycle which demanded an unbroken continual practice of traditional songs, whether by the professional *meshorerim* (singers) or by the entire community. Music was extensively used on the Sabbath and the many holiday services,[4] which were complemented by the frequent events in the extended families such as elaborate wedding ceremonies, graduation of the boys (bar mitzvah), circumcisions, and funerals, as well as by communal events, such as the inauguration of a new synagogue or of a new Torah (Pentateuch) scroll.[5] Such functions were open to outsiders only on rare and irregular occasions. The earliest on record took place in December 1885 when the poverty-stricken Yemenite Jews entered the first houses built for them in the village of Silwan. The two Hebrew newspapers reported that there were many guests on that occasion who were very excited to hear the Yemenite traditional songs.[6] Yet such events were rare exceptions, and in general the Yemenite way of life and spoken dialects were not understood by members of the New Yishuv.

Brief quotes of tunes and motives from Idelsohn's Thesaurus became fashionable among Jewish composers in Germany and in Palestine, but they hardly advanced beyond the external orientalism shown, for example, in Heinrich Schalit's *Freitagabendsliturgie.*[7]

The members of Engel's group were mostly interested in the heritage of the East European Jews. Yemenite and Babylonian tunes were occasionally included in sets of pedagogical arrangements of eastern European Jewish songs, such as Stutschewsky's compilation of thirteen

---

[4] The Jewish yearly cycle includes the Solemn High Holidays of New Year (Rosh Hashanah), The Day of Atonment (Yom Kippur), the Feast of Tabernacles (Sukkoth), which are celebrated in close sucession in Sept.–Oct.; The Feast of Lights celebrating the victory of the Maccabeans (Hanuka) in Dec.; Purim celebrating the miracle related in the Book of Esther in Mar.; the High Holiday of Passover celebrating the Exodus in Apr.; the High Holiday of Weeks (Shavuoth) in June and the fast days of mourning over the destruction of the Temple in July–Aug.

[5] See A. Shiloah, *Jewish Musical Traditions* (Detroit, 1992), 181 ff.; Y. Adaki and U. Sharvit, *An Anthology of Jewish Yemenite Songs* (Jerusalem, 1982), and a recording by N. and A. Bahat, *Jewish Yemenite Songs from the Diwan* (Jerusalem, 1982), Eastronics AMTI B201.

[6] *Havatzelet*, 10, and *HaZevi*, 9 (1885). Silwan is an Arab village on the steep slope opposite the Mount of Olives. The first Yemenite immigrants who arrived in 1882 lived there in hideous conditions, some in caves.

[7] Heinrich Schalit (1886–1976) was an organist and a composer of Jewish liturgical music. Born in Vienna, he lived in Munich from 1907 until his immigration via Rome to the United States in 1939. See Michael Schalit, *Heinrich Schalit, the Man and his Music* (Livermore, Tex., 1979), and Hirshberg, 'Heinrich Schalit and Paul Ben-Haim in Munich', 131–49.

Ex 11.1. Stutschewsky, *Thirteen Jewish Folk Tunes*, No. 5

Ex 11.2. Weinberg, *The Pioneers*, 'Yemenite Song'

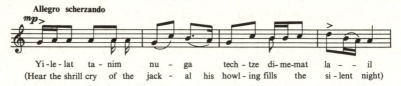

Jewish folksongs for violin (or cello) and piano published by Juwal in Tel Aviv; these included a single Babylonian tune derived from Idelsohn's Thesaurus (see Ex. 11.1), but its tonal harmonization made it difficult to notice its distinctiveness in the small compilation.[8]

Only rarely did the few composers of Engel's circle attempt to achieve direct contacts with the music of the Yemenites. One result of such a direct contact was the tune of the 'Yemenite Song' (see Ex. 11.2) in Jacob Weinberg's opera *The Pioneers*[9] of which the composer wrote that 'Mr Idelsohn and Mr Saminsky consider it a tune of the Georgian Jews. It is possible. Yet I heard it from the Yemenites in the village of Silwan'.[10] Weinberg's observation revealed his method of work. He first went to Silwan with the intention of selecting the proper tune for his opera through a direct encounter with the community. Then he contrasted his transcription with earlier publications, inadvertently exposing the difficulty of formulating precise definitions of the ethnic origin of certain traditional tunes within the ethnically heterogeneous society in Palestine.

The attitude of the European Jews to the Yemenite culture was a blend of Romantic idealism and patronizing colonialism. On the one hand the Yemenites were considered to be a cheap labour force. The well-to-do women of Tel Aviv coined the phrase 'to take a Yemenite' as a synonym

---

[8] J. Stutschewsky, *13 Judische Volksweisen* (Berlin and Tel Aviv, n.d.), no. 5.

[9] (J. Fischer & Bro., New York, 1932).   [10] 'My Concert', *Do'ar Hayom* (4 May 1927).

for 'to hire a cleaning woman'. On the other hand, the Yemenites were also considered to possess a deep and sincere religious attitude, folk wisdom, and an exotic folklorist aura, as implied in a glowing review of a ball which the young Yemenites organized to assist 'the hunger-stricken Jews in Yemen'.

It was a real pleasure to witness how the young generation of Yemenite Jews comes closer to a high cultural level. All the numbers in the performance were in good taste, albeit devoid of any real depth. They provide a genuine, almost photographic, reflection of Yemenite life. Their dances were full of grace and rhythm, and their oriental ornamental tunes were pleasant to listen to. . . . Such a ball makes one envision a regular Yemenite stage which would be guided by a qualified hand. Several numbers were encored at the request of the audience, which was different from that of other theatres.[11]

The Yemenite Mediators

While still catering to a special audience, the Yemenite ball marked the onset of a complex mediation process which implied a significant change of behaviour, attitude, and context on the part of both eastern performers and western-trained audience and musicians. Interest in Yemenite music was until then unidirectional and limited to a few scholars and composers. As soon as Yemenite performers began to appear on the public concert stage the interest became mutual.

Significantly, the first two stage personalities of the Yemenite community were young women: Bracha Zefira and Sarah Asnat-Halevi. There was much in common in their years of apprenticeship. Both were orphaned in their early childhood and both broke the community pattern according to which girls were kept at home until their marriage at a very young age.

Bracha Zefira (1910−90) was born in a Yemenite family in Jerusalem.[12] Her mother died bearing her, and her father, a poor scribe of sacred objects, became the victim of typhoid fever when she was 3 years old.[13] Zefira refused to disclose her birth date, which was found after her death in an official statement of her passport details, where the date is given as

---

[11] *Ha'Aretz* (28 Jan. 1929). The idea of a Yemenite stage was indeed implemented but only in 1949 when the choreographer and folk composer Sarah Levi Tanai founded the Inbal dance theatre.

[12] Her Hebrew name went through various transliterations. She adopted the spelling 'Zefira' in a legal letter to Columbia Records, New York, 12 July 1947 (Zefira Collection, Archive of Israeli Music, Tel Aviv University).

[13] A recorded interview, 1980.

15 April 1910.[14] The charity organization Orphan Aid placed her with a foster family of Jews from Bukhara and three years later moved her to a Sephardi widow whom she was forced to help in her work as laundry woman.[15] Still, unlike other Yemenite girls of the period, Zefira studied in an elementary school in the old city of Jerusalem. Naturally endowed with a superb musical memory, she absorbed traditional songs of different ethnic groups. At the age of 11 she was sent to the Shfeyah boarding-school.[16] There she began the first stage of her career in the course of which she served as a mediator between East and West. The school principal Hadasah Rosenblit, a sensitive woman who felt a special empathy towards the Yemenite girls, heard the girl singing the Yemenite *Hamavdil* and encouraged her to perform the song on all Saturday-night school assemblies.[17]

Restless and ambitious, Zefira left school after three years and returned to Jerusalem where she studied piano and music theory at the Palestine Conservatoire for about two years. She was then admitted to Menahem Gnessin's theatre school where she was trained for three years,[18] subsisting on a meagre income as a singer at the satire theatre Hakumkum.[19] In 1930 she made a bold decision and used her limited savings to study theatre in Berlin although she did not know German at all. The famous director Jessner was impressed by her audition and enroled her in Rolf Reinhardt's school. She occasionally visited the Jewish Community Centre where she met the pianist Nahum Nardi,[20] a young Russian Jew endowed with a brilliant technique and a special gift for improvisation. They married and embarked on an ambitious concert tour in the Jewish communities of Poland, followed by performances in Berlin, where Zefira was much encouraged when Albert Einstein attended the concert and then invited her for a discussion at his house. The tour continued in

[14] A letter to Mr Prins, Amsterdam, 19 Nov. 1948 (Zefira Collection, Tel Aviv University).

[15] Dora Rosolio, 'Bracha Zefira', *Dvar Hapoelet*, 7 (24 June 1940), 79. Dora Rosolio, David Rosolio's wife, was a highly respected music educator.

[16] Shfeyah was an agricultural school and a youth village about 20 km. south of Haifa. It opened for boys in 1923, and a year later also for girls.

[17] Bracha Zefira, 'Hadasah Rosenblit in Memoriam', *Davar* (22 Oct. 1945). *Hamadvdil* is a traditional paraliturgical song signifying the termination of the holy Sabbath.

[18] Menahem Gnessin (1882–1952) was a pioneer of the Hebrew theatre. He first came to Palestine in 1903 and founded an amateur troupe in 1907. He then returned to Russia where he directed an amateur Jewish theatre. In 1923 he moved to Berlin where he established the Theatre of Eretz Yisrael (TEI). He immigrated with the entire cast to Palestine in 1925, shortly before Zefira joined his theatre course.

[19] Lit. 'The Kettle', the troupe was founded by the poet Avigdor Hameiri. The programmes consisted of light skits and songs.

[20] Nardi was the Hebraized form of Naroditzky.

Latvia, Belgium, Holland, and France.[21] Their programme consisted of three ethnic divisions of songs—Yemenite, Bedouin, Sephardi—as well as children's songs by Nardi. Piano pieces, such as a Gavotte by Gluck and a Rhapsody by Liszt served as piano interludes. A charismatic stage personality endowed with a dark beauty, Zefira enriched her performances by means of colourful oriental costumes and stage lighting.[22] The Sephardi composer and scholar Leon Algazi, who resided in Paris, was spellbound:

Miss Zefira creates with her facial expression, with her gestures, a refined scene of the highest order. She achieves this with her special undefinable charm of the oriental voice which we have never heard before in Europe and also by her exquisite manner of Hebrew pronunciation. Upon listening to this 19-year-old child, I say to myself that Miriam, Deborah, and Shulamit, must have spoken and sung in that way. Hebraism then becomes real, alive, and it is enough for me to listen to this authentic accent in order to feel myself Hebrew in my thought, in my heart, in my blood.[23]

Zefira and Nardi returned to Palestine in 1930 and immediately set up a busy schedule of public concerts. Zefira's reputation abroad did not prevent initial difficulties; for instance, the owner of a Tel Aviv auditorium refused to rent it to a Yemenite, an action resulting in an angry press rebuke.[24] In April 1931 the couple embarked upon a tour in Egypt, where they performed for an entire week during the intervals of the matinee and night shows at the Rialto Cinema in Alexandria. The Arabic posters hailed her as 'the famous eastern singer' and announced a programme of 'stunning Bedouin songs'[25] but the local English reviewer defined her as a 'Yemenite singer' and noted that

her debut . . . was made to a full house, when she was received with great enthusiasm, while the calls for encores indicated the appreciation of the audience. Sung in Hebrew, the selections have a charm peculiar to that language, which, however, it is unnecessary to know in order to appreciate the talent of Mlle. Zefira.[26]

---

[21] Yosef Nedava, 'Bracha Zefira', an unidentified press clipping (Zefira Collection, Tel Aviv University).

[22] Most of the songs were preserved in recordings by CBS-CP-1112. Nardi published his arrangements much later, after his separation from Zefira, but the notation does not record his brilliant improvised playing.

[23] An excerpt from L'Univers Israelite, 1929 (Zefira Collection, Tel Aviv University).

[24] Nedava (Zefira Collection, Tel Aviv University).

[25] A poster (Arabic) and notices in French and Greek (Zefira Collection, Tel Aviv University).

[26] Egyptian Gazette (24 Apr. 1931) (Clipping at Zefira Collection, Tel Aviv University).

Zefira's repertory and performance style caught the self-confident western-educated critics in Palestine by surprise. David Schor, devoted as he was to the cause of Jewish folk songs, criticized Zefira's oriental quality of voice, claiming that 'she has no voice, and what little she has is blighted by the intonation characteristic of Yemenite, Sephardi, and Arabic singing.'[27] Yet, some of the columnists objected to the reserved reactions of the professional musicians: 'Will the real critics forgive me: I attended the concert of Bracha Zefira and Nahum Nardi ... and I enjoyed it very much.'[28] Another columnist warned against a hasty judgement:

The unwary listener faces two traps in attempting objective criticism of a Sephardi singer. The critic, who is usually European and unaccustomed to that style of singing, is sometimes impressed by its exoticism, and his unfamiliarity inspires sky-high praise ... On the other hand, it sometimes happens that the reviewer, unaccustomed to oriental singing and whose taste is not sufficiently developed to enable him to perceive the fine distinction between one song and another, ... finds them all boring ... In my opinion, this obligates the critic to keep his counsel until he gets used to the new style of singing.[29]

Members of the Sephardi community, on the other hand, immediately realized the unifying social potential of Zefira's contribution. The Sephardi author Yehudah Burla observed that 'the listeners, immigrants of different origins who are used mostly to European singing, are attracted by and attached to her singing. The audience is sensitive to those folk qualities, and all their bones shall say: this is an act of creation on this stage!'[30]

Bracha Zefira set the wheels in motion and touched a sensitive nerve of the Sephardi and Yemenite intellectuals who were constantly on guard lest their cultural heritage be jeopardized, as Sarah Asnat-Halevi soon realized when she tried to jump on the bandwagon. She was also an orphan, educated at the Shfeyah boarding-school where her theatrical talent was discovered. She then studied dance and music in Tel Aviv, and married an Ashkenazi artist, the actor Moshe Walin. Her friends urged her to follow Zefira in initiating her career in Europe. After successful performances in Bucharest and in Vienna she returned to Palestine where she emulated Zefira's programme of ethnic and folk

---

[27] *Davar* (24 Oct. 1930).   [28] LANI (a pseudonym), *Ha'Aretz* (4 Feb. 1932).

[29] Haim Weiner, *Ha'Aretz* (9 June 1933).

[30] *Ha'Aretz* (11 Mar. 1932). The author paraphrases Psalm 35: 10. Born in Jerusalem, Burla (1886–1969) was a member of a respected Sephardi family. Many of his stories deal with the cultural encounter of different immigrant groups in Palestine.

songs. Yet, Yehudah Burla, the Sephardi author who had just praised Zefira's pioneer endeavour, signalled an alarm regarding the new artist:

The art of eastern singing is now a barren neglected land. This singing has sounded strange and remote to the ear and feeling of our western audience. Such a situation is understandable: singing is the emotional expression of the race. . . . It is clear that an education and training is required in order to become accustomed to the singing of another race. When a real talent like Bracha Zefira has appeared together with a musician of the statue of Nahum Nardi we have had hopes that with effort and dedication they would gradually unveil the treasures of the expression of eastern singing . . . But recently another alleged new artist, Sarah Asnat-Halevi, leaped on to the stage and confused the public. Her singing is a far cry from being eastern.[31]

Burla's unprecedented assault on the young artist caught the editor of *Ha'Aretz* by surprise and he invited a response from the singer's most dedicated advocate, the prestigious poet Avigdor Hameiri. The latter provided literal translations of reviews by the most pedantic Viennese critics as proof of the singer's talent:

She evokes the legendary world of the East in front of our eyes. She is a little Hebrew Sheherezade from Yemen who tells us A Thousand and One Nights in Hebrew. Does she only tell them? She lives them anew, she reveals this world to us, she infuses life into remote legends, beyond the sea and the mountains.[32]

Another columnist went as far as to admonish the audience for its reserved response:

Sarah Asnat-Halevi is unlucky with our audience. Or maybe our audience is unlucky with her. And maybe our audience is so spoiled that it has waited for the critics, and when they were late in coming, the audience began to wonder whether the new genre is beneficial or damaging to our artistic life. This silence must stop for the sake of the truth and for the sake of art. . . . We must protect her, since she is blessed with artistic talent.[33]

The intensity of the disagreement revealed the deep seriousness with which the issue of east–west encounter was treated in the intellectual circles of the Yishuv. The western-educated musicians and columnists were embarrassed to find themselves totally unprepared for a serious evaluation of the new public genre of eastern songs, whereas the Sephardi intellectuals became aware of the danger of an uncontrolled and commercial exposure of their treasured heritage. The young singer herself was

[31] *Ha'Aretz* (14 Apr. 1933).   [32] *Ha'Aretz* (22 Apr. 1933).
[33] A. S. Juris, *Ha'Aretz* (8 June 1933).

totally unprepared to become embroiled in the polemics. She went to the United States after her second European tour in June 1934. There she participated in the New York revue *The Palestine Show*[34] and later tried her luck in Hollywood. She returned to Palestine only in 1947,[35] thus focusing all attention on the persistent Zefira.

A new stage had been reached with Zefira's participation in the momentous inauguration broadcast of the PBS in March 1936 which marked the official recognition of the East by the establishment. From that moment onwards reviews and commentaries became more penetrating and frank. The increased public exposure raised the issue of the purity of the ancient and proud tradition. The Yemenite columnist Shalom Levi Nahum reproached the radio programme director for his inaccurate presentation of the Yemenite songs which were ascribed to the medieval Sephardi poets Yehudah Halevi and Shlomo Ibn Gabirol rather than to anonymous ancient Yemenite poets. He also admonished the radio announcer for his faulty pronunciation of archaic words in the Yemenite dialect. It soon became clear that the promoters of Yemenite music were inadvertently at cross-purposes. Their wish to expose multi-ethnic audiences to Yemenite music required compromises which even the purists felt forced to adopt. Shalom Nahum remarked that the Yemenite singer Leah Jenteli pronounced the text in the accent of Aden which substituted the vowel 'a' for 'o' thereby making it difficult for the mixed audience to follow her otherwise beautiful rendition of the Yemenite songs.[36] Karl Salomon, the director of the Music Programmes of the PBS,[37] tried to find the middle road on the more sensitive issue of arrangements for western instruments:

A Yemenite tune sung or played by a Yemenite in its pure form may excite the eastern Jew or the lover of eastern music, and if the piece is sung with piano accompaniment he would treat it as sacrilege. Other Jewish circles, however, would enjoy the tune in the arrangement. The Hebrew music programme should therefore present both versions.[38]

While the purists were on guard protecting the genuine heritage, the fierce protectors of the Hebrew language[39] unexpectedly re-emerged in August 1939 and fired from the opposite direction. The columnist of *Ha'Aretz* reported that having gone to a concert by Zefira and Nardi in Tel Aviv he found the auditorium locked and dark, and the crowd

---

[34] Most of the music on the show was by Stefan Wolpe and Yedidia Gorochov. See Ch. 10, above. Programme at the Stefan Wolpe Archive, Toronto.

[35] *Ha'Olam Haze* (23 Oct. 1947).   [36] *Ha'Aretz* (21 Nov. 1937).

[37] See Ch. 8, above.   [38] *Ha'Aretz* (20 Dec. 1936).   [39] See Ch. 2, above.

waiting at the gates angrily told him that the Tel Aviv municipality had imposed a last-minute ban on the concert because of the inclusion of two Sephardi songs in Judeo-Espagnole (Ladino) in the otherwise Hebrew programme.[40] The columnist took a middle road. He requested the municipality 'to maintain a constant watch and take immediate action against any non-Hebrew performance on our stages as part of a renewed campaign for the perpetuation of Hebrew in our life.' Yet, he questioned the municipality's inconsistent policy which allowed non-Hebrew performances by reputed visiting artists supported by their consuls, but 'is capable of flexing its muscles against the little Yemenite and her companion, who have become so popular in the country'.[41]

The joint career of Zefira and Nardi culminated with a contract with Columbia Phonograph signed in July 1937[42] and a concert tour in the United States. However, soon after their return the temperamental couple separated. The personal decision inadvertently sparked a new and innovative stage of east–west encounter. Rather than finding another pianist, the young artist boldly approached nearly all members of the local composer community and commissioned arrangements for the traditional songs she had been performing. Though still burdened with resettlement difficulties, most of them responded favourably to the opportunity to meet the authentic east in their own study. Paul Ben-Haim, Marc Lavri, Oedoen Partos, Menahem Avidom, Haim Alexander, and Hanoch (Heinrich) Jacoby co-operated with her, a co-operation involving the arduous task of listening to the eastern songs and of transcribing them into western notation. Zefira insisted on performing with some of the finest instrumentalists of the Palestine Orchestra. Their participation encouraged the composers to make arrangements for a variety of instrumental combinations, from solo piano and string quartet to mixed chamber ensembles and a full symphony orchestra. Outside Tel Aviv and Jerusalem Zefira performed with piano only, travelling with Paul Ben-Haim who was also her principal arranger.[43]

Zefira's offer also raised ideological objections. Joseph Gruenthal (Tal) declined, claiming that 'arrangements would detract from the innocence of the songs and impose sophistication over them'.[44] Alexander U. Boskovitch who strove for an internalization of the eastern expression

---

[40] Ladino has been the spoken dialect of the numerous eastern Sephardi communities in the Balkans, Turkey, and the ancient Sephardi families in Palestine. Thousands of Sephardi Romances are in Ladino.

[41] Signed Y. K.-Y. *Ha'Aretz* (30 Apr. 1936).

[42] Mentioned in an undated letter from Zefira to Columbia Records.

[43] Hirshberg, *Paul Ben-Haim*, 161–76.

[44] A recorded interview with the author, 14 Feb. 1976.

into a stylistic synthesis avoided arrangements which would have kept the ethnic traditions separated from each other. Yet he treated Zefira's voice as a means of expression and composed four original songs specifically for her.[45]

A fortunate personal encounter led to the expansion of her repertory. While performing in Egypt she became a close friend of the Jewish composer Alberto Hemsi (1897–1974). Born in Turkey, Hemsi studied at Milan's conservatory. In 1927, after four years of activity in the island of Rhodes, he settled down in Alexandria, Egypt, where he was active for thirty years as a conductor of the synagogue choir and as a teacher at the conservatory. He was dedicated to fieldwork expeditions in which he had collected Sephardi traditional songs which he arranged and published through his own publishing house, Édition Orientale de Musique. He met members of the Palestine Orchestra and the composer Paul Ben-Haim on the occasions of their frequent concert tours in Egypt.[46] Hemsi's arrangements of Sephardi songs for voice and chamber ensembles became an integral part of Zefira's repertory.

Zefira allowed no one else to use the notated arrangements and consequently they were always heard with her own nuances, timbre, and intonations which could not be represented in European staff notation. She published the annotated compilation of her tunes only in 1978 as a summation of her life's-work,[47] but she never allowed the publication of the instrumental arrangements.[48]

Cast aside, Nahum Nardi reacted angrily and claimed legal rights to the entire repertory, thereby raising the issue of the authorship of traditional material.[49] The legal fight echoed in the music criticism when Menashe Ravina wrote that Zefira performed '*her* eastern songs. We are allowed to say that the songs are hers, because it was she who has sung them to the composers and convinced them to make the arrangements

---

[45] 'Adonai Ro'i' (The Lord is my Shepherd, Ps. 23), 'Tephila' (Prayer, Avigdor Hameiri) for voice and orchestra, and the songs 'Shnei Hatulim' ('Two Jokes', Alharizi) for voice and piano (IMI).

[46] The displacement of the Egyptian Jewry following the war of 1956 forced Hemsi to settle in Paris, where he published his ten-volume *Coplas Sefardies*. A. Hemsi, 'Fortune Smiles on my Songs', *Tatzlil*, 15 (1975), 146; 'The Eliyahu Hanavi Synagogue Choir in Alexandria', *Tatzlil*, 16 (1976), 43; A. Bahat, 'The Composer Alberto Hemsi', *Tatzlil*, 14 (1974), 39. Hirshberg, *Paul Ben-Haim*, 204–5.   [47] *Kolot Rabim* (Many Voices) (Ramat Gan, 1970).

[48] A few came out as choral arrangements, and some were published in versions for voice and piano without her permission, such as Ben-Haim's *Melodies from the East* (IMP, Jerusalem, 1970).

[49] Nardi, 'A Response to Marc Lavri', *Ha'Aretz* (11 Aug. 1939). The issue of 'folk' song became of crucial importance following the establishment of the Palestine Performing Right Society (ACUM). See Ch. 10, above.

for orchestra.'[50] When Nardi persisted Zefira countered by securing a written document from the Sephardi notable Moshe Cordoba who confirmed in writing that 'Itzhac Navon and I have orally transmitted to Zefira nine ancient tunes of Sephardi, Persian, Turkish, and Arabic origins,'[51] which were then arranged by Ben-Haim, Partos, and Lavri.

Zefira regarded her first performances with the Palestine Orchestra as marking the apex of her career.[52] Yet she was relegated to the popular summer series of 1939, performing only four songs in an otherwise popular Russian programme featuring Tchaikovsky's *Nutcracker Suite*, Rimsky-Korsakov's *Caprice espagnole*, and Liadov's *Kikimora*. Zefira was paid £3 (roughly 20 per cent of a monthly salary of an orchestra player) for the two performances.[53] The concert in Tel Aviv was an outdoor event held at the vast Levant Fair. David Rosolio remarked that the conductor Marc Lavri's 'appearance with Bracha Zefira demonstrated that singing and songs of this kind are totally unsuited for accompaniment by an orchestra'.[54] Thus the unfavourable milieu and the acoustics conspired to degrade the momentous event of the first performance of a Yemenite singer with the Palestine Orchestra. None the less, the orchestra continued to contract Zefira for summer and youth concerts in which she later assumed the central role, as in a concert on 16 August 1942 in which she performed seven arrangements and three original compositions by Lavri, Boskovitch, and Hemsi. The orchestra's part was limited to a suite by Salomone Rossi,[55] Saint-Saens' *Suite algerienne* and two movements from Ben-Haim's Symphony No. 1, all carefully selected for being Jewish, 'oriental', and Palestinian respectively. Zefira, however, was never invited to perform on the prestigious subscription series.

The process of mediation which Zefira effected was gradual, with changes in some parameters balanced by stability in others.[56] The most crucial change took place when Zefira performed to the ethnically heterogeneous audience at her boarding-school. Her public performances

[50] *Davar* (17 Aug. 1942).

[51] A letter from Cordoba, 6 May 1947 (Zefira Collection, Tel Aviv University). The ACUM documents contain no evidence of any legal proceedings between Zefira and Nardi.

[52] Interview, 1980.

[53] The concerts were held in Tel Aviv on 26 July and in Jerusalem on 8 Aug. 1939. A letter from Professor Kestenberg, 31 July 1939 (Zefira Collection, Tel Aviv University).

[54] 'Summer Symphony Concerts', *Palestine Post* (11 Aug. 1939).

[55] Arranged by Peter Emanuel Gradenwitz.

[56] See J. Hirshberg, 'Bracha Zefira and the Process of Change in Israeli Music', *Pe'amim*, 19 (1984), 29–46 for a schematic analysis of the process which follows the theoretical model in A. Shiloah and E. Cohen, 'The Dynamics of Change in Jewish Oriental Ethnic music in Israel', *Ethnomusicology*, 27 (1983), 227–52.

with Nardi further modified the context into that of a popular public concert and the external element of a harmonic piano accompaniment was added. Gradually Zefira began to consider her activity a national mission. She defined herself as a 'Hebrew' singer and expanded her repertoire through fieldwork projects, initiating working sessions with singers of various ethnic groups, listening to songs, and recording them in her superb memory, in return for small favours and even payments in cash. For example, she recounted how she used to meet the ageing and nearly blind Itzhac Navon and listen to his rich repertoire of Sephardi songs in return for escorting him on his daily excursions to the municipal park.[57]

Zefira's co-operation with western-trained composers finally provided the professional critics with the criterion for an evaluation of her endeavour. Admitting having reserved his judgement until the commencement of the new phase, David Rosolio wrote a detailed evaluation of her work. He contrasted the first stage of Zefira's work when she had presented the songs as raw material with the second stage of her work with Nardi. The first stage was limited to a very small audience of connoisseurs, whereas Nardi had pulled the songs into the public realm, frequently forcing on them alien elements. The audience liked the results but the link with the sources of the songs was severed. Rosolio considered the new stage as a synthesis of the two approaches, so that the arrangement supports and reinforces the original character of the songs. Rosolio especially praised Oedoen Partos who 'composed an "accompaniment" which was in fact an independent piece from which the folksong grew in a natural and organic manner'.[58]

The critic Olya Silbermann went into more detail when she criticized the arrangements for string quartet as 'unsuitable to eastern songs' and preferred the use of mixed wind–string ensembles or solo instruments such as the harp.[59]

It appears that the composers who co-operated with Zefira harboured ambivalent feelings about the young and hot-tempered Yemenite woman, and consequently they were reluctant to admit the extent of their indebtedness to her. The author, critic, and musician Max Brod, who was in the position of an outside viewer, indicated in the first comprehensive study of music in Palestine that 'the significant originality and greatness of this woman has not received its proper evaluation'.[60]

[57] Interview with Zefira, 1980. Zefira had no access to a tape recorder, still a rare commodity in the country, and was never interested in mechanical devices.

[58] Ha'Aretz (2 Aug. 1940).   [59] Ha'Aretz (16 May 1941).

[60] Die Musik Israels (1951; rev. edn. Kassel, 1976), 58.

Bracha Zefira was acknowledged as having paved the way for other Yemenite singers. Thus Esther Gamlielit's broadcast of traditional songs was praised as matching 'her older sister Bracha Zefira'.[61] Naomi Tzuri departed from the realm of traditional eastern songs and turned to a voice-teacher who trained her in the European bel-canto tradition, breaking through the ethnic barrier. Her programme of Italian arias and Lieder by Beethoven, Schubert, and Mahler at the venerable Tel Aviv Museum made the pedantic David Rosolio marvel that 'no one had anticipated that a Yemenite woman would successfully penetrate the spirit of western musical culture'.[62]

The emergence of the professional Yemenite singers had a manifold effect. In the social domain music provided a new option for Yemenite women whose lifestyle was otherwise conservative and enclosed, though it was at first limited merely to a few daring individuals. The Yemenite singers added prestige to the Yemenite community, further enhanced by their international tours. Their influence on the musical scene was even more immediate and comprehensive. They triggered the creation of a new genre of concert arrangements of the ethnic traditional song. By grouping together songs of different Jewish ethnic groups, they gave a boost to the ideology of the national melting-pot. Their concerts provided the western-educated audience with an easy introduction to the hidden sphere of the ethnic context-dependent repertory. Finally they allowed the immigrant composers to reach beyond orientalist fantasies and dependence on written transcriptions to a direct interaction with the sound and nuances of the genuine eastern song.

Far from being easy, the process was infused with feelings of suspicion and prejudice on all sides. The immigrant composers, hard-pressed to overcome their own resettlement difficulties, treated the genre of folk arrangement as a secondary occupation, whereas the young Yemenite women found themselves struggling for success in the competitive world of entertainment in times of economic crises and war. Another limiting outcome was the tendency to standardize a label called 'oriental singing' within the broad context of western cultural events, such as a large-scale benefit concert held by a women's organization which featured the Shulamit school's pupils' orchestra, four pianists, and three opera singers, with Esther Gamlielit as the sole representative of 'eastern singing'.[63] The full implications of the endeavours of the young Yemenite singers were felt only much later, after the foundation of the State of Israel.

[61] G. Swet, 'On the Radio', *Ha'Aretz* (21 Dec. 1942).
[62] *Ha'Aretz* (2 Mar. 1942).   [63] Notice in *Ha'Aretz* (3 Feb. 1992).

The route towards a desired national style by way of stylistic syntheses and compromise was viewed by the purists as a threat to the indigenous Yemenite music, and the Yemenite singer Yehiel Adaqi countered by launching a series of broadcasts of Yemenite songs with fellow singers in which he 'did not turn to get help from the "Ashkenazis" in dressing the melodies with harmonies or orchestral frame. Adaqi keeps the flame of folklore glowing and he presents it in its original form'. So remote were the music and the texts that Ravina suggested the reduction of the number of songs on the broadcast and the spending of some time for explanation of the 'incomprehensible texts'.[64]

Westerners Meet Arabic Music

The encounter with the East took a new turn upon the immigration of Ezra Aharon in 1934 and of Robert Lachmann's and Edith Kiwi's a year later.

Ezra Aharon (1903–95) was an oud-player and a singer employed at the royal band in the Iraqi court. In 1932 Iraq sent him as an official performer to the Cairo Conference of Middle Eastern and European musicians which became a landmark in the history of ethnomusicology.[65] Two years later he received an offer to perform at the Levant Fair in Tel Aviv. While the Iraqi government was mostly involved with internal affairs, the pan-Arabic movement increased its power in Iraq after September 1934 through vicious anti-Semitic and anti-British propaganda.[66] When rumours of Ezra Aharon's intentions to immigrate leaked out, his life was threatened and he instantly escaped from Iraq to Palestine.[67] Still apprehensive, he refrained from exposure by performing at the Levant Fair, but organized instead an intimate concert for a small audience in Jerusalem where he performed Arabic songs. The circle of Hebraists in Jerusalem headed by Dr David Yellin warned him that he would have no Jewish audience for songs in Arabic. Aharon took the hint and the Hebraists helped him adopt Hebrew poems to the Arabic tunes. His next concerts took place at the large Edison auditorium and were introduced by Dr Yellin. Still alone in his field and unemployed, Aharon received a timely encouragement when the prestigious ethnomusicologist

---

[64] *Davar* (6 Aug. 1946).   [65] Nettl, *Study of Ethnomusicology*, 345.

[66] M. Apel, 'Iraq and Palestine', MA thesis (University of Tel Aviv, 1983).

[67] A recorded interview with Professor Amnon Shiloah, 1981. I am indebted to Professor Shiloah for allowing me to use the valuable material.

Robert Lachmann (1892–1939) immigrated to Palestine.[68] Dismissed by the Nazi regime from his post as librarian at the music department of the Berlin State Library and head of the Phonogram Commission, Lachmann was invited by Professor Magnes, president of the Hebrew University, to found an archive of oriental music in Jerusalem. Lachmann brought along his up-to-date recording equipment as well as his earlier recordings made during the 1920s in North Africa and at the Island of Djerba. He also salvaged about fifty of Idelsohn's cylinder recordings of Jewish music. Lachmann had attended the Cairo Conference where he had made recordings of the Arabic musicians, among them Ezra Aharon. Soon after his immigration he happened to meet Aharon in a street in Jerusalem.[69] Lachmann not only resumed his recording project with Aharon but also sent him a few pupils who helped him make ends meet.

The inauguration of the PBS in 1936 finally provided Aharon with the proper home base for his musical work. The PBS commissioned Aharon to produce a regular programme of Sounds of the East.[70] Aharon organized a small ensemble consisting of Jewish musicians of eastern origin who played Arabic instrumental music. He also gathered a choir for which he composed songs in Hebrew. Arie Sachs frequently joined the Arabic broadcast with piano interludes. Finally, Karl Salomon encouraged Aharon to occasionally merge his ensemble with the Studio Players so that the oud and the kanun were heard together with violin, flute, and cello. Aharon even experimented with harmonization, overcoming the difficulty of the intonation of the three-quarter tone by assigning the third degree in *maqam rast* and the second in *maqam bayat* to the Arabic instruments while the western instruments harmonized them by the first degree.[71] Though a purist in his nature, Aharon responded to the ideological challenge and wished to provide the Arabic music with a new national Jewish style, encompassing Hebrew texts, western instruments, and harmonization. Though bold and interesting, Aharon's experiment had little reverberations outside the PBS circles. It appears that the western musicians did not realize the full potential of Aharon's ideas. His own compositions, however, received much more public attention. In

---

[68] E. Gerson-Kiwi, 'Robert Lachmann, his Achievement and his Legacy', *Yuval*, 3 (Jerusalem, 1974), 100–8.

[69] Interview with Amnon Shiloah.

[70] Ezra Aharon later received a full appointment at the Department of Eastern music which he held until his retirement in 1968.

[71] Interview with Shiloah. *Maqam rast* starts with a tetrachord of one whole tone followed by two three-quarter tones. *Maqam bayat* begins with two three-quarter tones followed by a whole tone. They are most prevalent in Arabic music.

1937 he set Psalm 21 to music in honour of the coronation of King George VI and in 1939 Salomon Rosowsky requested to see Aharon's songs.[72] Aharon notated only his short songs, whereas he coached his longer compositions in the Arabic manner of oral tradition.

Abrasive Encounter

The encounter of Yemenite and Iraqi musicians with western-trained composers and performers was fraught with personal, aesthetic, and social conflicts. Aharon published only a few of his noted songs, allegedly for fear of having others perform them without paying him.[73] Zefira wrote that

at one rehearsal I gathered all my courage and asked the strings to play without vibrato and to split the chords into arpeggios, instead of playing them with a single bow stroke, and even drum with their fingers on the back of the instruments. I pointed out that these effects would perhaps bring us a little closer to the style of the song. . . . They did not consider me qualified to tell them how to play, especially with regard to those elements which were not actually in the score . . . this kind of argument with performers and composers left me, after such rehearsals, depressed and pessimistic with regard to achieving a common approach. When it came to making music, it was impossible to wean them off their previous concepts even though we were all searching for a way to merge our approaches.[74]

In fact, such instrumental devices had just made their appearance in contemporary European compositions, especially Bartók's, which had just been played in the concert series of the newly founded branch of the Society for Contemporary Music,[75] and, needless to say, drumming on string instruments was common in Spanish guitar-playing. It appears that the resistance was sparked off by the supercilious attitude of experienced European performers toward the young Yemenite singer, more than by their opposition to innovative techniques as such. Bracha Zefira herself candidly admitted that she 'was scared of the German immigrants'.[76] In

---

[72] Letters of acknowledgement from the High Commissioner, 10 May 1937, and from Rosowksy, 23 July 1939, in the possession of Ezra Aharon.

[73] Interview with Shiloah. Ezra Aharon was either not aware of the existence of the Performing Right Society (ACUM) or did not trust it.

[74] *Kolot Rabim*, 21–2.

[75] The violinists Lorand and Alice Fenyves performed Bartók's duets in the course of the second concert of the Society, Jan. 1939, and the Jerusalem String Quartet included one of Bartók's quartets on the fifth concert in June of the same year. See Ch. 10, above.

[76] A recorded interview, 14 Jan. 1979.

order to penetrate what looked to her as the prestigious shrine of western concert life Zefira attempted to include a European repertory in her programme. She used Ravel's *Cinq Mélodies populaires grecques* as a proper starting-point, but the critic's reaction was that her voice did not suit this music and that she 'should keep to her own field of eastern song'.[77] In 1947 Ben-Haim celebrated his fiftieth birthday with a festive concert of the PBS orchestra to which he invited his friend, the bass singer and the director of the music department Karl Salomon, to perform his songs, pushing aside eight years of collaboration with Zefira, who was deeply hurt.[78] Zefira's daily encounters with the western-trained musicians grew increasingly abrasive and she became suspicious and irritable.

Frequently, the best intentions came to a halt as a result of cultural misunderstandings. In 1940 the young dancer Yardena Cohen, who came from a German family, turned to a revolutionary project of reviving ancient biblical dance. Her choreographies depicted biblical female characters, such as Hanah and Shulamit. Dispensing with the costumes and the white shoes of the classical ballet she danced barefoot, dressed in Arabic gowns. In order to complete the transformation she located Ovadia Mizrahi, Eliyahu Yedid, and Haim Hayat, three folk musicians of Iraqi descent, who were fishmongers at Haifa market-place and played the oud, the Arabic flute, and the darbouka (the Arabic drum). Yardenah Cohen felt elevated by the new tunes 'which infused the joy of movement into my veins, and I felt myself liberated from all limitations . . . Only the basic element remained—pure dance.'[79] Yet her musicians did not share her naïve elation.

They always insisted that I first listen to the contents of the song and to the meanings of the words and refused to understand that I was interested in melody alone. . . . I then prepared the composition according to my feeling and tried to teach them to memorize and rehearse it hundreds of times. All this effort towards the formation of a dance was accompanied by screams, reprimands, and tears, many tears.[80]

Obsessed with her own vision of the East, the young dancer made every possible mistake in her relations with the musicians, who were first hurt by her belittling of the traditional texts of their songs and then were forced to rehearse in the western manner which was remote from their habit of improvising on the spot. Busy making a living, they occasionally failed to show up for her performances with no previous notification. The disenchanted dancer tried to turn to Ezra Aharon as a well-known

---

[77] Olya Silbermann, *Ha'Aretz* (16 May 1941).   [78] Interview, 1980.
[79] *Betof Ubemahol* (*With a Timbrel and with a Dance*) (Tel Aviv, 1963), 31.   [80] Ibid.

and reliable professional musician. The first meeting ended in a serious misunderstanding. Aharon, who arrived well dressed, accompanied by a boy who carried his oud, was deeply insulted by Yardenah Cohen's offer to accompany a female dancer, an activity which was much below his position as the leading eastern musician in the country and a former royal musician.[81] Yardenah Cohen then gave up and retreated to more familiar territory. In the summer of 1944 she turned to the composer Alexander Boskovitch who notated the melodies of her dances and arranged them for piano.[82]

Ethnomusicology Established in Palestine

Though limited to a few specialists in Palestine, the Cairo Conference created the proper milieu for work on the music of the East. In April 1937 Radio Cairo broadcast a live concert of new orchestral Egyptian music to most countries in Europe and the event was reviewed in much detail in Palestine, since 'the problem of national music, and especially of a national symphony, is of interest to us now and therefore deserves attention'.[83] Immediately after his immigration Robert Lachmann embarked upon an ambitious project of field recordings. Though owning the best recording machine, Lachmann was forced to economize, using cheap tin-foil records which precluded their repeated use for decades.[84] Lachmann's prestigious position sharpened ethnic and national sensitivities. In March 1937 he presented a radio lecture with live illustrations by three Yemenite male singers. The Yemenite musician Yehiel Adaqi applied his purist attitude and complained that Lachmann authorized the participation of singers 'who lacked authentic integrity'. Consequently, one of the songs was performed with a wrong tune and another lost its plaintive affect.[85]

Lachmann recorded about a thousand items before his premature death in 1939. His project was continued by his colleague, Edith Gerson-Kiwi (1908–92). Her initial training was European, having studied piano with

---

[81] In his interview with the author, 21 Mar. 1977, Aharon was reluctant to discuss his encounter with Yardenah Cohen.

[82] Hirshberg, 'Alexander U. Boskovitch'. Boskovitch started his joint work with Yardenah Cohen on 5 Aug. 1944. A letter from Boskovitch to Y. Cohen, kept at her private collection. The MS of Boskovitch's arrangements is at the Boskovitch Archive, JNUL.

[83] Ha'Aretz (11 Apr. 1937).

[84] In 1992 the Jewish Music Research Centre at the Hebrew University and the Phonogramm Archiv in Vienna initiated a joint project of a digital reproduction of Lachmann's recordings.

[85] Davar (7 Mar. 1937).

Dounias-Sindermann, harpsichord with Wanda Landowska, and musicology with Willibald Gurlitt and Heinrich Besseler under whom she completed a dissertation on the Italian madrigal.[86] Yet, her immigration and her association with Lachmann turned her interest in the direction of ethnomusicology. She embarked upon an extensive fieldwork project, travelling across Palestine with her cumbersome tape recorder and making hundreds of recordings in the diverse ethnic communities of Palestine. In 1942 she joined the faculty of the Palestine Conservatoire in Jerusalem where she taught a survey course titled 'Eastern Music', using Curt Sachs's *Anthologie sonore* series for illustrations of world music.[87] Her first publication on the music of the East was published in Jerusalem in 1945.[88]

Having originated with Idelosohn's pioneer research work in 1907, the east–west encounter took root mostly in the realm of systematic research and fieldwork. The composers, while motivated and eager, met with too many musical and personal obstacles on the road eastward. The two academies of music in Jerusalem and Tel Aviv taught regular survey courses on non-western music but did not hire regular teachers of Arabic or other eastern instruments. Barriers were lowered but not dismantled.

---

[86] *Studien zur Geschichte des italienische Liedmadrigal im 16. Jh.* (Heidelberg, 1933; Wurzburg, 1938).

[87] Curt Sachs (1881–1959) started the *Anthologie sonore* project in 1933 when he moved to Paris following his dismissal on racial grounds.

[88] *The Musicians of the Orient* (Jerusalem, 1945). Gerson-Kiwi became a professor at the Musicology Department of Tel Aviv University when it opened in 1966. Her enormous archive of field work recordings has been donated to the National Sound Archives, JNUL, which issued its computerized catalogue in 1993.

12

Individualism versus Collectivism
Music and the Kibbutz

THE kibbutz[1] movement was the most powerful manifestation of the ideology of communal life and of a voluntary rejection of private property and pecuniary greed. The communal spirit penetrated all walks of kibbutz life, such as insistence on joint meals at the common dining hall which also accommodated most social and cultural functions. From 1921 to 1948 the number of kibbutzim in Palestine leaped from 11 to 130 and their population increased from about 700 in 1921 to 54,000, that is, from less than 1 per cent of the Yishuv in 1921 to more than 7 per cent. Kibbutz life was idolized in urban society among many of those who were not willing to join communal life themselves. Consequently, the kibbutz movement was permeated by the optimistic vision of paving the way to utopia. Yet the way was fraught with obstacles, doubts, and soul-searching.

Music played a dual role in the kibbutz. On the one hand, music was recruited at the service of social cohesiveness, mostly manifested by social song and dance, frequently depicted and extolled in literary works, as in David Maletz's *Ma'agalot*: 'It was a nice "party". But real joy and elation were reached late at night . . . They drank a little and sang a lot and also kept dancing. They danced in circles and then resumed their songs.'[2] On the other hand, music provided the individual experience which balanced the collective ideology. Most of the kibbutz members in the 1920s and 1930s were young immigrants whose trauma of immigration was compounded by the entry into communal life. European music was capable

---

[1] Kibbutz, pl. kibbutzim, lit., 'assembly' or 'gathering'.

[2] Pp. 76–7 (Tel Aviv, 1945, repr. 1983). Maletz (1899–1981) immigrated in 1920 and settled in kibbutz Ein-Harod) in Jezre'el Valley (the Emek).

of softening the shock. An anonymous young woman wrote in the official organ of the kibbutz movement: 'It feels that during a concert the separation between people falls down, the hard crust which covers the hearts is removed.'[3]

The social pressures of communal life were especially hard on young, idealistic individuals, who were constantly searching for an outlet for their personal yearnings. Some literary works of the 1920s and 1930s tried to express such suppressed feelings which were frequently released through musical experience. It was the violin which symbolized such conditions, as in Maletz's novel, in which two tormented young men confronted each other. The idealistic Shlomo Tamari toils in the fields in the blistering sun, and then he locks himself in his lonely shack were he plays the violin at night. Menahem, madly in love with Hanah, prefers Tamari's impassioned violin sounds, 'which registered in Menahem's memory as striving with desperate efforts up, up, longing and praying with the last drop of blood' to the 'relaxing, peaceful. miraculously calming tune of the gramophone'.[4]

Despite many common features and challenges, each kibbutz had a music history of its own based on a large number of variables. For example, ideology and politics were of much more consequence for daily life in the small collective communes than in the more heterogeneous urban communities. The countries of origin of the kibbutz members affected the extent of their attachment to European musical heritage. Those dominated by immigrants from central Europe created enclaves similar to the Jerusalem Music Society[5] whereas those coming from eastern Europe were more likely to feel attachment to Yiddish folk songs and hasidic traditions. The geographical location of a kibbutz also affected the nature of its musical activity. Kibbutzim which were relatively close to Tel Aviv could establish a regular encounter with urban musical life whether through invitation of guest artists or through visits to concerts in town, whereas remote kibbutzim had to rely much more on their own resources. Finally, the power of individual initiatives was decisive in the kibbutzim, where a handful of members determined the cultural profile of the commune. The present chapter seeks to maintain a balance between the presentation of general aspects of music in the kibbutz movement on the one hand and characterization of specific well-documented kibbutzim on the other.

---

[3] *Mibifnim, The Kibbutz Me'huad Monthly* (Ein Harod, 1935), 69–70. The Kibbutz Me'huad, (United Kibbutz) has been one of the national associations of the kibbutz movement.

[4] Maletz, *Ma'agalot*, 135.   [5] See Chs. 3 and 7, above.

The Kibbutz Chorus—Elevation to the Spiritual Realm

An anonymous member wrote in a kibbutz publication that 'singing is the refuge from daily toil. . . . While singing one reaches full unity with one's comrades.'[6] Writing in the *Givat Brenner Newsletter*, Shimon B. advocated the establishment of a chorus as a miraculous solution to the social ills of the kibbutz:

So often have we heard our members complain about the tenuous social situation. Many of us have given up and consider all further discussions of this topic as worthless. But I think that there is a very simple cure for all such bitter pessimists which is: a chorus! . . . One might ask: Our collective life, the dining hall, our shared work, the common education of the children and the very basic element of the kibbutz which is mutual aid, are they not sufficient to educate for social life together? . . . My answer would be: work is not always gratifying. There are different kinds of jobs. There are arguments, inequality . . . and the proof is that people who work together in the same field do not always become friends. At times collective work causes resentment. I have attended the recent rehearsal of our chorus . . . and I was delighted. They all sang together. Here they are all really equal, members of one chorus. The melody, the harmony, the rhythmic sounds, the incredible effort to blend one's voice with all other voices, to create in both piano and forte a gentle and beautiful composition which is above the realm of daily good and bad. This is the primary factor in education for sociability.[7]

Despite the elevated ideology, kibbutz choruses often worked by fits and starts, such as in kibbutz Givat Brenner.[8] During the first years of the kibbutz a few members organized a small *ad hoc* twenty-five member chorus for special functions. The initiative to establish a regular large chorus came from the outside when the violinist and composer Yehudah Shertok (Sharet) from kibbutz Yagur volunteered to direct choruses in new kibbutzim, such as Givat Brenner. One of the chorus members described him as

endowed with incredible will and energy, which he also requested of us. Rehearsals began two or three weeks before the performance. We worked every

---

[6] Quoted in *Davar* (9 Dec. 1938).

[7] B. Shimon, 'Why Chorus?', *Givat Brenner Newsletter* (17 Dec. 1941). As a rule, kibbutz members signed by first names only in internal publications as a mark of familiarity.

[8] T. Cohen, 'Musical Activity in kibbutz Givat Brenner 1928–1948', seminar paper (Hebrew University, Jerusalem, 1993). Givat Brenner, adjacent to the settlement of Rehovot, about 20 km. south of Tel Aviv, was founded by thirty-three members in 1928. Its development was exceptionally quick. By 1936 it numbered 676 adults and the number had doubled by 1945. Gurevich and Gertz (eds.), *Statistical Handbook*, 51.

night until midnight or 1 a.m. following a full day of exhausting work. I remember that once he started to rehearse a new song after midnight. I uttered a brief sigh which reached his ears, and he gave me hell.[9]

Shertok soon found out that the members could not cope with his demands and he angrily left the chorus. The leading members pleaded with him to return and he stated his conditions in a long letter which reflected his high expectations from the kibbutz chorus:

1. Participation which would reach a number proportionate to the large membership of Givat Brenner. I do not expect masses but not a priestly sect either.
2. Full and regular attendance in the choral lessons. The chorus would work as much as possible in three fields: (a) Learning of songs which would be passed on to all members through communal singing. (b) Rehearsing of more elaborate songs for performances. (c) Instructing the elements of music . . . The only excuses for missing a lesson would be illness or work at the same time in the kitchen or on guard duty. Committee meetings, lectures, reading a book or a newspaper, meeting a guest, or just fatigue are important by themselves but totally unacceptable as a reason for absence.[10]

The chorus must have been unable to cope with Shertok's demands since it soon disbanded. After a few abortive attempts Dr Benjamin Pintus, a new member of the kibbutz who was a well-trained musician, discovered the proper balance of cordiality and pedantry needed to inspire such a voluntary ensemble.

Most members of Givat Brenner were immigrants from Germany and Austria (280 of 527 members in 1942). The chorus devised a careful balance between preservation of the German musical heritage and the commitment of the kibbutz to collective ideology and to Hebrew repertory. Yehudah Meinzer told that they never sang in German, only in Hebrew,[11] such as when a chorale from Bach's *St. Matthew Passion* was sung with a Hebrew contrafactum which turned it into a Sabbath song.[12]

Some of the German-born members in the country were concerned that the links with European culture might be severed. One of them praised the choral conductor Ernst Horowitz: 'Do we really have to abandon European cultural values? The recent programme included

---

[9] Lea Felter, documented for Givat Brenner archive, Jan. 1978.

[10] Letter to the Culture Committee, 27 Jan. 1936 (Givat Brenner Archive). A few additional minor conditions followed.

[11] Tzila Amit, an interview with Yehudah Meinzer, 1 Feb. 1990 (Givat Brenner Archive).

[12] Programme of 27 Jan. 1939 (Givat Brenner Archive). The original title of the Chorale was not given in the programme notes.

Mozart alongside Engel and Wolpe. The European culture is not super-fluous for us. It has the potential to develop our own culture.'[13]

Orchestras and Quartets: Between Ambitions and Compromises

Whereas any group of some thirty motivated kibbutz members could aspire to assemble a modest chorus, the ingrained requirements of in-strumental specialization made similar orchestral endeavours ex-tremely difficult to achieve. The founders of Givat Brenner started a small orchestra soon after the inauguration of the kibbutz with disappointing results:

The orchestra causes us terrible problems. If only one or two of the members were willing to make a little effort . . . It could and should be the most im-portant element in our [cultural] activity. . . We can't force the players, but we have the right to request that they occasionally share their potential with us.[14]

The Fifth Aliya infused new life into the orchestra of kibbutz Givat Brenner. In 1935 the orchestra invited Hans Eisenstadt, music-teacher from Ben-Shemen Youth Village and a brilliant musician, to conduct the ensemble, and the players from the adjacent kibbutzim Na'an and Schiller as well as from the village of Gedera were invited to join. Yet, the elaborate logistics of transportation and the resulting high expenses often disturbed the regular rehearsals. In 1938 the Viennese-born violinist Yuval Ebenstein reorganized the ensemble as a chamber string orchestra. Ener-getic and industrious, he enlisted financial support from the Rehovot branch of the Federation of Hebrew Workers which enabled him to engage soloists from the Palestine Orchestra such as Lorand Fenyves who played Vivaldi and Horst Salomon who was the soloist in one of Mozart's horn concertos.[15] In 1943 Yuval Ebenstein left the kibbutz and the orchestra ceased its regular activities for three years, when the chorus conductor, Benjamin Pintus, regrouped it as a modest chamber ensemble. The erratic history of the Givat Brenner orchestra indicated that high motivation and ideological support alone were of limited value in the absence of a proper musical and administrative director.

In October 1936 several members of the kibbutz Afikim were invited to an instrument exhibition which raised in some of them the interest to

---

[13] Quoted in *Davar* (9 Dec. 1938). Stefan Wolpe was presented as a local folk composer. See Ch. 10, above.

[14] B. Yitzhac, 'Newsletter of the Cultural Committee, 1931', in *The First Years, in Commemoration of 60 Years of Givat Brenner* (Givat Brenner, 1988).

[15] A concert on 13 Sept. 1939. Programme at Givat Brenner Archive.

try and learn how to play.[16] They gathered a small ensemble which performed in April 1937 a short concert which attracted additional players from neighbouring kibbutzim. In an internal report the Afikim orchestra, though labelled 'uneconomical', was described as having the potential to calm the nerves at the worst time of the Arab revolt, since 'it would suffice if the orchestra project succeeds in taking our minds for a moment off the horrid memories'.[17] Another report quoted in the same article described the conditions in which the orchestra struggled for existence:

Shots in Bitania and our violist has been wounded. Attack on Gesher and the orchestra players have been called to duty. The High Commissioner visits Kineret and one of our members has been placed on guard duty. New members have settled in Massada and Ein Hakore and we have gained three new violinists. . . . We have transportation problems. Many hours are lost waiting for the bus and the carriage. The culmination of our activity—three intensive days of rehearsals. It is extremely hot and our fingers which are accustomed to the spade and the hammer hardly respond . . . A sudden message: The oboe-player Alexander's wife has had a baby. Should he go to Afula? Two hours later—the flautist had a son born. Should he . . . No. Both have stayed and have continued to play.[18]

The performances of the renamed Jordan Valley Orchestra in many kibbutzim attracted additional players from the Galilee and the orchestra dared to attempt symphonies by Haydn, Schubert, and Beethoven. In 1946 the orchestra organized a nine-day seminar in which its thirty-five members rehearsed orchestral and chamber works for eleven hours a day and also attended lectures on musical topics. The orchestra proudly celebrated its first anniversary with a festive concert at its first home, Afikim.

By 1947 the kibbutz movement reported the regular activity of three symphony orchestras. The Jordan Valley Orchestra was a regional ensemble which numbered 32 players from the Jordan Valley, the Jezre'el Valley, and the Upper Galilee. The kibbutzim of Hefer Valley established a thirty-member orchestra. The erratic Givat Brenner orchestra included members from three or four adjacent kibbutzim as well as from the village of Gedera.[19]

[16] Afikim, in the Jordan Valley near the ancient town of Beth-She'an, was founded in 1932 by a large Zionist group from Russia. In 1936 it numbered 277 adults. Gurevich and Gertz (eds.), *Statistical Handbook*, 51.

[17] *Davar* (9 Dec. 1938).

[18] Ibid. The kibbutzim mentioned in the report were all adjacent to Afikim. Kineret was the oldest, founded in 1913. The others were younger than Afikim. Afula was the nearest town, situated in the Jezre'el Valley (Emek).

[19] *Newsletter of the Cultural Centre of the Federation of Hebrew Workers*, 16 (2 Nov. 1947).

The kibbutz orchestras were amateur ensembles. Any attempt at musical work on a serious professional level collided with the kibbutz economics. Each kibbutz member was assigned duties which were defined as profitable for the collective, and music was regarded as a leisure activity. Moreover, the financial conditions of the kibbutzim never allowed them to release members from daily work in order to play in concerts. The sweeping kibbutz ideology lured certain professional immigrant musicians who were determined to alter their way of life. Some of them soon returned to the urban centres. The pianist Arie Sachs, for example, joined a group of young pioneers resolved to establish a new agricultural collective settlement. Yet, their project required an initial investment which they tried to raise working in town, and they convinced Sachs that he would make more money for the group as an experienced pianist than as an agricultural novice. They miscalculated, since having worked for a while as a jazz pianist in Jerusalem cafes, Sachs soon found his place at the newly founded radio station and abandoned his agricultural dream.[20] Still, many musicians willingly gave up their professional musical careers and permanently settled in a kibbutz. They continued to practise their instruments whenever possible, and some of them found the kibbutz audience ready to support their enterprise. Musical activities by kibbutz members needed little public relations and consequently were only irregularly documented, mostly in local reports. Permeated by the central European spirit, Givat Brenner supported chamber music groups, including two regular string quartets. Yehudah Meinzer who immigrated to Givat Brenner as a boy in 1938 attended a *Hausmusik* session at the Youth Club, a wooden cabin, on Saturday afternoon.

It was terribly hot although it was already October. Five members played Schubert's Quintet, Op. 163 . . . In accordance with my strict German education I politely knocked at the door and asked for permission to enter. They agreed and I listened with full attention and excitement. They played barefoot, dressed in khaki shorts and nothing else. . . . Schubert had never thought his work would ever be played in this way. I was especially impressed with their involvement. There were endless arguments about how to play this and how to interpret that.[21]

Menashe Rabinowitz, whose position at the Centre for the Promotion of Music made him a friend of the kibbutz movement, considered it his duty to review the kibbutz musical scene.[22] As such he was admitted to

[20] Interview with Arie Sachs, Sept. 1978.
[21] Yishai Be'eri, an interview with Yehudah Meinzer, 20 Dec. 1983 (Givat Brenner Archive).
[22] See Ch. 5, above.

the 1926 anniversary celebration of Ein-Harod although outsiders were denied entry because of an epidemic in the country. He sadly reported that the Emek String Quartet

which has just recently toured the country and raised high hopes among workers, did not perform this time. A string trio played instead . . . a three-violin arrangement of the andante from Beethoven's Seventh Symphony. I have never heard such perfection. . . . Yet, it was not only that the fourth member was absent, but even the three who did play were coerced to do so . . . Not only a trio or a quartet has been lost, but an entire musical centre.[23]

Rabinowitz blamed the dispersal of the quartet on the social pressures within the young kibbutz society which demanded that each kibbutz member strive for total absorption in profitable kibbutz duties, and music was not considered as such. With no support many of the few kibbutz musicians active in the 1920s lost their motivation to maintain regular chamber ensembles. The solution was found on the higher hierarchical level of the kibbutzim, which were grouped according to several political affiliations.[24] The Viennese-born violinist Yuval Ebenstein convinced the cultural committee of the United Kibbutz to sponsor a kibbutz string quartet which went on a concert tour in twenty-six settlements. The quartet maintained its socialist attitude even in the urban milieu of Tel Aviv, where its performance took place at the club of the waterfront workers. Menashe Rabinowitz argued that the ideological attitude permeated also the performance style of the kibbutz quartet:

every bow stroke reflects the love of the music. All is gentle and delicate. If one considers chamber music as an endeavour to absorb the individual into the ensemble, the kibbutz quartet has reached the utmost in this respect. It sometimes looked as if the players restrained themselves too much out of consideration for the others.[25]

A Piano in each Dining Hall

Despite the dismal economic conditions of the young communal settlements, much effort was invested in the purchase of a single piano which was placed as a rule in the common dining hall where members

[23] 'Music and Workers in the Emek', *Davar* (7 Oct. 1926).
[24] Such as Hakibbutz Hame'uhad (*United Kibbutz Movement*) and the more leftist Hakibbutz Ha'artzi Hashomer Hatz'ir. The central organizations facilitated communications and mutual help among the affiliated kibbutzim.
[25] *Davar* (6 Mar. 1939). The quartet members were Yuval Ebenstein, Haim Bar, Menahem Taub, and Haim Rothschild.

lined up to practise or just bang on the instrument. A member of Givat Brenner whimsically wrote that

the violin and the flute excelled in their beautiful sound since they responded to their owners alone. And then the piano cried out loud (cried because it suffered from lack of protection from the *Hamsin* heat, etc.): this is your fault. You are individualists while I allow everyone to plow my back, to bang at will. You should all admit that I am the only one loyal to the kibbutz way.[26]

Yehudah Meinzer told that the choral conductor Benjamin Pintus acted 'like a bulldozer' to force Givat Brenner to allocate the money for the purchase of a baby grand which would permit the holding of professional piano recitals.[27] In 1939 a small group of immigrants from Italy joined the kibbutz and contributed a second piano, and yet another was moved over by a well-to-do family from Tel Aviv whose daughter, a fine young pianist, joined the kibbutz.

Piano recitals embodied the dual role music played in the kibbutz. While serving as a social attraction which gathered all members in the dining hall, it also allowed one to concentrate on one's individual experience. Such events were poetically depicted in semi-documentary literary works.

One day a famous pianist chanced the Emek[28] and visited our kibbutz for a day or two. Menahem, of course, did not miss this wonderful opportunity for arranging a concert. He toiled for several hours, both before and after dinner, to prepare the Dining Hall: he used the tables to erect a stage on which he placed the piano, he decorated the stage with flower pots from the greenhouse, he lit the second *lux*[29] which was reserved for the Sabbath dinner, and arranged rows of benches. The concert began. There was an absolute silence. The listeners sat with longing glances and absorbed the music with their whole being. The pianist performed one piece after another with short intervals during which the sounds of dogs barking and hyenas crying penetrated the hall through the open windows. And to the ringing of the chimes of a caravan of camels passing by down the hill she played Tchaikovsky's Arabic Dance.[30]

The kibbutz created a code of manners of its own, which was an overt negation of bourgeois values. The most extreme symbol was the rejection

---

[26] Celia, *Givat Brenner Newsletter* (26 Oct. 1937). *Hamsin* ('fifty' in Arabic) in the very dry and hot wind which blows from the Arabian desert mostly in May and June and again in September allegedly for fifty days in each season.

[27] Tzila Amit, an interview with Yehudah Meinzer (1 Feb. 1990).

[28] Lit. 'valley', it connoted the fertile Jezre'el Valley in the north of the country. During the 1920s it became a poetic symbol of the vibrant revival of Jewish agricultural settlement in Palestine.

[29] In contemporary dialect, a powerful kerosene lamp.

[30] Yehudah Ya'ari (1900–82, immigrated 1920), 'Menahem's Wedding'.

of applause, looked on as hypocritical and as a sacrilege negating the spiritual experience of music. Newcomers were likely to be shocked upon their first encounter with a kibbutz concert. The composer and pianist Joseph Tal (Gruenthal) has reported on his first experience playing a recital at a kibbutz. Soon after his immigration he was hit by an unidentified viral infection which left him exhausted and unable to pursue his job as a photographer.[31] He was invited by friends to rest for a while at the kibbutz Beit-Alpha, of which he told:

.I arrived in the evening and suffered from fever and from the hot weather. The kibbutz had just received an upright piano and the members asked me to play a recital. It was 10.30 p.m. and I was not sure I could stand the effort, but I just could not refuse. People came from the neighbourhood, for instance from Ein Harod, Heftzibah, and other places. They came by wagons, on donkeys, by bicycle, it resembled a pilgrimage. The dining hall was packed to capacity. I had no music with me but I felt I could rely on my good training as improviser should my memory fail me. I started with Beethoven's D minor Sonata,[32] a serious and a long work. It went well, and I started to enjoy it. I was sitting with my back to the audience, and when the sonata was over I expected some applause. There was absolute quiet. I did not even dare to turn my back, fearing that they had all left. Nevertheless I decided to continue to play for myself. I played a Bach–Liszt Toccata. When it was over the same thing happened—no sound at all. This time I turned and I would never forget the experience. They were all sitting there as if transfigured and moved to another world. I went on very late, sick and weak as I was. When the recital was over they filled a table with all the delicacies they had on the kibbutz, and then I received the regal accommodation of a tent all for myself.[33]

The boycott of applause, however, was occasionally lifted by spontaneous excitement, such as at a performance of the chorus of kibbutz Givat Brenner when 'the audience deviated several times from its habit and responded with an applause'.[34]

Listening Together to Radio and Gramophone

With no radio station in Palestine before 1936, radio sets were kept by a few fans who knew how to locate high-quality short-wave transmissions from abroad.

[31] See Ch. 10, above.   [32] Op. 31/2.

[33] A recorded interview with Joseph Tal, 14 Feb. 1976. See also Tal, *Der Sohn des Rabbiners*, 159.

[34] Givart Brenner Diary, 3 Mar. 1946. From 1936 the kibbutz distributed among its members a mimeographed newsletter which documented all of the kibbutz activities and allowed members to express their opinions.

The kibbutz members go by carriage and by foot to listen to the radio. They gather on the benches in quiet anticipation. The magician sits at the miracle box, touches here, turns a button there, his face serious as if in a sacred service. . . . The clock hits Nine. Nine thirty. Ten. The way home takes an hour and a half. One has to work tomorrow. Where is the music?[35]

When the PBS was founded in March 1936 the British government distributed radio sets in rural settlements. Kibbutz Givat Brenner first placed the set in the common dining hall where the constant noise prevented any proper listening to music. Information about music broadcasts was not readily available, and one of the members complained that members sit at the radio and 'aimlessly turn the knob in search of something worthy of listening to'.[36] Yet broadcasts of important events were treated with special attention. In preparation for the transmission of Toscanini's inaugural concert of the Palestine Orchestra the kibbutz rescheduled its weekly General Assembly; dinner was served earlier than usual and the dining-hall doors were locked at 8.30 p.m. for the entire length of the broadcast concert in order to allow for attentive listening.[37] Soon Givat Brenner acquired two additional radio sets which were placed in small 'radio cabins' where music lovers crowded to listen to concerts 'despite the rain in winter and the mosquitos in summer'.[38] When the Palestine Orchestra halted its live broadcasts,[39] the members of Givat Brenner were encouraged to protest in writing 'since for the Hebrew village which has no chance to bring over such an orchestra, its omission from the Jerusalem broadcast would be a severe loss'.[40]

Unlike the protagonist in Maletz's novel *Ma'agalot* who prefers the impassioned violin to the relaxing gramophone,[41] most kibbutz members had no reservations about listening to records, whether alone in their small corner or at a record concert. The kibbutz Tel-Yosef, for example, held gramophone concerts three times a week.[42]

The Givat Brenner Archive contains many documents pertaining to the gramophones and records played in the life of the commune. The kibbutz ideology by definition recognized no private property and each member was expected to pass his belongings to the collective with the exception

---

[35] 'Musical Life in the Country', *Davar* (14 May 1929).

[36] Celia, *Givat Brenner Newsletter* (26 Oct. 1937).

[37] *Givat Brenner Newsletter* (29 Dec. 1936). The General Assembly was a central institution running the life of any kibbutz so that a postponement was not a casual matter. See also *Ein Harod Diary* (30 Dec. 1936), quoted in Shahar, 'Music and Composer on the Kibbutz', MA thesis, (Bar-Ilan University, Ramat-Gan, 1981), 51.

[38] Interview with Shulamit Lakhish (Givat Brenner Archive).   [39] See Ch. 8, above.

[40] *Givat Brenner Newsletter* (6 Apr. 1939).   [41] See this Ch., above.

[42] *Tel-Yosef Diary* (16 Mar. 1936), quoted in Shahar, 'Music and Composer', 51.

of strictly personal effects. Significantly, gramophones and records consti-tuted a grey area between collective and private effects and the kibbutz was unwilling to pressure members to turn their precious collections to the public use. At the same time the kibbutz used the availability of private collections as an excuse to refrain from purchase of records from the tight kibbutz budget. The sad history of the public gramophone in Givat Brenner was summarized in the kibbutz's newsletter:

There were happy days when the gramophone was placed in a public place and was available to anyone floating on the wings of song. The outcome of these years was 200 broken records. The cultural committee decided to lock the gramophone and to appoint someone to look after it. They elected Adolf Levinger who merged his private records with the public collection. . . . What a miracle: Givat Brenner gained a fine collection. It was a miracle especially when it was discovered that every kibbutz had a budget for gramophones, records, and needles, and here the cultural committee spent not a single penny even on needles. . . . With the increase of immigration there appeared private gramophones here and there but none of their owners was willing to give them to the public as has been customary with money or other things. The owners even asked for permission to use the records from the public collection. The single [kibbutz] gramophone could not satisfy 500 members. We worked out a plan to pass all private gramophones to the cultural committee . . . but most of the owners refused. As a result Adolf withdrew his own collection which comprised the bulk of the public record library and we were left with nothing.[43]

The pressure on the cultural committee soon increased. Gramophone concerts were held each Saturday afternoon, and listeners complained that the reduced collection rendered the record concerts repetitive, that an electric gramophone should substitute for the manual ones, and that the committee should understand that concerts 'are not directed to members who are bored on the Sabbath but to those for whom music satisfies an emotional need'.[44] The budgetary difficulty was finally resolved by an ingenious idea borrowed from capitalist economy. The kibbutz established a resort hotel and gramophone concerts turned out to be popular with the hotel guests who were willing to pay a small fee which was used to improve the collection. When World War II broke out, the black-out against air bombardments rendered gramophone concerts the only possible cultural activity.[45] The war cut the supply of gramophone needles and one of the members discovered a certain wood which was

[43] A. Ettinen, *Givat Brenner Newsletter* (17 July 1936).
[44] *Givat Brenner Newsletter* (23 Dec. 1939).   [45] *Givat Brenner Newsletter* (18 June 1940).

used to make needles which had to be replaced after playing a single side.[46]

One of the members of kibbutz Givat Brenner told a moving story of her first musical experience in the kibbutz. Born in Tel Aviv, Shulamit Lakhish was a member of a socialist youth movement which sent her for a month of volunteer work in Givat Brenner:

I worked with a kibbutz member who had the key to the record collection. Just before I went to Givat Brenner I had heard [Beethoven's] 'Kreutzer' Sonata a few times. The memory was fresh and I longed to listen to it again. I asked the member whether the kibbutz owned the 'Kreutzer' Sonata and he replied that they did. . . . I assembled all members to listen to the Sonata at the Culture Club. I anticipated the first chord. It did not come. . . . I said: 'This is not the "Kreutzer" Sonata.' He answered: 'But look' and he showed me the record jacket which said 'Kreutzer' Sonata. But it was another piece . . . I left in tears.[47]

Menashe Ravina, the arch-advocate of active music-making, reluctantly admitted that

there was no kibbutz without a gramophone, and the very few kibbutzim whose dining hall still lacked that potent device roamed *en masse* to their fortunate neighbours and drank from that musical font. The gramophone is the instructor, the promoter of music among the people, the educator, the teacher.[48]

Ravina's main objection was not to the gramophone *per se* but to the absence of a direct experience of live music without which the recorded music lacked reference to live music.

An anonymous member of the kibbutz Genosar,[49] wrote 'The Gramophone Song' in which Karlsbad was the pet name given to the record-player. A contrafactum of a favourite hymn of the Pioneer Youth Movement, it reads, in literal translation omitting the frequent repetitions of words:

Refrain:
The gramophone, the gramophone, it transcends any other instrument in the world, because what would become of us all without it?
First stanza:
If you fell asleep late and did not awake to the bell toll, Tritumba will loudly sound the gramophone.

[46] Yishai Be'eri, an interview with Yehudah Meinzer, 20 Dec. 1983 (Givat Brenner Archive).
[47] An interview with Shulamit Lakhish, 8 Oct. 1992 (Givat Brenner Archive).
[48] 'Musical Life in the Country', *Davar* (14 May 1929).
[49] Kibbutz Genosar, overlooking the scenic Lake Kineret, was founded in 1937 (Genosar Archive).

Second stanza:
And if your heart is broken since she turned you away, forget your sorrow, and listen to the gramophone.
Third stanza:
And when boredom takes over, as it frequently happens, avoid a conversation, avoid the newspaper, listen to Karlsbad and rejoice.

International and Urban Guests

Special events, such as concerts by renowned guests, reached beyond the small realm of a single kibbutz and attracted listeners from entire regions. The violinist and critic Yariv Ezrahi documented Jasha Heifetz's concert in Nahalal in a long poetic review. His exalted tone was sparked off by the combination of Heifetz's playing and the unique context of the kibbutz concert and was further enhanced by the idealization of kibbutz life which permeated the outlook of urbanites.

It was a dull day. The sun was hidden behind a thin curtain of fog. The horizon did not smile from far beyond. The birds were not singing, and the green meadow did not shimmer. And the new grey edifice of the Community House which was filled to capacity was dominated by a silent expectation of a fairy-tale about to be told. In the first rows one could see the lovely heads of the children of Nahalal. A few mothers held their babies . . . The hall could not accommodate all of them. Thirsty souls looked inside through the windows. Inside they clustered at every niche, or hung from the walls like bats. . . . An auto appeared out of the fog which enveloped the road to Jerusalem. With no sign of fatigue after the long travel the violinist climbed on to the stage to the sound of stormy applause. The tension mounted. . . . The violinist lifted the bow, and suddenly one baby cried, and then a second, and a third . . . 'Take them out'—everybody was angry. . . But Heifetz's good face was covered with a wonderful smile . . . The tunes of Grieg's Sonata started to fill the yearning hearts and Heifetz's miraculous fountain sprayed the arid fields of Nahalal with precious drops of refreshing sounds. . . . After Grieg a few more lovely pieces followed one another, and the audience gulped them down like fresh dates and thanked the artist, in the manner of the members of Nahalal, with glances more than with hands. Only next to me, close to the stage, there stood a healthy-looking young man whose applause resembled gunfire. At the end of each piece he shocked the ears with his clapping and screaming 'encore, encore'. . . . I covered my eardrums and thought: 'Our boys have powerful hands. Give them music and their applause will convert rocks into paradise.' . . . The violinist concluded with Achron's *Hebrew Melody*. . . . It sounded as if all Diaspora yearning for the homeland burst out of Heifetz's violin, moans of our brethren, consolations, weeping, and hopes. . . . But while shedding tears we clenched our fists: 'our

people will live forever. We will build our home.' The lullaby became a prophecy. With the last sound we opened our eyes. The dream had come true: we
were in Nahalal.[50]

The cumbersome transportation from Tel Aviv and from Jerusalem to
far-away kibbutzim required an overnight stay, which allowed the artists
to acquaint themselves with the kibbutz. After his concert in Ein-Harod
Bronislaw Huberman was

shown all that was interesting, such as the school, the kindergarten, the babies'
home for different ages, and so on. I saw there was everything, a piano, a library,
sports-grounds, botanical and zoological collections, but I missed one thing:
where is the synagogue?

His question incited a long discussion with the schoolmaster, who explained the method in which the kibbutz was teaching the Bible as 'the
spiritual treasury' of the Jewish people, with no need of the

vestments of liturgy. . . . I have sometimes dreamed of a phase of humanity's
evolution where the good would be done and taught just for the sake of the
good. And here I met for the first time a striving for it. I cannot tell how deeply
I was touched by that conversation.[51]

The German violinist Adolf Busch visited Givat Brenner and his car
sank in the mud on the way out.

Ernst has just arrived with his car from Tel Aviv and pulled them out and invited
them to our home. We became very friendly with him and with his wife. They
gave us tickets for the performance in which Adolf played Brahms's Violin
Concerto. . . . We had to go early before 6 p.m. because there was a [road]
curfew afterwads. . . . After the performance Adolf sent a note inviting Ernst to
the artists' room. He took the four strings off his violin and gave them to Ernst.
It was such a wonderful gesture, not only because they were costly but because
it was so human.[52]

According to notices in the newsletter of Givat Brenner, one of the
most musical kibbutzim, despite the high motivation of the audience, the
kibbutz could organize no more than four concerts per year.[53] The inner
need for music was filled by frequent travels to concerts in the adjacent
village of Rehovot and in Tel Aviv. The Cultural Committee complained

[50] *Ha'Aretz* (21 Mar. 1932).

[51] Bronislaw Huberman, Address at Gershon Agronsky's house, Jerusalem, 22 Jan. 1934, pub. in
Hadassah Newsletter (Jan. 1935), rep. in Ibbeken and Avni (eds.), *Orchestra is Born*, 9–10. See Ch. 8,
above.

[52] An interview with Miriam Engel, 5 Feb. 1993, in Tamar Cohen, *Musical Activity in Kibbutz
Givat Brenner 1928–1948* (Jerusalem, 1993).

[53] Excluding holiday celebrations and informal *Hausmusik* sessions. Ibid.

that members used to 'decide on their own to halt their work and go to concerts in town'.[54] A false rumour spread in Givat Brenner that the kibbutz would receive sixty tickets to Toscanini's dress rehearsal with the Palestine Orchestra sent most members rushing by carriage and by foot to Tel Aviv where they were met with locked doors. 'The rehearsal started and there was lot of commotion. Hundreds of people crowded outside. Toscanini stopped . . . and instructed to let everyone in.'[55]

For city-dwellers in general, and for urban artists in particular, the kibbutz connoted a synthesis of a rural pastoral, social utopia, and fulfilment of the national dream. Having settled in Jerusalem as a teacher at the Palestine Conservatoire, Joseph Gruenthal thought that it would be

important for the young immigrant students to see more of Palestine rather than only hear about Arab unrest and the perils of daily life in Jerusalem. Thus I hit on the idea of preparing with the Academy Orchestra a nice programme and of organizing a concert tour in the kibbutzim across the country. This was not an easy undertaking since funds were not available and what the kibbutzim could pay barely covered the transportation costs . . . Such an orchestral concert was a sensation for each kibbutz.[56]

Encouraged by the enthusiastic reception, Gruenthal mounted a full stage production of Handel's *Perseus and Andromeda* which was premièred outdoors in the kibbutz Kineret, 'in a subtropical summer night with the air rich with fragrance and with all kinds of insects'.[57] Such concerts generated many unforeseen incidents. The members of the kibbutz Kyriat Anavim erected a makeshift stage of straw bundles covered with wooden boards. While trying to cue the horn-player, Gruenthal noticed to his horror that the musician had sunk with his chair in between two straw bundles, whereupon musicians and audience all burst into wild laughter.[58]

Concerts by chamber ensembles from Tel Aviv and Jerusalem were regularly held in the kibbutzim. Nathan Shahar has compiled a sample list of fifteen chamber groups and recitalists who performed in Ein Harod, Yagur, and Tel Yosef in the years 1936–48. They included the venerable Jerusalem Quartet, two of Thelma Yellin's trios, Frank Pollack who arrived with his harpsichord, Oedoen Partos both as violinist and violist,

[54] *Givat Brenner Newsletter* (23 Aug. 1935).

[55] An interview with Leah Felter, Jan. 1978 (Givat Brenner Archive).

[56] Tal, *Der Sohn des Rabbiners*, 209.

[57] Ibid. 217. The lead role was taken by Hilde Zadek, who later became a soloist at the Wiener Stadsoper. Kineret overlooks the Lake of Galilee.

[58] Ibid. Kyriat Anavim is located about 15 km. west of Jerusalem.

and other ensembles of members of the Palestine Orchestra.[59] The kibbutzim provided an important outlet for the saturated supply of chamber
music ensembles active in Tel Aviv and Jerusalem.

An interim stage was the collaboration of guests with local musicians,
such as a Brahms programme held in Givat Brenner by a pianist from the
adjacent village of Gedera with a singer, a cellist, and a clarinet-player
who were kibbutz members.[60]

Concerts by large professional ensembles were organized less frequently
and on a regional basis, such as the open-air theatre of Ein Harod which
hosted a production of Bizet's *Carmen* and a performance of the Palestine
Orchestra under Leonard Bernstein on the occasion of his sensational first
visit to the country.[61]

The kibbutz musicians were catalysts of instrumental training to the
kibbutz children. Eva Salomon from Givat Brenner warned the parents of
the dozen children in the small school in 1937 that 'although Givat
Brenner is blessed with musicians, music education has been completely
neglected'.[62] The kibbutz first limited instruction to piano lessons only.
Benjamin Pintus objected to the exclusivity of the piano which could not
encourage the development of a children's orchestra and chamber
groups.[63] The kibbutz then released Theo Bloch, a semi-professional
clarinet-player, from his duties as farmer and placed him in charge of
musical education, although he himself 'was in need of training'. He
immediately enrolled as a student at the Music Teachers' Training College
in Tel Aviv: 'I studied for two days in Tel Aviv and for two days I taught
in Givat Brenner . . . I had to be on the watch not to discharge in Givat
Brenner more than I have accumulated in Tel Aviv.'[64] Bloch himself
instructed ear-training, group singing, and recorder groups, and he also
acted as a mediator between instrumental teachers from town and the
Cultural Committee in their constant financial squabbles.

Adult members who wished to keep in shape had to go through the
arduous task of convincing the General Assembly to grant them practice
time. Two farmers from Ein Harod 'needed two hours every day for
violin practice. It was hard to arrange since they work in the fields. It has
been decided to grant them a half-day three times a week.'[65]

---

[59] Shahar, 'Music and Composer', 58.   [60] *Givat Brenner Newsletter* (4 Mar. 1938).
[61] On 25 May 1945 and 10 May 1947 respectively. Bernstein conducted his *Jeremiah Symphony*
and performed also as a pianist. *Davar* (5 Apr. 1947).
[62] *Givat Brenner Newsletter* (16 Feb. 1937).   [63] *Givat Brenner Newsletter* (4 Nov. 1941).
[64] T. Bloch, 'Music in our School', *Givat Brenner Newsletter* (14 Oct. 1946).
[65] *Ein Harod Diary* (12 May 1944), quoted in Shahar, *Music and Composer*, 53.

Inventing Traditions

Most of the founders of the many new kibbutzim during the 1920s and 1930s went through the double trauma of immigration and of a radical change in their way of life. As a means to soften the trauma they resorted to the process of inventing traditions, which 'is taken to mean a set of practices, normally governed by overtly or tacitly accepted rules and of a ritual or symbolic nature, which seek to inculcate certain values and norms of behaviour by repetition, which automatically implies continuity with the past'.[66] The most consequential invented tradition of the kibbutz movement was the communal holiday celebration.

The strictly prescribed observance of the religious Jewish holidays is divided between the synagogue and the family[67] with the focus changing from one holiday to another. For example, the solemn Day of Atonement (Yom Kippur) is observed in its entirety in a day-long synagogue service, whereas the Passover festive meal (the Seder) is a family event.[68] The High Holiday of Rosh Hashanah (the Jewish New Year) is celebrated through a long synagogue service followed by festive family meals at home, including partaking of symbolic foods such as apple dipped in honey. The collective kibbutz ideology contradicted both the religious service and the family meals. The religious holidays were reinterpreted as modern revivals of ancient biblical agricultural rites, especially the three High Holidays associated with the agricultural cycle: the Feast of Tabernacles (Sukkoth) marking the autumn harvest and the beginning of the rainy season; Passover, which combined the spring festivity with the national symbol of the Exodus, and the Feast of Weeks (Shavuot, Pentecost) associated with the spring harvest.[69] The reinterpretation of the traditional Jewish yearly cycle was complemented by the celebration of national and local events, such as the kibbutz anniversaries, which required the inventing of brand new traditions. The celebration of the holidays became a recurrent issue of discussions and deliberations

---

[66] E. Hobsbawm, 'Inventing Traditions', in id. and T. Rank (eds.), *The Invention of Tradition* (Cambridge, 1983), 1.

[67] Shiloah, *Jewish Musical Traditions*, 162–3 and *passim*. See Ch. 11 n. 4 for a list of the Jewish yearly cycle.

[68] The Seder (lit. 'succession of events'), consists of reciting, chanting, and group singing of the Passover book, the Haggadah (lit. 'saying') which includes symbolic enacting such as partaking of the symbolic foods of Passover, with a large traditional family meal dividing the ceremony into two parts.

[69] Leviticus 23; 10ff.

within each individual kibbutz and in the kibbutz movement as a whole.[70] Attempts were made to infuse some of the festive days with cultural contents only remotely connected with the holiday itself, such as lectures on literary topics. Writing in the *Givat Brenner Newsletter*, one of the members suggested enriching the lectures through the participation of the orchestra and the choir.[71] To illustrate, the celebration of Rosh Hashanah in Givat Brenner in 1937 started with a festive dinner followed by a concert of the kibbutz chorus, quartet, and orchestra. The long and varied programme consisted of a movement from a Beethoven quartet, a choral movement by Mendelssohn, readings from the Bible and ancient Jewish legends, a chorus by Handel, an orchestral suite by Pachelbel, an excerpt from Bach's *St Matthew Passion*, an aria from Handel's *Rinaldo*, a chorus from Haydn's *Creation*, a cantata by Josef Haas, and finally dances by Mozart.[72] The traditional In Memoriam prayer of the Day of Atonement in 1939 was enriched by a performance of Cherubini's Requiem in memory of the members of the kibbutz who had passed away or were killed in the wave of hostilities of 1936–9. No reservation was expressed about the inclusion of a Catholic Requiem in the most solemn Jewish holiday.[73] Givat Brenner was personified on its thirteenth anniversary in 1941 as a Jewish child celebrating his bar mitzvah, the initiation rite. Despite the gloomy news from the war, the event was celebrated outdoors with the members well drilled as to how to take care of the children in case of an air attack. The national anthems and the speeches were followed by a Mozart programme of the orchestra with soloists from the Palestine Orchestra.[74]

While performances of concert music conformed to the solemn atmosphere of traditional holidays, they were out of place in social parties. An anonymous member of Givat Brenner complained that the refusal of the kibbutz musicians to merge a scheduled concert with a party in commemoration of the woman worker forced the organizers of the party to rely on cheap popular records as its only cultural content.[75] He was immediately rebuffed by P. Lisser who insisted that art music should be performed only in proper contents, and should not be used 'to fill gaps and holes in meaningless parties'.[76]

---

[70] Numerous articles on this issue were published in the periodicals and in kibbutz pamphlets. An attempt at reaching a consensus was made with the publication of *Liymei Mo'ed Vezicaron* (For Holidays and Memorials), (Hakibbutz Hameuhad, 1937).

[71] Yitzhac (no last name given), *Givat Brenner Newsletter* (10 Feb. 1936).

[72] *Givat Brenner Newsletter* (5 Sept. 1937). The structure of such programmes resembled that of concerts held in Tel Aviv and Jerusalem earlier in the century. See Chs. 2 and 3, above.

[73] *Givat Brenner Newsletter* (22 Aug. 1939).   [74] *Givat Brenner Newsletter* (4 July 1941).

[75] *Givat Brenner Newsletter* (14 Mar. 1937).   [76] *Givat Brenner Newsletter* (28 Mar. 1937).

The European orientation of the repertory of the holiday celebration in Givat Brenner sparked ideological controversies similar to those which raged in Tel Aviv and Jerusalem at the same time. The Rosh Hashanah concert in 1940 featured a piece by the local composer Moshe Rappaport (1903–68), which was the first performance of 'Hebrew music' by the kibbutz orchestra. Theo Bloch responded to members who expressed reservations about the modern work that their obsession with indiscriminate listening to records had blurred their sensitivity to new directions in music and 'might suffocate any attempt at a national Hebrew creativity'.[77] Ideological criticism also came from the opposite direction, especially after the outbreak of World War II. A kibbutz member who introduced himself as a 'non-musician' and 'non-musical' objected to a Mozart programme on the fifteenth Kibbutz anniversary since 'Mozart's church tunes—without denying their great artistic value—may be pleasant to listen to on any other evening, but they do not fit the celebration of the anniversary of a Hebrew village in this country. Where are the songs of the struggle for survival of our people?'[78] It appears that such reservations usually came from the direction of the uninitiated, whereas the kibbutz musicians kept protecting the mainstream repertory as a rule, such as when the pianist Fritz Weissmüller wrote that 'we should admit that music was created by others, by foreigners. If we wish to create Jewish music we should understand that we would never be able to ignore the artists of the past and their masterpieces.'[79]

While the Feast of Tabernacles and of Weeks were celebrated outdoor, the Passover Seder turned into an elaborate and colourful indoor celebration in the decorated dining hall. The commune, frequently referred to by members as 'the kibbutz family', substituted for the nuclear family. Relatives and friends from town were invited as guests. The Seder service book, the Haggadah, was rewritten, preserving some of the traditional texts to which an array of communal, choral, and solo songs and dances were added. Two of the veteran kibbutzim, Yagur and Ein Harod, took the lead,[80] serving as a model for other kibbutzim. Yoseph Ahai who provided the Hebrew translations and contrafacta to all feasts in Givat Brenner acknowledged the priority of the Seder celebrations in Yagur, Afikim, and Givat Hashlosha. He indicated that the Seder in Givat Brenner was remarkably traditional by comparison to Yagur 'although Givat Brenner is mostly detached from traditional Hebrew education. On

[77] *Givat Brenner Newsletter* (13 Oct. 1940).
[78] Zalman Hen, *Givat Brenner Newsletter* (20 July 1943).
[79] *Givat Brenner Newsletter* (21 Apr. 1944).
[80] Shahar, 'Music and Composer'. Y. Sharet, *Seder shel Pessah Nosah Yagur* (Tel Aviv, 1951).

the other hand, the Givat Brenner Seder included allusions to the kibbutz itself whereas Yagur turned away from any local references.'[81] Shmuel Gadon of Givat Brenner objected to the use of foreign tunes in the Seder and Yosef Ahai responded that 'of course I am fond of our own tunes, but in my opinion an event attended by 1,000 people requires a great masterpiece'.[82] Yet the objection to foreign tunes was not ignored and two years later the folk composer Yedidiah Gorochov, then temporarily employed in Givat Brenner, replaced them with his own tunes.[83] The holiday celebrations in the kibbutzim was thus based on models set by four or five large kibbutzim adjacent to urban centres, each kibbutz adding local variants of its own.

The kibbutz composer was the central personality in the planning and execution of the feast. Shalom Postolsky initiated a holiday tradition of the Feast of Weeks in the kibbutz Ein Harod in the late 1930s. Mattityahu Weiner (Shelem) who objected to Postolsky's interpretation, made a thorough study of Jewish sources and composed his own 'pageant in its entirety. The texts, the structure of the ceremony, as well as the melodies.'[84] His kibbutz, Ramat-Yohanan, adopted his version in 1945, and since then it has been repeated with few changes.

The most impressive and influential of the kibbutz celebrations has been the Seder of the kibbutz Yagur. Founded in 1922 by a small group of ten members, it absorbed a group of about 100 workers from Haifa in 1926. In 1933 it merged with a neighbouring settlement of immigrants from Poland, thus becoming the largest in the country, numbering 794 members in 1936 and more than 1,000 in 1941.[85] The only precedent for such a growth had been that of Tel Aviv in the mid-1920s,[86] with its effects on the social texture of a collective settlement reaching much deeper than in an urban society. Well-organized holiday celebrations were treated as a powerful tool for social integration. Created by the kibbutz composer Yehudah Shertok (Sharet), the Yagur Seder received its final form in the early 1930s with only minor subsequent alterations.[87] Its codification in print took place only in 1951. Sharet's detailed and

---

[81] 'About Four *Haggadahs*', *Givat Brenner Newsletter* (16 and 19 Apr. 1937). Yagur, located 12 km. south-east of Haifa, was founded in 1922, Givat Hashlosha, 2 km. east of the village of Petah Tikvah, was founded in 1925. In 1936 it numbered about 550 members.

[82] *Givat Brenner Newsletter* (20 Apr. 1942).   [83] *Givat Brenner Newsletter* (4 Apr. 1942).

[84] B. Bayer, 'Creation and Tradition in Israeli Folk Song: Some Specimen Cases', *Aspects of Music in Israel* (Israel Composers' League, Tel Aviv, 1980), 52–4. M. Weiner *Hava'at Ha'omer* (The Harvest Feast) (Tel Aviv, 1947).

[85] Gurevich and Gertz (eds.), *Statistical Handbook*, 51.   [86] See Ch. 3, above.

[87] B. Bayer, 'Passover Yagur Seder', *Dukhan*, 8 (1966), 83–98. By the early 1960s the ceremony which involved about 2,000 kibbutz members and guests had been transferred from the dining-hall to the new kibbutz auditorium.

flowery introduction and commentary to the publication is a unique documentation of the process of the shaping of the Seder through interaction between the composer and his congregation. Sharet expressed reservations about the printed version which was intended 'not for reading and not for the individual in his intimate corner but to the public'.[88] The notation is descriptive rather than prescriptive and no reconstruction of the event is feasible on the basis of the printed version alone. Sharet viewed the kibbutz Seder as an outcome of the need to fill the spiritual void which each individual member had experienced at the approach of the Jewish high holidays. The rejection of the orthodox observance had first led to aborted attempts to substitute light parodies or secular entertainment for the Seder, following which the kibbutz return-ed to the traditional texts. Yet while the customary Haggadah has been a richly illuminated book appealing to the individual eye, the kibbutz Seder was exclusively directed to the ear.[89] The composer co-operated with a group of kibbutz members in revising the Haggadah, substituting biblical verses, Talmudic texts, and medieval rhymed poems (*piyutim*) for seg-ments less suitable for public recitation or singing.[90] Yet modern literary texts were not included. Sharet endorsed the kibbutz custom to open or close the Seder with a separate harvest ceremony having its own songs, which were not included in the printed Yagur Seder.

Sharet directed the Seder for 'an active congregation'. Yet he noted that 'congregational singing throughout the evening would have detracted from its power and reduced full participation.'[91] Thus, full congregational singing was limited to climactic points and most of the texts were assigned to smaller groups which consisted of a mixed chorus seated in the front of the dining hall but on the same level with the entire congregation, a children's chorus, solo singers and speakers, with in-strumentalists joining in some of the songs. Designation of instruments was optional, a typical rubric being 'a soprano instrument (oboe)'[92] since the availability of instrumentalists varied from year to year. Sharet ob-jected to any stage action, tempting as it was under the circumstances, since he insisted on keeping the small groups as integral parts of the congregation.

The music of the Seder stemmed from a broad array of sources:

1. Biblical cantillation of the *Song of Songs* which was placed at the opening of the Seder, each verse performed by a member of the chil-

---

[88] Sharet, *Seder*. Bayer, 'Passover', 96, has noted that the tradition has been so well entrenched that the kibbutz members continued to use mimeographed sheets of texts without music also after the publication of the printed version.
[89] Sharet, *Seder*, 5.   [90] Ibid. 43.   [91] Ibid. 11.   [92] Ibid. 22.

Ex 12.1. Sharet, Seder music (Lithuanian style)

Ex 12.2. Sharet, Seder music (nigunim style)

dren's chorus. Sharet used the Lithuanian version as notated by Yehudah L. Ne'eman. (See Ex. 12.1.)[93]

Sharet suggested coaching the children's chorus not by oral repeats but through a systematic instruction of the system of Masoretic accents. He also recommended the diversification of the cantillation and the use of the accents of the eastern Jewish communities, which, however, he did not introduce into the printed version.

2. Traditional Passover melodies (nigunim). Sharet's treatment of one of them sheds light on both the collective aspect of the shaping of the Seder and on the extent of ideological conflicts stirred by the invented tradition. Sharet described the tune for the verse 'but the more they afflicted them, the more they multiplied and grew'[94] as a 'foul version' and as a 'wine which had soured'. He expressed his disgust with the alien practice of performing this nigun in 'sweetened parallel thirds' which the folk had absorbed from 'street songs, from the radio, from conservatory harmony exercises and from clichés of traditional music.'[95] Still, he had no choice but to give in to 'public taste', his only attempt at improvement being the arrangement of the nigun in an imitative style. (See Ex. 12.2.)

3. Folk song settings of Haggadah texts by Postolsky, Gorochov, Karchewsky, and Engel such as Postolsky's 'we were Pharaoh's bondsmen in Egypt'.[96] (See Ex. 12.3.)

---

[93] Ibid. 13. Ne'eman was a cantor and an ethnographer of cantillation. His Lithuanian tradition prevailed among the Orthodox Ashkenazi congregation of Jerusalem. The Hebrew term is *Te'amim*. See A. Herzog, 'Masoretic Accents', *Encyclopedia Judaica*.

[94] 'Vekha'asher ye'anu oto ken yirbeh vekhen yifrotz' (*Exodus*, 1: 12).

[95] Sharet, *Seder*, 60–1.   [96] 'Avadim ha'inu' (Deuteronomy 6: 21). Sharet, *Seder*, 15, 43, 52.

Ex 12.3. Postolsky, Seder music ('Avadim hayinu')

A - va -dim ha -yi nu   a - va - dim   a - ta be- nei ho-rin___   be - nei ho - rin

Ex 12.4. Sharet, Seder music ('Uvnei Yisrael')

4. Sharet's own settings, most of them in two parts, such as the setting of 'and the children of Israel went out with a high hand'.[97] (See Ex. 12.4.)

Sharet's commentary not only provided the most detailed performance instructions but also warned against the pitfalls of holding such an extended public ritual. The dainty opening with the children chanting verses from the *Song of Songs* always evoked verbal reactions and comments in the enormous audience, with the resulting chatter drowning the next speaker. Thus Sharet urged the speaker to continue immediately and securely with no time-gap after the final verse of the children.[98]

The Yagur Seder has thus exemplified the most ambitious process of an invented tradition which achieved a careful balance between individual endeavour and public input and reception.

The process of invention of traditions involved the reconciliation of a set of opposites, modestly and candidly presented by Yosef Ahai of Givat Brenner. The celebration through a concert by the kibbutz ensembles supported by professional guests was as a rule a gratifying experience, but it did not impress the sense of a holiday. 'I think that the difference between a concert and a feast is the extent of active participation.' Yet, it was difficult to achieve active participation of large audiences without the support of well-organized performing groups, which then attracted attention thus discouraging active participation. Invented traditions required repetition and regularity, whereas the kibbutz by definition was conceived as an innovative society, alert to internal and external changes. Yosef Ahai

---

[97] 'Uvnei Yisrael yotzim beyad ramah' (Exodus 14: 8), Sharet, *Seder*, 36.   [98] *Seder*, 54.

pointed out that 'many years passed before we rendered the Seder into a truly festive event. And what has helped us? In my opinion—tradition— our tradition. After many years of an exploration we have omitted the temporal and the local, freed ourselves of the secular, and reached the idea of the eternal holiday.'[99]

[99] *Givat Brenner Newsletter* (7 Sept. 1943).

$$\boxed{13}$$

In the Cause of Jewish Music

Joel Engel's premature death and Jacob Weinberg's emigration in 1927 dealt a heavy blow to the publication and performance of Jewish music in Palestine. The international operations of Juwal publishing house were taken up by Hanigun society in Palestine,[1] while the violinist and composer Joseph Achron sponsored Jibneh publishing house in Vienna which concentrated on Jewish art music. Both were soon taken over by Universal Edition, which, however, dispensed with its Jewish department in 1933. Subsequent attempts to sustain publication of Jewish music did not get off the ground.[2]

Entering a Dead-End Alley

While Engel and his colleagues proudly cultivated their deep roots in the traditional heritage of European Jewry, a small group of musicians and amateurs in Jerusalem adopted an opposing, radical approach, advocating a total rejection of all western values as a necessary step for the creation of genuine Jewish music in Palestine. Spearheading the group was the physician and musician Mordecai Sandberg (1898–1973). Born in Romania, Sandberg immigrated to Palestine in 1922, where he became increasingly dedicated to the cause of new Jewish music. The programmes of his concerts were dedicated to Jewish music and especially to his own works. In 1927 he founded what was described as a branch of the International Society for Contemporary Music in Jerusalem with the

---

[1] See Ch. 5, above.

[2] A letter from Stutschewsky to Salli Levi (WCJMP Archive, JNUL), repr. in Bohlman, *World Centre*, 127.

purpose of advancing his own system of writing in microtones, which idea was very much in vogue in the 1920s.[3] Sandberg had a quarter-tone harmonium built to his order by Straube in Germany.

The first lecture-concert illustrating the system took place in Jerusalem on 26 May 1927, featuring new works for mezzo-soprano, cello, piano, and the 'bichromatic harmonium' by Sandberg himself and by the German composer Wille Moellendorf. Sandberg's notation of vocal music followed Idelsohn's manner of writing from right to left (see Ex. 13.1).[4]

While some of the listeners expressed curiosity, Salomon Rosowsky hastened to cool them down, indicating that the idea had been introduced in Europe twenty years earlier and that it had never taken root there. Moreover, Rosowsky doubted its relevance to music in Palestine since he claimed that Arabic music was based on the division of the whole tone into three rather than four parts.[5]

In 1930 Sandberg and his friend M. S. Geshuri, an amateur folk composer who worked as a clerk at the Jewish agency, initiated a short-lived ideological periodical named *Halel*[6] which presented the platform of the group as a total rejection of all Jewish music written outside Palestine since 'Hebrew music can be created only in the Land of Israel . . . and must be common to all Hebrew, Western and Eastern Jews . . . and not the property of any Diaspora group, however large and culturally rich it may be.'[7] The rejection of western values did not prevent Sandberg from compiling a collection of European compositions in microtones as a further support for his approach. The mainstream circle of musicians in Palestine ridiculed Sandberg's ideas. David Schor complained that Sandberg 'considered himself the founding father of new music'[8] and Menashe Ravina opened a review of a fine piano recital with the sarcastic remark:

A scream burst out in our musical world: let us have tone material, quarter-tones, thirds of tones, etc. There came the two works [in the recital]—Bach's fugue and Beethoven's variations—and proved to the prophets of musical apocalypse that their words were false and that there was no limit to the potential of the sounds.

Rejected by his fellow musicians, Sandberg turned to international contacts. In 1938 he went to London to present an illustrated paper at the

---

[3] See Austin, *Music in the 20th Century*, 381–2 for a comprehensive chronological chart of research and composition in micro-tones at that time.

[4] See Ch. 1, above.   [5] *Ha'Aretz* (3 July 1927).

[6] The *Halel* (lit. 'praise') is a prayer composed of a sequence of psalm verses chanted on the High Jewish holidays. The periodical *Halel* published only five issues.

[7] S. Barkai, *Halel* (1930), 25.

[8] A letter to Stutschewsky, 18 June 1930 (Stutschewsky Archive, AMLI Library, Tel Aviv).

Ex 13.1. Sandberg's right-to-left notation with quarter-tone inflections

Music and Life 1938 Congress. The review in *The Times* commented that most of microtonality 'sounds so out of tune' and the critic of the *Daily Mail* observed that 'Mr Sandberg takes life and himself too seriously'.[9] Sandberg proceeded to give lectures and concerts in New York where he was left stranded at the outbreak of World War II and separated from his children who remained in Jerusalem. Having lost his position and house in Jerusalem he settled down after the war in the United States.[10] The attempt to rationalize the quarter-tone composition as a venue for new Jewish music remained a passing episode in the musical life of the Yishuv.

Between Folksong and Art Music

In a cultural milieu which idolized folksong, nearly all composers of art music found themselves torn between their traditional sophisticated European training and their sense of commitment to the genre of the invented folk song of the Yishuv.[11] Most of them encountered severe difficulties crossing the barrier, and in practice there was only a very limited overlap between the 'core' group of folksong composers and those of art music. Marc Lavri was the only one who wrote in the two genres, deliberately attempting to blur the line of demarcation. His first composition in Palestine was the folksong 'The Song of The Emek'[12] which extols the pioneer spirit of the settlers. It was immediately developed into the symphonic poem *Emek*, the first locally composed work which the Palestine Orchestra performed.

Other composers compromised on making polyphonic arrangements of folksongs written by others, as a proper outlet for their ideological drive.[13] The leaders of the avant-garde among the immigrants, Stefan

---

[9] *The Times* (21 May 1938); *Daily Mail* (19 May 1938).

[10] Sandberg organized several concerts in New York. See *New York Times* (9 June 1957). He was unable to resume his general practice in the United States so that he immersed himself in the monumental project of setting the entire Bible to music. In 1970 he moved to Toronto where he presented a series of lectures at York University. His two microtone instruments have been temporarily placed at the Department of Music, York University, Toronto. Data and material kindly provided by the composer's widow, the painter Mrs Hannah Sandberg, and by Professor Austin Clarkson, Toronto, Apr. 1993. A full catalogue of Sandberg's enormous output compiled by Austin Clarkson, Judith Sandberg-Maimon, Karen Pegley, and Jay Rahn is due to be published in *Musica Judaica*.

[11] See Ch. 9, above.

[12] Emek, lit. 'valley', connoted in the 1930s the fertile Jezre'el Valley in the north of Palestine which symbolized pioneer productive agricultural settlement. The composition was premièred on 13 June 1937.

[13] See Ch. 9, above.

Ex 13.2. Nardi, arr. Sternberg, 'Who will build'

Wolpe and Erich Walter Sternberg, were especially industrious in the realm of folksong arrangements, even though their knowledge of the Hebrew language was minimal. Their predilection for folksongs was strongly supported by their pre-migration interests. For Wolpe it was a partial realization of his socialist world-view, whereas for Sternberg it meant a continuation of his comprehensive training under Paul Hindemith who directed him not only towards dense chromatic polyphony but also towards the realm and ideology of *Gebrauchmusik*. Such was Sternberg's anthology of ten songs arranged for two parts. Contributing one song of his own and arranging songs by other composers, Sternberg's primary device was the two-part canon at different intervals, as in the arrangement of the pioneer song 'Who will build' (see Ex. 13.2).[14]

Folksongs of Palestine soon acquired international status, symbolizing identification with the builders of the Jewish homeland. In 1938 the American branches of the Zionist youth organizations Massada and Hechaluz published the series *Folk Songs of the New Palestine* which comprised six booklets consisting of a total of thirty arrangements for voice and piano. Significantly, the subtitle made a distinction between the composers who were 'the true builders, the pioneers', and the arrangers who were introduced as a select 'group of the eminent Jewish composers'.[15] Moreover, while all composers of the compilation were residing in Palestine at that time, only two of the dozen arrangers did so. Thus the composers personified the idolized pioneer whereas the arrangers represented the identification of world Jewry with the Yishuv. The series was edited by the musicologist Dr Hans Nathan, a recent *emigré* from Germany to the United States.[16] Wolpe's arrangement of

---

[14] E. W. Sternberg (arr.), *Manginot* (Tunes)—*Ten Two Part Songs* (Tel Aviv, 1936). *Mi yivneh*, by Levin Kipnis and Nahum Nardi was first performed by Bracha Zephira (see Ch. 11, above). It is a eulogy of the pioneers who build homes in Tel Aviv, plough fields in the Galilee and plant vineyards and orchards in Rishon Le'Zion and Rehovot.

[15] Pub. by Nigun (New York).

[16] The composers were Postolsky, Walbe, Zeira, Rabinowitz, Gorochov, Sambursky, Nardi, Shertok, Sarah Levi, Weiner, Karchewsky, Ezrahi, and Chitrik; the arrangers were Erich W.

Ex 13.3. Gorochov, arr. Wolpe, 'Our Baskets on our Shoulders'

Gorochov's children's song 'Our baskets on our shoulders'[17] indicated that despite the simple, almost naïve style, Wolpe consistently avoided major–minor chords (see Ex. 13.3).

The World Centre for Jewish Music

The Central European immigration infused new life into the emotionally loaded field of Jewish music, and the boldest new initiative was the World Centre for Jewish Music in Palestine.[18] Its promulgator was Dr Sally Levi (1894–1951), a dental surgeon by profession. Active as choral director in the Jewish community of Frankfurt, he immigrated to Palestine in 1935 and became Stefan Wolpe's composition student.[19] Levi's drive was catching and the prestigious columnist and critic Hermann Swet helped him mount an extensive international correspondence campaign with all prominent Jewish musicians as well as with non-Jews who were dedicated to anti-Fascist struggle. Within less than four years the World Centre received 1,269 letters in response to Salli Levi's call, both sides trying to defy personal and economical hardships and communication difficulties in a world on the threshold of war.

The purposes of the World Centre as outlined by Salli Levi in 1937 hardly differed from those of the Hanigun Society eight years earlier[20] in that they spanned the full gamut of musical activity, from publication and

Sternberg, Aaron Copland, Paul Dessau, Kurt Weil, Darius Milhaud, Ernst Toch, Stefan Wolpe, Lazare Saminsky, Frederick Jacobi, Leon Algazi, Arthur Honegger, and Max Ettinger. See Hans Nathan's letter to Hermannn Swet and Sally Levi, 3 May 1938 (WCJMP Archive, JNUL), printed in Bohlman, *World Centre*, 30.

[17] 'Saleinu al Ktefeinu'.
[18] See Bohlman, *World Centre*, for an annotated documentary history.
[19] See Ch. 10, above.   [20] See Ch. 5, above.

research to concert management and formulation of a network of international communication among Jewish musicians[21] such as Joachim
Stutschewsky, who viewed it as a revival rather than as a novelty.[22] The
World Centre reached the apex of its endeavour with the publication of
the first and only issue of its periodical *Musica Hebraica*.[23] The World
Centre cleverly organized its inaugural ceremony on 1 March 1938[24]
when the organizers could present the publication as a proof of their
competence, immediately earning the official endorsement of the
National Committee.[25]

The World Centre claimed credit for sponsoring performances of
large-scale Jewish compositions. The first of them was the local première
of Hugo Adler's *Balak and Bilam*. Hugo Adler (1894–1955) was the chief
cantor of Mannheim and 'one of the most effective organizers for the
World Centre in Germany'.[26] The oratorio *Balak and Bilam* which had
been premièred in Mannheim in a German translation of the biblical
text four years earlier, was performed in Hebrew by the PBS chamber
orchestra and Shem choir conducted by Max Lampel on 21 June 1938,
with Karl Salomon as one of the soloists. The performance at the
auditorium of the Jewish Agency in Jerusalem was broadcast live and was
followed by an announcement of the foundation of an association of
Friends of the World Centre. Swet wrote two long previews in which he
welcomed the composition as a new stage in freeing Jewish music in
Germany from the 'spirit of assimilation which had prevailed in Jewish
music since Sulzer and Lewandowsky'.[27]

The most ambitious initiative of the World Centre was the first performance in Palestine of Ernst Bloch's *Sacred Service*[28] on 18 June 1940 at
Edison auditorium in Jerusalem with a live broadcast. Karl Salomon,
director of the music department, conducted a seventy-member chorus
and the PBS orchestra which was doubled for the event to fifty members.
Despite the black-out for fear of German air raids, 'several hundreds
listeners attended, among them the leaders of the Jerusalem society'.[29]
The tense military conditions prevented the arrival of the management of

---

[21] Bohlman, *World Centre*, 8.

[22] Letter from Stutschewsky to Levi, 11 Apr. 1938 (Bohlman, *World Centre*, 127).

[23] Announced in *Ha'Aretz* (24 June 1938) (Bohlman, *World Centre*, 158–72 and *passim*). The
editors presented the publication as a double issue.

[24] Bohlman, *World Centre*, 124.   [25] Menashe Ravina, *Davar* (25 Sept. 1938).

[26] Bohlman, *World Centre*, 12, 59.

[27] Previews by Hermannn Swet, *Ha'Aretz* (13 and 20 June 1938).

[28] Composed 1930–3 at the commission of the Zionist leader Felix Warburg, it was dedicated to
his son Gerald.

[29] *Jerusalemer Stadtsblatt* (21 June 1940).

the Palestine Orchestra from Tel Aviv.[30] The event carried a special symbolic meaning in that 'the seventy members of the chorus included many Christian Arabs and Englishmen who jointly celebrated the Sabbath morning service in Hebrew'.[31] The Palestine Orchestra followed suit and included the *Sacred Service* in the second of its subscription concerts of the 1940/1 season with the same conductor and chorus.

Joachim Stutschewsky later claimed that the 'Board of the World Centre exerted no real influence on performances in the country and on the radio.'[32] Yet there is evidence to the contrary. The World Centre not only initiated the performance but also assumed responsibility for 30 per cent of a possible deficit not exceeding £15, thus convincing the PBS to guarantee the rest. Paul Jacobi, legal consultant of the World Centre, also conducted long negotiations with the management of Edison auditorium, assured exemption from taxation, and solicited a donation of £5 for the performance.[33] A last-minute crisis erupted when the soloist, Vittorio Weinberg, was deeply insulted after having found out from Salomon that his honorarium would be only £3. In a highly temperamental letter the prestigious singer rejected the proposal as 'a shit swindle'[34] and announced that he would not agree to anything below £15. Rosowsky immediately stated that his own support for the project would be contingent on Weinberg's participation. The crisis was soon resolved and four days later Weinberg confirmed his participation.[35] The ticket sale did not cover the expenses and the World Centre paid £15 which nearly exhausted its resources. While capable of sparking a special event, the World Centre was not in a position to sustain any regular concert activity.

The policy of the World Centre soon raised ideological qualms. Joachim Stutschewsky, who initially strongly supported the World Centre in his correspondence from Vienna, was bitterly disappointed soon after his immigration to Palestine:

I myself was fully dedicated and excited. . . . While in Vienna I had only a sketchy knowledge of this organization. When I reached Jerusalem I started to learn the details and after many meetings and discussions I became increasingly sceptical. . . . This idea which was announced in the Jewish world with much pathos and initial exaltation was revealed upon close scrutiny to be a daring imaginary dream, with no footing in reality, a terrible illusion.[36]

[30] Letter of 18 June 1940 (WCJMP Archive, JNUL).   [31] Ibid.   [32] *Memoirs*, 206.
[33] A letter from Paul Jacobi to the executive committee of the World Centre, 25 July 1940 (WCJMP Archive, JNUL).
[34] '*Dreckischen Schwindel*'. A letter to Sally Levi, 23 May 1940 (WCJMP Archive, JNUL).
[35] A letter from Jacoby, 25 July 1940. The letter did not state Weinberg's final honorarium.
[36] *Memoirs*, 205.

Stutschewsky reproached Levi and Swet for appointing to the international advisory board famous musicians who were 'detached from all
live roots of Jewish folk and Jewish spirit, . . . and isolated in abstractions
of other cultures'. After lengthy arguments Stutschewsky angrily abandoned what he considered to be 'the sinking ship'.[37] Upon the outbreak
of the war the World Centre ceased to exist.

Philip Bohlman has commented that when judged from the point of
view of western historiography which structures histories on the basis of
impact and influence, 'it would be easy enough . . . to conclude that the
music history of the World Centre simply did not happen. Influence and
impact are more or less absent.'[38] Bohlman has justly pointed out the
value of the rich documentation for the more comprehensive study of the
'multitude of histories' of the musical activity in the Jewish communities
in central Europe on the eve of World War II.[39] Yet also when judged on
its own merit the World Centre should not be deemed an utter failure
with no mark in history. The initiators meant no less than the first step
in the 'invention' of tradition which 'we should expect more frequently
when a rapid transformation of society weakens or destroys the social
patterns for which "old" traditions had been designed'.[40] The World
Centre was designed to provide a timely substitute for the crumbling
musical institutes in the individual Jewish communities. There is no doubt
that the conditions on the eve of World War II were ill-suited for the
development of such an ambitious international endeavour. It is likewise
doubtful whether under more benign conditions a similar organization
would have been conceived at all. Only the desperate efforts of the Jewish
Diaspora artists to maintain a semblance of 'business as usual' could
convince hundreds of well-established musicians to maintain a regular
correspondence for many months with an amateur musician practising
dentistry in Jerusalem. Thus although the World Centre may be regarded
as the most surrealistic chimera of the pre-war years, one should not
ignore the fact that the response of hundreds of correspondents suggests
that it helped the Jewish musicians to forge a sense of solidarity in a dark
reality of crumbling Jewish communities, a mass refugee movement, and
a growing premonition that the worst was still ahead.

Bloch and the New Image of Jewish Music

A shift in the structure of the repertory by Jewish composers performed
in Palestine in the late 1930s effected a significant transformation of the

---

[37] Ibid. 207.   [38] *World Centre*, 238.   [39] Ibid. 239.
[40] Hobsbawm, 'Inventing Traditions', 4.

elusive and controversial concept and image of Jewish music. Joachim Stutschewsky's prolonged stay in Germany, Vienna, and Switzerland permeated his pathos-filled Russian temperament with a cool, down-to-earth central European disposition. Thus, upon his angry withdrawal from the grand visions of the World Centre he channelled his fervent energy into a more tangible local project of concerts of Jewish music. Stutschewsky's decision to immigrate was based on the premiss of a secure position at the PBS. Yet he soon found out that there would be none. The British director invited him to prepare ten broadcast concerts of Jewish music, but the constant rotation of PBS directors prevented the realization of the series.[41] Stutschewsky turned to the National Committee which created for him a position of Superintendent of Music.[42] However, the new position entailed no executive power whatsoever. Disenchanted with the bureaucracy in Jerusalem, Stutschewsky decided to move to Tel Aviv which offered him better opportunities as a freelance performer, organizer, and cello-teacher. There he convinced the Cultural Centre of the Federation of Hebrew Workers to sponsor a series of bi-weekly concerts of Jewish music, alternating with concerts of non-Jewish chamber music. The first concert was a replay of Hanigun concerts,[43] with works by Achron, Rothmüller, Brandmann, Zeitlin, and Stutschewsky himself. But then Stutschewsky turned his series into a venue for new music, such as works by Erich Walter Sternberg, Ernst Bloch, and Paul Ben-Haim.[44] The shift had far-reaching consequences, changing the image of Jewish music from that of arrangements of Jewish folk songs to that of complex modern music. Stutschewsky discovered that attendance at his concerts of Jewish music was disappointingly small, especially when compared with a sold-out concert of Russian music. He whimsically contemplated cheating the audience by advertising an evening of Russian music and performing Jewish music instead.[45] His attempt to expand the series to Jerusalem was especially painful, since the first concert was attended by only forty people, fifteen of whom had come by invitation, and the second concert was cancelled when two tickets only were sold.[46] To make matters worse, a radio survey suggested that the listeners were generally indifferent to Jewish music and did not wish to hear it on the radio.[47] Still, Stutschewsky was not ready to relent:

---

[41] Stutschewsky, Memoirs, 201.   [42] Ibid.; O. Silbermann, Ha'Aretz (21 Oct. 1938).

[43] Held on 22 Oct. 1938. M. Ravina, Davar (4 Nov. 1938). See Ch. 5, above.

[44] Davar (27 Jan. 1939). Paul Ben-Haim's String Quartet which was premièred in this concert was his first major piece written in Palestine. See Hirshberg, Paul Ben-Haim, 149 ff.

[45] Stutschewsky, Memoirs, 212.

[46] Id., 'Jewish Music and the Yishuv', Mishmar (29 Sept. 1943).

[47] H. Swet, Ha'Aretz (21 Mar. 1937).

'I looked for new compositions, selected the programmes, held numerous rehearsals, distributed brochures at stores, dropped notices at mail boxes, in short, I was "a jack of all trades"'.[48] His persistence earned him the respect of the musicians' community which marked his fiftieth birthday with a festive broadcast concert in which he was introduced as the 'standard-bearer of the independent national Jewish style',[49] but the audience remained uninterested. Hermannn Swet admitted that the Jewish compositions were hardly ever heard outside the enclave which Stutschewsky had formed at Brener House. Reacting to a broadcast of compositions by Heinrich Jacoby and Oedoen Partos, Swet supported the inclusion of new Jewish compositions under the label of contemporary music:

Nowadays, in a period of a colossal national war, the music of Mozart, Handel, and Purcell is no longer sufficient. We live in another age represented by Hindemith and Stravinsky and to a certain extent by Arnold Schoenberg. An effort is needed to understand those works, but they are worth the effort.[50]

When focused on the music of Ernst Bloch, the image of Jewish music sharpened. Huberman was one of Bloch's admirers. Technical difficulties prevented him from mounting an immediate performance of Bloch's recently composed *Sacred Service* and the newly founded Palestine Orchestra included instead a single movement from his *Three Jewish Poems* (1913) in one of its first concerts.[51] Olya Silbermann hailed Bloch's achievement as a major breakthrough in Jewish music, since the composer 'returned to Judaism via modern music, with no external influences of Diaspora Judaism'.[52]

The two successive productions of the *Sacred Service* coincided with Bloch's sixtieth birthday. The event was previewed in great detail and accompanied by broadcasts of a few of Bloch's chamber works.[53] Having cast aside both the traditional orthodox ritual and the assimilated German reformed service, the intellectual circles of the New Yishuv adhered to the *Sacred Service* as representing their own understanding of their Jewish roots, substituting the concert hall for the synagogue. Karl Salomon previewed the work as a 'secular Mass which is not intended for synagogue service. Though based on prayers and on biblical and traditional verses, it has nothing to do with the ritual. The music is modern in its

---

[48] *Memoirs*, 212.   [49] H. Swet, *Ha'Aretz* (2 Feb. 1941).   [50] *Ha'Aretz* (14 Sept. 1941).

[51] Together with Lavri's *Emek* (13 June 1937). Composed in 1913, the *Trois poèmes juifs* was one of Bloch's first works in his *Jewish Cycle*. See A. Knapp, 'The Jewishness of Bloch: Subconscious or Conscious', *Proceedings of the Royal Music Association*, 93–6 (1970–1), 99–112.

[52] O. Silbermann, *Ha'Aretz* (16 June 1937).

[53] *Ha'Aretz* (24 Nov. 1940). Some, such as the Quintet, were broadcast from records.

technique but spiritually Jewish.'[54] Menashe Ravina labelled the piece 'religious',

albeit very different from that which is called 'cantorial music'. Its power and expressive depth contrast with the shallow coloraturas and whimpers of the cantor. The *Sacred Service* . . . is permeated with an Israeli religious spirit and shows the damage caused to Jewish music by the rejection of musical instruments in the synagogue and the preference for the solo cantor over the choir. Art music originates with combination of sounds, with the chord. The church preserved the choir, the organ, and the orchestra, which enrich the religious expression and carry the prayer to the highest spheres.[55]

Ravina, who listened to the performance on the radio, praised the PBS for finding the right way: 'The symphonies by Beethoven, Mozart, and the other giants may be also broadcast from records . . . A record is often preferable to a performance by a second-rate orchestra. But a new, original, Israeli work cannot be played from records.'[56] Imperceptibly, Ravina created a semantic opposition 'Israeli–Jewish' with the term 'Israeli' connoting innovation.[57]

It appears that the previewers' emphasis on the innovative aspects of the *Sacred Service* sparked the reservations of the audience-at-large towards new music, and Rosolio sadly concluded that 'many of our listeners missed this opportunity'.[58]

The new image of Jewish music was further sharpened by the intensive sequence of premières of newly composed orchestral works. Despite its tenuous relations with the local composers,[59] the Palestine Orchestra did perform within the brief time-span of the years 1937–43 a considerable number of new compositions, including Lavri's *Emek*. Sternberg's *Twelve Tribes of Israel* and *The Story of Joseph*, Ben-Haim's First Symphony, Heinrich (Hanokh) Jacobi's Viola Concerto, and Boskovitch's Oboe Concerto. In 1942 the Palestine Orchestra announced the Huberman Prize Competition which instigated the composition of Boskovitch's Violin Concerto and Ben-Haim's *In Memoriam*,[60] both of which were performed in the same year. The interaction of musicians, critics, and audience with the new repertory substituted ideological evaluations of concrete artefacts for hazy visions of a desired national style.

---

[54] *Ha'Aretz* (18 June 1940). The same definition was given by Hermannn Swet and by Sidney Seal in their radio previews. *Palestine Post* (17 June 1940).

[55] *Omer* (24 June 1940).   [56] Ibid.

[57] Only in 1948 was the term 'Israeli' loaded with official political and territorial meaning.

[58] *Ha'Aretz* (12 Dec. 1940).   [59] See Ch. 8, above.

[60] Boskovitch's Concerto was performed on 27 Feb. 1944 and was then withdrawn by the composer for further revision which was never completed. Due to the war conditions the competition was held only once.

14

Between East and West
The Ideological Strife

THE musical scene of the *Yishuv* was an arena of soul-searching and ideological controversies repeatedly focusing on the same nagging questions:

- What has been the extent of the contribution of Jews to world music?
- Is a Jewish ancestry a sufficient condition for rendering a composer Jewish?
- Would any piece by a Jewish composer qualify as Jewish music or should it also feature specific Jewish properties? And if Jewish properties are required, what would they be and who would determine them?
- Would the folk music of the Jewish Diaspora be relevant to the national revival in Palestine?
- What would be the role of western techniques and devices in the development of the desired national style?
- Would a thorough study of the music of mid-eastern Jewish communities and of Arabic music be conducive to the search for a genuine Jewish style?
- Would a Jewish style in music eventually emerge as a natural consequence of a high-quality compositional activity or is there a need for a deliberate and co-ordinated effort in order to forge such a style?

Such questions had a direct bearing on all facets of the musical scene, including compositional strategies, music criticism, concert programming, and educational curriculum.

Wagner and Judaism in Music

The prolonged argument sparked off by Richard Wagner's *Judentum in der Musik*[1] took a peculiar turn when it reached the musical scene in Palestine. Wagner's main thesis which denied the natural competence of members of the Jewish race to make any valuable contribution to German music incited two conflicting responses. The first was the statistical argument, attempting to discount the racial claim by illustrating the extensive contribution of Jews to all realms of European music. The second was the substantive argument which requested the definition and application of genuine Jewish properties as prerequisites for identifying a composer, a musical artefact, or a musical tradition as Jewish.

One of the earliest expressions of the statistical argument was presented by Gdal Salesky who listed 66 composers and 248 performers of allegedly Jewish origin who had left their mark on European music.[2] The statistical argument required solid criteria for national definition, whereas in a world dominated by migration there was no agreement whether national definition should be determined according to the country of origin or the country of resettlement of the composer. To further complicate matters, none of the two options addressed the question of Jewish identification. The critic Menashe Ravina focused on the problem in his review of an anthology of fifty-one modern piano pieces published in New York in 1940, in which Igor Stravinsky was defined as Russian, whereas Ernst Bloch was introduced as an American. The pianist and composer Leopold Godowsky (1870–1938) who had settled in the United States only in 1912 was also labelled as an American. Ravina contended that

I have no doubt that Godowsky is a Jewish composer and as to Ernst Bloch, I have no doubt that he is one of the greatest Jewish composers of our generation. Thirteen nations contributed to the American-published book, and the nation of Israel is not mentioned among them at all . . . We must collect our musical treasures and classify them according to their sources. It is high time to do so.[3]

---

[1] First published under the pseudonym Richard Freigedank in *Neue Zeitschrift für Musik*, 33 (1850) and then as a separate book in 1869. English trans. in Richard Wagner, *Prose Works*, ed. William Ashton Ellis (London, 1895–9). An easily available edn. in A. Goldmann and E. Sprinchorn (eds.), *Wagner on Music and Drama* (New York, 1964), 51–9.

[2] *Famous Musicians of a Wandering Race: Biographical Sketches of Outstanding Figures of Jewish Origin in the Musical World* (New York, 1927). Salesky deliberately used the term 'race' which was deleted from the post-World War 2nd edn., titled *Musicians of Jewish Origin*.

[3] *Davar* (12 May 1947).

The definition of a composer as a Jew implied an intrinsically racial inquiry into one's family history, often leading to questionable results based on flimsy evidence. For example, Salesky included Ravel among the Jewish musicians merely on the basis of his Kaddish. Huberman followed suit in his programme notes for the inaugural concert of the Palestine Orchestra. A backlash soon followed. Hermann Swet quoted personal communications by Joel Engel and Adolf Weissmann, who had refuted Ravel's alleged Jewish ancestry. Yet Swet agreed that Ravel 'had left for us a few works of very high value for the young Jewish music',[4] thus further compounding the problem by admitting the existence of a Jewish piece by a non-Jewish composer. The same question was raised on the occasions of the performances of Prokofiev's *Overture on Hebrew Themes*.[5]

The statistical approach not only carried the risk of awkward mistakes and racism but also raised the spectre of diluting the spiritual and cultural meaning of Jewish content in music. A diametrically opposed view was taken up by those who willingly adopted Wagner's final conclusion that the emancipation of the Jews was a chimera, and that a truly Jewish music would emerge only within a Jewish social and spiritual context, thereby supporting the cause of Jewish nationalism.

One of Abraham Z. Idelsohn's earliest Hebrew articles written soon after his arrival in Palestine[6] in 1907 was a three-instalment analysis of Wagner's pamphlet. Idelsohn used Wagner's rejection of the emancipated Jew as a justification for his own hostility towards the two extreme types of the Diaspora Jew. On the one hand, Idelsohn followed the secular movement of the Jewish Enlightenment in his contempt for the extreme Jewish orthodoxy 'which has no roots in the soil of the land but only in the heavens, which has no present tense, which connects past with future, . . . which cannot listen to a woman's voice and is banned from playing an instrument'.[7] Idelsohn continued to enumerate all rabbinical bans on mundane pleasures which symbolized the mourning over the destruction of the Temple. His ideological opposition was undoubtedly strengthened by his bitter personal experience with the Jerusalem orthodoxy.[8] According to Idelsohn, the orthodox attitude could never reconcile itself with the German nation which is 'deeply rooted in its land and has neither past nor future . . . and which finds beauty only in the

---

[4] *Ha'Aretz* (2 Jan. 1938).
[5] M. Ravina, 'On the First Concert of Hanigun', *Davar* (25 Dec. 1929).
[6] See Ch. 1, above.
[7] 'Richard Wagner and the Jews', *Hashkafa* (4 Apr. 1908).
[8] See Ch. 1, above.

world'. He respected Wagner as the embodiment of the German spirit and as a sincere revolutionary who fought for the abstract ideal of freedom and the emancipation of Jews. Idelsohn fully endorsed Wagner's protection of the purity of the German spirit against the penetration of the liberated Jewish elements, and he reprimanded those who kept attacking Wagner at a time when nearly the whole world, including Jews, admired his dramas. Idelsohn's own response to Wagner's admonishment was that

We should admit that it was all truth! We should turn to self-appraisal and accept his difficult words as instruction, because one may learn much from one's friends, but even more from one's enemies. [Wagner's] pamphlet shows us how far we had departed from a natural way of life. I suggest that there is only one way to retrieve our honour and respect—the revival of natural life, of national life, since there is no humanity without nationhood![9]

The debate on the very essence of Jewish music was rekindled in 1926 when the German scholar Heinrich Berl published his polemical and sincere *Das Judentum in der Musik*.[10] Anticipating suspicions of partisanship, Berl introduced his book with a statement that he himself was not Jewish, and that he had deliberately borrowed Wagner's term in order to dismantle the latter's arguments.[11] Berl's point of departure was the theory of the Romantic crisis as presented by Ernst Kurth and by Paul Bekker, each in his own way,[12] as the dissolution of instrumental harmony into linearity. Berl maintained that harmony of European music was understood through analysis, whereas the Jews were an oriental people whose musical personality was synthetic and emotional and therefore dominated by vocal melody.[13] Berl described the 'Asiatic crisis' as the penetration of the Orient into the Occident through Judaism, which might free European music from its Romantic crisis and lead it to a new classicism. Berl applied inspired rhetoric in his laudatory discussion of the great Jewish composers of the past, from Meyerbeer's autonomous melody to Mendelssohn's emotional Jewish soul. Berl commended Bizet, whom he erroneously considered half-Jewish, and Offenbach for leading the fresh anti-Wagner 'protest' of the young French.[14] He completed the list with Mahler and Schoenberg who had turned new music away from harmony to pure melody. The Jewish Diaspora was abnormal since it lacked the 'landscape' (*Landschaft*) which was essential for the emotional aspect of

---

[9] 'Richard Wagner and the Jews', *Hashkafa* (6 Apr. 1908).   [10] (Berlin, 1926).

[11] Berl, *Judentum*, 10.

[12] Ibid. 21. Berl dedicated his book to Paul Bekker, whom he deeply admired.

[13] Ibid. 92.   [14] Ibid. 89–91. Berl followed Nietzsche in his admiration for *Carmen*.

music of any people. Therefore, Berl considered Zionism as the only solution to the Jewish crisis.[15]

Arno Nadel[16] countered that 'there is only one Jewish music which we all know . . . this is synagogue music',[17] whereas the Jewish composers of the nineteenth century and of the modern era went through psychological processes which dissociated them from the Jewish organism. Berl countered that he could not consider the third movement of Mahler's First Symphony as anything but the purest Judaism. Moreover, Berl insisted that if no modern Jewish music had existed, a revival of Judaism would not have been possible.[18]

Menashe Ravina came across Berl's book during his study period in Europe in 1927.[19] Ravina stated that 'there have been so many Jewish composers that there was an opinion that the German Chorale maintained its original Jewish origins better than our synagogue prayer.' According to Ravina Jewish composers in Europe could not hide their Judaism.

Their works are mostly hybrid and incomplete, but thanks to the genius of the composers they exert a great influence on the general music. This influence is both beneficial and damaging. It diverts western music from going its own way, but at the same time protects it from an unnatural one-sidedness. As long as Jewish music does not exist on its own as a healthy music which expresses the life of the Hebrew nation, it will be no more than a commentary, but it would not provide any direction. There is hope that the Hebrew people would resume normal life and establish a centre in their homeland . . . and then the Hebrew music would also reach a revival.[20]

Ravina thus coined the pair of contrasting terms 'general music–Jewish music' which became common in later writing on music in Palestine.

Contrasting Diaspora and the Land of Israel

The first concert of Engel's works which took place on 28 February 1925 prompted a debate on the role of traditional Jewish folk song. Engel himself commenced with a long ideological essay.

What is this Hebrew music, on which the new generation of Hebrew composers struggles so much? And how could one prove that it is Hebrew? Indeed, it is

---

[15] Ibid. 17.
[16] Nadel (1878–1943) was a poet and a musicologist. Born in Lithuania, he resided in Berlin from 1895 until his death in a Nazi concentration camp.
[17] Quoted, ibid. 153.   [18] Ibid. 154–5.   [19] 'Judaism in Music', *Davar* (3 June 1927).
[20] Ibid.

impossible to prove. . . . Music is not logic. One either accepts it and lives with it, or rejects it. I, like any other sincere Hebrew composer, have the subjective privilege of defining my music as Hebrew, that is, of considering it connected in some way to the roots of national creation. But there is a deep chasm between the subjective privilege and the objective fact. Who would be able to bridge this chasm? The people, only the people. . . . Final judgement in such matters may be reached only by life itself, by the daily toil of the Hebrew masses . . . . Yet the snag is that the masses are detached from our new Hebrew music. Some of them—the majority—do not know it at all, and others, mostly the 'intellectuals' and the 'important' people cannot distinguish it from the Hebrew folk song, and they look down on it. There is no reason to do so. First, because the Hebrew folk song, though simple, is beautiful, and there is no reason to belittle it. Second, because the new Hebrew music has matured and released itself from the nappies of the primitive folk song.[21]

Engel's romantic concept of music embedded in the people contrasted with the presence of a heterogeneous migrant community, large segments of which had never been linked to the Yiddish folk song of eastern Europe, whereas another group, mostly of intellectuals, had deliberately detached itself from Jewish Diaspora culture.[22] David Rosolio raised a suspicious eyebrow:

Although 'Hebrew music' has become almost a commonplace among us follow-ing the performances of Achron, Gnessin, and others, the concert of Engel's works last Saturday outlines the need to discuss the concept itself, its meaning, and its implications. . . . The endeavour to create Jewish music is new. Com-posers such as Halévy, Mahler, and Schoenberg worked in the sphere of general music, so there is no wonder that Engel's music is influenced by other com-posers. Engel's chief source is the folk song of the Diaspora Jews. One must ask whether the Diaspora soul may provide the source for a new culture, which would express the revival of the Jewish soul in the Land of Israel.[23]

While the statistical attitude was occasionally applied in politically oriented arguments and in concert programming, the substantive approach prevailed and directed the controversies from questions of the composer's ancestry to the semiotics of music. Being Jewish and designating a piece as 'Hebrew' was no longer enough. John Foldes, a Jewish composer active in Manchester, composed a *Hebrew Rhapsody* based on allegedly Jewish folk dances. Menashe Ravina formed an ironic hypothesis about the unfortunate composer's method of work:

[21] *Ha'Aretz* (12 Feb. 1926).
[22] Most explicitly through the struggle for the exclusivity of Hebrew. See Chs. 1, 2, 11, above.
[23] 'Hebrew Music', *Ha'Aretz* (8 Mar. 1925).

It is interesting to observe the naïvety with which a Diaspora composer approaches the solution of the question of Hebrew music. He first chooses the easiest form: fantasy, rhapsody, pot-pourri, suite . . . In order to collect his varied material he has most probably gone to the Hebrew club in his home town where he has notated the songs and dances of the young people. Since he does not know the folk tunes of Eastern Europe, he has accepted each new tune as a Hebrew one from the Land of Israel and as having eastern roots. Returning to his desk, he comes under the exotic influence of the tunes and he arranges them for orchestra . . . turning them into a 'rhapsody' whose designation as 'Hebrew' merely marks the Hebrew club which served as its origin.[24]

The polarization of Diaspora versus the Land of Israel was epitomized in the attitude towards the use of the augmented second. In his study of the Society for Jewish Folk Music Sabaneev observed that

there were cases in which the collectors and harmonizers purposely altered the primitive diatonic content of a melody to the 'orientalized,' with the characteristic 'Jewish augmented second' which was regarded as an infallible attribute of the genuine Jewish melody.[25]

The interval was frequently frowned upon, either as improper to the spirit of the revived national spirit or as a folklorist platitude. Commenting on the première of Ernst Bloch's *Shelomo*, Menashe Ravina objected to the instrumental recitatives which permeated the work:

There is a marked difference between the sung biblical recitative and the one played on the cello. The biblical recitative limits the range of sounds and is syllabic. In the Rhapsody the composer has made endless use of chromatic progressions into which he has interpolated the augmented second which taints music with a folklorist character improper to the solemnity of the book of Ecclesiastes.[26]

The anonymous horra dance song 'El yivneh hagalil' (The Lord will build Galilee) was published several times in folksong compilations in two versions, or else as two related tunes. One of them was dominated by the augmented second (see Ex. 14.1). Michael Gnessin preferred the Dorian mode in his *quatre-mains* arrangement, thus avoiding the augmented second (see Ex. 14.2).[27]

---

[24] *Davar* (3 Oct. 1938).   [25] 'Jewish National School in Music', 457. See Ch. 5, above.

[26] *Davar* (9 Jan. 1939), a review of Stutschewsky's local première of the work with piano accompaniment.

[27] Jibneh edn. (Jerusalem, 1923). The arrangement was made for the dancer Baruch Agadati and was dedicated to the pupils of Shulamit school (Jacob Michael Collection, JNUL).

Ex 14.1. 'The Lord will build Galilee'

El   yiv-neh ha-ga-lil____   Bar-uch yiv-neh ha-ga-lil

Ex 14.2. Gnessin, 'Ora' ('El Yivneh hagalila')

Collectivism versus Individualism

The most thorny issue for the immigrant musicians was the absence of a recognized tradition of folk music of the Jews in Palestine. The Romantic view of folk music as an outcome of a cumulative process over an extended period of time contrasted with the relentless pressure to establish a new genuine culture here and now which emanated from the feeling of 'absence' which

always accompanies us on the way towards the realization of our identity. We lack national folk instruments. At times I envy the Russian peasant for his mouth harmonica. It is a very primitive instrument. I used to reject it as detrimental to musicianship, especially when I realized that its chords were constant and that they frequently contradicted the Russian melody. . . . But still . . . Could you imagine a happy Russian peasant without his harmonica? . . . When I envision the German wanderer I must mount the *Laute* on his back . . . We are too intellectual and we degrade the value of simple folk spirit. What have we discovered by means of our fake intelligence? A new, special musical instrument—the tin can. Once there was a tin can in the kibbutz. It was empty. And its sound powerful and noisy. They sent comrades to fetch it. And they made noise and the horra dance commenced. . . . Is the tin can the musical instrument which should substitute for the harmonica and the guitar?[28]

The supreme position held by the members of the Society for Jewish Folk Music was dissipated after Engel's death. The dynamics of reappraisal showed in the sincere criticism of the first concert of Jewish music sponsored by the revived Hanigun Society in 1930:

Hebrew music is pallid and dated. For three hours they sprinkled sounds with no reverberation; gloomy, depressing shadows of sounds. The works by

---

[28] M. Ravina, 'Folk Instruments', *Davar* (17 May 1928).

Rosowsky, Milner, Alman, Krein, Weinberg, Kugel, and Goldstein which were played here sound like translations, compilations, bits and pieces, a sound here and another there. However we admire the memory and contribution of the late Engel (and he was the giant in the group), his work was still mostly a folklore collection presented with popular simplicity. . . . The Society will get nowhere in that way. It is the way of poverty, of a suffocating traditionalism devoid of creative spirit.[29]

Fighting Alien Corruption

A recurring motive in the search for the visionary pure style was the fear of foreign repertories, genres, and musical flooding of the fragile nascent national style. Significantly, mainstream art music was generally accepted as essential to musical life in Palestine. Other repertories and practices, however, frequently triggered reservations. A concert of Russian music for bayan[30] and balalaika in 1930 provoked Menashe Ravina:

There exists an art of twilight, of decadence, of the *Cherry Orchard*, a parochial art . . . It is a potent art and its influence is great. . . . The most powerful proof against the entire bayan art is Glinka. . . . Seventy-three years have elapsed since Glinka's death. Magnificent Russian music has developed since then, music which has taken the entire world by surprise with its expression and sincerity. And what a miracle! The romance is still alive and kicking. Well, it lost its motherland, but it continues to wander abroad and to look for proper provincial grounds. Its way is well paved: Russia, Volga, nostalgia, longing . . . And the balalaika is playing. . . . Fading pianissimo, imitation of motherland sounds, tremolo, vibrato. All with a refined taste. But this is no art. It is a craft capable of addressing wishes which need no fulfilment, longing with no purpose. Twilight. Decadence. Parochialism.[31]

Synagogue music was likewise harshly judged. The cantor and composer Leo Liub formed a boys' and men's choir which performed at a public service on the High Holidays in 1934. While praising the choir itself, Ravina wrote that

there is nothing one can say about the compositions. A few sparked some interest, but in my opinion most of them . . . belong to the world of waltzes and military marches. Those elements must have permeated synagogue singing to

---

[29] Norman, 'A Concert of Hebrew Music', *Ketuvim* (2 Jan. 1930).

[30] The bayan is a chromatic accordion with a button keyboard. It has been a popular instrument in Russia, possessing a repertory ranging from popular songs and choral accompaniment to highly virtuosic arrangements of classical music.

[31] 'Bayan Art', *Davar* (3 Jan. 1930).

Ex 14.3. Zeira, 'A Sad Song'

Ha - tish - ma ko - li   re ho - ki she - li   ha - tish - ma ko - li   ba   a - sher hin - kha

(Will you hear my voice, you who are far away, will you hear my voice wherever you are)

such an extent that the directors of religious singing no longer notice this alienation. I felt deeply insulted.[32]

Contemporary European synagogue music was deemed incapable of offering anything to the quest for a genuine national Jewish style.

Most frightening of all was the overpowering influence of the sound film. Ben-Michael wrote in Sandberg's short-lived eccentric periodical *Halel* that 'the sound film is a new enemy of the Hebrew melody, and the enemy is now attacking the heart of the Hebrew musical culture, the Land of Israel'.[33] Yet he soberly rejected all calls for an artificial boycott as ineffective, since 'a technical device is neither good nor bad. It is man who renders it useful or destructive.'[34]

In the summer of 1934 the Levant Fair organized a contest for amateurs playing folk instruments. Menashe Ravina deplored the absence of any tradition of genuine folk expression: 'Most of them played European tunes derived from foreign folk songs or from the music hall repertory. Not a single original song, no new melody'.[35] Reviewing a broadcast recital Gershon Swet observed that

all composers of the Palestinian songs which [soprano] Miriam Segal performed yesterday (with the exception of [Paul] Ben-Haim), namely Verdinah Shlonsky, Mordechai Zeira, Emanuel Pugachov [Amiran], and Marc Lavri are Russian immigrants who did not free their songs yet of the influence of the Gypsy romances. Occasionally the Land of Israel wins over that of Russia, but most of the time the latter reigns supreme and only the Hebrew lyrics indicate the origin of the songs.[36]

Zeira's song on the programme, 'A Sad Song' to a poem by Rahel, may illustrate the residue of Russian traits which Swet referred to (see Ex. 14.3).[37]

By 1934 the polemic literature about Jewish music had swelled to such an extent that Joachim Stutschewsky felt the need for a detailed survey of recent writings on Jewish music. He was surprised to discover that 'non-

---

[32] *Davar* (21 Sept. 1939).
[33] 'Sound film in the Land of Israel', *Halel*, 2 (1930), 29. See Ch. 13, above.
[34] Ibid.   [35] *Davar* (17 July 1934).
[36] 'The Voice of Jerusalem', *Ha'Aretz* (23 Feb. 1940).   [37] M. Ze'ira, *111 Songs*, 165.

Jews take the stance that Jewish music exists, whereas Jewish musicians deny this'.[38] Stutschewsky opposed the attempts to search for Jewish traits in the music of composers who overtly denied their Jewish roots. Yet he also rejected the territorial condition as a prerequisite for a national style, since 'the Jews, despite their dispersal and wandering from country to country, have had "national life" and special traditional qualities of their own'. Stutschewsky expressed his hope that the Jewish artist 'would liberate himself from foreign influences and would endeavour to imbue his works with contents of their own, into which the essential traits of Judaism would be integrated in a natural way'. Stutschewsky concluded that Jewish music was formed in the Diaspora, whereas the Jewish community in Palestine was too young to establish life-patterns of its own. He refrained from any stylistic specifications since

It does not matter whether Jewish music moves in free rhythms or in regular metres, whether it is based on triads or on other harmonic systems, whether it stems from synagogue chant or from folk tunes, whether it is scored for strings, winds, or piano. We grasp this music as Jewish because it expresses the internal experience of the Jew. Music is not only form but first and foremost content . . . The composition which would establish the direction of the era has not been written yet. . . . The Jewish musician of our time is still motivated by two forces: birth and attachment to one's people on the one hand, and influences of his environment and education on the other. Consequently one is still unable to create the immortal work which is independent of time. . . . I do not mean Jewish music which would separate us from the masterpieces of other nations but Jewish music which would emanate from our innermost soul and would create forms and patterns of our own, and would still appeal to other peoples and would receive is own position in world music.[39]

Concert Programmes and National Ideologies

The realm in which the statistical attitude kept its prominent position was concert programming. Within the mere four seasons of its regular activity, the frail Palestine Opera mounted operas by the Jewish composers Meyerbeer, Halévy, and Anton Rubinstein. Engel's preview of the première of Rubinstein's *The Maccabeans* turned into a rebuff of the statistical attitude:

National culture is never created by translations. . . . Opera in the Land of Israel will become a Hebrew opera . . . only when it is partly and later fully based on

[38] 'Is there Jewish Music', *Ha'Aretz* (8 June 1934). Stutschewsky sent the article from Vienna.
[39] Ibid.

Ex 14.4. Rubinstein, *The Maccabeans a* Greek anthem *b* Jewish anthem

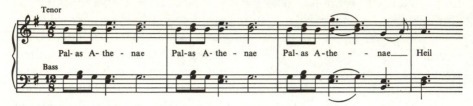

a   Four Greek Priests

b   Chorus of the Jewish People

a Hebrew repertory. . . . For the time being the Palestine Opera attempted to produce old Jewish operas by Halévy, Saint-Saëns, and Rubinstein. They may be called Jews only in the relative sense, since basically their work was detached from their people. Even when they approached Jewish [subjects] they did it as aliens, not with inner conviction.[40]

Engel's rejection of the statistical approach was expressed in his criticizing Rubinstein for using the same musical types for both the Greek and the Jewish anthems in his *Maccabeans*, as a consequence of which the music leads one to ask 'why do the Jews reject the Hymn to Athena despite its kinship to their own hymn?'[41] (See Ex.14.4.)

The statistical approach also elicited the question of whether a Jewish origin should override a qualitative evaluation. A certain musician who had bluntly refused to perform a piece by a Jewish composer touched off an angry rebuff. Hermann Swet countered with a demand to be 'more discerning. . . . The Jewish label alone is not sufficient'.[42]

The rise of the substantive approach opened a Pandora's box of its own, mostly that of identifying Jewish properties in music. The severity of the problem came to the fore when an attempt was made for the first time in the country to test the audience's response. The music department of the PBS broadcast a series of unnamed musical excerpts and asked the listeners to write as to whether they were Jewish or not. Some of the listeners described Varlam's aria from Mussorgsky's *Boris Godunov* as

[40] 'Rubinstein's *Maccabeans*', *Ha'Aretz* (13 Dec. 1925).   [41] Ibid.
[42] *Ha'Aretz* (19 Apr. 1936). Neither the musician nor the composer were mentioned by name in the newspaper.

having a Jewish character, whereas works by Joseph Achron were not perceived as such. Hermann Swet praised the initiative but rejected the premisses of the experiment:

We now touch on the heart of the great question: What is Jewish music? Is it based on a Jewish folksong? On a Hasidic nigun or dance? Or else on a cantillation of a prayer? What shall we say if the nigun or dance are not Jewish at all, such as German or Russian lullabies? Is it an adequate reason to disown the entire piece as non-Jewish? And what about abstract music devoid of any deliberate national character? . . . The essence of a musical composition is not dependent on its thematic elements or on its folk-national tints. Symphonies by Cesar Franck and Saint-Saëns are French and it does not matter at all whether one notices any folk tunes in them. . . . And looking from the opposite direction at works such as the *Overture on Jewish Themes* by the great Russian composer, Sergei Prokofiev, a truly magnificent work, Rimsky-Korsakov's wonderful *Song of Songs*, Glinka's 'Hebrew Song' from *Prince*, and Mussorgsky's *Joshua*— are they all instances of Jewish music? Could we add them to our national heritage?[43]

The Vision of the East

Unable to discriminate the Jewish properties in the music of the West, all eyes were turned to the East as the promised *font et origo* for the desired genuine Jewish style. The East was contrasted with the West in general and with the European Jewish Diaspora in particular. The columnist Itamar Ben-Avi was among the first who established this contrast in his review of the amateur production of the Hebrew version of Goldfaden's Yiddish play *Two Yoktan Yokshan*.[44] The production opened with a

small orchestra of flutes, tambour, and cymbals which played beautiful sounds; and when one shut one's eyes, one could imagine hearing snatches of the songs of future farmers in the field . . . The curtain rose, and a few of the pupils recited French national poems. . . . The orchestra [played] again; and this time it was a Hebrew tune of the Diaspora; it was a tune attesting to our inferiority among nations, to our neglect of art and of the beautiful in life. Still, it charmed me and filled me with *Weltschmerz*.[45]

Ben-Avi's conflicting response illustrated the dichotomy of the immigrant, hovering between his nostalgia for the culture he had cast aside and his vision of a new and independent national culture.

[43] H. Swet, *Ha'Aretz* (21 Mar. 1937).
[44] Goldfaden's play was a Jewish adaptation of Molière's *The Miser*. For Ben-Avi, see Ch. 2, above.
[45] *Hashkafa* (31 Jan. 1902).

Realizing this dichotomy, the poet and columnist Yehudah Karni requested that the immigrant artist undergo a deep transformation:

You must keep quiet for a while, and in your silence try to free yourself of all impressions and sounds in which you had been engulfed in the Diaspora. . . . The wild cry which one hears in this country at an Arab wedding is more significant for the Hebrew art of the future than the formal European tune, and the dances of our road construction workers are more important than the most modern foreign dances. We must learn from the Sephardis and from the Yemenites.[46]

As a modified borrowing from Spengler, the concept of the decay of the West became a recurrent issue in writings on music.[47] Indeed, no opportunity was overlooked to contrast the decadent West with the dawn of the East. In the broadest terms the East included the Russian Five and their disciples as a fresh revival which infused new life into the ageing European music, or else the transparent Mediterraneanism of Debussy, Ravel, and de Falla. Concert programmes more often than not elicited ideological comments. Salomon Rosowsky's programme notes to a performance of Tchaikovsky's Sixth Symphony, the 'Pathétique', concluded with the comment that

the people of the Land of Israel, who rejoice in creativity, are far removed from Tchaikovsky's spirit and emotions. They would be able to overcome the lure of his gloomy sounds, and yet would also appreciate the incomparably painful 'song of death' which is eternal in its sadness and beauty.[48]

In his review of Golinkin's performance of orchestral excerpts from *Lohengrin* Rosolio commented that 'Wagner's sources of inspiration are embedded in German ancient lore, which is foreign to us'.[49]

The German heritage on which most musicians in Palestine had been trained was thus perceived as a wonderful art, albeit culturally remote. Yet, confusion prevailed whenever the vision of the East had to be spelt out in tangible musical terms as the desired alternative. Pianist Arieh Abilea described the musical scene which he found upon his immigration in 1921 as 'bare and desert-like'.[50] Unlike Idelsohn, he and most of his colleagues lacked the expertise and the orientation to look for the rich heritage of the Eastern ethnic communities residing in the alleged desert. During the 1920s the East was a mere visionary image, frequently evoked

---

[46] *Hedim* I (1922), 37–8.

[47] *Der Untergang des Abendlandes* (Decline of the West, i (1917), ii (1922)). The trans. of the title follows Kohn, *Mind of Germany*, 330. See Ch. 4, above.

[48] Concert of 22 Jan. 1930.   [49] *Ha'Aretz* (28 Jan. 1930).

[50] Recorded interview, 1975.

through the biblical spectacles which the Hebrew theatre cherished. Jacob Weinberg wrote the score for the production of Beer-Hoffmann's *Jacob's Dream* and was promptly reprimanded for his music which was 'more European than ancient Eastern'.[51]

The sudden increase in the immigration of composers in the 1930s and the influx in productivity of new compositions in Palestine turned the ideological controversies from foggy visions to specific artefacts and intensified the sense of urgency. The crystallization of a genuine national style was still relegated to the distant future, but each step on the way, as represented by each new composition and performance, was viewed as either contributing to or detracting from the progress towards the desired goal.

[51] *Ha'Aretz* (16 July 1925).

15

The Semiotics of the East

THE semiotics of all arts, music, and letters in Palestine during the 1920s and early 1930s was grounded in the representation of the Yishuv's collective spirit. Topics ranged from the romanticized countryside scenery to pioneer heroic deeds.[1] Difficulties arose as soon as the flowery ideology had to be put into practice by way of concrete musical patterns. Any attempt to balance the sophisticated training of the composers in European compositional techniques with new inspiration from the East hit against their lack of expertise and experience in the music of the East.

First ventures in composing art music in Palestine were entrenched in European orientalism and in the emulation of the sonorities of Arabic music. Jacob Weinberg's opera *The Pioneers* wished to convey the ideological message of the rejection of the Jewish Diaspora and the victory of the Zionist dream.[2] The story of this naïve folk opera takes place in an idealized contemporary scene, devoid of any dramatic conflict. The first act takes place in a Jewish community in a small town in Poland, dominated by orthodox customs and class hierarchy. A motivated group of young people headed by Ze'ev, the son of a poor shoemaker, plans to migrate to Palestine and to form a kibbutz there. Ze'ev's girlfriend, Le'ah is reluctant to abandon the comfortable home of her well-to-do parents, who pressure her to marry into a rich family, and Ze'ev emigrates

---

[1] The same applied to all other arts as well as to the development of modern Hebrew and daily customs. See I. Even-Zohar, 'The Emergence and Crystallisation of Local and Native Hebrew Culture in Eretz Israel, 1882–1948', *Cathedra*, 16 (1980), 165–89.

[2] See Ch. 3, above. A vocal score was published by J. Fischer & Bro. (New York, 1932; libretto in English, Hebrew, and Yiddish). A full stage production never took place in Palestine or in Israel. The soprano Miriam Melzer has made a fine recording of the great coloratura aria for the *Voice of Israel* in 1988 and the cantorial class of the Hebrew Union College in Jerusalem has mounted a semi-staged performance of two scenes from the opera in 1993.

Ex 15.1. Weinberg, *The Pioneers*, Hasidic Sabbath Song

na na na   na na na na   na na na na   na na na   na na na na

Ex 15.2. Weinberg, *The Pioneers*, leading motive

without her. The scene then moves to a kibbutz in the north of Palestine where the young pioneers cherish their new simple and communal way of life and turn to nationalistic pantheism as a superior alternative to the orthodox way of life in the Diaspora. Le'ah realizes in the mean time the shallowness of her life in Poland and follows Ze'ev to the kibbutz. Finally the parents of both Ze'ev and Le'ah also immigrate to Palestine and settle in the city of Haifa. A family reunion in the kibbutz puts an end to old class barriers and all join in an exalted national hymn. Curtain.

Weinberg explicitly stated that he 'took special care to emphasize the contrast between the elements of Palestine and those of the Diaspora'.[3] In this respect he was one of the first promoters of a generally accepted set of semiotically meaningful musical patterns and types, which permeated much of the music of Palestine in the following two decades. The Diaspora is represented in the opera by East European cantillation formulas and by a full quote of an Hassidic Sabbath song (see Ex. 15.1).[4] The leading motive of the opera depicts the pioneers through the Romantic version of the Dorian mode, that is, minor with no leading tone (see Ex. 15.2). Le'ah, the leading role, is represented in a grand coloratura aria echoing Rimsky-Korsakov's *The Golden Cockerel* (see Ex. 15.3).

Another early attempt to reach eastward via the Steppes of Central Asia was Verdinah Shlonsky's *Images palestiniennes*, composed in 1929.[5] Based on a single verse from Abraham Shlonsky's poem *Night in Cana'an*, the first song exploits the full paraphernalia of European Orientalism, such as extended piano arabesques, modal patterns, and open fifths at the lowest range of the piano (see Ex. 15.4).

[3] A letter to Idelsohn of 20 Dec. 1931 (Idelsohn Archive, JNUL, Mus. 7 (632)).
[4] I am indebted to Professor Eliyahu Schleifer for the identification of the song.
[5] See Ch. 10, above. Verdinah Shlonsky who was then a student in Paris won the Nadia Boulanger Prize for this work.

Ex 15.3. Weinberg, *The Pioneers*, aria

Rise— up my— love— my— fair one and come—— a-way and come— a-way for——

lo   the— win - ter is   past———   the

Ex 15.4. Shlonsky, *Images palestiniennes*, first song

Lai-la   ho lai - la   lai - la   ho lai-la   lai - la lai la bicna;—— an

Ex 15.5. Lavri, *Emek*

As in the earlier cases of European national schools, dance and march became the dominant modes of expression. The most pervasive and soon the most abused musical type was the horra dance which Marc Lavri transferred from his folksong 'Emek' into his symphonic poem of the same name,[6] whose première by the Palestine Orchestra was duly acknowledged as the first symphonic horra.[7] The typical patterns of the horra included short symmetrical phrases in common time, regularly repeated syncopated rhythms, square phrases, short melodic motives in small range, avoidance of leading tones, and a simple diatonic harmony with open fifths substituting for major–minor triads (see Ex. 15.5).

The employment of dance patterns was in most works stylized and implied, as had been the case in many of Debussy's works. One of the

[6] The Emek, lit. 'valley', was the Valley of Jezre'el in the lower Galilee which turned into an emblem of agricultural dedication of the early pioneers.

[7] Olya Silbermann's preview, *Ha'Aretz* (16 June 1937).

Ex 15.6. Wolpe, *Dance in Form of a Chaconne*

Ex 15.7. Ben-Haim, Symphony No. 1, Finale

Ex 15.8. Ben-Haim, *Variations on a Hebrew Theme*

earliest examples was Stefan Wolpe's *Dance in Form of a Chaconne*[8] where syncopated dance rhythms form the counterpoint to a recurring chaconne subject in whole-note values. Wolpe was also among the first composers in Palestine who emulated the plucking of the kanun and the oud in Arabic music through frequent clashes of minor and major seconds (see Ex. 15.6).

As early as 1940 Paul Ben-Haim was careful to limit himself to a mere hint of the horra rhythm in the Finale of his Symphony No. 1, where it followed a quote from his oratorio *Joram*, composed in Germany in 1933. The temporal progression represented Ben-Haim's own migration from Germany to Palestine. Ex. 15.7 illustrates the horra motive.[9]

In the first exposition of the folk song 'My Motherland, the Land of Cana'an' which Paul Ben-Haim quoted in his piano trio, *Variations on a Hebrew Theme* (1939), the traditional device of strict imitation leads to a negation of harmony by forming parallel fifths and cross-relations (see Ex. 15.8).[10]

Wolpe's response to the Arabic music which fascinated him from the first moment of his arrival was reflected in the heterophonic techniques

[8] Composed 1938; pub. by Soundway Press.   [9] Hirshberg, *Paul Ben-Haim*, 197.
[10] Pub. by IMP, Jerusalem. Hirshberg, *Paul Ben-Haim*, 155–8.

Ex 15.9. Wolpe, 'If it be my fate'

permeating the song 'If it be my fate' to a poem by Rahel (see Ex. 15.9).[11]

The agglomeration of such patterns soon created an image and a point of reference for the music of Palestine. The inevitable backlash was immediate when the immigrant composers resisted any semblance of ideological pressure which could threaten their individuality. Anticipating ideological critique, Erich Walter Sternberg saw fit to defend his new work, *The Twelve Tribes of Israel*, well before its première in 1942. Sternberg described the composers in Palestine as immigrants

from the four corners of the earth and coming from different schools . . . It is my contention that the composer has only one duty. He should not care whether what is required from him is Palestinian folklore, synagogue chants, or melodies decorated with Russian embellishments, but should go his own way and speak his own language from within.[12]

Stefan Wolpe found it necessary to allude to this problem in the programme notes for a concert held in New York in 1949, ten years after his emigration, when he wrote of his Palestinian Songs that

[11] The poetess Rahel (pseudonym of Rahel Bluwstein, 1890–1931) immigrated from Russia in 1909 and lived in the agricultural settlement Kineret. She soon earned an honourable position among the modern Hebrew poets. Many composers of folk and art music set her introverted, sensitive poems to music.

[12] *Musica Hebraica* (1938). See Ch. 13, above.

they represent a unique experience for me in the sense that some of the inherent traits of these songs are akin to elements in the music of Palestine . . . I in no way intended to adapt myself to a folklorist language in connection with which I have no fetishistic prejudices.[13]

The sudden influx of new large-scale works composed in Palestine placed the music critics in a delicate position. In their extensive reviews they attempted to maintain a separation between ideological judgement and evaluation of the artistic craft. The music critics not only refrained from expecting the use of semiotically loaded patterns to be a necessary condition for ideological evaluation of a new composition, but were also reluctant to accept such use as sufficient. David Rosolio wrote ironically that Lavri 'elaborated the horra [in the symphonic poem *Emek*] according to all rules of effect, but with no consideration of rules of structure'.[14] Whenever they were faced with a well-made composition which lacked explicit oriental patterns, the critics looked for some hazy 'Jewish spirit'. Such was the case of Sternberg's *The Story of Joseph*, a long suite for a string orchestra written in an elaborate contrapuntal technique, which was the first major orchestral composition composed in Palestine.[15] Performed in 1939 soon after its completion, it sparked two conflicting reviews which reflected the extent of vagueness of the concept of 'Jewish music'. David Rosolio considered the composition as a first step towards the creation of Jewish art music. Having briefly described the structure of the Suite, Rosolio pointed out that

much more important has seemed to me the salient Jewish idiom of the piece. Sternberg has not used any folk tune, neither of the Jewish Diaspora nor of Palestine. The piece is totally free, the fruit of the flight of imagination, and its melodies and harmonies are permeated with elements which are in almost full harmony with the biblical text on which it is based. The composer has reached an intensive distillation and has found a pure artistic expression of the genuine Jewish feelings and moods. This is one of the very few works in our literature which may be defined as Jewish music. This work looks forwards rather than backwards, such as in all those which invoke time and again the *melos* and harmony of the Diaspora song.[16]

Menashe Ravina's impression was markedly different. While praising Sternberg for avoiding the temptation of turning the Finale into a horra dance, Ravina considered the composition as 'absolute' music:

[13] Programme notes of the Fifth Annual Festival of Contemporary American Music, New York, 1949 (Stefan Wolpe Archive, York University, Toronto).

[14] *Ha'Aretz* (25 June 1937).

[15] A full score published by Novello & Company (London, 1942).

[16] *Ha'Aretz* (2 Jan. 1939).

Ex 15.10. Sternberg, *The Story of Joseph*, 'Hymn'

Sternberg avoided the interpolation of Eastern motives. Despite the biblical subject he departed from an individualistic approach with no compromise with that which is considered modern Eastern. This has been his wish as a composer. But if this is so, he should not have depicted 'The Rise of Joseph' as the procession of a European sovereign into a Christian church, as in the chorale that ends the work (see Ex. 15.10).[17]

A similar polarity obtained in the reviews of the première of Sternberg's *The Twelve Tribes of Israel*. Rosolio observed that the composition incited in him a 'deep emotional satisfaction—since we have reached a work permeated by a deep Jewish feeling and put together with fine and perfect spiritual and technical tools,'[18] whereas Peter E. Gradenwitz hailed the mastery of the composer without alluding to the Jewish issue at all.[19]

Boskovitch and the Collective Ideology

None of the composers in Palestine could ignore the uniqueness of their historical position as the founders of a new national style. From the vantage point of ideologically committed musicians, the heavy burden of the European training on the one hand and the vagueness of the concept of national music on the other, threatened their ability to meet the historical challenge. The composer Alexander U. Boskovitch took the initiative and made a valiant attempt to formulate a comprehensive platform for the Jewish composer in Palestine. Shortly before his immigration Boskovitch had published a paper entitled 'The Problems of Jewish Music'[20] which provided the point of departure for his extensive

---

[17] *Davar* (23 Feb. 1939).   [18] *Ha'Aretz* (11 May 1942).

[19] *New York Times* (16 Aug. 1942). The musicologist Peter Emanuel Gradenwitz (b. 1910) came with the German immigration of the 1930s having completed an extensive research of the Stamitz family. *Stamitz, das Leben* (Prague, 1936) and several articles in *Musica Divina*, *Music and Letters*, and *Musica*. See 'Stamitz', *MGG* xii. 1162.

[20] 'A Zsido Zene Problemai', *Kelet es Nyugat Kozott* (Between East and West (Cluj, 1937)). The book was published in a limited edn. by a group of Zionist students in Cluj. Only two copies are known in Israel. See Hirshberg, 'Alexander U. Boskovitch', 95.

theoretical formulations. Although his first comprehensive presentation was not published until 1953,[21] Boskovitch had begun to disseminate his ideas and ideology about ten years earlier through public lectures and numerous informal discourses with young students and friends. A handwritten brief lecture to a gathering of Jews from Hungary in Tel Aviv on 16 December 1943 has provided the first documentation of such presentation.[22] Boskovitch's point of departure was that music was a function of its time and place, contradicting the romanticized view of music as a universal language. Music created at one period would be a total anachronism in another period. Hence writing in the most perfect Palestrina style in the twentieth century would amount to no more than a composition assignment. Likewise, music appropriate for the misty seclusion and melancholy of northern Europe would be out of place in the Mediterranean countries 'where everything is sharply delineated'. Consequently the cantorial liturgy and folk songs of the Jewish Diaspora would not fit the spirit of the Yishuv in Palestine. Boskovitch made a distinction between the 'static landscape' which was the visual scenery of each country, and the musically more viable 'dynamic landscape', namely the soundscape of the spoken languages and the rhetoric of their utterance. In this respect Boskovitch resembled Wolpe and Ben-Haim in their strong emotional responses to the scorching Mediterranean sun, the sand dunes of Tel Aviv, the scenery of the dry mountains of Jerusalem, and the excited vocal gestures of spoken Arabic and Hebrew in Palestine.[23] Boskovitch appears to have followed Nietzsche's ideas as presented in *Jenseits von Gut und Böse*, especially in his concept of 'dynamic landscape' which directly derives from Nietzsche's distinction between the German 'who reads not with the ear but merely with the eye' and the 'ancient man' who delivered his speech 'in a loud voice: that means with all the swellings, inflections, and variations of key and changes of tempo in which the ancient *public* world delighted'.[24] It is therefore unclear why Max Brod has denied the existence of any link between Boskovitch's use of Mediterraneanism and Nietzsche's line of thinking.[25]

[21] 'The Problems of National Music in Israel', *Orlogin*, 9 (1953), 28–93. Boskovitch's premature death halted the final stages of his work on a comprehensive book on the problems of Israeli music. The MS has been edited by Herzl Shmueli and is due to be published in the Hebrew language in H. Shmueli and J. Hirshberg, *Alexander U. Boskovitch, his Life and Works*.

[22] In Hungarian, (Boskovitch Archive, JNUL). I am indebted to Avigdor Herzog for his generous help in the translation of the handwritten MS.

[23] See Ch. 10, above. Ben-Haim's reactions have been preserved in his extensive correspondence 1933–4. See Hirshberg, *Paul Ben-Haim*, 102–10.

[24] *Beyond Good and Evil* (1886) trans. M. Cowan (Chicago, 1955), #247, p. 183. The topic is discussed all through the Eighth Article, 'People and Fatherlands' (#240–54).

[25] A passing comment in Brod, *Die Musik Israels*, 58.

Ex 15.11. Boskovitch, 'The Lord is my Shepherd'

Despite the sharp oppositions of time and place, Boskovitch acknowledged the factor of the deeply ingrained national identity which he illustrated through a hypothetical example of two shepherds, one Arab and the other Jewish, who would play their flutes on adjacent hills in the northern mountains of Palestine. Though acting in identical time and place, their reactions to their surroundings would be different because of their dissimilar backgrounds. Such a qualification was of crucial importance since it forestalled any seemingly easy solution of the problem of the national style through an unqualified emulation of Arabic music.

Boskovitch rejected the avant-garde view that the composer was ahead of his time, claiming that the artist was nourished by the spiritual attitude of his own time. He requested that the Jewish composer in Palestine act as spiritual leader, in a way similar to that of the celebrant in the synagogue,[26] and as such the composer must express and represent the emotions and thoughts of the entire collective and suppress any urge to use his music as an outpouring of his individual inner feelings. The direct derivation from the static and dynamic landscape implied that only composers living in Palestine would be able to create the national style, whereas Jewish composers living in Europe would always identify to a certain extent with the surrounding society.

Boskovitch's compositions of the 1940s were directly related to his platform, especially the second movement of the Oboe Concerto (1943), the *Semitic Suite* (1945), and the four songs written for Bracha Zefira.[27] The orchestral song 'Adonai Ro'i' (The Lord is my Shepherd) is based on an austere ostinato pattern with no modulation (see Ex. 15.11).

---

[26] The celebrant is named in Hebrew *Shli'ah Tzibur*, lit., 'sent by the congregation'. Any knowledgeable layman may be 'sent' to lead the service. It is both a duty and a measure of honour conferred by the congregation.

[27] 'Adonai Ro'i' (The Lord is my shepherd), 'Tephila' (Prayer: poem by Avigdor Hameiri), and 'Two Hitulim' (Two Jokes: poems by the medieval Jewish poet Alharizi). The *Semitic Suite* (piano version) and the songs were published by IMI. An autograph and copies of the Oboe Concerto and of the orchestral score of the Semitic Suite in Boskovitch Archive, JNUL.

Ex 15.12. Boskovitch, *Semitic Suite*, 'Toccata'

While on tour with the Palestine Orchestra in Egypt, the oboe-player Bram Blez, who had played the première of the Oboe Concerto, was strolling with the violinist Lorand Fenyves in the Cairo market when they stopped to get a shoeshine. Blez hummed one of the tunes from the Oboe Concerto and the Egyptian boy repeated the tune immediately. Fenyves took it as an indicator of Boskovitch's absorption of the aesthetics of Arab music.[28]

The title of the *Semitic Suite* was an ideological declaration in itself, stressing the region of the Near East rather than the Jewish people, the Arabs being Semitic as well.[29] Though a relatively short work, its composition spanned four years of painstaking revisions and rewriting. Four of its seven movements are in heterophonic style devoid of any tonal directionality, and they emulate the sound of Arabic orchestras, especially the second 'Toccata' (see Ex. 15.12).

As could be expected, the *Semitic Suite* called for a purely ideological review. David Rosolio was in accord with Boskovitch who

recognized the problem that one cannot continue in this country writing works which are based on purely western concepts. The landscape, the lifestyle, the environment, all require a change and a fundamentally different approach. But it seems to me that Boskovitch's method jumps overboard. The central issue is a *synthesis* of two styles . . . and one cannot solve a problem by ignoring it. Boskovitch writes in an undiluted eastern style and discards the western style altogether. It is an interesting but an unsatisfactory solution.[30]

Rosolio's reservation represented an absence of consensus concerning the extent of proximity to Arabic music as a gauge of progress towards the desired genuine national style. Moreover, it reflected an apprehension that the quest for a new style in the East might sever the links with the great western tradition.

The Mediterranean Style: A Myth or A Reality?

Summing up the brief history of art music in Palestine, Max Brod has credited Alexander Boskovitch with the concept of a Mediterranean

[28] An interview with the violinist Lorand Fenyves, Jerusalem, 31 Dec. 1976.
[29] An earlier version of the suite was named *Seven Experiments in Semitic Style*.
[30] *Ha'Aretz* (1 Mar. 1946).

Ex 15.13. Boskovitch, *Semitic Suite*, 'Folk Dance'

Folk Dance

style.[31] Brod characterized the style both positively, through a list of recurrent patterns including harsh rhythms, irregular metres, ostinato repetitions, abundant use of variation techniques, linear and frequent unison textures, and negatively, enumerating rejected devices, such as elaborate polyphony, major–minor tonality, and the interval of the augmented second which had been semiotically loaded with the connotations of the Diaspora. The list is by no means free of contradictions. For example, while it is true that irregular metres were frequently employed in the music he has referred to, the opposite was true as well since regular metres and short square phrases characterized the horra-like dances. The *Semitic Suite* which must have been one of Brod's paradigms contains both metrically irregular (Ex. 15.12) and regular movements (Ex. 15.13).

Moreover, Brod has acknowledged the fact that none of those devices was unique to the early music of Palestine and that they had been part and parcel of the European Orientalism since the nineteenth century.[32]

Brod was Boskovitch's close friend and for a while took composition lessons with him, so that the concept must have come up in the course of their frequent discussions. Yet Boskovitch himself neither spelled out the specific term in any of his writings, nor did he use it in titles of any of his works. After the completion of his *Semitic Suite* which was the closest manifestation of the regional ideology, Boskovitch entered a long period of nearly fourteen years during which he produced no major work in the field of concert music. Though partially caused by an array of personal and professional reasons, his long 'silence' was interpreted in professional circles as an artistic crisis and soul-searching.[33]

Other composers hardly used the term either. Paul Ben–Haim inscribed the heading 'Mediterranean Concerto' in the title-page of his long and elaborate Piano Concerto (1949) but he must have had second

---

[31] Brod, *Die Musik Israels*, 58.   [32] Ibid.

[33] None the less, *Shir Hama'alot* (Song of Ascents, 1959) his first composition which marked the end of his 'silence', retained most of the devices of his early period, with a sudden stylistic shift to a serial technique occurring only a year later with the *Concerto da Camera* of 1960. See Hirshberg, 'Alexander U. Boskovitch', 95.

Ex 15.14. *The Twelve Tribes of Israel*, opening

thoughts since he erased the title from the autograph score before the première and never quoted it in the programme notes.[34] The concept was adopted as a title for the first time only in 1951 by Menahem Avidom (Mahler-Kalkstein) for his *Mediterranean Sinfonietta*. Composed after the establishment of statehood and the renewal of links to the western world, it must be regarded as a consequence of the antecedent period of composition in Palestine.

The musicologist Peter E. Gradenwitz formulated a taxonomy of the nascent music of Palestine which he categorized into 'The Eastern European School', 'The Central European School', and the 'Eastern Mediterraneanism'[35] thus presenting Mediterraneanism as a coherent school of composition. Yet such a labelling appears to have been a gross simplification of a much more elaborate situation. The collective biography of the immigrant composers has shown that they did not arrive as a group and that none of them was recognized as an authority. Wolpe was the only one of them who started a semblance of a 'school' which dispersed immediately after his emigration in 1938.[36] All of the composers were subjected to both an internal need and external pressures to react to the unique conditions in Palestine. Yet they had also experienced the trauma of displacement and felt an urge to retain their links with their western heritage, which they continuously practiced as performers and teachers. Most of them circumvented the conflict by writing in several distinct stylistic tracks running parallel. The avant-garde composer Erich W. Sternberg reacted to his immigration by a return to German late Romantic techniques and rhetorics in his large-scale orchestral works, such as in the opening gesture of *The Twelve Tribes of Israel* (Ex. 15.14).

At the same time he maintained his predilection for elaborate atonal harmony in his works for piano and in his chamber works which he designed for the small sophisticated audience of the Society for Contemporary Music, as in his Toccata (Ex. 15.15).

[34] Hirshberg, *Paul Ben-Haim*, 238–9. Despite the erasure the inked title still showed and to further blur it Ben-Haim wrote over it the date 1949.

[35] P. Gradenwitz, *Music and Musicians in Israel* (Tel Aviv, 1952). Gradenwitz includes Verdinah Shlonsky among the Central Europeans although she was born in Russia and trained in France, and, moreover, she did use most of the devices characteristic of the so-called 'Mediterranean style'.

[36] See Ch. 10, above.

Ex 15.15. Sternberg, Toccata

Ex 15.16. Ben–Haim, *a Five Pieces for Piano*, 'Pastorale' *b* 'Akara' (The Barren)

a Five Pieces, 'Pastorale'

b Akara (The Barren)

Even those composers who were fully dedicated to the collective cause of a new national style were reluctant to deprive it of western traits. The prolific Paul Ben-Haim used to compose in separate stylistic tracks at the same time, as illustrated by a comparison of the 'Pastorale' of *Five Pieces for Piano* (1943) (Ex. 15.16*a*) with 'Akara' (1945), a romantic Lied setting of a delicate Hebrew poem by Rahel (Ex. 15.16*b*).[37]

Moreover, none of the works in which the so-called 'Mediterranean' devices prevailed was completely cut off the European heritage. Not only were all of them scored for European instruments and ensembles, but they also retained tonal traits, such as an implicit tonic–dominant polarity in Ben-Haim's 'Pastorale'.[38] Moreover, the penchant for European music to closed forms showed even in works based on continuous, non-

---

[37] Hirshberg, *Paul Ben-Haim*, 187.
[38] From *Five Pieces for Piano* (1943). See Hirshberg, *Ben-Haim*, 210.

directional Arabic models, such as the second movement of Boskovitch's Oboe Concerto. The oboe solo unfolds in a gradual expansion of the modal range, closely emulating the technique of the introductory section of the Arabic *taqsim*, moving above a monotonous ostinato pattern in the strings. Yet, upon the arrival at the highest notes of the range the ostinato stops for a few measures, articulating a motivic and a registral recapitulation (see Ex. 15.17).

The fallacy of the concept of a Mediterranean style is demonstrated most clearly in those works which were deliberately loaded with semiotic patterns, such as in Marc Lavri's *Dan the Guard*, the first locally composed opera to be produced in Palestine.[39] As in most national operas, the story contrasts individuals with homogeneous collective groups. The opera takes place in a small unnamed kibbutz in the north of Palestine which is threatened by hostile Arab neighbours.[40] The hero is the young idealist Dan, who struggles against the dark feelings of jealousy which rise within him when he discovers that his girlfriend Efrat is also loved by his best friend Nahman. Dan cannot bear the realization that his individual feelings might encroach upon his loyalty to the collective spirit of the kibbutz. In his final monologue while on a night-shift he overcomes his urge to shoot his friend. A subplot depicts the elderly Velvele who deliberately breaks all religious *mitzvoths*[41] with the intention to divert on to himself the divine ire which might befall the young members who had abandoned all religious commitments and dedicated their lives to building their kibbutz. Velvele is the only victim of an attack of Arab marauders and the moving scene of his death presents him as the sacrifice who saved the younger generation of the kibbutz.

Lavri has made use of the entire paraphernalia of semiotically loaded patterns and types in order to represent the different collective groups, such as the augmented second for the old Polish Jews (Ex. 15.18*a*), a horra dance in parallel fifths for the festive event of the communal laundry (Ex. 15.18*b*), whereas operatic clichés, mostly derived from Puccini, have been used to depict the pure young heroine (Ex. 15.18*c*).

[39] Libretto by Max Brod, based on S. Shalom's play *Shots at the Kibbutz*. The composition was completed in 1944 but many revisions took place during the rehearsals. The opera was premièred on 17 Feb. 1945 and produced thirty-three times in eight cities and towns in Palestine. The score has never been printed and no revival has taken place since then. See J. Hirshberg, 'The Opera *Dan the Guard* by Marc Lavri', *Tatzlil*, 17 (1977), 123–34.

[40] Although the final choral song which Lavri has interpolated into the opera hints that the kibbutz was the isolated Hanita in the wild mountainous Upper Galilee which had become a symbol of pioneer heroism.

[41] Observation of the Jewish religion first and foremost implies a strict maintenance of an elaborate system of laws, ordinances, and regulations named *mitzvoths* which cover all facets of individual and communal life.

Ex 15.17. Boskovitch, Oboe Concerto *a* beginning of exposition *b* end of retransition *c* recapitulation

Ex 15.17. *Continued*

Ex 15.18. Lavri, *Dan the Guard a* Diaspora motive *b* Dance *c* Aria

a Diaspora motive

Bunem

Sim‑has toy‑re _____ oy _____ Sim‑has toy‑re

b Dance

Chorus
Kibbutz
members

Mim - ro - mim bra‑kha ____ yo‑ re‑det pri zo - me - ah ba ‑ shma‑ma

(Blessing descends from above. Fruit grows in the wasteland)

c Aria

Efrat

Lo Av li kan ve ‑lo em _____ gal‑mu‑da a‑no‑khi

(I have no father, no mother. I am alone.)

Olya Silbermann recognized Lavri's tenuous situation, being placed 'in a difficult historical situation which forced him to create something out of nothing—deriving from the nascent reality of life in the Land of Israel on the one hand and from the fading hasidic folklore on the other. No wonder he was influenced by the master of opera—Puccini.'[42] Lavri's deliberate manipulation of discreet semiotic figures suggests that the so-called Mediterraneanism did not constitute a coherent musical style but a set of semiotically loaded musical patterns which were frequently juxta-

[42] *Mishmar* (28 Mar. 1945).

posed with other similar sets, such as that of Diaspora-related patterns. Nor did Mediterraneanism effect any significant change on the level of selection of musical genres. The Romantic national schools in Europe had established a preference for operas, songs, symphonic poems, and dance suites as the best tools for representation of national expression. Yet at the same time all nationalistic composers persisted writing in traditional classical genres such as string quartets, symphonies, and concertos as a measure of respect to and links with the mainstream Classical–Romantic tradition.[43] With the exception of the persistent Marc Lavri none of the composers in Palestine dared to cope with the insurmountable difficulties of producing an original opera in Palestine. Yet, contrary to expectation, they did not favour dance suites and folk songs either. In the years 1942–5 Boskovitch composed two large-scale concertos compared with two suites and four songs. From 1936 to 1945 the prolific Ben-Haim composed eighteen arrangements for Bracha Zefira,[44] sixteen Hebrew Lieder, and four instrumental dance suites, compared with two long and elaborate symphonies, three large-scale chamber compositions, and the violin-concerto movement *In Memoriam*.[45]

The alleged Mediterranean style was thus nothing more than an aggregate of rhythmic, melodic, and harmonic patterns and types which were semiotically loaded through their recurrent use in some of the compositions of the 1930s and 1940s. Highly communicative, they gradually acquired the description of 'Mediterranean style' and later of 'Israeli music', as has been deduced from a listeners' survey taken in 1976 in which the second movement of Boskovitch's Oboe Concerto was identified as 'Israeli' by more than 90 per cent of the subjects, contrasted with Sternberg's *The Twelve Tribes of Israel* which only about 20 per cent took as Israeli.[46]

The extensive repertory of those two decisive decades has exemplified that which Leonard Meyer has described as stasis[47] much more than even a semblance of any ideological consensus. Its heterogeneity provided the point of reference for the intensive ideological controversies and polemics which saturated the musical scene in the following years, especially when music was recruited to enhance the cultural image of the young State of Israel.

[43] As in the case of Smetana's operas and symphonic poems contrasted with his autobiographical string quartet, and Ernst Bloch's conscious contradiction of his *Jewish Cycle* with works such as the Concerto Grosso.

[44] See Ch. 11, above.   [45] Hirshberg, *Paul Ben-Haim*, 397–411.

[46] Id. and D. Sagiv, 'The "Israeli" in Israeli Music: The Audience Responds', *Israel Studies in Musicology*, 1 (1978), 159–71.

[47] *Music, the Arts, and Ideas* (Chicago, 1967).

Epilogue
Guns and Muses

THE termination of World War II in 1945 was followed by momentous political, social, and psychological changes in the Yishuv. Relieved of imminent danger of extermination, the Jews of Palestine suffered the trauma of realizing the horrifying scope of the holocaust. The Yishuv united in a struggle with the British administration to relax the strict immigration quota and admit the scores of thousands of Jewish war refugees from Europe. At the same time the international debate over the solution of the problem of Palestine was renewed under the auspices of the United Nations, accompanied by an alarming increase in violent clashes between paramilitary groups of Jews and Arabs, assaults on British soldiers, and terrorist attacks on civilians. The British army acted against the underground paramilitary groups by imposing frequent curfews. The situation deteriorated much more after the United Nations Partition Resolution of November 1947.

Musical life flourished against the grim conditions 'as if the public has been longing for cultural values as means to forget the troubled reality. Concert auditoriums, theatres, and of course cinemas are full.'[1] Musical life turned into a symbol of optimism and normality, such as when the pianist Frank Pollack played a brilliant Mozart programme 'while the sounds were intermingled with the roar of bombs and the barking of gunfire—incredible!'[2] Yet, Olya Silbermann once admitted that

I find it difficult to continue to write about music during the recent weeks, to continue to report about the local musical scene or to depict musical events in the world – when this world is bad and treacherous. When one hears music

---

[1] D. Rosolio, *Ha'Aretz* (15 May 1947).   [2] Id., *Ha'Aretz* (26 Mar. 1948).

which affects one in its sublimity and hidden beauty . . . one wishes to believe in a better future which could emerge from the ashes of the ruins.[3]

Frequent terrorist attacks on the narrow highways forced the Palestine Orchestra to use armoured vehicles in order to safely transfer its overseas guests from the small international airport to Tel Aviv, a distance of a mere eight miles. Consequently, each guest artist had to weigh the danger against the challenge and those who defied the danger could

rely in advance on having a grateful audience. We should remember that the news in the foreign press depicts a scene which is far from reality. The reader of such press cannot know that 'shots on Tel Aviv' do not hit the auditoriums of Ohel Shem or of Tel Aviv Museum, although one can hear them only too well. Such a reader cannot know the position of the Yishuv: life as usual, come what may.[4]

The flautist Uri Toeplitz has made a special note of the dedication of the Italian conductor Bernardino Molinari who refused to leave the country when his seaside hotel came under fire from neighbouring Jaffa. He joined the orchestra in an armoured bus for a perilous journey for a concert in Haifa.[5] Next came Jascha Horenstein and Izler Solomon who were likewise praised for their courageous participation.

Music served as a source of collective prestige when the situation allowed the élite of the new generation of locally born and trained young musicians to go for studies and concert tours abroad. The end of isolation was marked by a special concert in Paris of 'music from the Land of Israel' given by the orchestra of the Société des Concerts du Conservatoire conducted by Charles Munch, the programme including European premières of Boskovitch's *Semitic Suite*, Lavri's Piano Concerto, and Ben-Haim's First Symphony. The soloist, the young pianist Penina Salzmann, was soon joined on international concert tours by other young soloists from Palestine such as Menahem (Max) Pressler and Alexis Weisenberg, who were viewed as cultural ambassadors of the nascent nation.

On Friday 14 May 1948, David Ben-Gurion, chairman of the Zionist Executive, declared the birth of the State of Israel in an official ceremony held at the small auditorium of the Tel Aviv museum, home of the venerable chamber music concert series. The Palestine Orchestra, its members standing in the cramped lobby, was honoured to close the event with the national anthem 'Hatikva.' On the next day the Göteborg

---

[3] *Mishmar* (9 Apr. 1948).

[4] Rosolio, *Ha'Aretz* (5 Mar. 1948). Ohel Shem was then the auditorium of the Palestine Orchestra.

[5] Toeplitz, *History of the Israel Philharmonic Orchestra*, 112.

Symphony performed Sternberg's *The Twelve Tribes of Israel* with a live broadcast which was marked in Israel as a 'significant demonstration' of the international recognition of the artistic potential of Israeli music.[6]

The declaration of the State sparked a full-scale war between Israel and the neighbouring Arab countries. Jerusalem came under a prolonged siege and the only highway from Tel Aviv was cut off. In July the Israeli army opened a makeshift mountainous road and the Palestine Orchestra took the arduous route in armoured vehicles to Jerusalem. Playing two successive public concerts and a concert for the soldiers in two days, the orchestra was enthusiastically hailed by the exhausted and starved audience.

On the threshold of the 1948/9 season the orchestra renamed itself as the Israel Philharmonic Orchestra. In his concluding review of the stormy season Menashe Ravina noted that 'this has been one of the periods in which we were happy that there have been *no* significant changes in our artistic life' and that despite all difficulties the orchestra performed twenty-five premières, among them five Israeli compositions.[7] The phoenix-like opera under a new management produced Massenet's *Thaïs* and Rossini's *Barber of Seville* as a first step towards its revival as the Israeli Opera in 1948. The PBS went through a thorough reorganization and became the Voice of Israel.

The combination of hardships of a difficult war with the optimism of the making of a new state turned every musical event into an extreme symbol as well as into a topic for the renewal of old ideological debates. When the young and charismatic Leonard Bernstein opened the 1948/9 season of the Israel Philharmonic with a festive Beethoven programme, Rosolio highly praised the brilliant performance but reprimanded the orchestra[8] for ignoring his proposal to announce an international competition for a work by a Jewish composer which would open the season.

Between December 1948 and July 1949 Israel signed separate cease-fire agreements with Jordan, Egypt, and Syria. Basic problems remained unsolved for decades, but daily life in the country finally reached a semblance of normality. With the immediate arrival of enormous waves of refugees and immigrants from middle-Eastern and European countries Israel resumed its role as an immigration country. The old controversies erupted again and were soon supplemented with two new issues: namely the role the new government of independent Israel should assume in

[6] M. Ravina, *Davar* (6 July 1948).   [7] *Davar* (29 Oct. 1948).
[8] *Ha'Aretz* (5 Apr. 1948).

supporting the professional, experienced, and mature musical establishment which the Yishuv had formed, and the complex national, political,
social, and educational role which music should play in the building of
the new nation. A new chapter in the social history of music had begun.

Bibliography

I. Libraries, archives, local music publishers

AMLI (Americans for Music Libraries in Israel), Central Music Library, Tel Aviv; Archive of the Hebrew University, Jerusalem; Archive of Israeli Music, Tel Aviv University; Archive of the Israel Philharmonic Orchestra; CZA Central Zionist Archive, Jerusalem; Givat Brenner Archive; Haifa Music Museum and AMLI Library, Haifa; Gur Theatre Archive, Hebrew University, Jerusalem; IMI Israeli Music Institute, Tel Aviv; IMP Israeli Music Publications, Jerusalem; JNUL Jewish National and University Library, Jerusalem; Lavon Institute (formerly The Labour Archive), Tel Aviv; Merkaz Letarbut shel Hahistadrut, The Cultural Centre of the Federation of Hebrew Workers; Menashe Ravina Collection, private, Tel Aviv; Municipal Museum, Rishon Le'Zion; WCJMP, Archive of the World Centre for Jewish Music in Palestine, JNUL; Stefan Wolpe Archive, Paul Sacher Foundation, Basel, Switzerland and York University, Toronto, Canada.

II. Periodicals and daily newspapers

Aherout, lit. 'The Freedom'. The original awkward transliteration followed the French pronunciation of the title. Defined as a 'national paper'. First published three times a week, daily from its fourth year (Jerusalem, 1909–17) (H).

Davar, a daily newspaper, the official organ of the Histadrut, Federation of Hebrew Workers in Palestine (Tel Aviv, 1925–) (H).

Do'ar Hayom, a daily newspaper (Jerusalem, 1919–36) (H).

Dukhan, a Periodial Devoted to Topics of Jewish Sacred Music, Israel Institute for Sacred Music (Jerusalem, 1944–) (H).

Dvar Hapoelet, a weekly of the women workers (Tel Aviv, 1933–76).

Ganenu, Hovrot Lehinukh Hapaotot Began Hayeladim Ubebeit ('A Journal of Children's Education at the Kindergarten and at Home'), the Federation of Kindergarten Teachers (Jerusalem, 1919–22) (H).

Gazette de Jerusalem, ed. Luncz (Jerusalem, 1882).

Ha'Aretz, a daily newspaper (Tel Aviv, 1919–) (H).

Haboker, daily (Tel Aviv, 1935–66) (H).

Ha'Olam, the official organ of the Zionist Federation (1907–50) (H).

Ha'Olam Haze, weekly (Tel Aviv, 1937–93) (H).

Ha'Or, ed. Eliezer Ben-Yehuda (Jerusalem, 1891–1915) (H).

Hapo'el Hatza'ir, weekly of the workers' party of the same name (Tel Aviv,

1908–70) (H).

Hashkafa, ed. Eliezer Ben-Yehuda (Jerusalem, 1897–1909) (H).

Havatzelet, monthly, later semi-weekly, weekly, twice or three times a week (Jerusalem, 1863–1911) (H).

HaZevi, ed. Eliezer Ben-Yehuda (Jerusalem, 1885–1915) (H).

Hedim, a literary periodical (Tel Aviv, 1922–8) (H).

Ketuvim, a literary weekly, Tel Aviv (1926–33) (H).

Mibifnim, The Kibbutz Meuhad Monthly (Ein-Harod, 1924–) (H).

Musica Hebraica, journal of the WCJMP, 1–2 (Jerusalem, 1938).

Orlogin, ed. Abraham Shlonsky, a literary periodical (Tel Aviv, 1950–7) (H).

Palestine Bulletin (Jerusalem, 1925–33).

Palestine Post, replaced the *Palestine Bulletin* in 1933 (since 1948 *Jerusalem Post*).

Te'atron Ve'omanut (Theatre and Art), a periodical (Tel Aviv, 1925–8) (H).

Turim, a literary weekly (Tel Aviv, 1933–4) (H).

Warte des Tempels, Die, weekly of the German Templars (Jerusalem, 1839–77; 1913–17 pub. as *Jerusalemer Warte*) (Ger.).

III. *Fiction, printed documents*

BARASCH, ASHER, *Ke'Ir Netzurah* (As a Beleaguered Town) (Tel Aviv, 1945).

BEN-AVI, ITAMAR, 'Galin Kan', in *Hoveret Ha'Opera Ha'Arzisre'elit*, 10–13.

COHEN, YARDENAH, *Betof Ubemahol* (With a Timbrel and with a Dance) (Tel Aviv, 1963) (H).

EISENSTADT-BARZILAI, JOSHUA, 'An Opinion about the State of the *Yishuv* in Palestine in 1894', *Ahiassaf Calender* (1894).

GOLINKIN, MARK, 'Heikhal Ha'Omanut', in *Heikhal Ha'Omanut* (The Temple of the Arts) (Tel Aviv, 1927).

—— 'Arba Shnot Avoda Operait Be'Eretz Yisrael' (Four Years of Operatic Work in Palestine), in *Heikhal Ha'Omanut. A Guide to Music in the Land of Israel* (no ed.) (Tel Aviv, 1942).

GUTMAN, NAHUM, *Shvil Klipot Ha'tapuzim* (The Orange Skin Alley) (Tel Aviv, 1958).

—— *Ir Ktanah Ve'anashim bah Me'at* (A Small City and a Few People in it) (Tel Aviv, 1959).

—— *Hoveret Ha'Opera Ha'Artsisrelit* (The Booklet of the Palestine Opera) (Tel Aviv, 1935) (H).

IDELSOHN, ABRAHAM Z., 'Richard Wagner and the Jews', *Hashkafa* (Apr. 1908).

KESHET, YESHURUN (JACOB KOPLEWITZ), *Kedma Veyama* (East and West) (Tel Aviv, 1980) (H).

MALETZ, DAVID, *Ma'agalot* (Circles) (1945; Tel Aviv, 1983).

SHALOM, S., *Yeriyot el Hakibbutz* (Shots at the Kibbutz) (Jerusalem, 1940).

SHARET, YEHUDAH, *Seder shel Pessah Nosah Yagur* (Passover Seder in Yagur's Version) (Tel Aviv, 1951).

YA'ARI, YEHUDAH, 'Hatunato shel Menahem' (Menahem's Wedding), in *KeOr Yahel—Ya'ari's Stories*, ii (Jerusalem, 1969), 105–14.

IV. *Folksong Anthologies*

ADAQI, YEHIEL, and SHARVIH, URI, *An Anthology of Jewish Yemenite Songs* (Jerusalem, 1982).

BENARY, N. (ed.), *Liymei Mo'ed Vezicaron* (For Holidays and Memorials) (Hakibbutz Hameuhad, 1937).

BRONZAFT, MOSHE (GORALI), *125 Songs for Public Singing and Choirs* (Jerusalem, 1940).

HATULI, BINYAMIN (OMER) (ed.), *Se'u Zimra* (Sing ye) (Tel Aviv, 1938).

LUNZ, ABRAHAM MOSHE (ed.), *Kinor Zion* (The Violin of Zion) (Jerusalem, 1903).

STUTSCHEWSKY, JOACHIM, *13 Jüdische Volksweisen* (Berlin, n.d.).

WEINER (SHELEM), MATTITYAHU, *Hava'at Ha'omer* (The Harvest Feast) (Tel Aviv, 1947).

ZEIRA, MORDECAI, *111 Songs*, ed. Shlomo Kaplan (Tel Aviv, 1960).

V. *Books and Articles*

ADLER, ISRAEL, and COHEN, JUDITH, *A. Z. Idelsohn Archives at the Jewish National and University Library* (Jerusalem, 1976).

—— BAYER, BATHJA, and SCHLEIFER, ELIYAHU (eds.), *The Abraham Zvi Idelsohn Memorial Volume* (Jerusalem, 1986) (Eng. and H).

AMIKAM, BETZAL'EL, 'The Third Aliya', in Benjamin Eliav (ed.), *The Jewish National Home* (Jerusalem, 1976) (H).

APEL, MICHAEL, 'Iraq and Palestine', MA thesis (University of Tel Aviv, 1983) (H).

AUSTIN, WILLIAM W., *Music in the 20th Century* (New York, 1966).

BACHI, ROBERTO, 'A Statistical Analysis of the Revival of Hebrew in Israel', *Scripta Hierosolymitana* (Jerusalem, 1956), 179–247.

—— 'Demography', in *Encyclopedia Hebraica*, 6 (1957), 665–707 (this appears as part of the article 'Eretz Israel', edited by B. Netanyahu) (H).

BAHAT, AVNER, *Oedoen Partos, his Life and Works* (Tel Aviv, 1984) (H).

—— 'The Composer Alberto Hemsi', *Tatzlil*, 14 (1974), 39–42 (H).

BARTLETT, WILLIAM HENRY, *Jerusalem Revisited* (1855; Jerusalem, 1976).

BAYER, BATHJA, 'Creation and Tradition in Israeli Folk Song: Some Specimen Cases', *Aspects of Music in Israel* (Israel Composers' League, Tel Aviv, 1980), 52–4.

—— 'Passover Yagur Seder', *Dukhan*, 8 (1966), 89–98 (H).

BECKER, HEINZ, 'Fried, Oskar', *MGG* iv. 945.

BEKKER, PAUL, *Beethoven* (Berlin, 1911).

BEN-ARIEH, YEHOSHUA, *A City Reflected in its Times—the Old City* (Jerusalem, 1977) (H).

—— *Jerusalem in the 19th century* (New York, 1986); this is a revised, updated, and abbreviated trans. of the Hebrew original. *A City Reflected in its Times—New Jerusalem—The Beginnings* (Jerusalem, 1979).

BEN-ARIEH, YEHOSHUA, 'The Yishuv in Eretz Israel on the Eve of Zionist Settlement', in Kolat (ed.), Ottoman Period, 75–138 (H).

BEN-HAIM, EFRAIM, 'Autobiography', Tatzlil, 5 (1965), 127 (H).

BEN-HAIM, PAUL, 'My Immigration to the Land of Israel', Tatzlil, 11 (1971), 185–9 (H).

—— 'Autobiography', Tatzlil, 13 (1973), 172–3 (H).

BEN YEHUDAH, BARUCH, The Story of the Herzlia Gymnasium (Tel Aviv, 1960) (H).

BENTWICH, MARGERY, Thelma Yellin, Pioneer Musician (Jerusalem, 1964).

BERL, HEINRICH, Das Judentum in der Musik (Berlin, 1926).

BIGGER, GEDEON, 'The Development of the Urban Area of Tel Aviv 1909–1934', in Mordekhai Naor (ed.), The Beginnings of Tel Aviv, 1909–1934 (Tel Aviv, 1973), 42–61 (H).

BLUMBERG, ARNOLD, Zion before Zionism (Syracuse, 1985).

—— (ed.), A View from Jerusalem 1849–1858: The Consular Diary of James and Elizabeth Finn (London, 1980).

BOHLMAN, PHILIP V. The Land where Two Streams Flow (Urbana, Ill., 1989).

—— 'The Immigrant Composer in Palestine 1933–1948: Stranger in a Strange Land', Asian Music, 17 (1986), 147–67.

—— The Study of Folk Music in the Modern World (Bloomington, Ind., 1988).

—— The World Centre for Jewish Music in Palestine 1936–1940 (Oxford, 1992).

BOSKOVICS, ALEXANDER U. (Sandor), 'A Zsido zene problemai' (The Problems of Jewish Music), in Kelet es Nyugat Kozot (Between East and West) (Cluj, 1937), a publication of the Jewish Students' Relief Society, 31–7.

—— 'The Problems of National Music in Israel', Orlogin, 9 (1953), 28–93. (H)

BROD, MAX, Die Musik Israels (Tel Aviv, 1951; rev. edn. Kassel, 1976).

—— and COHEN, YEHUDAH W., Die Musik Israels (a revd. edn. with a second section Werden und Entwicklung der Musik in Israel) (Kassel, 1976).

CARMEL, ALEX, German Settlement in Palestine at the End of the Ottoman Period (Jerusalem, 1973) (H).

—— The History of Haifa under Turkish Rule (Jerusalem, 1977) (H).

CARMI, T. (ed.), The Penguin Book of Hebrew Verse (Harmondsworth, 1981).

CARMI, ZE'EV, The Trade Union in Israel (Tel Aviv, 1959) (H).

CENTRAL BUREAU OF STATISTICS, Government of Palestine, Department of Customs, Excise, and Trade, Statistics of Imports, Exports, and Shipping 1928–1945 (Library of the Central Bureau of Statistics, Jerusalem).

CLARKSON, AUSTIN, 'Stefan Wolpe's Berlin Years', in Edmond Strainchamps and Maria Rika Maniates (eds.), Music and Civilization: Essays in Honor of Paul Henry Lang (New York, 1984), 371–93.

COHEN, ERIC. See SHILOAH, AMNON.

COHEN, JUDITH, 'The Opera "Jiphtah" by A. Z. Idelsohn', Tatzlil, 15 (1975), 127–31 (H).

COHEN REISS, EPHRAIM, Memories of a Son of Jerusalem (Jerusalem, 1967) (H).

COHEN, TAMAR, 'Musical Activity in kibbutz Givat Brenner 1928–1948', seminar paper (Hebrew University, Jerusalem, 1993) (H).

COHON, IRMA, 'Idelsohn: The Founder and Builder of the Science of Jewish

Music—the Cantor of Jewish Song', in *Memorial Volume*, 36–45.

CRAVEN, ROBERT R. (ed.), *Symphony Orchestras of the World* (New York, 1987).

DEVERELL, F. H., *My Tour in Palestine and Syria* (London, 1899).

DEVEREUX, GEORGE, 'Ethnic Identity, its Logical Foundations and its Dysfunctions,' in George de Vos (ed.), *Ethnic Identity* (Chicago, 1975), 42–70.

DIXON, W. H., *The Holy Land* (London, 1869).

EDEL, YITZHAC, 'Autobiography', *Tatzlil*, 8 (1968), 57–62 (H).

EFRATI, NATHAN, 'The Jewish Community in Eretz Israel during World War I', Ph.D. thesis (Hebrew University, Jerusalem, 1985) (H).

EHRLICH, CYRIL, *The Music Profession in Britain since the Eighteenth Century* (1985; Oxford, 1988).

—— *Harmonious Alliance* (Oxford, 1989).

—— *The Piano* (Oxford, 1990).

EISLER, HANS, 'Our Revolutionary Music' (1932), in Manfred Grabs (ed.), *Hans Eisler: A Rebel in Music* (New York, 1978).

ELBOGEN, ISMAR, *Der jüdische Gottesdienst in seiner geschichtlichen Entwicklung* (Leipzig, 1913); Hebrew trans. by J. Amir (Tel Aviv, 1972).

ELIAV, MORDECHAI, 'Notes on the Development of the "Old Yishuv" in the 19th Century', in Y. Ben Porat (ed.), *Chapters in the History of the Jewish Community in Palestine* (Jerusalem, 1973) (H).

—— (ed.), *The First Aliyah* (Jerusalem, 1981) (H).

ETTINGEN, SHLOMO, 'Transportation', *Encyclopedia Hebraica*, 6 (1957), 954–82 (this appears as part of the article 'Eretz Israel', edited by B. Netanyahu).

EVEN-ZOHAR, ITAMAR, 'The Emergence and Crystallisation of Local and Native Hebrew Culture in Eretz Israel', 1882–1948', *Cathedra*, 16 (1980), 165–89 (H).

—— 'Processes of Contact and Synthesis in the Formation of the Modern Hebrew Culture', *Perspectives on Culture and Society in Israel* (Tel Aviv, 1988), 129–40 (H).

FINN, E. A., *Home in the Holy Land* (London, 1866).

GELBER, YOAV, *New Homeland* (Jerusalem, 1990) (H).

GERSON-KIWI, EDITH, *Studien zur Geschichte des italienische Liedmadrigal im 16. Jh.* (Heidelberg, 1933; Wurzburg, 1938).

—— *The Musicians of the Orient* (Jerusalem, 1945).

—— 'Engel, Joel', *New Grove*, vi. 167.

—— 'Robert Lachmann, his Achievement and his Legacy', *Yuval*, 3 (1974), 100–8.

—— 'A. Z. Idelsohn: A Pioneer in Jewish Ethnomusicology', in *Memorial Volume*, 46–52.

GILADI, DAN, 'The Yishuv during the Fourth Aliya', Ph.D. thesis (Hebrew University, Jerusalem, 1968) (H).

—— 'Tel Aviv during the Fourth *Aliyah*', in Mordekhai Naor (ed.), *The Beginnings of Tel Aviv 1909–1934* (Jerusalem, 1984), 77–84 (H).

—— 'The Settlements outside the Baron's Sponsorship', in Kolat (ed.), *Ottoman Period*, 503–38 (H).

GIVAT BRENNER KIBBUTZ, *The First Years; In Commemoration of 60 Years at Givat*

Brenner (Givat Brenner, 1988).

GOLDMANN, A., and SPRINCHORN, EVERT, *Wagner on Music and Drama* (New York, 1964).

GOLINKIN, MARK, *From the Temples of Japheth to the Tents of Shem: Memoires* (Tel Aviv, 1957) (H).

GNESSIN, MICHAEL, 'An Autobiography', in R. Glazer, *M. P. Gnessin* (Moscow, 1961 (Russ.)), Hebrew trans. in *Tatzlil*, 2 (1961).

GRADENWITZ, PETER EMANUEL, *Stamitz, das Leben* (Prague, 1936).

—— *Music and Musicians in Israel* (Tel Aviv, 1952).

—— 'Huberman, Bronislaw', *MGG* vi. 815.

GROSS-LEVIN, MIRIAM, 'Opera in Palestine', *Journal de jeunesse musicale d'Israël* (1958), 4–5 (H).

—— *Guide to Music in the Land of Israel* (Tel Aviv, 1942).

GUREVICH, DAVID, *Statistical Abstract of Palestine 1929* (Jerusalem, 1930).

—— GERTZ, AARON, and BACHI, ROBERTO, *The Jewish Population of Palestine* (Jerusalem, 1944).

——, —— (eds.), *Statistical Handbook of Jewish Palestine 1947* (Jerusalem, 1947).

HABAS, BRACHA, (ed.), *The Book of the Second Aliya* (Tel Aviv, 1947) (H).

HAGLUND, ROLF, 'Göteborg Synfuniker', in Craven (ed.), *Symphony Orchestras*, 301–4.

HEMSI, ALBERTO, 'Fortune Smiles on my Songs', *Tatzlil*, 15 (1975), 146 (H).

—— 'The Eliyahu Hanavi Synagogue Choir in Alexandria', *Tatzlil*, 16 (1976), 43 (H).

HERZL, THEODORE, *The Complete Diaries of Theodore Herzl*, ed. Rafael Patai (New York, 1960).

HERZOG, AVIGDOR, 'Masoretic Accents', *Encyclopedia Judaica*, xi (Jerusalem, 1971), 1098–1100.

HIRSHBERG, JEHOASH, 'The Opera *Dan the Guard* by Marc Lavri', *Tatzlil*, 17 (1977), 123–34 (H).

—— 'Heinrich Schalit and Paul Ben-Haim in Munich', *Yuval*, 4 (1982), 131–49.

—— 'Bracha Zefira and the Process of Change in Israeli Music', *Pe'amim*, 19 (1984), 29–46 (H).

—— 'Israel Philharmonic Orchestra', in Craven (ed.), *Symphony Orchestras*, 202.

—— *Paul Ben-Haim, his Life and Works* (Jerusalem, 1990).

—— 'Alexander U. Boskovitch and the Quest for an Israeli National Musical Style', *Studies in Contemporary Jewry*, 9 (1993), 92–109.

—— and SAGIV, DAVID, 'The "Israeli" in Israeli Music: The Audience Responds', *Israel Studies in Musicology*, 1 (1978), 159–71.

HOBSBAWM, ERIC, 'From Social History to the History of Society', in Felix Gilbert and Stephen R. Graubard (eds.), *Historical Studies Today* (New York, 1972), 1–26.

—— and RANK, TERENCE (eds.), *The Invention of Tradition* (Cambridge, 1983).

HOFFMAN, SHLOMO, 'A. Z. Idelsohn's Music: A Bibliography', in *Memorial Volume*, 31–50 (H).

HORNBOSTEL, ERICH, and ABRAHAM, OTTO, 'Über die Bedeutung des Phonographen für die vergleichende Musikwissenschaft', *Zeitschrift für Ethnologie*, 36 (1904), 222–33.

HOROWITZ-BEN-ZE'EV, GRETLA, *Memoirs of Rishon Le'Zion* (Haifa, 1973) (H).

HUBERMAN, BRONISLAW, 'Mein Weg zu Paneuropa', *Paneuropa*, 2 (1925).

—— *Vaterland Europa* (Berlin, 1932).

IBBEKEN, IDA, and AVNI, TZVI (eds.), *An Orchestra is Born* (Tel Aviv, 1969).

IDELSOHN, ABRAHAM Z., 'My Life', *Jewish Music Journal* (1936), repr. in *Memorial Volume*, 18–23.

—— *Gesänge der jemenischen Juden* (Leipzig, 1914).

—— *Jiphtah; Musical Drama in Five Acts* (Jerusalem, 1922).

—— *Gesänge der babylonischen Juden* (Jerusalem, 1922).

ISRAELISCH-DEUTSCHEN GESELLSCHAFT ARBEITSGEMEINSCHAFT JERUSALEM *Kurzbiographien von Mitgliedern der Israelisch-Deutschen Gesellschaft Arbeitsgemeinschaft Jerusalem* (Jerusalem, 1991).

KAMINSKY, JOSEPH, 'An Autobiography', *Tatzlil*, 12 (1972), 69–71 (H).

KARK, RUTH, *Jaffa—A City in Evolution 1799–1917* (Jerusalem, 1984) (H).

KARTOMI, MARGARET, 'The Processes and Results of Musical Culture Contact: A Discussion of Terminology and Concepts', *Ethnomusicology*, 25 (1981), 227–49.

KATZ, RUTH, 'Exemplification and the Limits of "Correctness"', in *Memorial Volume*, 365–72.

KAUFMANN, FRITZ MORDECAI, *Die schönsten Lieder des Ostjuden* (Berlin, 1920).

KIWI, EDITH. See GERSON-KIWI, EDITH.

KNAPP, ALEXANDER, 'The Jewishness of Bloch: Subconscious or Conscious', *Proceedings of the Royal Music Association*, 93–6 (1970–1), 99–112.

KOHN, HANS, *The Mind of Germany* (New York, 1960).

KOLAT, ISRAEL (ed.), *The History of the Jewish Community in Eretz Israel*, i. *The Ottoman Period* (Jerusalem, 1989) (H).

KOSHNIR, DAVID, 'The Last Generation of Ottoman Rule', in Kolat (ed.), *Ottoman Period*, 1–74 (H).

KRENEK, ERNST, *Gustav Mahler* (1941; New York, 1973).

KUNZ, EGON, 'The Refugee in Flight: Kinetic Models and Forms of Displacement', *International Migration Review*, 7 (1973), 125–46.

LAVRI, MARC, 'Autobiography', *Tatzlil*, 8 (1968), 74–7 (H).

LISSAK, MOSHE, *The Élites of the Jewish Community in Palestine* (Tel Aviv, 1981) (H).

LÜHE, BARBARA VON DER, 'Hermann Scherchen in Palastina', in Hans Jorg Pauli and Dagmar Wunsche (eds.), *Hermann Scherchen, Musiker* (Berlin, 1986), 35–41.

MARGALIT, ISRAEL, and GOLDSTEIN, JACOB, 'Baron Edmond de Rothschild's project 1882–1899', in Kolat (ed.), *Ottoman Period*, 419–502.

MAYER, LUDWIG K., 'Graener. Paul', *MGG* v. 663.

MAZOR, YAAKOV, and TAUBE, MOSHE, 'A Hassidic Ritual Dance: The *mitsve tants* in Jerusalemite Weddings', *Yuval*, 6 (1993).

MAZOR, YAAKOV and HAJDU, ANDRÉ, 'The Hasidic Dance Niggun', *Yuval*, 3 (1974), 136–266.

MEYER, LEONARD, *Music, the Arts, and Ideas* (Chicago, 1967).

MUELLER, JOHN, *The American Symphony Orchestra: A Social History of Musical Taste* (Bloomington, Ind., 1951).

NETTL, BRUNO, *The Study of Ethnomusicology* (Urbana, Ill., 1987).

NEUMANN, B., *Die Heilige Stadt und deren Bewohner* (Hamburg, 1877).

NIETZSCHE, FRIEDRICH, *Jenseits von Gut und Böse* (1886), trans. Marianne Cowan as *Beyond Good and Evil* (Chicago, 1955).

OLIPHANT, LAURENCE, *Haifa or Life in Modern Palestine* (London, 1887).

PELEG, FRANK, 'The Harpsichord, Past and Present', *Tazlil*, 9 (1969), 157–9 (H).

PORTER, J. L., *Jerusalem, Bethany, and Bethlehem* (London, 1887).

REYES-SCHRAMM, ADELAIDA, 'Music and the Refugee Experience', *World of Music*, 32 (1990), 3–21.

RINGER, ALEXANDER, *Arnold Schoenberg: The Composer as a Jew* (Oxford, 1990).

RINOT, MOSHE, 'Education in Eretz Israel', in Kolat (ed.), *Ottoman Period*, 621–714 (H).

ROGERS, MARY ELIZA, *Domestic Life in Palestine* (1862; London, 1989).

ROSOLIO, DORA, 'Bracha Zefira', *Dvar Hapo'elet*, 7 (24 June 1940), 79 (H).

ROTHMÜLLER, ARON MAARKO, *The Music of the Jews* (London, 1953).

RUBINSTEIN, ELIAKIM, 'From *Yishuv* to a State: Institutions and Parties', in Binyamin Eliav (ed.), *The Jewish National Home* (Jerusalem, 1976), 129–205 (H).

RUPPIN, ARTHUR, *Memoirs, Diaries, Letters*, ed. Alex Bein (London, 1971).

—— *Three Decades of Palestine* (Jerusalem, 1936).

SABANEEV, LEONID, 'The Jewish National School in Music' (1924), trans. S. W. Pring, *Musical Quarterly*, 15 (1929), 448–68.

SALESKY, GDAL, *Famous Musicians of a Wandering Race: Biographical Sketches of Outstanding Figures of Jewish Origin in the Musical World* (New York, 1927).

—— *Musicians of Jewish Origin* (New York, 1949).

SAMBURSKY, DANIEL, 'Autobiography', *Tatzlil*, 9 (1969), 180–2 (H).

SCHALIT, MICHAEL, *Heinrich Schalit, the Man and his Music* (Livermore, Tex., 1979).

SCHLEIFER, ELIYAHU, 'Idelsohn's Scholarly and Literary Publications: An Annotated Bibliography', in *Memorial Volume*, 53–180.

SCHMELZ, UZIEL, 'Some Demographic Peculiarities of the Jews of Jerusalem in the 19th Century', in M. Ma'oz (ed.), *Palestine in the Ottoman Period* (Jerusalem, 1975).

—— 'Population Characteristics of Jerusalem and Hebron Regions according to Ottoman Census of 1905', in Gad Gilbar (ed.), *Ottoman Palestine 1800–1914* (Leiden, 1990), 23–39.

SHAHAR, NATHAN, 'Music and Composer on the Kibbutz', MA thesis (Bar-Ilan University, Ramat-Gan, 1981) (H).

—— 'The Eretz Israeli Song 1920–1950: Sociological and Musical Aspects', Ph.D. thesis (Hebrew University, Jerusalem, 1989) (H).

—— 'The Eretz Israel Song and the Jewish National Fund', *Studies in Contemporary Jewry*, 9 (1993).

SHAKED, GERSHON, *Hebrew Narrative Fiction 1880–1980*, ii (Jerusalem, 1988) (H).

SHAVIT, ZOHAR, *The Literary Life in Eretz Israel 1910–1933* (Tel Aviv, 1982) (H).

SHAW, S. J., and SHAW, E. K., *History of the Ottoman Empire and Modern Turkey*, ii. *Reforms, Revolution and Republic—The Rise of Modern Turkey* (Cambridge, 1977).

SHELEM, MATITIAHU (WEINER), 'The First Shearing Songs', *Tatzlil*, 7 (1967), 180 (H).

SHILOAH, AMNON, *Jewish Musical Traditions* (Detroit, 1992).

—— and COHEN, ERIC, 'The Dynamics of Change in Jewish Oriental Ethnic Music in Israel', *Ethnomusicology*, 27 (1983), 227–52.

SIKRON, MOSHE, *Immigration to Israel* (Jerusalem, 1957).

SLONIMSKY, NICHOLAS, 'Leichtentritt, Hugo', *MGG* viii. 506.

SPENGLER, *Der Untergang des Abendlandes* (Decline of the West), i (1917), ii. (1922).

STERNBERG, ERICH WALTER, 'Autobiography', *Tatzlil*, 7 (1967), 177–9 (H).

STONE, LAWRENCE, 'Prosopography', in Felix Gilbert and Stephen Graubard (eds.), *Historical Studies Today* (New York, 1972), 107–40.

STUTSCHEWSKY, JOACHIM, *Memoirs of a Jewish Musician* (Tel Aviv, 1977) (H).

TAL, JOSEPH (Gruenthal), *Der Sohn des Rabbiners* (Darmstadt, 1985).

THALHEIMER, ELSA, *Five Years of the Palestine Orchestra* (Tel Aviv, 1942).

THOMSON, W. M., *The Land and the Book* (London, 1878).

TISCHLER, ALICE, *A Descriptive Bibliography of Art Music by Israeli Composers* (Detroit Studies in Music Bibliography, 62; Warren, Mich., 1989).

TOEPLITZ, URI, *The History of the Israel Philharmonic Orchestra Researched and Remembered* (Tel Aviv, 1992) (H).

TSCHAIKOV, MAUREEN, 'Musical Life in the Christian Communities of Jerusalem', M.A. Thesis, (Hebrew University, Jerusalem, 1993).

VOS, GEORGE DE, 'Ethnic Pluralism: Conflict and Accommodation', in id. (ed.), *Ethnic Identity* (Chicago, 1975), 1–41.

WAGMAN, YAHLI, 'Verdinah Shlonsky—In Memoriam', *IMI News* (Apr. 1990).

WAGNER, RICHARD, *Entwurf zur Organisation eines deutschen Nationaltheaters für das Königreich Sachsen* (1848), *Gesammelte Schriften und Dichtungen* (Leipzig, 1871–80).

—— *Prose Works*, ed. William Ashton Ellis (London, 1895–9).

WEBER, MAX, *The Rational and Social Foundations of Music* (New York, 1958).

WEINBERG, JACOB, 'Autobiography', *Taztlil*, 4 (1966), 68 (H).

WERNER, ERIC, 'Abraham Zvi Idelsohn: In Memoriam', *From Generation to Generation* (New York, 1969), 161–8.

WOLPE, STEFAN, 'The Palestine Songs', Programme notes of the Fifth Annual Festival of Contemporary American Music, New York, 1949, the Stefan Wolpe Archive, York University, Toronto.

YODELEVITCH, DAVID, *The Book of Rishon Le'Zion* (Rishon Le'Zion, 1941) (H).

YORMAN, PINCHAS, *The ACUM Story* (Tel Aviv, 1977) (H).

ZEFIRA, BRACHA, *Kolot Rabim* (Many Voices) (Ramat Gan, 1970) (H).

ZENCK, MARTIN, 'Das Revolutionäre Exilwerk des Komponisten Stefan Wolpe—mit kritischen Anmerkungen zur Musikgeschichtsschreibung der dreissiger und vierziger Jahre', *Exilforschung*, 10 (1992), 129–49.

Index